CRY
HAVOC

SIMON MANN

CRY HAVOC

'WHEN I SET OUT TO OVERTHROW
AN AFRICAN TYRANT, I KNEW I
WOULD EITHER MAKE BILLIONS OR
END UP GETTING SHOT...'

JOHN BLAKE

Published by John Blake Publishing Ltd,
3 Bramber Court, 2 Bramber Road,
London W14 9PB, England

www.johnblakepublishing.co.uk

www.facebook.com/Johnblakepub `facebook`
twitter.com/johnblakepub `twitter`

First published in paperback in 2012

ISBN: 978 1 85782 663 0

British Library Cataloguing-in-Publication Data:

A catalogue record for this book is available from the British Library.

Design by www.envydesign.co.uk

Printed and bound by CPI Group (UK) Ltd

1 3 5 7 9 10 8 6 4 2

www.captainsimonmann.com
twitter.com/CaptSFM

Papers used by John Blake Publishing are natural, recyclable products made
from wood grown in sustainable forests. The manufacturing processes conform to
the environmental regulations of the country of origin.

Every attempt has been made to contact the relevant copyright-holders,
but some were unobtainable. We would be grateful if the appropriate people
could contact us.

Dedication

I started this book in Chikurubi Prison as a love letter to Amanda and I dedicate it to her, but also to everyone who tried to help me escape my two prisons.

ACKNOWLEDGEMENTS

In this book I have tried to be honest about how I felt about what was being done, or not being done, to get me out. Sometimes I was very angry. So I wrote that. Now that I am out I feel differently. Now I feel just thankful.

There are people who, even today, I find out tried to help me, but I didn't know. There are people who tried to help me who don't want me to ever know. There are people who disliked what I was about, but who tried to help me despite that.

This is for them all. Thank you. However they tried. To Amanda. To Edward, my dear but now dead brother. To my sister, Sarah. To Peter, Jack and Sophie. To all the many others. Big help or small. Successful or not. Thank you, just the same.

I also want to thank all the many people who have helped with this book. Particularly Jim Nally who worked slavishly as Creative Editor. I gave him 200,000 words that I had written and Jim turned it into the fabulous book it is now. And Adrian Sington. Ever loyal and hardworking agent, without whom all would have been lost, many times over and everyone at John Blake, and mostly John Blake himself.

Some names, identifying characteristics and locations in this book have been changed for legal reasons.

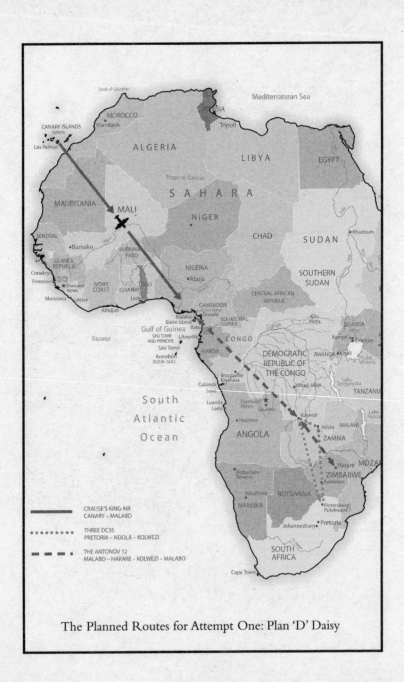

The Planned Routes for Attempt One: Plan 'D' Daisy

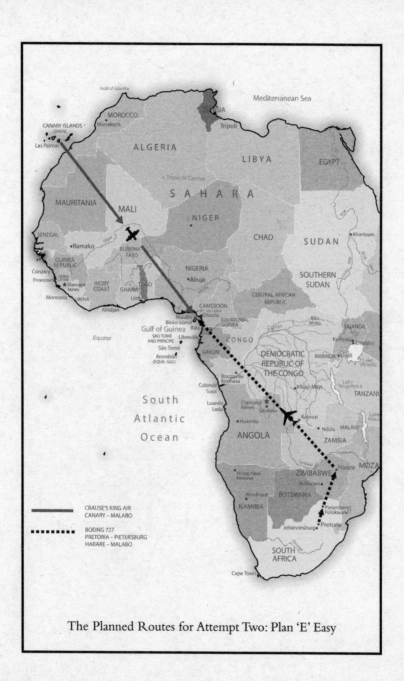

The Planned Routes for Attempt Two: Plan 'E' Easy

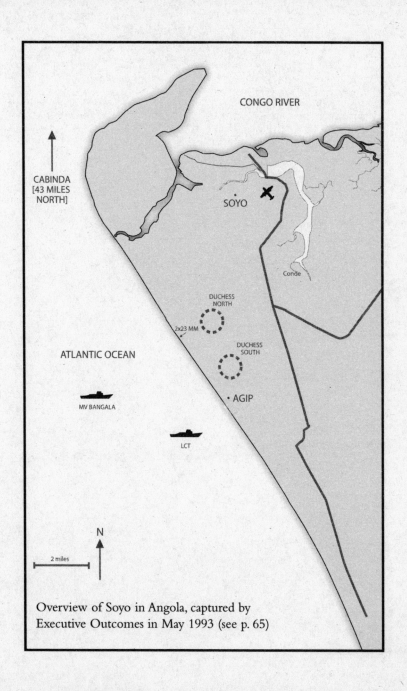

CONGO RIVER

CABINDA
[43 MILES
NORTH]

SOYO

Conde

DUCHESS
NORTH

2x23 MM

DUCHESS
SOUTH

ATLANTIC OCEAN

AGIP

MV BANGALA

LCT

N

2 miles

Overview of Soyo in Angola, captured by
Executive Outcomes in May 1993 (see p. 65)

PROLOGUE

This is about oil. Oil wars. In Africa mostly.

Many of the words in this book were written by hand. In ballpoint pen on heat-sticky school exercise books, in Chikurubi Maximum Security Prison, Harare, Zimbabwe – Chik Max. When I started to write, this was a love letter to my wife, Amanda. A present for her. The story of our love.

Prison security stole it.

Having been started over, and having been again stolen, then again restarted, the letter had become more than the story of our love affair. It was the story of my life, even if our love was the best part of that.

At any day then, I might have been taken to Equatorial Guinea (EG) to be killed. In Zimbabwe, my trial yet lay ahead. The prosecution was asking for the death penalty. Perhaps, therefore, this book was the only way that I could tell my seven children who I was, what had happened, why I had done these things.

Perhaps this book was a way that I could make some money for Amanda. She and the children were not eating air. Food costs money. Your man in prison costs money. Lawyers drain away money. Lawyers guzzle money.

In 2007, security took away the book again. This time I had fooled them. They took away 800 pages of unsorted and muddled drafts, but the best copy was hidden – ready to be smuggled back to England. The book escaped.

CHAPTER ONE

SATURDAY 6 MARCH 2004: D DAY MINUS TWO: EN ROUTE WONDERBOOM TO PILANSBERG SOUTH AFRICA

Gun-smoke grey vapour rips past; a silver spate river of cloud. A jagged mountain ridgeback lies too close beneath the thin metal hull of our Hawker biz jet. The Kruegersberg Ridge. Rock-crag fingers claw my arse.

Up front, the three pilots bicker and shout. Pien is number three. His arse is on the jump seat, but this is his airplane. Pien doesn't give a toss about 'cockpit human resource management' – he knows this Instrument Approach. He knows the Kruegersberg Ridge. The other two have got us below the published approach height; I can see it. That's a fuck-up. Pien bollocks them. Fly up!

Imprecisely, we are flying a Precision Instrument Approach into Pilanesberg, near Sun City,* a playground for wealthy whites.

From our base, Wonderboom, Pretoria, that's a 20-minute hop. This odd route is part of today's cunning plan, by which we will fly out of South Africa without being clocked by Immigration. I mean, we will be clocked, of course, but this makes it easier for the powers that be to scrub around their seeming dopiness in failing to detect a large number

---

*The Apartheid government couldn't tolerate vices like gambling, topless dancing and inter-racial sex. Not in the homeland of the Volk. Sun City, in South Africa's North West Province, was founded in 1979 by tycoon Sol Kerzner in the heart of the bush, Bophuthatswana – one of a series of nominally independent homelands set up by the Apartheid government. As a result, Sun City could sidestep South Africa's puritanical laws. Today it is again part of South Africa.

of mercenaries leaving the country at the same time. That's if we make it as far as a landing at Pilanesberg.

Rock reefs rip up through cloud below. I don't need an altimeter; through my port-side window I can see that the ground is too close. The flying is shit; this cockpit tantrum is an omen.

Here I am, about to give the 'GO GO GO' on the most risky job of my ramshackle career. The lives of many now hang from this beam of fate: victory or an abyss. But bad omens hurt.

Thankfully, ten minutes later we've landed. We ask to clear Pilanesberg Customs and Immigration, outbound. We josh black officialdom. But Pien has bribed them.

We take off for Kinshasa,* Cathedral of Crime, heart of the 'Heart of Darkness'.

We reach the cruise. Our Hawker is straight and level – MACH 0.74, 440 knots TAS (true airspeed), Flight Level 340 (approximately 34,000 feet ASL [above sea level]) – en route from Pilanesberg to Kinshasa. One thousand four hundred and thirty nautical miles (NM); Estimated Time En Route (ETE) 3 hrs 30 mins.

The cabin is fridge chilly. I zip my jacket to the neck. If I tell the air crew to warm us, then in five minutes we'll be toast. After their toddler tantrums I don't want to talk to them.

Sitting back in my wanker's black leather biz jet executive power chair, I close my eyes, breathe deeply, count to ten. I listen to myself. Who I am, what I am about.

Tugged, scratched, I pull myself through tangled jungle thorn. Tearing with haste. Hunted. Never sure which way. Harried, soaked. Sweat and dirt grime. With this piece and that, I've cobbled together a monster child. I drag him along with me, through sopping, super-heated thicket. Can I shoot the little bastard now, after all this? I wish. That's how I feel.

More calm, my mind runs through the night before. Dinner with Frank Thomas. Red-faced, fat. I find him pompous, sly, often drunk. Blimp. He is a liar and traitor by profession – a private spook – but he hasn't betrayed me yet ... and he is clever. It was Frank who introduced me to some of the great and the good in Constantia, Cape Town.

*Kinshasa, capital of the Democratic Republic of the Congo (DRC), was formerly Leopoldville, after Belgian King Leopold II. In the late 19th century, Leopold ran the region as a personal fiefdom. His agents raped it for slaves, ivory and gold, killing anyone in their way. Sir Arthur Conan Doyle called it 'a crime against humanity', journalist Richard Dowden a 'place of physical and spiritual horror'. It is truly Joseph Conrad's Heart of Darkness.

Frank is on my payroll for this Op – a Coup d'État against the .
who rule EG: a private-venture Assisted Regime Change (ARC)
the rage. Frank has already been paid $10,000. He's my spy and secret
agent – into Nigeria, that is – and he's set up and ready. He'll go to the
capital, Abuja, straight after the coup has struck. He's already been up
there once for me.

After that, he is earmarked to ride shotgun to those EG locals who
will be running security and anti-corruption in the new interim
government. That's the one I'm about to put in power. I hope.

Frank is also my snout into South African National Intelligence
(SA NI)* In fact – come to think about it – he is more like one of the
Liaison Officers we had in Northern Ireland than a snout. Jesus. An LO*
between me and NI? But that's the way this bloody thing's going.

Frank's fat face of last night swims in front of my shut eyes. It looks
flushed across the dinner table, as if through a Vaselined lens, soft focus,
candle-lit.

'Well, ha ha ha, Simon! Dicky and the Director…'

'The Director, Frank?'

'The Director of NI.'

'Go on!'

'Well, ha ha ha… They think it's funny how you're dashing in and out
of the country … up and down Africa … up and down like a whore's
drawers.'

This is Frank-speak. Blimp telling me how closely I am being
watched.

But I know that I am being closely watched from other – better –
sources than Fat Face. For God's sake: I've seen the transcripts of my
own phone calls with Amanda, complete with snotty handwritten shit
down the margins.

But I've also been shown the top-secret INT (intelligence) report that
tells SA NI of our coup plot. Of course, that report's spook author – not
Frank – had been unaware that he was in fact telling them about a coup
that – in the lush imagination of NI at least – is their coup anyway.

I'd not only seen that intelligence: I'd ordered it to be hacked off the

*SA NI is the South African equivalent of MI6 or the CIA.

*LO, a Liaison Officer, like an SBLO – a Special Branch Liaison Officer – between the SAS and the Northern Ireland Police Special Branch.

computer of the creep in question, a spook who was sending reports to both MI6 and the CIA.

Frank stuffed in more food.

'Mmm… mmm… So, it looks like everything will work out then, doesn't it?'

'What do you mean, Frank?'

'I didn't think it would work.'

'You've said that before … often.'

'I thought that Severo Moto wasn't well enough known – to become the new President of Equatorial Guinea, I mean. But now you're going … and everything's gonna be all right! … So when are you all off, then?'

'Tomorrow morning – to Kinshasa – to see the Greek… By the way, thanks for the intro, Frank.'

'He's good … but his partner is the Boss, don't forget… That means even the Greek has to do what he's told.'

'Sure … then Harare – direct from Kinshasa…'

'What are you flying?'

'Pien's Hawker … so we've got the range… D Day is the day after…'

We both paused, knowing that D Day might mean D for Death, or – God forbid – capture. For me it might mean that. Not for Frank.

'Can you get me the contact details for Severo Moto, Simon? The Director asked me to ask you.'

'I'll clear it – then let you have the numbers tomorrow.'

I think: South Africa's thumbs-up for what's going on couldn't come clearer.

During dinner my mind keeps hopping to Amanda, the woman I love. The child inside Amanda – one she had told me about only a few days before – would be our fourth. I'm in love with her. How many times had the two of us had dinner together here in the Sandton Towers, Jo'burg's finest?

I think of when I drove the children to school just last week. When I said goodbye to them, the idea like a burr in my head had been that I might never see them again. I may not.

For the thousandth time I scan my virtual instrument panel of this Op: a Coup d'État – a putsch – against the gangster regime who boss EG. My feet are cold: I want to see a red light. One would do. With just one clear red I can jack it in, shoot the bastard child.

We are living dangerously. Sixty-nine mercenaries fly from South Africa to Harare tomorrow night. They will rendezvous in Harare with me and the weapons. Then we fly into Malabo, capital of EG, to execute Plan E: a coup against the gangster regime which tyrannises the poor bastards who scratch away their lives in that oil-rich shithole. Plan E for Easy. Sure.

On D Day – the day after tomorrow – in the early hours, we'll take out EG's self-appointed President Teodoro Obiang, one of the most brutal tyrants in Africa. We're flying in with the exiled opposition leader, Severo Moto. He'll take Obiang's place. Moto's mission is to take democracy and the rule of law into EG. To spend their petrodollars on clean water, education programmes, blitzing malaria – the good stuff.

Our plan – our hope – is for a bloodless coup. Just in case it isn't, we'll be bombed up with enough guns and ammo to win a war.

It is 2004 and regime change is in vogue. The US and UK governments have just unseated another despot: Saddam Hussein in Iraq. We too are doing the right thing. But, as I feign sleep in the Hawker, it's as I say. My feet are cold. We are living dangerously.

We've already tried this Op once, two weeks ago – Plan D for Daisy. But the little flower fucked up. After Daisy was all over – without tears, just – we had to laugh. The little flower turned into a rolling goat fuck. Better than anything else – giggled the troops – had been the sight of three DC-3s (the WWII vintage Dakota – except these all had the old South African Defence Force (SADF) conversion, their two piston radials each replaced by Pratt & Whitney PT6 gas-turbine prop engines) sitting all afternoon on the apron of Ndola International, Zambia, stuffed with 70 mercenaries and their kit, waiting for the 'Red ON … Green ON … GO!' A 'GO' that never came.

There are geeky anoraks who would find that sight a bigger, better thrill than Farnborough Bloody Air Show. To others it would smell as fishy as a Grimsby trawler. Not even to the village idiot would it have looked kosher.

And – of course – that meant that the news of this – and of other strange goings-on earlier – had spread; not only to those intelligence agencies betting on the Op, but also to a motley gang of African warlords. Apparatchiks on the Beltway. Whitehall. Rebel armies. Hedge fund managers. Merchant bankers. And, of course, Big Bad Oil – what I call 'the Barrel Boyz'.

If we can make this Op work, then each of these will want a better share of the new EG's massive oil production. But – if it all turns to rat shit – then they'll all deny us. Or they'll switch sides, running to Obiang to tell on us. The tyrant. School playground bully *Numero Uno*.

In West Africa, it's a war. As everywhere, that war is about oil. We are the pawns in the war. Our Op is one part of a great web of top-flight skulduggery – a part where I am being shouted at. Get a bloody move on – GO!

So, yet again, I scan my virtual instrument panel for this Op. It is how I try to weigh our pros and cons.

China – a nod and a wink – GREEN

US – more than a nod and a wink – GREEN

UK – more than a nod and a wink – GREEN

Spain – telling me: get on with it – FLASHING GREEN

South Africa – telling me: get on with it – FLASHING GREEN

I have five green lights now: the intelligence agencies of China, the US, the UK, Spain and South Africa … although none of them will ever say so.

Two of those greens flash urgently: Spain and South Africa.

But the real deadline now driving this job is 14 March: the Spanish General Election.

My boss in all this (but by no means the Head Shed) has said that, if we are not 'in' by the 14th (and it's already the 6th), then we will have to go to HOLD.

But HOLD won't be HOLD. HOLD will be Op CANCELLED.

You see: international recognition – for our new interim EG government, with interim President Severo Moto at the helm – is life-and-death critical to the job. Recognition by Spain – as the old colonial power – is the essential diplomatic trigger. It's the *sine qua non* to secure the recognition of the US, the EU and then the African Union (AU). Recognition *de facto*, then *de jure*: the final seal. Without that international recognition we could all look very silly. Dead. We have a promise of that recognition from the Spanish powers that be. But the Spanish elections are on 14 March and who knows who will be in power after that. That's why 14th is cut-off day. That's why we are helter

6

skelter to GO. So all I need, to stop this thing – to give in to my cold feet, to let loose the top of my bottle – is just one red light.

But red lights? None. Orange lights? Plenty. Green lights? Five.

Our plan – a long way down the road from Plan A – is now Plan E. E for Excellent. But E is makeshift. Rushed. Shoestring. Intelligence-industry scuttlebutt. Actually, Plan E is a heap of shit.

Inside our Hawker, cold air blows against the back of my neck. Up front sit our three tetchy airmen.

Alongside me sits Charles West – a mercenary who's fought with us, with our set-up Executive Outcomes (EO), from the start – and a man named Lyle, here on Charles's say-so. Charles tells me that Lyle knows Eastern Bloc weapons and ammo inside out. As does he.

I open my eyes. I had dozed off. We're coming in to land. Kinshasa is always hairy: very busy, pilot-driven, a Tower of Babel. Air Traffic Control (ATC) has no radar, but, with luck, a handheld radio and a blackboard. There are no radio-navigation aids. Towering A-bomb Cumulonimbus thunderheads menace all around; columns of dragon smoke.

As the Hawker halts, refuellers rush up. So does the Greek. He is the cause of all this efficiency. He drives up in his own 4x4 and parks beside us, airside.

I need a favour from the Greek. I need a back-up aircraft for the Op. The machine earmarked for the job of transporting the South African troops from Wonderboom to Harare, then all of us – plus weapons – on to Malabo is still in the United States.

I bought the machine days ago. Pien sourced an unbelievably good deal. It was an ex-US Air Force VIP Flight Boeing 727-100, going for just $300K. It had low hours and low cycle times (the number of take-offs and landings). And, of course, it had been well looked after. It was dead cheap because it had no civilian engineering paperwork.

Trouble is, it's stuck in Miami, Florida.

I know the Greek's boss owns a Boeing 727. Frank told me. I know the Greek's boss has a dislike for Obiang.

We shake hands, then talk.

The Greek is typecast: pasty white, podgy, white nylon shirt, midday stubble. Soft-spoken. He looks out of place among the black African madhouse chaos of Kinshasa International airside. Yet he is the Main Man. He listens, then tells me quickly, quietly: he is willing to let me use his aircraft tomorrow night – a Boeing 727 – for our coup, and at a good price. With as good an answer from the Greek as I could have wished for, we shake on it. I pay cash for the jet fuel, then we fly off: Harare, here we come.

Waiting for us at that airport are weapons and ammo, sold to us by a key middleman in the Op, one Captain Brodie. Lately of the Zimbabwe Air Force, Brodie is a veteran of their rape and pillage of the DRC for diamonds – and anything else that's worth taking. But Brodie is also a senior – but covert – officer in Mugabe's notorious Central Intelligence Organisation (CIO). Bob's Gestapo.

These men are good friends of Mark Thatcher – himself one of the high-profile secret backers of this Op. ZDI are supplying me with 100 AK-47s, 20 PKMs, 20 RPG-7s, nine 60mm mortars, six Dragunov sniper rifles, ten 9mm Star handguns and box upon box of mortar bombs, grenades and ammo. Two and a half tons and 250, 000 US dollars worth in all. Charles and Lyle are here with me to make sure we get what we've paid for.

Tomorrow will be the first time that the key components of the party attacking EG – men, weapons, the 727 – will be all in the same place.

I had two golden rules for this operation. Golden rule number one is that favourite of the Provisional IRA: men and weapons come together for the least possible time. They meet for the Op – that's all. Tomorrow golden rule number one is going to be broken, but it's that or jack this in.

Anyway, my 727 is stuck in Miami. The ferry crew flying the thing to South Africa phoned in. They are Aircraft On the Ground – AO fucking G – with a 'no fly' equipment failure. Just to make sure that I go pear-shaped, the ferry captain is also grousing about paperwork. I know that the paperwork can be torn up, then sorted out later. If there is a later.

I've dealt with ferry crews before. They're always a waste of rations. They land somewhere sun 'n' fun – like Miami – then bingo: the airframe goes unserviceable (U/S). What I need to do is get hold of someone in the States who'll ride shotgun, to get crew and aircraft into the sky. Flying south. Fast.

I know just the man. But Bill comes at a cost, and at a risk. Anthony – my Jo'burg-based PA – is trying to get hold of him, but we're running out of time.

MARCH · 2004 . . . MARCH · 2004 . . .

The whole picture is looking shonky. The plane picture worse. My 727 has to be flown out of Florida for South Africa in the next few hours. Finding a plane is only one of my 'No Go' headaches.

Already in EG is my number two – Niek du Toit – and an advance party of ten men. Tomorrow night – before me and my 69 men land at Malabo International – his ten must secure the airport's control tower. This must be done silently. Maybe by force.

With the control tower in his hands, Niek can radio us the all-clear: that our runway is not an ambush. He can also operate the runway lights. Switch on the instrument landing system – if serviceable.

Niek's team has to get six vehicles onto the airstrip. Those wagons are to carry me and my 69 to our targets. Each vehicle will have a driver and a co-driver from Niek's team. They will have recced the route to our targets. Palace, police station and barracks, media and communications. The Central Bank. Key Points (KPs). All of these have to be locked down.

Niek is taking the biggest gamble right now. As I keep telling him, by his being in EG so much, he has been putting his head inside the mouth of a hungry lion. A man-eater. Tomorrow night he'll be taking over an international airport for a plane that may or may not fly in.

If he and his team are captured while we're in flight, then – maybe – the first we'll know of that is when we land. By then it will be too late to avoid the water barrels, chains or rocks laid across an ambushed runway. Caltraps.

Another of my old gang is Crause Steyl. He is in the Canary Isles with President designate Severo Moto, plus a chartered King Air 200 turbo prop. His job is to fly our new *El Presidente* into Malabo, landing a half-hour after us: the cavalry. That just gives us time to form up. Moto's brass band. His guard of honour.

Since day one of this Op – plotting with the Boss in London – golden rule number two has been that we must not move around Africa without our 'Pres des' in tow. If we are caught without Moto on board, then we are the big bad mercenaries. They'll throw away the key. With Moto, then, what we are about is clear and in the flesh. Black flesh. Then we are the bodyguard – the close protection – such that Severo Moto can take his place as an interim President, pending free and fair elections. We are PC.

Tomorrow, golden rule number two, like number one, is going to be broken. But it's either that or jack in the Op. Fucking hell.

What my men don't know – what only the Boss and I know – is that, inside Obiang's fortified palace, courtiers and security disloyal to him are primed and ready. As soon as they get the Boss's phone call, the plotters will arrest Obiang, his closest supporters and any security people still loyal. That call will only be made once he knows that I'm gear-up out of Harare, en route to Malabo. With airport and palace held, the EG army – mutinous, disloyal, and now caught off-guard – will either surrender or run into the jungle.

Mark Thatcher – who is a helicopter pilot and a yachtsman – has our Escape & Evasion (E&E) plan. I've been through it with him more than once and he is gung-ho. It's Mickey Mouse but it's better than nothing.

In case it all goes wrong on the night, our opening night in EG, we've agreed frequencies, timings and days, locations, signals – either for a helicopter or for a boat. For Mark to come in and pick us up.

This whole Op may sound kamikaze to you… Maybe it is, but you don't know what we did in Angola in '93. Or Sierra Leone (SL) after that. Both those times, all the odds were stacked against us – plus superpower players – but we won through. Big time.

Anyway, ask around! You don't become a crack mountaineer by turning back when the weather changes, or because someone's hurt their toe. You get there by not jacking it in. You get there by wanting the top badly enough. It's 'Who Dares Wins'. Isn't it?

So, as Pien's Hawker rocks and rolls Harare-ward, that's how it is. I pray to the war god. My prayer to Ares. Let us be lucky one more time, please. Just one more.

Between prayers, my mind drifts to Amanda and the baby inside her – our fourth – that she only just told me about. I think of our son – Freddy – and our two lovely little girls, Lilly and Bess, so different from each other. I drove them all to school just last week.

When I said goodbye to them, I felt a heart stab: I might never see them again. But I have to block them out of my mind. I cannot allow myself to think of the pain I will cause them if this goes wrong. I've been here before: in the British Army, and all the other ones I've been in. If you're going to do this shit, you have to build a barbed-wire fence around your heart.

I feel the engine thrust come off. The pitch change, top of the drop. I take a deep breath, tune into what's happening in the cockpit. At least the toddlers are calm now. We're on long finals – follow the glide path and the localiser beam – down onto Harare's great 4,725-metre runway.

Right, lads, who wants to jack it in? Last chance. Now. Truck's over there…

Charles, Lyle and I walk the walk. Harare International Customs and Immigration. The night-time airport is deserted. We're the only show in town. They're bound to give us a load of shit.

We breeze through. Zero hassle. A sure sign – I cheer myself – that all's well. For an old 'Africa Hand' like me, such a walk-through can mean only one thing: that we have powerful friends. These must be friends who – thanks to Mark Thatcher – love us. The air crew – following shortly – will waltz through too. Harare? Piece of piss.

Charles, Lyle and I are driven along bare, scarcely lit streets. Not so long ago Salisbury. Metalled potholed roads are wet with rainy-season rain. Dim yellow streetlights glisten off the surface, as few and far between as other traffic.

I can feel the poverty that grinds these people as fiercely as the blast-furnace heat of an African midday.

A mobile phone rings.

Back at the airport, the three pilots are in shit. They are held. The plane's owner, Pien, is scared. Another old Africa Hand, Pien knows Africa better than anyone. He has done shit in Africa that makes my hair stand on end, and that's not because of the flying. Now he tells me that this is not the usual 'your money or your life' banditry.

They want money, of course, Pien tells me. US dollars, naturally, but there's something nastier at work. Another cold chill blows between my shoulder blades. My Africa Hand antennae, comfy after our stroll-through, are back on alert. Is this whole thing a set-up? An ambush? Have we just 'walked the walk' … into a gin trap?

I ring our fixer, Brodie, and tell him what's happened. He'll sort it out, he says. Relax. I wince once more at this month's ever-ready thought: the pond life with which I have to deal – so as to make this Op work – would fill a swamp. What is it they say? 'Lie with dogs – get up with fleas.'

11

Déjà vu. I check in to the Cresta Motel; just as I had two weeks earlier, for the previous, aborted, shot at this.

I set up my mini COMCEN once more: it's a comedy Communications Centre, made up of a battery of four mobile phones and their chargers, and two stacks of Pay As You Go cards. This is not some cunning, low-tech COMSEC (Communications Security) ploy: it's our African way of keeping in touch. Drums.

One phone has a UK SIM card on 'roaming'; another is a South African one – same detail. The other two are on different, heavily juiced-up local Pay As You Go networks. Most times one or other of the four will work, even if only for text. I also have a handheld Iridium satellite phone, never before used and therefore, I hope, 'clean'.

This motel room puts me into a cold sweat. All by itself. I had sat in an identical room two weeks earlier, as the ill-fated Plan Daisy – even more far-fetched and far-flung than this one – ran awry. Plan D. Yes, far-fetched and far-flung. But better – safer – than this one, Plan E. It didn't break golden rule number one – men and weapons come together for the least possible time. That's why it was safer. For Plan D, I sat through the long night: frantic to talk to the airport control tower, or the Operations Centre, or the loo cleaner, or any so-and-so, at half a dozen African airports, each unwittingly involved in that cunning plan.

All I wanted to know: where's my bloody airplane? That night the aircraft was an old Russian Antonov An-12 cargo plane. As I sat there – shouting at the darkness, the distance, the poor phone lines and the far-away second languages – my fever to GO GO GO had driven me crazy.

I had screwed myself up to fight – to kill or be killed if it came to it – only to find myself trying to sweet-talk some Air Traffic Controller, half asleep, in a far-off place, with no Air, no Traffic and fuck-all Control. Throughout that night a chunk of me had been fearful. Cold, wet, ball-of-sick-in-my-gut fear. That fear had been piano wire tied taut to the door. Waiting for that moment when Mugabe's famously nasty CIO came busting through to capture me. Or to shoot me.

Now, two weeks later, that cold, wet ball is back. Will the air crew get out OK? If not, we'll have to break them out – by force maybe or bribe more likely – then flee Zimbabwe. Bring Plan E to its own sorry end.

But fear not! Captain Brodie – of Zimbabwe Defence Industries (ZDI) – is secretly Central Intelligence Organisation, CIO, Gestapo, and therein lies our safety. Thatcher is sure of it. So is Niek. We're in with the Baddest of Bad Arses. He will look after us.

I start to wonder why Niek – up there at the coalface in EG – hasn't been in touch. Shit. Has he been captured? Even if we do speak, how can I tell that he isn't being forced at gunpoint to string me along? So that we fly into their trap? A runway ambush. Their touchdown Killing Zone (KZ).

Still no word about my 727, the one last heard of stranded in Miami. And still the Greek hasn't got back to me about our alternative option – his 727, idle in Kinshasa. If neither 727 comes good, then this is over. For ever.

I'm running myself ragged. Why not be a train driver, after all? Why not be safe at home? Why not be with Amanda?

Thank God there is a point to this Op. A point beyond mere money, I mean. EG is a rank tyranny and ongoing. Sure, we'll make money – loads – but EG is a mountain that needs climbing. The people of EG are under the cosh. EG has too much oil. It's like the fatal gift of beauty. An ancient Greek curse.

One-time Spanish colony EG is the third-biggest sub-Saharan oil producer. Yet the poor bastards come near bottom of the UN Human Development Index. Less than half the population drinks clean water. One in five children dies from malaria before they make it to five years old.

Since independence in 1968, the nation's two leaders – without an election between them – have been pilloried as being among the worst abusers of human rights in Africa. And the richest. Before Obiang's terror came that of his uncle, Francisco Macías Nguema. He ordered the mass murder of thousands of the Bubi tribe and political enemies. One third of the population fled. Francisco was a member of the Fang tribe, one of Africa's largest. The Fang extend from Cameroon, through Equatorial Guinea, all the way south to Gabon.

Obiang, of course also a Fang, took over by force – killing his uncle – then, some say, eating him. That was in 1979. Since then, Obiang and his gang have trousered the petrodollars, letting his own people starve. With no help from outside, those people will never win their freedom. Getting out from under tyranny without help has a snowball-in-hell's chance.

This civilian population will never know the most basic public health care. This state won't even fork out the $5 needed per new-born child for a mosquito net. A simple step that would more than halve the infant mortality rate, which stands at almost one in ten.★

I cannot think of a single reason not to putsch this bastard.

My SA mobile rings. It's the Greek calling from a far-distant very bad line in Kinshasa. His boss says no. Fuck. The notice is too short. If we have another go, then his boss will back us all the way, he says: 727, money, weapons.

I have no idea if any of that is true. It's too late now anyway. It's tomorrow or it's never. If Anthony, my PA, can't get this American crew to fly my 727 from Miami to South Africa, the Op is gashed.

The same phone rings again. It's Anthony. Hallelujah! My 727 is back on plan. Good ol' Bill: he has the ship ready for take-off from Miami. Paperwork done. Snags sorted.

0400 HRS ZULU,★ ETA LANSERIA RSA

I know that Pien has paid off the officials at the airport in Pietersburg (now called Polokwane) in the northern state of Limpopo, South Africa. The plane will land there, refuel, then clear immigration. It'll take off OK for Harare, with 69 known mercenaries on board. Bet your arse, it won't be just Pien's bribe that will make sure that happens smoothly. I know. I suspect that powerful agencies, too, have smoothed our path out of South Africa.

Hallelujah! At last. I get a call through to Niek up in EG. He is ready for us, he says, and all is well. Meaning that there isn't a wall of water-filled oil drums across the main runway at Malabo International. That tanks aren't out on the streets. Not yet.

Cryptically, Niek lets me know that the EG Army are going to help us, and that the South Africans are going to support Severo Moto. Both of these things I know, but how the hell does Niek? It's an open line, sure to be intercepted, so I can't ask: our stilted, veiled speech, our ad hoc codes, won't allow it.

I put the phone down. I run it through in my mind: was there any

---

★The precise figure is 92.3 deaths per 1,000 live births, and 155.4 per 1,000 live births in under-fives, according to the UN Population Prospects report, 2005–10.

★A military term for Greenwich Mean Time.

hint – any use of one of our trigger code words – to say that Niek was under duress? But I couldn't spot one. All clear. Or I'd missed it.

Suddenly my Op is happening.

I don't know whether to feel happy or just more frightened. I don't tell anyone that the Hawker crew is being held at the airport. Does Brodie have the political clout to spring my crew? He'd better have.

As on our first shot, two weeks ago, I stay in frequent comms with the Boss and Mark Thatcher. The Boss is having fun with our code. His code says that the Op's a party, the mercenaries the band, weapons the musical instruments. I wish I hadn't started that one. Thatcher is full of it: good luck, right behind you. His code is that we're oil-prospecting in Uganda. He's 100 per cent on board with our E&E plan. The plan I noted in my Smythson notebook.

'I'll be there for you, no matter what, Simon.'

All this time I'm thinking, what the fuck's happening to Pien and the other two?

Just then a mobile rings.

Pien. I can't make out what he's saying. I shout at him to slow down. He's gabbling. He's joyful. They've been let go. Pien knows the score. Brodie has sorted out the airport uglies in nothing flat: he has flexed supercharge muscle. Brodie has clout. We – therefore – are VVIP. In favour. I thank my stars that Mark Thatcher is on the boat. The Zimbabwe sector of this Op is going to be a walk in the park. Plan E for Easy is GO GO GO.

The evening wears on.

I want to get pissed, with Charles and Lyle, in the Cresta Motel bar, but I can't. To take my mind off the mission, I try to watch TV in bed, but it's garbage. I ring round my stations: Niek, Anthony, the Boss, Thatcher. I dare not call Amanda any more: I'm beyond love.

I think of Willard in *Apocalypse Now*, in his hotel room in Saigon during the Vietnam war. What did he say? 'When I'm here I wanna be home. When I'm home I wanna be here...' Boy, he got that right.

Then the thought strikes me: I've gone beyond doing this shit for a reason. All I'm doing is seeing this Op through for the Op's sake. I'm trail-stamping deep snow to the top of a meaningless mountain.

The task – the climb – the Op – has a life of its own. Groups carry out tasks. The group – the team – is a runaway juggernaut truck. Big wheels are turning now. Task and group. I'm the flea on one axle. I'm clinging on. In my heart of hearts I know it: this is how big fuck-ups happen. But each time I think that, I think back to our other times: the Ops before, when I felt the same. Because then – each time – by sticking it out – by keeping the top of my bottle screwed down…

Just keep going. We always win through…

0600 HRS ZULU (Z), SUNDAY 7 MARCH 2004: D DAY MINUS ONE FOR THE ATTACK: CRESTA MOTEL, HARARE, ZIMBABWE

Dawn comes. I've never been more than half asleep.

Anthony calls to say my Boeing 727 landed at Lanseria International, South Africa. Since then it's flown from there to Wonderboom in Pretoria. Some avionics have gone U/S – but none of the items is a 'no fly'. Our crew are right now taking over from the bronzed, fun-loving ferry crew. The 727 will be taking off on time, for the rendezvous (RV) at Harare. But this early morning – now – I don't know what to do.

Charles and Lyle were pissed last night, for sure. They're with me at this motel because this evening – out at the airport – they will check that ZDI actually deliver to us the weapons and ammo that we paid for. It has cost US$250,000. Cash. Charles and Lyle won't want to run this morning. I slip into my running kit, then set off for a fast 45 minutes.

As ever, to run is a blessing. Mindless joy and rhythm make me calm and focused. I feel good. The coup is going to be doing something right – and this time the Op is for all the right reasons.

Then, minute by minute, the day becomes more and more of a nerve-stretcher. As I lounge about, with nothing else to do, each hour becomes my rack. The time my inquisitor. All I can do is quiz myself. Over and over I run through my coordinating instructions.

Niek wants us into the Landing Zone (LZ) – Malabo International's main runway – between 0200 Z and 0600 Z the next day – ideally between 0300 Z and 0500 Z. Our Estimated Time En Route (ETE) is four and a half hours.

So we must take off from Harare between 2130 Z and 0130 Z –

ideally between 2230 Z and 0030 Z. I must allow an hour to refuel, and an hour and a half to load the weapons and ammo. Therefore, the 727 and the men must land at Harare between 1900 Z and 2300 Z tonight.

Our Harare gear-up time will trigger Crause's take-off from his refuelling point in Bamako, Mali. He is flying the King Air with the new President, Severo Moto, direct to Malabo International. They will have flown out of Gran Canaria, the Spanish island off Africa's west coast.

The two trigger messages – for Crause and Moto to take off – and for the palace coup to green-light – will be sent by me, from the cockpit of the 727, via my Iridium satellite phone, to the Boss. Then I will make two more calls: to Thatcher and to Anthony, both in South Africa.

While I'm still trying to lounge in the Cresta, Brodie calls me. He's in the lobby. Is something wrong? When he arrives it's 12.30. He insists I buy him a beer. He sips his Lion lager carefully. What's going on? I wait for his news. There is none.

Then the penny drops: he is babysitting his US dollars. This evening Captain Brodie (laugh! Captain of what?) will be given $20,000 by me – just for his own pocket – if it goes OK. He's already had $10,000.

A warmer into the bank.

Brodie is large. Between 50 and 60, I guess. Black and sweaty. A lugubrious face that belies real intelligence. Well dressed for a Zimbabwean. Always formal. Not afraid of eye contact. Hard and direct for what he wants. For what he doesn't want, ruthless. Not kind.

We talk of more business in the future. All the time my radar is probing. Is he a traitor? An entrapper? But the radar can't see through his thick black hide. Reading him is too hard, our differences too great.

My loyal soldier Charles West has had a panic attack. He triggers one off in me. Would the AKs come as standard? Four magazines, a bayonet and a cleaning kit? We didn't order them separately.

Maybe we – Niek and I – should have been specific when we placed the order. To this question Charles had added a few choice Boerer slurs, against black Africans in general, Brodie in particular. I ask Brodie, and he tells me, 'Four magazines with each weapon is standard. Standard is what you'll get.' Unshakeable.

Brodie says he'll be back at 1800 hrs to take us to see the weapons. Back in my room, I force myself to read a Jane Austen novel – *Mansfield*

Park. Same one I start again later in prison. Plenty of time to finish it then. I snooze. You can blame Jane or the beer. It's the least painful way to pass this time.

I look at my Breitling Emergency. It's after six. Suddenly the minutes that crawled by are racing. Too quick. Now I have to pack up, get the other two together and check us out of this dump. If we don't work fast, we'll get late.

A part of me refuses to believe that we are going to go ahead with this. I'm scared. I screw the top of my bottle down – yet again – only harder. I wish that I was armed already, but not to shoot anyone else.

From the start of our EO adventures – the business identity of our old mercenary outfit – rule number one had been 'Don't get captured'. To that end, there had always been a last few rounds. A last grenade.

We rush to be ready. I row with the hotel – over their not taking local currency, over their ripping us off. Then we wait. We're twisted up like corkscrews with the stress of this. Where the fuck is Brodie? We rush to wait. A thunderstorm bangs off all around us, then delivers its downpour.

Rainforest rain. Tropical greed. Exotic excess.

I phone Brodie. No answer. I phone the other ZDI man, a frightened little apparatchik named Daniel. No answer. The rain drives down harder. This rain means business.

Anthony had already called to say that the Boeing 727 took off – bang on time – from Wonderboom, in South Africa, for Pietersburg. Then he had called again. Our aircraft had taken off for Harare. Shit! The thing will be landing in ten minutes, for God's sake!

Where the fuck's Brodie? Where's our wagon? Where's Daniel?

The rain's a burst main.

A pair of yellow headlights leak through the downpour, followed by another. The splashy outline of a car pulls up. It's Brodie. Daniel is driving the second. We scowl. They smile. Relax. I smell that Daniel has been drinking. Brodie takes me aside.

'Do you have my twenty thousand ready – to give to me? I want my twenty thousand now.'

I love his spirit, and his openness. I laugh and smile at him. He and I are best friends.

'*Shamwari!* My friend! You don't think I'm going to leave Zimbabwe without giving you your money, do you?' Africans hate that kind of joshing. Brodie hates it. Clever me. Or should I read Brodie's plea for cash up front as a warning?

'Your money's on the plane,' I lie, voice dropped, serious now. 'It's in the cockpit – with the captain...'

Brodie's phone rings. He talks briefly, in *Shona*, the Bantu tongue of Zimbabwe, then he says, 'Your plane has landed...'

'...and my money better be on board,' he doesn't say.

'...it's taxied to the civilian side – for the fuel,' he tells me.

We pile into two cars, with our kit. I'm with Brodie. Charles and Lyle are with drink-driver Daniel. We drive through the thrashing rain. Roads are rivers. I think about Neil, the captain, and the co-pilot of my Boeing, flying the men into Harare.

Neil is the brother of Crause, the pilot charged with flying Severo Moto into Malabo, from the Canaries, via Bamako. Neil and Crause are both EO originals, with us from our first war, Angola 1992–5. I think of Neil, and how he would be loving it. Poking the new Boeing down the Instrument Landing System glide path. Down through this onslaught waterfall. Vic Falls, from above.

Reaching the civilian side of Harare International – all along on running-wet tarmac – we drive on, dodging potholes, skirting the perimeter fence, right round, until we reach Manyame Air Base.

The military side of the airfield. The guard room and gate look British. Strangely anachronistically British is what they are, still fresh from 1950. The old Rhodesia. Our convoy of two drives in. Damp soldiers eye us, then stand to attention. String puppets. No nit-picking checks. All salute.

Brodie's $20,000 rides on this. We're expected. I've bought the bloody place.

At the military camp, inside the old Rhodie Fire Force huts (the huts from which the Fire Force fought their nasty useless stupid war so well), I'm introduced to the Base Commanding Officer. Fine in his Sunday afternoon Hawaiian shirt, but looking worried.

He's been dragged off the golf course – unaware and unhappy – to sign off on something beyond his power. That's how he seems. Not happy. My alarm bell clatters. There are four or five people with him, also soldiers, also in their Sunday civvies. They alarm me more. I look around. What danger? Nothing stands out.

He nods us through. Airside. I push a squeaking metal door …
through to a hairdryer of wet warm air and a welcome sight.

The downpour has halted.

I see the aircraft – there she is! My very own Boeing 727. Here.
Twenty-four hours ago she was stuck in Florida. I'm hit by a freight
train of feelings: pride, excitement … then memories of the great days
of Angola and SL.

Fear uncoils its cold scales against the sides of my belly: what is going
to happen to us in the next 24 hours? Not everyone is working to my
Coordinating Instruction. Not the target, President Obiang.

But, as ever, it is doing which elbows dread behind.

Quickly, I walk across the ramp, then towards the rear air-stair (for our
kinds of shit, the rear air-stair is one of the Boeing 727-100's plus points.
Useful. We are not a customary airline!).

As I reach the bottom of the stair, the howl of the aircraft's auxiliary
power unit beats down on me from just above my head. The smell is
hot-wired: the reek of Jet A-1 kerosene makes my heart pump. I leap
up a gear.

'Napalm in the morning' if you like. But for me kerosene and hot jet
exhaust are the smell of 'Action Stations' … of 'Airborne!' … of air
power… 'Danger's no stranger – to an Airborne Ranger!'

On board the smell of Nando's greets me. I had forgotten how
Anthony and I had planned our in-flight catering for the troops. Men
call out to me. A few faces I remember from the old days, most I don't.
I greet them all as old friends. I make it to the cockpit.

'Hi, Neil – you fuelled up OK?'

'Hi.' Neil looks at me to check that we are really here. Doing this. 'We're
full of fuel. Topped off. Ready to go – and all paid for. Where's Charles?'

The refuel has been a scam, of course, our cash US dollars going
nowhere near the fuel's true owners. This is Zim.

'Charles and Lyle are checking the weapons. I'm going to them now,'
I say. 'Get our loading party ready, will you, please – down at the bottom
of the air-stair?'

This loading party is to shift the gear into the hold. Neil is ready for
that because he has read the handwritten orders I gave to Anthony back
in Jo'burg. I know that Neil has read those orders because I can see my
note in his hand. I say nothing, but I curse Anthony: I told him that note

20

must not come onto the aircraft. It's one more breach of security. One more of many. Too late to matter, I hope.

On my way back down the stair, I find our old flight engineer. Like many of the others – like Neil and the co-pilot – he is a veteran of our adventures. Gnome-like. Always sunburned. Wiry. White-grey hair, balding. Always nervy. Excited. A born pessimist. This night, and true to his trade, he looks like he's lost something precious. A ten-rand note maybe.

'Cheer up. It may never happen! C'mon, man – only two and a half tons of weapons and ammo… That's no sweat…'

'It isn't your two and a half tons … it's where you're gonna put them…'

He glances at his clipboard, scribbled with the hieroglyphics of weight and balance, of centre of gravity.

We both know how tight we're going to be for fuel: we'll be shutting down the centre one of the 727's three engines as soon as we're into our cruise climb. Even then we're too tight on range – and on take-off weight. Harare is 5,000 feet above sea level for a kick-off – and we're going to be heavier than maximum for this runway. This outside air temperature … in this wind … this tide.

The flight would be without a kosher ATC flight clearance. But over black Africa, pilot-to-pilot self-ATC is the norm. Worse than incorrect Flight Plans, and the wrong Over-Flight Clearances, we have no Alternate … no other airport to divert to.

If Malabo proves impossible, our best option is to fly south-west for just under 300 miles to São Tomé. We may have enough fuel. But then we will be flying into another war.

We've spoken with some of the rebels down there, three nutters from the Committee for the Liberation of São Tomé and Principe (CLSTP). They are our friends, and have promised us their help if we need it. If we land there, without doubt they'll use us to kick off their own coup.

'Whoops! Sorry! Wrong island. Wrong fucking President!'

There are other horrors. This is March. We are close to the Equinox. Flying into the Inter Tropical Convergence Zone (ITCZ). That equals shit weather. This time of year the ITCZ is bang on top of our target: Malabo, on Bioko Island (formerly Fernando Po), Equatorial Guinea. The armpit of Africa.

That's the weather. But what if Niek is nabbed?

What if our main runway – our Landing Zone – turns out to be our Killing Zone? What happens if we get ambushed on landing? We are on one wing and a prayer.

In Jo'burg we decided – Charles, Neil and me – that, if Niek is compromised, then we'll just fly in anyway. We'll crash-land if we have to – then take our chances. Leaving Niek behind is not an option.

Fucking hell. Why am I doing this? For the money? Sure. Right now, all the money in the world isn't enough. I've got loads of bloody money anyway. I'm a multi-millionaire in sterling, for fuck's sake.

Brodie, my Zimbabwe spook, waits for me at the bottom of the air-stair. He craves his 20 grand. All 20 shine back out at me from his greedy dark-brown eyes. In his car we drive 100 yards – round the corner to a run-down old Rhodie hangar.

Charles and Lyle wait outside, standing by the other car.

Charles gives me a hidden look: 'All clear.'

Inside the hangar – ill-lit and dirty – stands a flatbed trailer, sides up, without a pulling truck. No horse.

Brodie waves us to inspect the piled boxes.

'There are your weapons on the trailer. Check them, please.'

So we climb up the high sides. A sickening sinking weight thumps downward to my lower gut. I climb … peer over the sides… There isn't enough kit on here. Something's wrong.

I look across at Charles. He and Lyle have their knives out, opening a box. Some of the boxes look like the real thing but others don't. My mind reels. Stupidly I think what a long walk it is to Jo'burg. My skin soaks me in a chilled sweat.

I open what looks like a shoebox. Plain brown cardboard. Inside are one old 36 grenade, a few loose rounds of 9mm. They laugh at me. What the fuck is this?

I look back to Charles. He's holding an RPG-7 round: rocket and warhead. Lyle's looking at the rocket while Charles looks at me, his face a mirror of mine.

'What the fuck is this?'

'Get down off the truck!'

It's an order. I glance around the meanly lit hangar. A circle of ten men stand silent in a ring around the trailer. Black overalls, HK MP5s slung across their chests. Relaxed, alert, poised.

I know the look of these men. I've been one. They are pros, even if we are in the heart of black Africa. God knows … but where had they come from?

Three or four others huddle around Brodie. Their bulky awkwardness and cheap leather jackets give their game away: 'secret police'.

My strong heart slips, then I fall. A dark abyss without bottom sucks me down and down … down…

My hands are steel-cuffed behind my back. The cuffs pull my shoulders back. My neck and head forward. It hurts. They stuff me onto the back seat of some crap car.

Two goons wave the barrels of their 9mm Star handguns in my face. I'm sat between them. Their breath smells of cheap liquor, kaffir beer, moonshine, hooch.

God knows what they'll do to me.

We drive.

No formal arrest. No hope. I'm going to die, so I think of home. They tell me how I'm going to die. Nobody knows where I am, they tell me. They're going to shoot me. The crocs will hide me. There are plenty of crocodiles in Zimbabwe.

We drive some more, then turn off the bombed tarmac. The car lurches down a sandy dirt track, weak yellow headlights barely showing the way. I can sense a river ahead.

Crocodiles eat evidence.

What ways out of this? Who are these people? What's gone wrong?

God knows what's gone wrong. This is Africa.

Stay loose. We can get out of this, I tell myself. Thatcher can get me out. Thatcher and the Boss can get us all out.

If we live.

The dirt track grows bumpier, narrower.

'Are white men tougher than black men, Mann?'

I smell the hooch from inside him.

'We are going to kill you, Mann. Nobody will ever know where you died. Nobody will ever know what happened…'

'Are you afraid, Mann?'

They're bullshitting me. I hope.

I don't know. If they are, then I can't see why. What's their game? The crocs are not thinkable. I try not to think. I feel relief, strange flakes in

23

the Force Ten blizzard of thoughts and sadness charging by. Relief muddles me. We've fucked up. All is lost. There's no suspense now. That's a cop-out … but it's some kind of relief.

Sixty-nine men have been nicked with me. Fucking hell. I don't know that they have been nicked. I assume it. I know Charles and Lyle are in irons. I saw them collared along with me. I saw them taken to another car.

Brodie was nicked. He was taken to a third car. Maybe ZDI will sort this out for him and then, because we're his clients, for us? Maybe even without Thatcher's help… But I didn't believe in Brodie's arrest. There had been a touch of con about it.

The car stops. I feel sick.

'Get out! Kneel down!'

Their feet kick me, hands strike my head. Ten paces from the car. Downhill. They wrestle me into a kneel. River water. I can smell my death even though I don't believe in it.

They say they're going to shoot me … again. They shoot, now…

Click. Click.

They laugh.

My knees are wet in the sand.

My mind clicks.

When these goons had waved their Stars at me before, I had seen their hammers were back. They hadn't re-cocked a weapon since, so their bravado had been only that: they had no rounds in the chamber. They still don't.

'Are you afraid?' 'Are you brave?' 'How tough are you?' 'Do you think you are tougher than a black man?' 'Do you think you are better because you are white?' 'Who knows where you are?' 'Who cares where you are?' 'How long will it be before anyone misses you?' 'What can they do to help you – here in Zimbabwe?' 'Are you ready to die?' 'Would you like us to kill you – or shall we wound you … leave you for the crocodiles to finish you…?'

Even when they do shoot me I still won't believe it.

'Please kill me first. Please don't leave me to the crocodiles…' I say. But not to them. I say it to myself.

Fucking hell.

Am I scared? Yes.

CHAPTER TWO

OK. So just how does this whole fucking shambles kick off anyway? Sometime in late 2002, I'm introduced to Wayne Adams, a spivvy property something-or-other. A wannabe adventurer. He's short, heavy, fat. Tod slipper shoes, his ankles buckle. Greasy, pitch-black hair, too long. Greasy skin. Rich car. Rich clothes. Centre of the Universe.

Early 2003, he asks me (Africa Hand) to visit Gabon: he had become big mates with the President of that country – the late and unlamented Bongo.* The President, it turns out, had taken a shine to Wayne when they had met on holiday.

My seven-day trip to Libreville is as much a waste of time as I had feared. A pain in the arse. The city is a dump, a slum, despite years of oil boom. The palace of Monsieur Le President Bongo, on the other hand, is a thing of beauty.

When I meet Bongo, I feel like laughing and not because of his name or because he is such a short arse (even in high Cuban heels). What is revoltingly hilarious is that nothing matters to Bongo except the flat dollar-a-barrel tariff deals that he has with Big Oil.

The Barrel Boyz.

Deals like this are what an oil company calls a Sweetheart Deal – but only behind their slammed closed doors. They aren't so 'sweetheart' to the Joe Bloggses of Gabon. Bongo's dollar-a-barrel Sweetheart Deal

*Omar Bongo ruled Gabon for more than four decades until his death in 2009. Bongo had come to symbolise 'la FrancAfrique', France's shadowy system of maintaining control over former colonies through a web of opaque dealings.

25

costs his country ten dollars a barrel, if a cent. The stupid fucker Bongo may not even know that. He wouldn't care anyway.

Bongonomics.

By the end, the outcome of this business trip farce looks to be the waste of time that I had feared from the start.

Then, when I get back to London, I bump into an old girlfriend (at the time, I thought it a coincidence) who wants me to meet another, bigger big shot. The point of this meeting is to talk through the Gabon trip. To me that sounds like worse time flushed after bad, but I agree to meet the friend anyway. Big shots can be useful, and talking Bongonomics can be fun.

So, in February 2003, I find myself at a house in London. That the Gabon trip had been a set up doesn't cross my mind. I am too busy being flattered by this guy's great INT all about my career – especially of my feats in Angola and Sierra Leone. Then there is his thirst for my opinion on other African hotspot hell-holes.

When I meet the Boss, he somehow knows that I have twice been in Southern Sudan, as a guest of the rebels, the Sudan People's Liberation Army (SPLA), only months before. Somehow he knows that the first SPLA trip had gone walkabout – over the DRC border, into the north-eastern region of Kilo Moto. The second had gone walkabout in the Ethiopian Frontier Mountains.

It is after this chatty Grand Tour of the horrors of Africa that he says it: 'The one place where I would like to be King for a Day is Equatorial Guinea. Have you seen their crude oil figures? Their production? Their proven reserves? Billions!'

After more chat, the meeting is brought to an end. Something might be possible in the Sudan (agreed). Would I think about it and set out on paper what could work?

Back home I do think about it. I had liked the Boss. He is witty and smart. Very well dressed, but casual. Doesn't suffer fools, but says so. Knows the score.

On my computer, I give the Sudan (poor bastards) my best shot (again). I wittily codename my paper 'GORDON TWO' – when actually it must be 'GORDON FOUR' or 'GORDON FIVE'. You see, I had written up Sudan plans before, for other philanthropists.

The Sudan idea is to find some super – but frozen – asset – oil or gold – of which the Sudan has plenty. Once chosen, and agreed, then this asset could be brought out of the cold and into production, by the use of a private-venture military force – but acting under a government licence, and within a government partnership.

But which government? Khartoum tyrants? Or the Kenya-based SPLA rebels? Which one of those would be a question of where the asset is. North: Khartoum. Or South: Nairobi. Or both. Then it's just a question of picking the nastiest bunch of local *banditti*. Hire them for security. Train them a little. Arm them better.

By chance I have already spent time looking into just the job: a gold mine in the Ingessana Hills, north-west of a place called Bau, close to the Ethiopia border. The mine had been developed, then abandoned, by a Chinese outfit. Profits had been high, but it hadn't worked because of a pack of Shifta wannabe warlords.

Two sides of A4 set it out well enough. But somehow I'm not surprised when, at the next meeting with the Boss, advertised as a chat about 'GORDON TWO', he only nods – grandly – at my paper. Then he lays it down on the sofa beside him. What he really wants to talk about is President Teodoro Obiang Nguema Mbasogo of Equatorial Guinea. Tyrant. What about a coup to overthrow him? An ARC in the coin of that year of the Iraq invasion, 2003. What about an assassination of President Obiang? Would I lead such an Op? I had worked wonders in the Angolan war, and Sierra Leone's, and I had done so without public fame or notoriety. I had impressed him. Am I in?

If Obiang is the terrible tyrant that everyone says he is, then what could be better than mounting a coup against him? It would be a good Op to carry out even if there were zero money to be made out of it. Why should the people of EG have to live under the cosh as they do? Why should anyone?

And then there are the supertanker loads of petrodollars to be made, some by me, even if it is made clear that there will be no cherry-picking of oil assets. There are other reasons too. There is the big picture opportunity. Our days in Angola and Sierra Leone had been great – but I and others had felt that we had not gone far enough. Every step we took we saw how we could vastly help poor and suffering Africans. The Africans agreed. Some mighty powerful other agencies, however, disagreed.

These agencies care mostly about oil. They want West Africa to be fragmented, chaotic, at war. They do not want a West Africa OPEC.

What these Barrel Boyz want is fear and loathing… The Balkanisation of West Africa, as one CIA staff paper called it, while PowerPointing 'the benefits', bullet point by bullet point.

However, goes my thought: if I and the gang could be the power behind a democratically elected and vastly wealthy Equatorial Guinean throne, then we could be a real power for good in one of the worst parts of Africa.

There are other reasons. I am flattered to be asked. I want to make the money. I want to make a difference, make some lives better. I feel challenged to take on such a tough job. I want the danger and the hardship. I love the craic.

You see, I had made two fortunes winning the Angolan civil war, then spent one of them winning another: the Sierra Leone civil war. But Equatorial Guinea would be something else. I would be getting into it because I wanted to be in it, not because that was where the trade winds had blown me.

Anyway, as I say, it is 2003, and ARC is in vogue. I had played a part in the 'sexing up', the plotting, that had gone on, so as to bring about the Iraq invasion and the downfall of the arch tyrant Saddam Hussein. I had wholeheartedly put my shoulder to that wheel. So, in that case, why not private-venture ARCs?

I mean, how many people does any tyrant have to kill or torture before something can be done about the bastard? Walking past someone being beaten to death in the street, or mugged in a shopping mall, is not right. We all agree, even the *Guardian*. Walking past isn't something any of us would like to do. It isn't what our upbringing tells us to do. But, other than in scale, what's the difference between a bunch of yobbos mugging an old lady and a tyrant mugging a people? Both like their victims weak, that's for sure.

EG will be a tough mountain to climb. High, but it needs climbing. It will be hard. Dangerous. I want to trek back into the big mountains like a soak wants a drink. I want the job. I long to pull it off.

'I'm in – but not for an assassination.'

'Why not?'

'Because it won't work. Kill Obiang and what happens next? You could get the son – Teodorino – and be no further forward. You could get the army, God help us … a home-grown coup. Then where are you?'

I say it, and I mean it. What I don't say about the proposal is that an assassination is plain wrong. I feel that way, but I know the Boss won't be keen on that kind of talk.

To me, the rightness of being 'in' on an EG coup is clear enough. If Obiang had been a benign dictator, then I would not become part of a plot to overthrow him. Not for any money. But even though Obiang is a full-on certificated and practising tyrant, his assassination is a non-starter.

So I'm in.

We set to work, and that means brainstorming the options.

The Boss is interested to hear how things had worked in Angola and Sierra Leone. I stress over and over how speed had been the key.

'Speed and surprise are needed in the attack. But I'm talking about something else… I mean that we must be speedy, between the day when you give me the "Go!" – the day when you say that I have the green light – between then and the day when we actually do go. That was how we got away with what we did in Angola … and then again, in Sierra Leone. We were speedy. We moved faster than the leaks. Faster than all the government arseholes.

'You see: we're gonna have leaks – you can't stop leaks … the only way round the leaks is to be fast. The one thing you must not do is give me GO … STOP … GO … STOP… That way we'll be fucked.'

I say it. Then I say it again. I think he understands it. I really hope that he understands it. If this is to work, then that sort of speed and surprise will be the single most crucial factor.

I had become the 'Go To Guy' for military coups. The most notorious and best-paid mercenary of my generation. How had that happened? How had that murky world made me its bright star?

Number two Chester Square in Chelsea was the house of my birth. Where the family lived for six years after that. Number two is Blue Plaque: 'Matthew Arnold: 1822–1888: Poet and Critic: lived here.' I remember the London County Council blue disc. The house.

My parents had employed a nanny who'd taken me and my younger brother Richard for walks along Ebury Street, marching with the New Guard. From Chelsea Barracks to Buckingham Palace. For the Guard Mount.

Nanny had shown how, in some streets, every fifth or sixth house was a gaping hole. Bomb sites held me in grim amazement. Nanny told us about the Blitz: then the V-1 doodlebug (chugging motor … then the cut, a tense silence, followed by the great bang) and the V-2 rockets (no warning of any sort, just an immense explosion).

We were raised in the shadow of war. My grandfather Frank and father George – F.T. and F.G. – were both war heroes: the Great War for Frank and World War II for Daddy. Neither spoke about it much, but when they did it was frightening. What had gone on – in Daddy's case at least – was still talked about even when I joined the Scots Guards.

I don't know how Frank survived. Most junior infantry officers joining anywhere near the start of the Great War were killed well before the end of it. He was wounded three or four times. Each time he went back and fought again. The doctors told him that his cricket was over. He proved them wrong, by becoming captain of England.

Having joined the Scots Guards at the outbreak of World War II, my father fought in Operation Torch, the allied invasion of Libya. At the time, Rommel and the Afrika Korps were being forced to retreat westward by Montgomery's Eighth Army, following the Battle of El Alamein. Torch was planned to pincer Rommel at Tunis, which it did.

George then fought throughout the long and bloody slog up through Italy, thus ending the war in Trieste, on the Italian–Yugoslav border. By that time he was a major with two Military Crosses (MCs) and a Distinguished Service Order (DSO). He was regarded by the Scots Guards, and many others, then and much later, as the best fighting company commander there was.

With war heroes and bomb sites so close to home I became locked on to all things war. War comics, or trash mags, as they were called, were our schoolboy staple. Even Nanny had an incredible story to tell: her escape from the Gestapo, from occupied Belgium, and certain death in a concentration camp. Nanny was Jewish.

It was ever a surprise that our nursery short-haired miniature dachshund, Sammy, did not have his own tale to tell of wartime derring-do.

Later, Nanny was to further whet my appetite. She gave me adventure books by John Buchan – all about the South African Richard Hannay – and then she gave me C.S. Forrester's Hornblower novels. What Nanny didn't tell me was that these books were for enjoyment, to get me reading: that they were not training manuals for life.

The books had no warning label. They didn't say: 'Don't Try This at Home.'

One, I remember, *The Jungle is Neutral*, by Frederick Spencer Chapman, had a foreword by Field Marshal Earl Wavell that said: 'What English schoolboy doesn't dream of blowing up a Jap troop train, crossing a bridge?' That was the stuff of the day.

We would have Sunday lunch with Pop, our name for Daddy's father. There would be a crowd of his friends and Daddy's. Every man there had fought the Germans in one or other world war.

Nanny used to vary our walks. We loved Victoria railway station, filled with steam – bursting with noise and energy. There we would gaze up at the gigantic hissing locomotives. Some of the drivers knew us by name and would take me up into their cab. But, when I was eight, Victoria station took on a nasty new mask. It became the terminus for my train to prep school, North Foreland Court, Broadstairs, Kent (and right on top of the self-same 39 cliff steps used by Buchan).

North Foreland Court was a preparatory institution that took seriously its duty of preparing small boys for life's unpleasantness. I'm sure that it was the same one used by Evelyn Waugh in his *Sword of Honour* trilogy. A place where only prefects and headman's pets could sit on the radiators, to escape the ice.

At North Foreland, the Mann Pressure Machine was on. Full blast.

On day one, the headmaster told me how he had taught my father and my Uncle John, before taking me outside alone. I stood frozen as he pointed to the gym roof, all dark-red tiles except for a bright-pink one in the middle.

'Do you see that pink one?'

'Yes, sir.'

'Now! Look over there.'

He pointed to a distant cricket pitch and pavilion. The square roped off for winter.

'During the Fathers' Match of 1929, your Grandfather Frank hit a cricket ball from there, onto the roof, smashing the old tile.'

I tried to look awestruck.

My grandfather and father had both captained the England cricket team; Frank on the victorious tour to South Africa in 1922–3; Daddy doing it again in 1948–9. Then meeting Mummy on the boat home.

I tried hard to be good at cricket, but found myself knocked about in the nets. I just didn't have an eye for the ball. I hoped that I'd be good at war. The war that we knew was just around the corner. That way, I could live up to being a Mann in one way at least.

Those five years at North Foreland dragged by. They were ghastly. The food! I loathed the place, and could not forgive my parents for sending me there – aged eight; – then Richard – aged seven. We had such a lovely home. What was the point? Then, at last, it was Common Entrance, the exam to go on to Eton.

Three days before the exam results were due, I went to a country house cricket match with Mummy and Daddy. Daddy was playing. Captain, as usual. I was to go back to school alone – by train – that Sunday evening. Daddy took me to the nearby railway station. We walked onto the sleepy two-track stop. The station was a picture postcard: great leafy green trees all round, meadows framed between them. But I couldn't see that.

If I had failed the Common Entrance exam, I told myself, then I would disappoint. Then what would happen? Flogging? North Foreland had tried plenty. Deportation to the Colonies? Death? The hinterland behind such a failure was unmapped.

Catching a deep breath first, I asked, 'What happens if I've failed?'

My father looked at me, puzzled. Surely he hadn't forgotten?

'Common Entrance, Daddy. What happens if I've failed Common Entrance?'

There was a pause.

'Good Lord! Well … if you've failed… Well, I don't know. I don't know. Well, we'll have to think of something, won't we?'

The kindly train drew up, puffing. The carriages were the old-fashioned sort where each compartment had its own door, with no passageway. I opened a door, dived in and slammed it shut: a reassuring sound. I sat, secure from the outside world. Thankful to escape.

There didn't seem to be anyone else on board. I found the sash to let the window down. As I stuck my head out, my father, standing on the platform, smiled. 'Don't worry, old boy. We'll think of something.'

A toot rang out, then the steam engine puffed itself into movement. The three carriages clanked out from between the tended platforms, each with its hanging pots of startlingly coloured flowers.

England, Their England: we'd read the book at school, and laughed at A.G. Macdonell's funny and frightening cricket match. As I sat down a thought stepped up. I was going to have to look out for myself; and that might be fun. It was a signal along the track. I saw it. Knew it.

Later, from Eton, Victoria station became a sally port – for lubricious escapades into London. And then from Sandhurst – the Royal Military Academy – it was 'SAME DETAIL!', to use the old drill square shout. More London escapades. Rites of passage.

Strangely, it was the Navy that taught me a vital skill: to shoot straight. At North Foreland, there was an old RN Petty Officer who ran the spot-on, perfect .22 rifle range (not air rifle). He and his beard had survived Jutland, 1916, the greatest naval engagement of all time, won by Jellicoe's perfect command of the Grand Fleet.

'Mann!' Chief shouted. Sitting upon his little chair and Persian rug-covered table, he glared at my target. He peered down his Brassoed brass telescope. 'HOLY MOSES! The days of miracles are over … you wave that bloomin' rifle around like that, sir, 'n you ain't hittin' nothin'…'

I was nine. I had a rifle and a shotgun at home too.

At Eton it was ex-RN Chief Petty Officer Barnes. If he said Barnes it came out Ba-r-r-r-nes. One day, after we had been shooting the 7.62 mm SLR and GPMG, he explained to me how he ran his Flag Ship strict firing range, or anything else.

'An 'ard ship's an 'appy ship, sir … an' that's all thar is to it.'

Right.

I was 15 – by any normal standards already a trained soldier.

Even my O Levels and A Levels are down to the Army. I scraped three A Levels (History, Geography and English Lit) only because, in those days, if you didn't have the basic O Levels, and at least two A Levels, then you could not go to Sandhurst. You could not be a Regular Commission Officer. I had to have them.

I was one of the last to go through the old two-year Sandhurst, Intake 50, whereby one of those years was called 'Academic'. I spent my time foxhunting in Leicestershire and deb-delighting in Annabel's – whenever I got away, and whenever I could scrape together enough cash.

Improbably, I won the Soviet Studies Prize in my academic year. I had a talent for it – I must have had, given how little reading I did – and became friends with two of our five-star VVIP lecturers, Peter Vigor and Christopher Donnelly.

Chris went on to be the Senior Intelligence Officer in NATO under Secretary General Lord Robertson. Chris and I were to meet again, along the murky corridors that led to the Iraq invasion in 2003.

Peter Vigor was a Sovietologist of vast depth, many papers and several books. His family had traded with the Russians since Tudor times. Peter had been chosen to go with Nixon, on his world-changing Moscow visit of 1972. He knew well many senior generals of the Red Army, and of the KGB, at the height of the Cold War. The strange thing was Peter looked just how a casting director would want George Smiley to look, in a film of Le Carré's spy novels. We became friends, so later he came out as my guest to Münster, Germany, to lecture to the Scots Guards Battle Group.

Then, at last, I was commissioned as an officer in the Scots Guards, as my father and grandfather had been before me. I turned up in Münster with skis on the roof of my car, as advised. I parked outside the Commanding Officer's office, as advised. I marched in to report, as required. The result was as hoped. They were short of skiing instructors, so, despite the wails and curses of the adjutant, Roddy Gow, a skiing instructor I was. Straight away. Yes, sir.

I too was to march up Ebury Street, from Chelsea Barracks, to change the Guard at Buck's and Jimmy's. When I did so, I always had in mind the places they had marched to: Pop: Ypres Salient, Passchendaele; then Daddy: the capture of the Siegfried Line, the Battle of the Bou, the Battle of Anzio, Monte Cassino, the Arno and Florence, Gothic Line.

Perhaps that's why I felt unfulfilled and bored. I felt that way despite operational tours in Northern Ireland, then at its miserable worst. I felt that way despite the Cold War rigours of the 4th Guards Armoured Brigade, stationed as we were in Münster, on the North German Plain (good tank country). Opposed as we were to the 2nd Guards Red Banner Tank Army (dissected by Peter Vigor's technical description and his humorous broadbrush account of the likely views held by those officers and men).

I was proving nothing. Not to myself at least. I was a soldier, but I wanted something more. I wanted to find a cause. I wanted to slay a worthy dragon.

Then a friend suggested I see David Stirling. He had been a young officer, a lieutenant, in the Scots Guards – of course – in Cairo, during

Rommel's North Africa campaign. Then and there, somehow, he had founded the SAS.

Stirling had been the subject of the best book Nanny had ever sent to me at Eton – *The Phantom Major*, by Virginia Knowles. I couldn't believe that such a legend existed in the flesh. Still alive and kicking. Stirling had a huge reputation. Founder of the SAS. Wild man. Adventurer. Freedom fighter. Hitler had said of Stirling and the SAS: 'These men are dangerous.' How's that for a write-up?

When this friend suggested: 'Why don't you go and talk to David Stirling?' I thought he was mad. It's like saying to a wannabe teenage girl: 'Well? Why don't you go and have a chat with Madonna?'

But I did track down David's phone number. Then, armed with the foolhardiness of youth, I called him. Shock horror, he asked me to go and meet him. At his London club for a cocktail. I walked into White's needing a cocktail. But I needn't have been afraid. Stirling was amazing: amazingly charming, amazingly friendly, amazingly dangerous.

By then it was the autumn of his no-holds-barred life, but he wasn't about to settle into quiet retirement. Stirling was a ringmaster of what would now be called private military companies. A circus.

It was there, during that first meeting in White's – the *sanctum sanctorum* of the Empire's club-land – that he popped a question: would I like to help out with a Coup d'État? One that he was putting together. One against the communist rule of the Seychelles? The ousting of the quasi-Marxist-Leninist tyrant France-Albert René. A bad ass if ever there was one.

I was 21. It pleased me that such schemes should be kicked off somewhere like White's Club, but it didn't surprise me. My reading of John Buchan made that normal. The plot sounded precisely like the kind of thrill I craved, not least because – as cover for my job as the Op Rupert – I was to pose as a millionaire playboy. With yacht. With squeeze.

Count me in.

I left White's signed up, a little pissed and feeling as though I too had smoked one of Stirling's great Cohiba Esplendido cigars. He had puffed away throughout. My overexcited heavy breathing had made me inhale a Che Guevara lungful too.

This amazing man had also signed me up for White's itself.

'You'd better be a member here, you know … you've gotta be a member of one of these bloody places...' He saw my hesitation, and misunderstood it. (I was in fact worrying about what my father, who hated all London clubs with venom, would say.) '...well, yes – I know White's is a shits' club, of course it is, but at least we're the best shits...'

My only act of courage in this Seychelles Op was to leave my post in the Scots Guards. Or try to. I wrote a letter of resignation to Regimental HQ Scots Guards. I could not reveal the reason for my resignation.

The Lieutenant Colonel commanding the Scots Guards at that time was a dragon: Colonel Sir Gregor MacGregor of MacGregor, the 6th Baronet MacGregor of Lanrick, in the County of Perth. A small, toxic, red-haired, farting, foul-mouthed, stentorian dragon. One of his kinder nicknames was 'the King'. This was because – by his say-so – if the Scots monarchy were ever to be restored, then it would be he who wore the crown. I know other Scots who make the same claim, but it fitted Gregor, his fireworks and his Blimp self-caricature.

When I went to see this dragon king, I dressed in the anachronistic fashion dictated by the then Standing Orders of the Brigade of Guards: black lace-ups, highly polished, three-piece pinstripe suit, stiff detachable white collar, NOT a Brigade of Guards tie, bowler hat, properly furled brolly.

Already ringing in my ears were the rockets of my father and three uncles. One was John Mann, MC and DSO, like Daddy. The other two, as it happens, were Peers of the Realm: Lord MacLean (Chips, the Lord Chamberlain) and Lord Vernon (descendant of Admiral Vernon, and the first ever hereditary peer to declare himself for Labour). All four of them had been wartime Scots Guards.

The dragon rat, Gregor, had phoned my family – told them that I was trying to resign – and asked them to straighten out their crazy child. The network was working. The Mann Pressure Machine at full RPM. The phone ringing. I was surprised that my wonderful godfather, Lord Inchcape, hadn't joined the chorus too.

'This is fucking nonsense, Mann! What the fucking hell do you think you are doing? ...mmm, boy? What? Resign? What? Bloody hell!'

'Sir, as my letter states, I do wish to resign.'

'Well, you bloody well can't. So fuck off!'

'But, sir, I insist.'

(Loud) 'You! You! You insist! Ha ha ha. Fuck off!'

(Quiet) 'Excuse me, sir, but if you will not allow me to resign, then I will do something that will force you to make me leave!'

Now – let me tell you – up until that point in my life, this was the ballsiest thing I'd ever done. Gregor was a frightening man. And in the post of a god.

(Louder) 'Make me! Make me! Mann – if you do anything – no matter what – I will not ask you to resign: I will place you under close arrest! Then prosecute you! Then have you thrown into Colchester military prison. Do you understand?'

(Quieter) 'Yes, sir.'

(Loudest) 'Now get out of this office – before I lock you up for INSUBORDINATION!'

(Quietest) 'Yes, sir.' And out I went. Flimsy. Beaten.

Of course, looking back, the old bastard had done me a favour. He'd done the right thing too. Stirling's Seychelles putsch never went anywhere. In fact, the same scheme was still bubbling around at his South Audley Street offices years later, when I worked there too.

Despite all that, the founder of the SAS and I became friends. More than that, he became a sort of extra, volunteer, godfather. He was one of those I looked to for fatherly path-finding. Approval. David – always – was a man of beautifully dangerous ideas.

Meanwhile, 'The Troubles' in Northern Ireland ground on. I did five tours there, one way or another. The early Seventies were a dangerous time. More than 100 British soldiers were killed each year by the Provisional IRA – as many as in the worst years of conflict in Iraq and Afghanistan. Despite that – from my first tour in 1973 to my last in 1980 – we felt we were going backward, not forward. We weren't winning.

I cannot say that it was enjoyable, or exciting, or satisfying – even if it was our chance to be on Ops. It was boring, sometimes sickening, frustrating ... but always dangerous. Even so, I wanted to see real action: I wanted to follow my first cousin Locky (now Sir Lachlan MacLean Bt, CVO, DL): I wanted to join the fabled SAS – of God-like status to us infantry. The SAS, I knew, were busy with Op Storm, the secret war in Oman; the war to beat off communist-backed insurgents trying to overthrow the old Sultanate, a friend of England.

So, in 1979, aged 27, I did finally reach my teenage goal: a mountain peak of my dreams and ambition. After six years in the British Army, I passed Selection into 22, the Regular Special Air Service Regiment.

Seven months later, in Belfast, one burst of machine-gun fire killed Captain Richard Westmacott, Grenadier Guards, my friend and Brother-In-Arms. He and I had climbed the same mountain – with the same goals – and with the same fires inside us – seeking just causes, worthy dragons.

Richard's killing began a skid for me. A skid downward. Outward. Out of the SAS, out of the British Army, out of my first civilian job, out of my first marriage, away from my children.

There then followed businesses, with too little business. Derring-do, that never did. A brief second marriage. This girl, that girl, then back to this one. The lower I skidded, the less I dreamed of causes or dragons, worthy or not.

War checked my fall, and turned my luck: the 1990 Gulf War. Peter de la Billière, an SAS general, remembered me. He put me on his London staff, as a captain, my old rank. De la Billière was the Commander of British Forces engaged in the first Gulf War (now sometimes jokingly referred to as the Great Gulf War, since World War II came after the Great War, World War I).

The General is a great man, and good to work for. My job – as a lowly Captain SO 3 – was always different day to day: sometimes lowly and humdrum, others stratospheric and interesting.

When General de la Billière retired, the SAS offered me a great post. More than a job, it was a closure for me. It would bring to an end the bad things that had stayed in my mind after the killing of Richard and my departure from the SAS. Two of the soldiers who interviewed me for the job, and gave me their thumbs-up, were from my old G Squadron troop.

Then, my best friend – brother – father – Tony Buckingham – took me out to lunch. His Angola offshore project had at last become reality. He incorporated Devon Oil and Gas (DOG), and asked me to join him. I had been key in getting Tony into Angola in the first place.

It was my dream job, and the chance for a new start as a civvy. I could trade my army salad suit for a pinstripe, try to earn some real money. The SAS offer had set me free. Despite Tony being wild for their job himself, I just didn't need it any more.

Tony. Shorter and rounder than me. Always laughing. Always suntanned. Noisy. Perma-rich. Lots of cars. Clouds of Cohiba cigar smoke. Toad of Toad Hall, meet JR Ewing.

Tony made me his office manager, with a small salary and a percentage of DOG's massive upside. That was in April 1992, when I set out as a wannabe oil tycoon. I enjoyed the challenge, the learning curve.

I met Amanda. I fell madly in love.

Then, the following January – less than a year into the job – everything changed.

I came back from lunch alone into Tony's office, the air thick with cigar smoke.

'Ah, Simon – rebels have attacked Soyo. They've taken it: the port and the town. It's been confirmed. There is no doubt.'

Tony paused to suck his Cohiba Esplendido cigar. Then he blew. 'Devon Oil and Gas's Angola project is kaput – over. I'm sorry, Simon. I can pay you this month … and next. That's it. You'd better start looking for something else.'

For weeks I'd felt a storm, somewhere out there, winding itself up to fall upon this patch of sea. On 16 January 1993, the storm had fallen. UNITA – the Union for the Total Independence of Angola and anti-government rebels – had set my dreams on fire, and those of who knew how many others. By returning to civil war, UNITA, at a stroke, had enslaved hundreds of thousands back into privation. Thousands were to die.

For me, with no DOG, the skids would slip once more. No pay cheque, no Amanda. I was 40 years old, without business qualifications, with a CV that made suits stare, that made insurance companies laugh, with a goods train full of baggage … and that was before the negative equity on my mortgage. My Harlesden railway worker's two up two down. For this Mann there was no brewing family dynastic fortune.

Fire crackled. A spark spat out.

'If UNITA have captured Soyo, why don't we capture Soyo back?' I let fly.

Stavros, at the far end of Tony's power desk, laughed. He stirred himself from his own Esplendido: 'You're fucking crazy!'

I ignored Stavros, as I knew Tony would. Tony sucked thoughtfully, then blew. 'How?'

'Put a scratch force together. Hit the place.'

'Simon, I mean "How?" … as in "How is this to be paid for?"'

'You're Captain Cash Machine.'

Stavros's laugh had wilted into a worried frown. 'You're fucking crazy!'

'Shut up, Stav.'

'Tony – look – with Soyo in UNITA hands the Angolan government are out by five million US per week in lost production. That Agip onshore production – the one at Soyo – pumps at least that. We can hit Soyo for the same amount as one week's lost revenue.'

Suck. Blow. 'Two weeks. Ten million.' Captain Cash Machine is right. Cohibas cost a bomb.

'Fine – two weeks. But … why not? Why should these bastards – UNITA – be allowed to get away with this?'

Suck. Blow. 'Are you sure, Simon?'

'With the right money? With the right support from the Angolans themselves? Sure I'm sure.'

'This scratch force – who would it be? Hereford?' asked Tony.

'Not Hereford. They're expensive. They don't know Angola. No. South Africans: they're used to the climate, and to the people … and I know they're available. Plenty of them.'

'How do you know them, Simon?'

'Here and there… I know where to go, once we have a green light from Angola.'

'Once we get the cash from Angola, you mean. How would our costs work, Simon?'

'Not more than US$2,000 a month, per man. One hundred men. And a success bonus. Two or three months, and then another two thousand, as the bonus. Something like that.'

'How would we go in?'

'I don't know. Hopefully Angolan government forces will take us in, and come in with us: maybe by sea … maybe by choppers.'

Stavros had just slurped, then puffed. 'You are kidding, aren't you? You're both out of your fucking minds. UNITA are a full-on guerrilla army, for fuck's sake!'

I turned on him. 'Look, Stavros, UNITA are just a bunch of thugs. Whatever they were before, they're just thugs now. UNITA put their chop on the UN's Bicesse Accords… Ronald Reagan's Crocker Plan. They signed the agreement. They promised to disarm, demobilise, live by the election. Win or lose. They promised everyone. Savimbi himself, the UNITA leader, even promised David Steel and me: just the three of us. Comrade General Dr Jonas Savimbi gave his word! UNITA lost that election – back last September, which the UN, the US, the EU – and everyone else – decreed "free and fair".'

Warming to my task, I kicked on: 'God knows! We all saw what an effort went into those elections. So what excuse does UNITA have for plunging a whole fucking country back into hell? Back into bloody civil war?'

I finish off by nudging Stav. This is us.

'But Stavros – these thugs, these criminals, are now attacking you! – us: our property, our livelihoods, our men. My bloody job. How many thousands of others are they hurting, right now? They're warmongers. Let them have war then! How does it go in *Julius Caesar*? "Cry 'havoc!' and let slip the dogs of war!"'

'You're the warmonger, Simon.' Stavros slurped, then puffed.

'No – I bloody well am not! There is nothing worse for Mr and Mrs Joe Bloggs of Angola than civil war – nothing. I've been too close to civil war in Africa, in Liberia … in '89. I saw it. Nothing is worse for the locals. I promise you: anything that speeds a government victory is good. If we go there, and fight for the government, then we'll be fighting for peace – that's what victory will mean – as well as our own shit.'

'What do you say to that, Tony?' drawled Stavros, laconically.

'He's right. I agree with Simon – 100 per cent.'

'You could both be killed,' Stavros snapped, frustrated now.

Tony leaned forward, stabbed his intercom, then bellowed: 'Katya, try to get Joaquim David, will you? He's in Angola. Try his Sonangol direct line, first – then the outer office number.'

Joaquim David – General Manager of Sonangol, the state national oil company of Angola – was among the half-dozen most powerful men in Luanda, Angola's capital city.

'Please! Tony!' Stavros cried. 'You're not really going to pitch this to Joaquim David, are you? He'll think we're crazy people. Jesus! You two are crazy people.'

We waited for Katya to get our call through to Joaquim David, known as JD, in Luanda. A task that often took days.

Stavros fiddled with a box of matches, pricking the soggy end of his Cohiba with one stick, then lighting yet again the other. Once he had the whole thing burning to his exact satisfaction, he turned to Tony: 'This UNITA business. Who is behind it? I mean: who is backing UNITA in this new phase of war? Shouldn't we look behind the obvious?'

'Let Simon and me worry about UNITA, Stavros. Why should anyone back them? They are in breach of an internationally agreed peace treaty. Shit! The Bicesse Accord that UNITA signed up to was also signed by the MPLA, as government, as well as Portugal, Cuba, the USA, the Soviet Union … and Old Uncle Tom Cobley and all, and Old Uncle Tom Cobbley and all!'

Stavros again slurped and puffed, eyes closed in thought.

I turned to Tony. 'What do you think the chances are? Of selling this to Luanda, I mean.'

'God knows. You know how oddball they can be. I like the idea, Simon. Don't worry: I'll give it my best shot, I promise you.'

I stood and walked around the big desk. I looked out over London: the picture-window view, behind Tony's chair, was the best point of the penthouse. The office block sat on the south-west corner of the Ebury Street and Lower Belgrave Street crossroads. The view from the window was northward, over Belgravia, towards the Hyde Park Hilton. Panning right from the Hilton and then eastward, you could see the Post Office Tower, then St Paul's and, further yet, the strange modern shapes of the City.

January cloud sat low, the skyscape already dark and grey by mid-afternoon. East, over the City and beyond, there hung a curtain of dark-grey, almost black cloud, squalls of rain falling upon Docklands and the river. Car headlamps were already lit, The yellow beams reflecting greasily off the rain-slicked tarmac.

It's slippery, I warned myself.

A large jet, a British Airways Boeing 747-400, lowered itself out of the cloud, its blazing landing lights showing first, then the aircraft itself, one red navigation light a bright spot on the port wingtip. The pilot in me watched as the machine, already low, was turned to intercept the ILS localiser radio beam. A Precision Instrument Approach into Heathrow, busiest airport in the world.

At that instant, I knew, hundreds of aircraft were being controlled in and out of London. As ever, the city's thumping energy caught me up into its beat: a titanic engine pushing and pulling goods – goods good and bad – all around the globe.

Once a slave colony of Rome, London itself later became the city to which all roads led. All ships sailed.

My thoughts swung to Luanda, then to Soyo. To the Angolans. I'd been there twice, and it felt good: *simpatico*, safe, welcoming. Now Soyo had fallen. Luanda must be cringing before the onslaught.

Jonas Savimbi had made clear what he planned for the people of Luanda: a plank of his manifesto had been that anyone who could not speak his native African language he would treat as white. He hadn't been talking about Portuguese.

I thought of the journey Tony and I had made to Soyo, only two months back, when everything was going so well. For the journey I had dug out my Penguin *Heart of Darkness*.

I'd traced the Congo River on my Michelin 1:500,000 road map and had seen how apt were Conrad's/Marlow's words '...an immense snake uncoiled, with its head in the sea, its body at rest coursing afar over a vast country, and its tail lost in the depths of the land'.

As we had flown into Soyo, the Congo estuary did look as if it was the head of an immense snake, or dragon, with Soyo perched upon the southern, the lower, lip of the monster's mouth. From the air I had seen across to the northern side, to the top of the dragon's head, to Banana Creek. That day, great towers of Cumulonimbus had menaced, from over the endless forest inland: columns of dragon smoke reaching up to 30,000 feet or more.

I puzzled upon what was happening. UNITA's attack on Soyo was an attack on Angola's oil production, that was clear. As Tony had said, it would have been carefully considered beforehand. What did it mean? I asked myself. For so long the Angolan war had dragged on, yet never once had the flow of oil been cut. The oil industry had always been carefully left alone. This could only mean that UNITA planned quick victory, through rapid mortal blows; and was this one of them?

Yet how could this be possible, if UNITA had disarmed and demobilised, as they had sworn to do? I remembered the meeting between Savimbi and Sir David Steel. I'd been there as David's bag carrier, but in truth as Tony's secret agent. Savimbi had been big, ugly, very black. He was magnetic, enigmatic, commanding. Here was power.

Suddenly the telephone rang. Tony jabbed at his button. Breathless but victorious, Katya announced Joaquim David on the line. For overseas calls Tony kept a stentorian and old-fashioned shout. He gave JD full blast:

'Hello! Joaquim? How are YOU?'

Next, Engineer Comrade Joaquim David, ever calm and courteous, asked after everyone. Tony and JD went over the Soyo news. Then Tony pitched our Soyo plan. I stared out of the window, praying to my heathen gods.

Please, Ares. Please, Athene. It hurt me to think how much was at stake. Today I could lose my job. Much more than that would follow.

Once JD had the proposal straight he paused an age. That was his manner. Then my heart sank as he described the idea as very bad. Very dangerous. JD asked again: was this serious? A before-lunch idea?

Tony reassured him.

JD promised that the President, and his Chief of Staff, General João de Matos, would at least hear the proposal. That was his duty, he said, however bad an idea he thought it. He rang off, promising at the least a speedy reply.

Half an hour later, sure enough, came his reply. JD's courteous tones, carried round the room by Tony's speaker-phone, could not hide his worry or his confusion. The President was sending his Gulfstream jet to Lisbon, as soon as such a flight could be made ready. *El Presidente* wanted the three of us to come to Luanda for meetings. Joaquim David, messenger, feared that the Soyo plan was to be given the go-ahead.

Forty minutes later I walked from the office to the motorbike stand in Eaton Square. The rain had almost stopped, but the road looked slippery. My mind was in too many places.

First, I'd been sacked. It was all over. Now it might be all on. Could it really be that, after everything, UNITA, Soyo, was to be my dragon? My worthy cause?

To seal out the wet, I pulled up the jacket's zipper tab as high as it would go. The BMW K1000 RS stood on its main stand. I pushed the start button and electronics set the engine running. A plus of being even a tyro tycoon was having a well-engineered bike.

I pulled down the full-face helmet, did up the chinstrap, then pulled on and Velcroed tight my leather gauntlets. The engine ticked over, warming itself. I swept the worst of the water from off the seat with the back of a gauntlet.

With the bike still on the stand, I swung my right leg over, steadied myself on the balls of both feet, then pushed the machine forward and off. I tried to kick myself into the frame of mind needed for a fast ride home on a slippery top, weaving through London's night-dark, high-speed, log-jam rush hour.

I was on my way to Amanda. How much I loved her. Fun. Laughter. Jokes. Beauty. Strength. Fine limbs. Wild hair.

Launching into the spray of speeding traffic, I grin to myself. All I have to do now is slay UNITA, win the gold, then woo the girl.

Piece of piss.

CHAPTER THREE

MARCH 2003: SPAIN

There's no point overthrowing a tyrant without someone to put in his place. Our man is an exiled opposition leader. Severo Moto. If the Brothers-In-Arms put Moto in power, Moto will see to it that the Brothers-In-Arms benefit from EG's great wealth. *Quid pro quo.*

But before anything can happen, Moto and I need to meet. I have to check out the President designate, and the President designate has to check out me. This blind date has been set up by a plot investor, Malaysian oil broker/Barrel Boy Mustafa Al-Senussi. So it is that a week later I'm checking in to this old guard five-star hotel in Barcelona: the Majestic. Barcelona. Old Spain. Rich. Courteous. It's the Ritz but more posh. The former townhouse of some Duke or other, and Mustafa's choice of RV.

Could there be a more obvious place for me, with all my baggage, to meet the exiled opposition leader of an oil-rich West African tyranny? And in the company of a Barrel Boy like Mustafa? For God's sake.

I walk into Mustafa's suite and struggle to keep a straight face. 'Nice *basha*,' is what comes to mind. His sitting room is the size of a tennis court. Mustafa is sitting at a table with the faithful Iqmad, another scion of a millionaire business dynasty, and another coup backer.

The other backers start grilling me – in a polite way – about how I'd go about toppling Obiang. Iqmad asks about an assassination. He fancies taking out Obiang, but I repeat the arguments. Killing Obiang could flush out all sorts of would-be new Emperors. We would have to sort out all of them. Plus, killing him makes us bandits.

Whenever I stop, Mustafa talks up why I'm right for the job in hand. He's selling me to the investors. But they want to show how tough and sharp they are. We move on to discuss other scenarios. Other options.

I talk them through the slow-burn guerrilla war option. We start in the jungle on EG's mainland, fight village to village, hiding in the jungle, until we reach the capital. I point out the obvious weakness of that approach. Obiang is a billionaire. When billionaires holler for help, help comes.

We could find ourselves fighting the entire Angolan Army, for example. But the biggest 'why not' – for the slow-burn guerrilla war option – is that of civilian casualties. Burned villages. Many.

I talk them through the option of landing on Bioko Island, establishing a Beachhead, then a defensible base, then advancing on Malabo, the capital. The trouble is that Obiang will flee.

I talk them through the 'Wham Bam Thank You Obiang' option. We land at night, with a crack unit, on Bioko Island, near Malabo. Our weapons are speed and surprise. (But without any Pythonesque 'Fanatical belief in the Pope'.)

We smash and grab the palace, with Obiang inside, then Army HQ, Police HQ, communications centres, bank, media centres. KPs. We seize power in a lightning strike. We mug Obiang of his personal fiefdom. A *blitzkrieg* smash and grab.

They ask me which option I favour, but I won't throw any out. I learned in the SAS: don't close an option until you have to. Talk them all through, throw away the dross, but keep all the others open. Anything can happen. We may find ourselves going into EG as Severo Moto's escort, after an army coup has already removed Obiang. We may have to put forward Moto, while the Colonels argue about what they should do next.

After an hour, I know I'm getting the thumbs-up from the investors. I'm the man for the job. We all know it. There's still one man I need to back me. The Prez Dez, S'Moto himself, walks in, with aide. Everyone goes quiet. More than anything, Moto has to make me want to back him.

First sights count all round. I try to get a read-out on him, in among the 'hello and how-de-do' small talk. He is small, and a little podgy. For an African of his age, he looks old. He seems serious, bright, intense. He is a church man – nearly ordained as a Roman Catholic priest – but I try not to rubbish him on that score. He is well turned out, but I know that the Brothers-In-Arms pay all those bills. Moto is what they call the ace card.

Then it's clear I'm meant to lead. Sell myself to Moto. Moto must sell to me. I want to get a feel for Moto. I want to know if he's for real. A good guy. I want to know that he isn't just another arsehole manic for power. Is Moto worth risking our necks for?

The thing is this: whenever I've been part of a private military venture before, either we'd been upholding the cause of a democratically elected government (Angola, Papua New Guinea) or we'd brought democracy back (Sierra Leone). One thing had always been sure and uppermost: we'd all believed. Each time I'd been sure, in my heart of hearts, that our actions would improve the lot of all the Mr and Mrs Bloggses of the country we were in, or going to.

I want to hear it from Moto. If we take down Obiang, then what is Moto's vision for his native Equatorial Guinea? Who is he?

To find out, I need an interpreter. Moto only speaks Spanish, some French, and of course Fang, his tribal lingo. But Mustafa isn't going to miss a trick: he steps in as interpreter, mainly in French. As back-up, Moto has his aide with him, who speaks English. Badly.

I ask Moto why he went into politics. He tells me he'd completed 80 per cent of his training to be a Catholic priest. He woke up one morning – bang! – he could do more good for his people in politics.

'On the Road to Damascus,' I joke.

He smiles, priest-like. He tells me how, early in Obiang's reign, they had been allies. Moto had worked in various ministries, until he fled for Madrid in December 1981. Moto's crime was to publicly call for political reform. Democracy. Later he went back, asking for free and fair elections.

Obiang threw Moto into Malabo's ghastly Black Beach prison. Obiang knew what that was like: his uncle had done the same to him one time. Moto learned his lesson. On his release, given on the pleading of the King of Spain and Pope John Paul II, he fled EG for Madrid. Here his party, the Progressive Party of Equatorial Guinea (PPEG), formed a government in exile. According to Moto, PPEG has won several elections in EG. Obiang refuses to accept the result. African democracy. A mess.

Of course, I knew this patter anyway. I'd done my homework. I have my sources. I'm sure Moto has already checked me out too ... but our dance isn't done.

There is one INT issue that is snagging me badly. Preying on me. My sources tell me how Obiang splits his time between one palace at the capital, Malabo, on Bioko Island, and another at Bata, the mainland capital, miles of sea away, 200 NM SSE.

We don't want to assault a stronghold that doesn't have the bad guy inside it. Which do we hit? How can we be sure he's there? With that, Moto smiles and whips out a mobile phone. He snaps the lid open and dials a number that he knows by heart. One that he hasn't stored in the phone's speed-dial memory. He puts the phone to his ear.

After a couple of seconds, he speaks just a few words in Spanish. He listens, then snaps the phone shut. He opens it again to check it has cut off. I like his attention to detail. It won't help him. If he's under surveillance, then those precautions mean shit.

He looks up at me, smiling. 'The President's at Malabo right now,' says Moto. 'He's planning to stay there the next two nights.'

I nod, then smile. Moto has a man at the heart of Obiang's court. He has someone next to the President secretly plotting against him.

Silence now. I wait for Moto to question me about our options for the Op. He doesn't. He's going to leave the rough and tumble to us, he says. I respect that. He's probably worked this out. Whatever we do tell him will be a *maskirovka*. A deception. The last people we're going to tell what is really going on are him and his staff ... not until we have to. He just asks that the coup be bloodless. He wants bloodless. I want bloodless. I tell him that we will want him to be alongside us on our way to the Op. He smiles. He wouldn't miss it for the world, he says.

After all, what are we? If not the bodyguard of a politician going home?

Unable to stop myself, I remember an ex-President of Sierra Leone I once lunched with, at the Italian next to Colonel David Stirling's old offices in South Audley Street. These days, that Italian is George's, owned by the Birleys.

This old boy had been elected President, but had later fled guerrilla insurgents. By the time of his having pitched up at our offices – sometime in 1989 or thereabouts – he was working as a Heathrow baggage handler.

At lunch, I was tired and bored. Of course, he had no money. Of course, neither did we. Bolshie, I sat watching him. Then I leaned across the table: 'I'll do it for you.'

He grinned at me.

'I'll do it the old-fashioned way, without money. I'll go into the jungle, recruit a few men and work my way to Freetown from there.'

His grin widened.

'Step by step...' I was talking his language '... but I have one need from you. I cannot do without.'

Less grin. 'And what is that, Captain Mann?'

'That you come into the jungle with me ... all the way ... to victory ... to Freetown.'

Bullshit fled. The grin had gone. We didn't hear from the arsehole again. He wanted his Presidency back. But for free.

Moto is different. I like Moto. He seems astute, assured, sincere. He is good enough for what's afoot. He's committed to democracy. He doesn't believe in eating people. A progressive leader.

Next, for a laugh, I try him with the curse of the twin skulls. A Fang belief that, if you take power wrongly, as Obiang did, by the murder of his uncle, then the curse will be on you. It will lead to Obiang's downfall. The joke – to some – is that Obiang's two sons fit the curse so well. Medieval Europe is the best model by which to look at African politics. Succession is the flash-point.

But Moto switches off, then and there. No curse. Looks upset.

Mustafa – who doesn't know about the curse – looks cross. Also because the twin skulls had come as a surprise to him too. I suppose that Moto – Man of God – doesn't go in for *sangoma* spells. The rattling of dried monkey balls. But this is West Africa. All religion is powerful, voodoo the more so. Home-brewed mischief.

Later, after Moto and his aide leave, Mustafa slaps his hand on his thigh. Shoves his cigars into a glass ashtray the size of a dinner plate. All's well. He has good news for the Boss. His investors, his mercenary soldier and his figurehead *El Presidente* have all got on. Mustafa has booked a

MARCH · 2003: SPAIN . . .

table for lunch. We leave the hotel and jump straight into the three hovering black Mercedes limos.

They're all for us: it's Mustafa the gangsta rappa. I love it, of course. But I don't fail to see red flashing lights.

The restaurant is super-rich only. Tables are out on the boulevard pavement. The valet lackeys would be shocked if we didn't pitch up in a fleet of limos. Princess Dolly and all. As we parade our way to the table, I can't help but hear the *Maitre d'* greet Mustafa, by name. His lost son.

When the food ordering and wine tasting rigmarole is all done, I lean to Mustafa's ear. 'Mustafa – our security – why don't we set up a website, you know? "Eg.coupsters.com", something along those lines?'

He peers at me over the rim of his wine glass. 'What's up Simon?' he asks, looking bemused, before taking a long, lazy mouthful of vintage Rioja.

'Well... You booked me into the Majestic in my name. You're checked in using yours. Anyone could have clocked Severo Moto strolling in and meeting us, the mercenary soldier and the millionaire businessman. Then there's this lunchtime circus...'

I pan the street, pavement, restaurant. 'I'd say we're about as covert as a remake of the chariot race in *Ben Hur*.'

Mustafa puts his glass down. He eyes me. He is a diamond buyer squinting through his loupe. How does it go: Carats – Colour – Clarity – Cut?

'Have a drop of wine, Simon. Stop worrying,' he tells me.

That winds me up tighter.

Mustafa takes aim. 'Of course the Spanish ... er ... *CESID*★ have seen us.'

'What?'

'*CESID* – Spanish intelligence ... they know.'

For God's sake. What the fuck is going on here?

'Spain are backing the coup,' smiles Mustafa, 'and have promised to give the Boss immediate *de facto* international recognition to Moto's interim government.'

The words sink in. For this Op, such recognition is a *sine qua non*. A formality without which there is nothing. Spain is the former colonial

★CESID – Centro Superior de Informacion de la Defensa

power of EG. If the Spanish recognise Severo Moto's interim government as legitimate, then the EU and the US will follow.

Mustafa went on. 'They want to send in a thousand *Guardia Civil*, as soon as Moto is in there, to ensure a peaceful handover of power.'

Mustafa's thin smile wipes itself away. 'But we must not let that happen. That would leave Spain too powerful in the new EG, ourselves less so.'

My mind spins. Yes. It's the Iraq invasion line-up, but guess what? Here we all are again.

There has been no cloak and dagger in Barcelona, and now I know why. This is Spain's own Op, and that means that it is also a CIA Op. After all, a nod is as good as a wink, if you're a blind horse. Isn't it?

I feel my body uncoil. This is good news.

In Angola, we were working with the democratically elected government. In Sierra Leone we were working towards democracy, with those in power. This EG Op isn't like that. The operation is against the *status quo*. We're with the rebels. The Op is against the heads. Much riskier.

Not now. Not with a fucking King on board. I drink the wine. Uncoil some more.

Then Mustafa tells me there are rumours that Obiang is ill. One of our investors is getting this from Obiang's personal surgeon in the Mayo Clinic, Jacksonville. Hippocratic Oath country.

If Obiang dies before we get in there, then we may be out of business. Our going in then would add to the no doubt already messy power struggle. Chaos. We'll do it if we have to, but it isn't first prize. The illness routine may or may not be true. In Angola, President Dos Santos used to pull his 'I'm about to die' stunt every eighteen months or so. It was a game: always useful for winning the hearts of the *povos* – or so he believed – and for gassing out of the woodwork the many plotters who would be the next *El Presidente*.

Then there is the curse of the twin skulls mumbo jumbo. If nothing else, that tells me that there is a strong likelihood – at any given moment – that other interests inside the borders of EG might mount a successful coup of their own. That too would spell disaster: if anyone is to overthrow this government, it's gotta be us.

'Time is of the essence,' says Mustafa.

MARCH · 2003: SPAIN...

This I've longed to hear. Investor urgency – an understanding that we must be swift once we start to roll – tastes sweeter than the vintage Rioja. A breakthrough. The investors have at least grasped the heart of how to do this.

Then Iqmad turns and says something to me. My ears are damaged – from high-velocity rifle fire – and the traffic noise doesn't help. I ask him to say again.

'What's your favourite?' he asks, in a conspiratorial undertone.

For God's sake. That's what I thought he had said the first time. Is he gay? I look at him. Quizzing. Maybe he is.

'Favourite what?'

'You know...'

I don't. I shake my head. 'No.'

'You know...' He glances down at his hand, held below the table height. He must be gay. Favourite? Favourite what? Favourite cock?

Then I see it: he's holding his hand as though it's a handgun. Then it dawns on me: the boy's a gun nut, a wannabe.

I laugh. 'No. No favourite ... just so long as it works.'

I can see that this isn't going to work. I look serious. 'But really: you can't do better than a 9mm Browning – you know – that's the SAS basic weapon.'

His face told me that you could do much better.

'But an HK MP7 is really good.'

Iqmad brightens up at that. He rattles off a load of gun nut stuff. I listen politely.

What a happy bunch of Coupsters we are.

I tell my new partners our proposed coup will need planning. Pricing. For that reason, my next move is a trip to South Africa. Soon. There I can make contact with the same men I had first met in London in the Eighties.

At that time, they had been soldiers in the SADF. They had been officers, but they had been working in Europe undercover: to bust import sanctions against the Apartheid regime.

When, in 1993, the Angolan government had first transferred money to Tony Buckingham and me, to mount the Soyo Op, we had gone to two of those men, now in Pretoria, South Africa: Eeban Barlow and Larnie Keller. The four of us had then founded Executive Outcomes,

MARCH · 2003: SPAIN . . .

using an off-the-shelf shell company of that name already owned by
Barlow. Tony and I had made sure that we were never directors,
employees or shareholders of EO. Everything has always been on a
handshake. We tell them what to do. We pay them for doing it.

EO has become something extraordinary, and frightening, to many
people (and governments) in Africa and beyond. Then – on 31
December 1998 – after victory in Angola, and victory again in Sierra
Leone – it was disbanded entirely.

The people I now need to see are my old EO crowd.

Lekker. Like a *krekker*!

CHAPTER FOUR

1993: ANGOLA

Like nowhere else on earth. Overrun with Barrel Boyz, desperadoes, gun-runners, Portuguese and a multi-national menagerie of misfits, fighting to expand vile political creeds (China, Cuba, South Africa), and old Cold War superpowers clinging to fading glory (USSR and the US).

The Cold War's last hurrah. A fireworks party. And Star Wars' Last Chance Saloon. Driving all this chaos and violence were Angola's fuck-off riches. In Angola, it's about oil. Lots. It's about diamonds. The best.

Angola had been ravaged by civil war for two decades. Half a million people had died. Four million had been displaced. That civil war started in 1975, when the Portuguese, beaten by the guerrilla war for independence, fled.

The civil-war fighters were the governing MPLA – the Marxist Popular Movement for the Liberation of Angola – versus UNITA, the anti-Marxist National Union for the Total Independence of Angola.

In 1975, backing the MPLA were the Soviet Union, with their running dog Cuba. Backing UNITA were the US, China, France and their paper-tiger running dog South Africa. Angola had been the Cold War's hottest proxy war. More than once I was shocked to see – from the air – miles of burned-out Russian tanks. They looked like the relics of a World War II battle. A Kiev. You couldn't go to the battlefields on the ground. *Achtung Minen*.

The fighting had been very bad. Vast areas were still No Go owing to these anti-tank minefields and booby-trapped anti-personnel mines. In great tracts of forest no bird sang. They'd all been eaten. Russian KGB Alpha troops had fought in the front line against their CIA equivalents: Delta. Greek alphabet soup.

Cuban had fought South African. At one point, the SADF had been within 20 kilometres of Luanda, before being ordered – by their proxy war masters the CIA, in Langley, Virginia – to halt. Turn round.

The White House had woken up to what the CIA were about to pull off – an outright victory, by means of the white South African Apartheid regime. The White House had come to its senses.

Our EO South Africans loathed the US for that betrayal. The cup of victory, for their hard-fought campaign, had been snatched from their lips by a bunch of fat suits in Washington. Or so they believed. The CIA weren't happy either. Langley had invested big time in Angola. Clout. Money. Blood. Pride. History.

(One CIA man that I knew was Chris Garner. I knew him through Nicholas Elliott. Garner used to plot at David Stirling's Mayfair offices. The Seychelles were a perennial target for Garner. He often used to brag about the Angolan visa stamped in his US passport. The stamp was UNITA, the signatory Jonas Savimbi.)

Then everything changed.

The so-called South African Border Wars of 1966–89 – over lands disputed with Angola and Namibia – were ended. On 31 May 1991, in Lisbon, Angola's President José dos Santos and UNITA leader Jonas Savimbi signed the Bicesse Accords, which laid out a transition to multi-party democracy, under the supervision of the UN. This had come about after the Trojan negotiations of Chester Crocker, US Assistant Secretary of State for Africa under President Ronald Reagan, and architect of its 'Constructive Engagement' approach. Under the Accords, all foreign troops and support for the war had to pull out of Angola.

The MPLA and UNITA troops were to come into UN demob camps and disarm. A new Angola Armed Force – the Forcas Armadas de Angola (FAA) – was to be formed, using men from both armies. After the entire population had been given photo ID cards, there were to be free and fair (and supervised) elections.

After two decades of carnage, Angola stood on the threshold of peace.

The Bicesse Accords also expedited the dismantling of the Apartheid regime and the old SADF. More specifically, under pressure from African National Congress (ANC) leader Nelson Mandela, the buckling regime of South African President F.W. de Klerk agreed to disband the SADF's notorious Civil Cooperation Bureau (CCB), a unit that carried out the government's dirtiest covert and clandestine work.

Quite a few of EO's best came straight out of the CCB. Do not pass Go! Do not collect your pension! Join EO!

On 29–30 September 1992, Angola held Presidential and Parliamentary elections. The MPLA secured 129 of the 200 National Parliament seats, UNITA 70. In the Presidential election, José dos Santos secured 49.57 per cent of the votes, UNITA leader Jonas Savimbi 40.6 per cent. Savimbi rejected the result, claiming the election had been rigged – the familiar African reaction to a drubbing at the polls.

Terrible things happened in Luanda next, as news of the election result came through. UNITA supporters and staff were hunted down and slaughtered. Savimbi himself narrowly escaped.

Using the massacres as their immediate cause – however it was that those massacres really came about – UNITA resumed the civil war. What triggered the massacres is still in dispute. MPLA are sure, and I agree, that the massacres were part of a plan set up in order to give UNITA a plausible cause for going back to war. They did.

Now supposedly without their Cold War backers, both the MPLA and UNITA needed to source money to continue fighting.

UNITA – which controlled two thirds of Angola's fabulous diamond fields – sold millions of US dollars' worth of uncut stones to diamond merchants. The MPLA sold billions of pounds' worth of offshore crude oil, for which the operating base was Soyo.

Barrel Boyz' Christmas.

When UNITA attacked Soyo in January 1993, it was an attack on the MPLA's jugular. For the MPLA, the loss of Soyo spelled the end. For me it spelled the beginning. Tony fired me, but I asked that we fight back. Against UNITA. For the MPLA government. To save our business. Our phone calls from Belgravia to Luanda and Joaquim David followed.

Let us take Soyo back.

So it was: and as JD had proposed, the President's Gulfstream flew us to Luanda. We were nervous. To our utter amazement, we discovered on arrival that our proposal had been hastily accepted.

A strange meeting took place, when JD introduced Tony and me to General João de Matos, Chief of Staff of the FAA. De Matos had to ask us, so he did: 'But how will you carry out this attack?'

DM, as he was known, was young, good-looking, mixed blood. A large man, a little overweight. Known to be very brave, to the point of foolhardy. Cool, quiet. Perhaps shy, or disdainful. His combat fatigues clean and pressed, boots polished. Always smoking.

'Simon. Answer the General, please.'

JD nodded at Tony's order. His hospital pass. Tony knew I hadn't a clue. How could I? Without INT. Without any recce.

'A classic Special Forces *coup de main* attack, sir,' I bullshitted. Then shut up. Nobody challenged me. Nobody said a word for long minutes. Nobody wanted to admit they didn't know what that was either.

Later, DM had asked what we needed. As part of my list, I asked for defence stores. DM interrupted: 'What do you mean by defence stores exactly?'

'Barbed wire, coils of Dannet, picks, spades, axes, right-angle pickets, wire cutters, wiring, gloves, sandbags, sheets of CGI…'

A hand holding a burning cigarette halted me. 'Let me tell you about African defence…'

I nodded that he should.

'We attack. They run away…'

I smiled. Arrogance? Or pride in his troops?

'…then … they attack. We run away.' De Matos smiled at my not knowing whether to laugh. He waved his cigarette through the air.

'Angola is a big place… Why defend somewhere to the end, when there is so much else to run away in?'

But it was the MPLA that was running away now. The war was going very badly. It was UNITA who were taking the places that must be held. Soyo was a damaging loss: it attacked the credibility which the all-important oil companies accorded the MPLA government.

MPLA control. Barrel Boyz' confidence.

Our military meeting ended. A business meeting began. Now Tony went in to bat.

Everything started happening at lightning speed. We flew to Windhoek in the President's jet. There we were to switch to scheduled. The President's jet would be too visible in South Africa. This plan backfired because, in Windhoek's terminal building, we bumped into half of G Squadron, 22 SAS. All ex. They had seen us come off the biz jet.

Ha ha. Very funny. Pres jet, eh, Boss?

But rumours were sure to start now, back in Blighty.

Once in Jo'burg, we hooked up with Eeban Barlow and Larnie Keller. Expecting us, they had already given me the ballpark numbers for pay and costs.

Money flew from account to account to account.

The four of us agreed to use Barlow's as yet unused company, Executive Outcomes, as the corporate vehicle with which to do this job. Our frantic logistical efforts rushed forward.

Amanda came down to South Africa for a romantic Valentine's Day weekend at Ngala, a swanky game reserve to the west of the Krueger's western boundary. She was so lovely and so much fun… Why go back into a war?

I asked her to marry me.

'Oh, don't ask me that now, Pilot. Go and have your lovely adventure. You can come back to London … then ask me some other time.'

Executive Outcomes recruited a 60-strong team of South African mercenaries. The first EO aircraft flew into Cabo Ledo, a deserted Soviet military camp and disused reinforced-concrete runway, 60 kilometres due south of Luanda, along the coast.

When the aircraft door opened, I bade welcome to our first EO troops in theatre.

'What took you so long?'

Working frantically with JD, I had set up their arrangements: water, rations, clean huts, vehicles, weapons, ammo, clothing and webbing, LOs and the rest. I had also made that all-important Afrikaner recce. Where, on the nearby beach, must we put the *braai*?

The next day, the MPLA made Tony and me brigadier generals in the Angolan Army. General João de Matos himself gave us our badges of rank. The ceremony was carried out on the orders of *El Presidente*. They badly wanted Soyo back.

We were brigadier generals for the same reason that all of the EO men deployed in Angola, from Soyo onwards, were formally enrolled into the recognised armed forces of the sovereign state, the FAA. At the time that seemed like common sense to me, and was done at my request. Without that formality, by what right could any of us open fire?

As the South Africans enrolled, Joaquim David noted that many of the men shared the same surnames. He took me to one side. 'I presume these are *noms de guerre*?' he said to me conspiratorially. He laughed with me that they were not.

Our enrolling into the FAA meant that none of us could legally be described as mercenaries – at least not according to the Convention for the Elimination of Mercenaries in Africa 1977. Alarmingly for the Afrikaners, this meant that the EO troops were now subject to Angolan military law. Despite my having squeezed from the Angolans an agreement that the South Africans must keep the right to veto any Soyo attack plan that looked too kamikaze.

So there it was: in the far-off lands of West Africa – the Heart of Mischief – I had found the dragon I sought.

I had set up an op of my own. Now I had to figure out how to win it.

Forget tyro oil tycoon: my career as a mercenary – gun for hire, dog of war, soldier of fortune, *condottiero*, call it what you will – had begun.

I thought how good it would have been to phone Richard Westmacott. Ask him to fly down, join the Op. He'd have loved it. We could have done with his ready wit and laughter.

2333 HRS ZULU, 14 MAY 1993. ANGOLA: MV BANGALA: 5NM SSE OF CABO LEDO

Black sea and black night rolled around the oilfield support vessel *Bangala*.

I peered at my watch: 2333 HRS ZULU: H HOUR MINUS 8.

Like a Hornblower, or a Jack Aubrey, I paced the *Bangala*'s work-deck. Rough old timber. Sacrificial beams already sacrificed.

Unlike a Hornblower, or an Aubrey, I was jumpy. The *Bangala*'s crew could mug me at any moment. So could their skipper, Geordie.

UNITA could dash out of the darkness. They have patrol boats. They patrol. They surely have plenty of weapons, heavy and light. I curse myself for having only my 9mm HK P9 handgun. Tony had given it to me for the Op, as a present. I have it in a waistband holster on my right hip. Side draw. If I'd had any sense I would have brought at least a PKM machine gun for myself, or an AK. I'm on my own. I'm feeling it.

I'm not even sure that the South Africans – that's Steven Mason and Co., now carrying out the recce – are really on side. It's possible that they have another set of orders entirely, either from their peers or – God forbid – from Pretoria. The Broederbond. UNITA. The CIA.

I peered at my wristwatch: 2337 HRS ZULU.

In half an hour it would be Tuesday. D DAY for Soyo. The attack was still planned for first light, some seven hours yet. Forty minutes earlier, my recce team had shoved off into the darkness, their rubber inflatable bobbing up and down on the swell. The south-west-facing beach of Soyo peninsula was less than a mile away, north-east, and as yet unseen through the darkness of night. As dark and opaque as a barrel of crude. The sea darker.

Six minutes back, Steven had signalled me on his VHF handheld: they were close to the beach. Steven plus three would land, to carry out the recce, while the other two would crew the boat. To sit at sea, a cable or two out from the beach. From there they would await events, and orders.

Orders? I ran over our ramshackle plan. Our orders, now in mid-stride, hurried, never ready from the start:

Ground and Situation: Enemy Forces: UNITA occupy the port, airport and peninsula of Soyo with 3,000 of their finest. Plus some guest stars, we suspect. They are dug in, and they have medium-heavy weaponry. This includes 82mm mortars and radar-controlled ZU 23mm 2AN twin cannons, plus small boats, captured from oil companies when they took the town. They also have Strela-3 Surface to Air Missiles (SAMs). The 23mms and the Strelas I know about. They fired at Jesus and me last week. I will not forget them.

Our London office – Devon Oil and Gas – has been warned that UNITA are ready for us, and will kill us if we attack. They know we're coming. God knows how many UNITA spies are within the FAA. Many of the FAA were UNITA only months before.

Elsewhere in Angola, UNITA control 80 per cent of the country. All of the country dwellers are UNITA; UNITA are the people of the land, as MPLA are those of the cities. Savimbi's UNITA are successfully attacking the FAA and MPLA wherever they can. UNITA (and whoever are backing them) are winning the war.

Situation: Friendly Forces: We have 60 South Africans plus the six-man recce party with me on the *Bangala*. Those 60, plus Tony, are by now in Cabinda town, city of the Angolan possession, the Cabinda enclave, just to the north, on the other side of the mouth of the Congo. With them are four Mi-17 support helicopters (SHs), two Mi-24 gunships and four Pilatus PC-9 trainers, now in the role of Close Air Support (CAS). They are armed with 64mm rocket cannon pods.

Back in Luanda, what's left of the FAA air wing are ready to join our Soyo attack. That will mean Fighter Ground Attack (FGA) sorties, flown at intervals by the ageing Sukhoi SU-22s, now down to four flying aircraft.

My friend, Jesus. My front-seater.

Meanwhile, there are 1,000 children in FAA uniform on a Landing Craft Tank (LCT) steaming towards Soyo beach under the gruesome command of one Colonel Pepe. They are to beef up our 60 South Africans. With these ten hundred 16-year-olds are two T54 tanks, our own 82mm mortars, ammo, fresh water, rations … and stores sundry.

Why did our enemy UNITA have 3,000 of their finest, but we 1,000 boys? How come?

UNITA had cheated the Bicesse Accords, that's how. Makes you think that their promises of peace had never been more than poppycock (a word which, incidentally, derives from the Boer War Afrikaans expression *pappi kak*, soft shit). UNITA had lacked candour. The troops that they had sent to the demob camps had been their dross, the weapons their cast-offs. Their good troops and their good weapons, they had kept hidden in the bush: a piece of information that must have been available to the CIA … except that it was probably a CIA idea, a CIA plan, in the first place.

The governing MPLA, on the other hand, had been much easier for UN Peacekeepers – and CIA busybodies – to keep an eye on. They had not cheated. Not only had they not cheated; they hadn't paid their men on demobilisation. As a result, when the call-to-arms came again, those unpaid men had said, 'No, MPLA. We will not fight for you again. With no pay.'

Mission: Our mission – and the terms of the deal by which we would be paid our money – was that we would take and hold Soyo for 90 days.

Execution: General Outline: Secure a helicopter LZ – on the south-west-facing shore of the peninsula – and a defensive position such that it would cover a beach landing point for the LCT. This would be achieved by a surprise helicopter assault at first light.

With the LCT and the 1,000 boys would be set up a beachhead, from which operations could begin. UNITA would be removed from the Soyo peninsula.

Tasks: Steven's night-time recce – launched from the *Bangala* by me – had the task of making a recce of the two possible LZ sites: Duchess North and Duchess South (see map on page xiii). This was to prevent the possibility of the Mi-17s flying into a UNITA defensive position, or an ambush. A support heli has no more defence against small-arms fire than does a family Volvo. The heli will be travelling slower, when it drops off troops.

An hour or two later – H HOUR PLUS TWO – the LCT carrying our 1,000 FAA boys would land on the beachhead to expand and reinforce the defensive position. The whole Op was in fact planned to go down around the very spot where the Agip onshore production facility had a massive round crude-oil storage tank.

The LCT's approach and landing on the beach was crucial, and one that needed seamanship. As she came to within a cable of the beach, she must let go her aft kedge anchor. That hook would then hold her stern off, as her bow ran up the beach, thus stopping her from broaching: turning sideways on to the surf.

Between the Mi-17s, the LCT and the *Bangala*, the landed force would be well supported from Cabinda. This was the base for our equipment – our sinews of war. Plenty.

Casualty evacuation (Casevac) and treatment for our white mercenary troops was to be by helicopter to the Malongo oil base hospital, just north of Cabinda town. A first-world facility manned and equipped to first-world standards.

This was all-important for our South Africans. Fighting as a mercenary is not the same as fighting for Queen and Country. There is no *Dulce et decorum est pro patria mori*. Those who were fighting for their country, or their bit of their country, the black FAA boys, would not be so treated.

I paced another six lengths of the *Bangala*'s work-deck. Each ran from her rounded open stern for'ard to the aft side of her meagre superstructure, itself placed as close to the bow as possible. This design gave the biggest work-deck.

I needed the heft of the HK against my hip. Without command my hand went to the pistol grip, touching it as though for luck. I thought back over the haste-crammed day.

Earlier that morning, Tony and I had loaded ourselves into one of the Mi-17s. The six-man recce party – including the commander, Steven – and their weapons, plus a rubber boat and outboard engine – were already on board.

We flew at low level up the 60 kilometres of road from Cabo Ledo to Luanda. Passing through the Mad Max shambles of Luanda International, with a boat and eight heavily armed white men, was a high point in our careers as diplomats and persuaders. In fact, it was only a chance meeting with a Sonangol employee, a man loyal to Joaquim David, who luckily knew something of what was afoot, that saved the day.

Two Sonangol oil company 4x4s took us to Ilha beach. Luanda Sunday traffic cared *nada* for our task; our haste. On the beach, families watched with smiles and frowns as the rubber boat was quickly pumped up. It was there that we found that hiding a PKM (the Russian equivalent of the GPMG, the NATO General Purpose Machine Gun) beneath one groundsheet doesn't work.

Tony and I were ferried first, out to our oilfield support vessel, the MV *Bangala*. We climbed up the boarding ladder. The rubber boat headed back empty to the beach, to pick up the rest of the party. Tony and I were met by the skipper of the *Bangala*, Geordie. From Hull, of course.

Six days earlier, we had been on board the *Bangala* for a recce. Joaquim had hired the boat commercially, under the pretence that we were working for Sonangol and that the boat was needed for oil work.

That morning, once we made our way to the bridge-house, Tony and I faced Geordie, his back to the wheel. His eyes went back and forth between us. Geordie's body language said, 'Fuck off.'

'Now fuck off, will ya!' he said.

I tried to smile sweetly, but Geordie was not done. 'I knew you two were naught but trouble the first time I clapped eyes on ya. Why'd

Sonangol want t' charter ship any'ow? In Luanda 'arbour? Don't make sense, do it? Now fuck off … afore I lose me job – an' me temper!'

I was ready for this.

'Geordie, I understand your position. But, in time of war, we are requisitioning this vessel. Charter rates will still apply. I am a brigadier in the Angolan Armed Forces, the FAA. Here is my ID card, and here is a letter of requisition from the Chief of Staff, General João de Matos.'

Geordie frowned and looked at the papers. It was obvious that I must be telling the truth.

'Can I call me boss?'

'No. No calls or signals off this boat, by any means, until further notice.'

'This is bloody piracy!' (Later on, Tony and I were charged with piracy, in a case initiated by the US owners of the *Bangala*, but this was dropped when JD told them that they would never work on the west coast of Africa again.)

'When the time comes,' I told our skipper, 'you can tell your company – or whatever – that the boat was seized at gunpoint – by eight heavily armed men; and they are heavily armed, Geordie. So are we.'

My hand moved to my hip. Geordie's eyes followed.

Tony and I had a very private chat, by the stern. Then, with the recce party aboard, and Tony back ashore, the inflatable was hoisted. Lashed down to the work-deck. Geordie weighed anchor, so we steamed forth out of Luanda roadstead: Geordie, his five-strong crew of villainous-looking Nigerians, my recce team and me.

On my orders, the *Bangala* turned south. Once out of sight, and once night had fallen, she would turn north, for Soyo. I did not really hope to fool the many watchers and spies by that, the oldest naval ruse in the book. It was for form. A matter of etiquette.

We would arrive off Soyo at around 2200 hrs Z, whereupon the recce party would go ashore.

Now, as I wait for news from that recce party, I walk up and down the *Bangala*'s work-deck. From just aft of the superstructure to the flush countered stern was 30 paces. Painted onto the superstructure, and facing the work-deck aft, was a fierce African votive mask with triangular filed teeth. I could just see the outline of the fangs as I neared the forward end of each beat.

Geordie had told me that the mask was of the Bangala people, a now extinct tribe of cannibals who once lived far up the great Congo River. They had been well known as crews for the Belgian river work boats.

I didn't want to be here, eyeing this portrait of a savage. I wanted to be on that dinghy, heading towards the LZ. I'd had a row with Tony over this. He had been adamant that I would not be with the men at Soyo.

For God's sake. He was more worried about how he'd break the news to my mother and father, whom he knew, than anything else. Or so he joked. Of course, I could have defied Tony. Gone in. But I couldn't defy the South Africans.

They'd made up their minds. This would be their mission. They would not allow me to get involved on the ground. For me to insist upon it would have caused a meltdown. And distrust. And that would make it more dangerous for all.

I didn't trust them anyway. Their not wanting me with them worried me. Made me paranoid. But I knew that it was their way. It just wasn't worth it. And so here I was, alone on the *Bangala*.

What I had to do, other than control the *Bangala* and command the recce party, was relay the signal from Steven to Tony, waiting in Cabinda with the assault group. That message had to be passed not later than 0300 hrs Z. Plenty could go wrong in the meantime.

The recce team could be bumped, shot, killed or captured. They could get into a firefight with UNITA. We knew that UNITA had boats. What was to say they wouldn't get caught before they even made the beach?

Geordie's binoculars were around my neck. Every tenth length of my walk up and down the deck, I'd stop and peer carefully all around the dark sea.

I looked further out to sea. Ten miles away, although seemingly much closer, two oil-production platforms flared gas, beckoning with reflected paths of flame. I kept my eyes from the flares to safeguard my night vision, as trained, but those gas flares made me think. The lamps of Europe had once burned spermaceti whale oil. They burned without the lamp owner giving much thought to the great whale fisheries of the Southern Ocean. So is gasoline burned today. Without much thought for what is going on in the places that it comes from.

Or how ivory had once been a part of so many goods. Or of the slave trade.

To my north and east – over Soyo peninsula – far away over the great river and its forests – the sky was utterly black, except when zig-zagged streamers of white fire silently ripped from cloud to cloud, cloud to ground. Flashing discharges lighting up vast cathedrals of Cumulonimbus, their thunder deadened by the distance. Unheard.

Soyo the fire dragon. I lit another Marlboro.

Beneath the *Bangala*, the swell moved her. This wave, black and oily in the night, came from the south-west. It ran, therefore, straight in upon the beach. I feared that the swell had grown since I'd launched the recce. The more swell, the more difficult would be the beaching of the LCT.

Then came whispers over the VHF. Steven: 'Enemy in sight.'

I looked towards the beach. I saw lights, then some sort of commotion. With a shock I felt fear's grasp upon me. Quick as mist blown over a mountain ridge. Excitement, comradeship, wealth ... all the drums and bugles ... they all ran away.

I stood alone on the deck. To steady myself I yet again scanned the sea – with care – pausing as I scanned – again just as I'd been trained.

Having walked up to the bridge, I lit another cigarette, saving my night eyesight from the match flare. I tried but failed to radio-check Tony using the *Bangala*'s HF set. I felt so alone.

Back on deck I began again my up-and-down sentry-go. I tried to measure the swell height against the hull, now sure that it was bigger, rougher, now sure that the *Bangala* was moving more than she had.

All the time I had to keep pushing the fear away. That's how it was: I kept screwing down the top of my bottle.

Again I scanned the sea, dodging the binos around the oil platforms' gas flares. Hanging on to my night vision.

Slaves. Ivory. Oil. The thoughts jarred me. This West African coast had been a hunting ground for ever. It still was.

'Slaves. Ivory. Oil. Diamonds. Gold. Ladies' underwear. Next floor is Lower Ground. This lift is going down.'

Like Harrods. But going down is right.

Night wasn't passing.

Darkness had come for ever.

I smoked, paced, peered, dreamed. Every so often I had to check myself for thoughts of love, of Amanda. But I threw out those thoughts. I had a job to do.

I had agreed not to call or radio-check Steven. Other than in an emergency. I'd heard nothing since his 'Enemy in sight'. Had they been captured? Killed silently? I didn't dare break his instruction for me not to radio-check him. I just had to keep on waiting. Pacing.

0245 HRS ZULU and still nothing. Nearly three. H HOUR MINUS FOUR.

Then it came: a whispered 'Duchess South'.

I repeated the code words back. Heard Steven say them over once again. Now we both knew that the other knew that the message was passed.

Now I had to pass the same message to Tony in Cabinda, using the ship's HF radio. When I turned it on, all I could hear was feedback, then screaming. By the sound of it, the Spanish deep-sea trawlermen were holding some sort of HF rave-up. For 20 minutes I struggled to get through to Tony.

No use.

It didn't matter.

Yesterday, as we had said our goodbyes on the stern of the *Bangala* and had our chat, I had told Tony what to do. I had shocked him: 'If you haven't heard from me, from the *Bangala*, by 0330 HRS ZULU on Tuesday morning, then tell them that you have; tell them that I said Duchess South for the LZ; that one is the best bet anyway...'

'Jesus, Simon! But ... OK: 0330 HRS ZULU and Duchess South.'

It was ruthless, but we had to make this happen. Of course, had something really gone wrong with the recce party, then I would have put a stop to the Mi-17s going in. But I was damned if I was going to let a shit HF radio signal fuck up all our plans. I was damned if I was going to let the South Africans, ours or Pretoria's, mess this up. By chance or otherwise.

As it was, I had been forced to trick the South Africans into agreeing to this heli assault. They hadn't believed the Angolans capable of producing the heli assets. I told them how their reluctance to attack was raising doubts. Were they here for pay, beer, *braais* on the beach? Were they using the excuse of FAA's poor combat intelligence as a way of exercising their 'No Attack' veto, when in fact they were taking orders not to attack from NI, in Pretoria? After all, South Africa was on UNITA's side. South African soldiers had fought for UNITA. Some of these men had fought for UNITA.

No, they said. But they hated the idea of a sea assault.

OK. So I asked them: if there was a heli assault organised for them, would they attack? Otherwise we might as well own up and pack up. On their mettle they agreed. Sure that the heli assets would not be forthcoming. Not from a bunch of blacks.

Then it was there: Tony's HF radio voice, answering my radio-check.

'Hello, Zero, this is One – Duchess South – over...' Crackle ... whistle ... Spanish shout.

'Zero – Duchess South – Duchess South – over.'

'One – Duchess South – out.' Message sent and acknowledged. Message passed.

Geordie agreed to steer the *Bangala* further offshore. As dawn approached, I didn't want to alarm any watching UNITA fighters. I took up my vigil on the deck once more. Mouth and throat smoked dry. I lit another cigarette. Paced the deck.

There was light, surely?

There lay the fire dragon: Soyo. Dark along the seashore, fast asleep. There ran a long beach, grey in the low light. A black, scraggly forest lay upon it.

Then – quickly after the night's long wait – there was the attack: four Mi-17s carrying the South Africans. Two Mi-24 gunships in support, firing into the bush below. One carried Tony – although I didn't know it then. The six-ship attack looked puny in such a big panorama. The 17s sank down into the black forest. The 24s circled.

Firing. Firing. Firing.

We watched.

Then the 17s rose out of the trees, turning to fly north, now lightened of heavily armed fighters. The 24s circled some more, strafing with their chin cannons, then followed.

As an afterthought – so it seemed – a twin 23mm, almost on the beach, opened up on the rear 24. I had seen these UNITA 23mms before.

Their tracer-laced fire had chased Jesus and me in our SU-22 as we made our kamikaze photo recce weeks earlier: our high-speed, low-level pass. The lines of burning steel trying to catch and kill. The recce sortie that had to be flown. The recce sortie that gleaned vital intelligence about UNITA positions at Soyo. The recce sortie that had told any reluctant South Africans that they were going to have to either shit or get off the pot.

If the South Africans were only here for the pay, beer and *braais* on the beach – or if they were secretly following orders from SA NI not to attack UNITA – they no longer had a legitimate excuse to hide behind. No longer could they use the lack of FAA Combat Intelligence about UNITA to delay the op. The choice was straightforward. Shit now, or trek back: from Luanda to Voortrekkerhoogte.★

I could hear the 23mms over the sea's noise. Over the ship's engine thrum. Over the distance. Each burst of fire was a machine roar, the sound of each round joined to the next.

Fire spat. Body-smashing. Chainsaw rip.

As the sleepy gunner chased his Mi-24 target, so 23mm tracers flew over the *Bangala*, over Geordie and me, and into the sea behind.

'I thought you said there were nowt 'ere t' shoot more 'an 1,000 yards!' wailed Geordie.

'Sorry, Geordie. Only kidding.'

'Fer fuck's sakes! I'm gettin' 'er art ta sea.'

'Quick as you like, Geordie.'

'Bloody right!'

As we sailed away from the beach, I searched out to sea, east–south-east, with the binos. As I scanned, I saw what I wanted ... then lost it. I had to be sure that I really could see the LCT ... but there it was: sailing towards the target.

I found it and held it. That was the vital element. Even though, to land in this swell, they were going to have to know what they were about.

Once sure of the LCT, I told Geordie to head north for Cabinda Roads, an order that made the poor man grin for joy. He wanted his ship well away from the firefight.

The *Bangala* skirted Soyo peninsula at a safe distance, then set course for Cabinda. She churned along at her best speed, a snail's six knots. I found myself cut off, in an eerie flat calm, knowing that a momentous storm – the attack that I'd kicked off – my dragon fight – was raging all around.

VHF radio contact with Steven had been lost as soon as we'd sailed from the landing. The HF had not worked since I'd sent the code words

★ The town in Pretoria named after the pioneering Voortrekker pilgrims who, between 1835 and 1854, left the Cape Colony and trekked into the interior of what is now South Africa.

through to Tony early that morning. Still armed with Geordie's binoculars, I climbed onto the lookout atop the bridge-house.

Aft, I scanned the peninsula for any signs of the action that must be taking place, but could see none. At least there were no UNITA patrol boats chasing us.

I tried to keep a sharp lookout on the waters ahead of the bow, since Geordie had asked me to. Great hardwood tree trunks, almost submerged, were a hazard in this, the mouth of the Congo estuary. Flotsam of the great forest upstream, and carried by the vast river, these trunks could do serious damage to the *Bangala* if she was struck. They were like rotten but still poisonous old teeth, fallen from the mouth of the worm – dragon Congo.

I looked upstream towards where I knew the city ports of Matadi and Boma must lie, but saw nothing. I could only just make out the waterway into Banana Creek.

Beneath us sank a vast deep. The Congo is so mighty that its waters have carved out a submarine canyon. The water we bustled through was sweet. Not salt. River water, despite our being miles out to sea.

As the vessel closed with the Cabinda shoreline, I was surprised to make out what looked like a modern port. I climbed down off my perch and joined Geordie on the bridge.

He saw me looking at the distant pier and cranes. 'Tha's na Cabinda. Tha's Malongo ... the oil terminal and port!'

This was our oil port. That with the first-rate medical facility. The one that Joaquim David had promised us: to take care of any of our own casualties. I looked in another direction, to where Geordie's grimy finger pointed: some houses clinging to the beachline, the dark forest ready to roll over them. There was no port at all: just a handful of rusty hulks anchored half a mile off.

'Cabinda's over there, man! Cabinda's shaller water for four cables out. There's no port – so it's all lighters: lighters off, an' bloody lighters on. We'm gonna anchor amongst them 'ulks.'

Geordie's eyes could not but glance to the oil port, now just five miles away. That was his home and, once there, the *Bangala* would be safe from the mischiefs of war. I feared that Geordie might take himself and his ship to safety at the first half-chance. I followed his gaze to the oil port, but could make out little at the distance.

Beyond the oil port, the coastline bent slightly eastward, out of view. Beyond lay Pointe-Noire, the sea port of Congo Brazzaville.

Pointe-Noire had been Evelyn Waugh's location for the plane crash, and temporary death, of that other brigadier general, the great but fictitious hero Ben Ritchie Hook.

The *Bangala* readied to drop her best bower anchor. I spotted a speeding launch heading out towards us. No doubt it was for me. Handing Geordie back his binos, I dived below to grab my ready-packed rucksack. As I came back on deck, the launch was already alongside us. Shouts and waves signalled that I must quickly board.

I turned to Geordie, striving to go eye to eye. I told him that the *Bangala* could be life and death to the men now ashore at Soyo. He and his vessel must therefore stand by, at anchor in Cabinda Roads. Those were his orders. He was under command – under requisition – in a country at war.

For this government, at least, a war of survival.

My heart sank. Geordie wouldn't hold my eye. It was little surprise, therefore, as the launch dropped me at the jetty and into a waiting army jeep, to see the *Bangala* slinking off towards her kennel: the oil port. Bitch.

Sick at what that loss might cause, I cursed Geordie; but I could not really blame him. I wondered if I should have used force to keep my 'requisition' on strength. Too late. I could not see how I could have stopped him. Not without great delay. I was soon to learn that the *Bangala*'s desertion was the least of my worries.

As I was driven from the jetty to the airport, the jeep driver spoke neither French (the European language of that part of the coast) nor Russian (a language of which FAA soldiers often had a few words – a hangover from the last phase of these endless civil wars). To my boiling frustration, I could glean no picture of what was going on.

I had a bad, hollow feeling in the pit of my stomach. A feeling soon made worse by the faces of Joaquim David and Tony. They were sitting on a broken-down piece of wall, at the back of the two shacks that usually served as Cabinda International's terminal buildings. Tony was smoking a Cohiba Esplendido. A Woodbine would have been in better keeping with his defeated air.

'Where've you been?' he asked.

'Came here as fast as that old tub would go. As we agreed. What's up?'

'We're facing a wipe-out...'

'Come, Tony – let us not be pessimists,' said JD. 'Simon, well done. Your role last night was successful. How is the *Bangala*?'

'The *Bangala* is in one piece, but unfortunately Geordie – against my pleas, and my orders – has buggered off to the oil terminal. I doubt if any threats, or promises, will win him back on strength!'

'*Shit, Simon!*' yelled Tony.

His anger hurt me.

'I'm sorry, Joaquim... Sorry, Tony. Only a full-on armed guard would have stopped him. Even if I had an armed guard to post on board then, what would be the use of that? What are we going to do if he won't sail for us? Shoot him?'

JD leaned forward. 'OK. Tony, allow me to bring Simon up to date, please?'

'Go ahead, Joaquim.'

'So, Simon, after you sent the code Duchess South, we made ready. Tony insisted upon riding in one of the Mi-24 gunships. In went the attack, as you no doubt saw...'

I grinned at Tony. 'Couldn't bloody well resist that, could you?'

He smiled a quick smile, the first break in his gloom.

JD went on, 'The heli assault went as planned – into the Duchess South LZ – which was clear of enemy and of obstacles – as hoped. The recce group was there – Steven and his men. They linked up with the main force. They all moved to the agreed position. From there they could cover the beach landing spot ... and they began to build defences.

'Then they were attacked – heavily, and by a strong and determined force. Since then – and now – attacks have followed: one, after another, after another. They have some lightly wounded, and are running low on ammo. They do not know how long they can hold on.'

'Shit! But where are the FAA? Where's the Landing Craft? I saw the LCT sailing into the beach...' I said.

'Well, of course ... so for hours your South Africans only just held off the UNITA attacks, which became stronger and stronger. Then – let's see – about three hours ago the LCT at last landed but ... but then – well – disaster has struck...'

Tony had been gazing into the distance, his face grim. Now he took up the sorry tale: 'You know how it's done, Simon. The LCT lets go her kedge anchor – about one cable's length off the beach – while they ram her bow into it. The kedge is there to stop the stern swinging in, to stop the vessel broaching to ... broaching in the surf...'

Tony stopped. Our eyes met. 'The fucking warp broke! Can you fucking believe it?'

'Go on.'

'The fucking thing broached to – waves pounding into it – 1,000 men on board – waves pounding into it, and UNITA shooting at it too.'

'Fucking hell!'

'Fucking hell is right. Somehow everyone got ashore. The South Africans gave covering fire. But all the ammo, rations, water, heavy weapons, the tanks – they're still on the thing: swimming and battered in a half-sunk wreck.'

'So what is happening now?'

'So far as we know, they are still all holding on...'

At that moment, a Pilatus PC-9 hurtled over our heads, followed by another. We stopped talking and watched the two aircraft. In Cabinda to provide Close Air Support (CAS) to our Soyo battle, 43 miles south, they now turned hard onto a curved left base to land.

JD spoke: 'We'll talk to these pilots while they refuel and rearm.'

'But you say we are holding on?'

'Yes. The South Africans have formed a defensive circle with a helicopter LZ at its centre. The outer circumference is held by our FAA children, and that includes the beach where the wreck is. We are flying the PC-9s non-stop to try to break up the UNITA attacks. We are flying the Mi-17s non-stop, with the Mi-24s in support: ammo in, casualties out. There are no serious South African casualties yet.'

I saw a look of worry – no, embarrassment – on Joaquim's face. It didn't suit him. Tony gave him a scowl of anger. The strength of that look shocked me.

'What's up? Is there worse?'

Joaquim looked at the ground: 'Tell him, Tony, please. I am too ashamed.'

I looked to Tony, amazed.

He growled out the story, while my heart sank: 'The oil terminal hospital is off limits. We can't use it for casualties.'

Neither man could look me in the eye. They both knew that the South Africans would refuse to carry on if they found out they were

76

fighting without a white man's casualty plan. It spelled disaster. Not only that: if we had been warned that this was to happen, we could have put other arrangements in place. Now, with a desperate battle in progress, we were more than 1,000 miles from the kind of medical support that we needed.

A lifetime away.

Tony went on: 'I've been to the Cabinda hospital, here, at Joaquim's suggestion. It's a cesspit … a disgrace. I wouldn't send my worst enemy there.'

JD walked off to the terminal shack 20 yards away, now FAA's forward Tactical Headquarters. To call it a TAC HQ was as ludicrous as calling it a terminal building – or calling Cabinda's hospital a hospital.

'Fucking hell! We're really in the shit now…'

CHAPTER FIVE

In Jo'burg, sure enough, I meet three of the old gang, former members of Executive Outcomes: Coebus, Crause Steyl (the pilot) and Niek du Toit.

Details of the op are secret. The fewer people who know about the plan, the better. As the British Army would have it, the Op and everything about it is 'NEED TO KNOW'.

I don't mention that the Op is a coup. I don't mention Equatorial Guinea. They won't ask. They know better. In this game we're all up to something, all of the time. Madcap, sketchy schemes are never far from the ears of a mercenary. In the improbable event of these madcap, sketchy schemes ever happening, then their most likely outcome is disaster.

As Conrad put it in *Lord Jim*: 'Nothing offered just then, and, while waiting, he associated naturally with the men of his calling in the port. These were of two kinds. Some, very few and seen there but seldom, led mysterious lives, had preserved an undefaced energy with the temper of buccaneers and the eyes of dreamers. They appeared to live in a crazy maze of plans, hopes, dangers, enterprises, ahead of civilization, in the dark places of the sea; and their death was the only event of their fantastic existence that seemed to have a reasonable certitude of achievement.'

Coebus is my first shot. He and I drink a beer at the bar of the Sandton Towers, where we have drunk many. We shoot the breeze for one bottle, then I ask, 'Come on, Coebus – how about it? One last op. A big one… You know how bloody bored you are.'

'For a government? Or against a government?' he asks. That's Coebus: straight to the jugular.

'Against the heads, this time … but it needs doing bad.'

'No, Simon – not one against the heads – not yet – maybe when the girls are older – when they've left school – they need me too much…'

I thought about it. Coebus is an old woman now. Or is Coebus right? To take his job as a single father so seriously?

For God's sake. That's not how the West was won. Was it?

Then I need my numbers. Pounds, shillings and pence. I'll get them from Niek and Crause. I've been out of the game a while. What are the costs? Men, weapons, aircraft. These ops are a business, even if they are life and death. I have to put together a cashflow.

Then – again back in the UK – the Boss and I discuss the possibility of us becoming the contractors for EG's fishery protection programme. This would give us good cover for having a boat, and crew, on the target. The Boss gives me a copy of a US proposal. Some outfit from Texas: BAT Systems.

I look at BAT's proposal. It's wildly over the top. So much so that it has to be a cover. Then two sources that I run it past tell me it's just that. BAT are a front for some ex-SEAL (Sea, Air, and Land) and ex-Delta guys. That BAT's EG coup plan had been close to execution when the CIA had got cold feet. Langley binned it. In the BAT bin.

I give this titbit to the Boss. He laughs. 'So! You heard about that one, did you? How interesting. You have some good sources, I see. Well done.'

I draw up our own fishery protection proposal, which the Boss then sends to his contact in EG. Our proposal goes down well. We even get praise from this contact down there – I assume he is the Minister for Defence, or Fisheries, or some such. Then a meeting is arranged with a man who is apparently a go-between, and a Mr Fix-It, with President Obiang.

The meeting was a waste of time, but I let it pass. I put it to the back of my mind. It would have amazed me then to know how Amil Hammam was to play a part in my story.

But right now I'm trying to work out how to get a recce into EG. Fast. The principal investors are all over me to get on with the job. At one point I say to them that I have revised my estimate downward, from 150 to 80. The least number of troops that I need to do the op.

'Eighty?' The Boss sneers. 'If you want to know what I think, you could do this with eight.'

Think about it. What does that mean?

Meantime, there is one job of overriding priority that I need to do in EG. Fast.

Niek du Toit, an ex-commandant, is someone that I met through a guy called Paul Heyns. Paul is dead now. Killed in February 2003 in the CAP 20 aerobatics aircraft he was training in. I sometimes used to fly with him, in his Pitts Special and other assorted flying machines.

Paul nearly killed me once. He was showing me how short a take-off his Short Take-Off Husky could do. From the pumps to the runway and across it. One hundred and fifty feet at the most. Except that we didn't take off – not without bashing into the dirt bank on the far side of the runway. Paul's only comment was that my briefcase was heavier than it looked. Paul wasn't just good at tight aerial manoeuvres. He was good at tight business ones.

Paul used to do the trickier EO procurements in the Angola and Sierra Leone days. I met Niek because he worked for Paul in his arms-dealing outfit, the South African government-licensed weapons-trading company Military Technical Services Pty Ltd (MTS).

Although Niek had worked for Executive Outcomes in Sierra Leone, our paths hadn't crossed. At that time there were 1,800 people in EO. Tony Buckingham and I were happy not to be well known. When I first met Niek – which must have been in 2000 – it was at a four-ball meeting at the Jan Smuts International Holiday Inn in Johannesburg: Paul, Niek, myself and one Mark Thatcher.

I check out Niek with Coebus, and Crause, and several others. Everyone says the same: very courageous, very professional. He is close to the old 32 'Buffalo' Battalion crowd.* That is good, because those men are black. They are good, not expensive and much less provocative. In the situation we will be in, of suddenly running an African country – albeit very briefly – black is gonna be beautiful.

*Known as 'The Terrible Ones', *Os Terriveis*, 32 'Buffalo' Battalion was one of the SADF's most feared units during the Border Wars with Angola and Namibia. It was made up mostly of Angolans recruited from the National Liberation Front of Angola (FNLA), a militant outfit who fought for and won Angolan independence from Portugal. Later, FNLA allied itself to the UNITA rebels.

MAY · 2003: ZURICH, SWITZERLAND

I like Niek du Toit's super-serious manner and his Afrikaner way of working. Nothing is too hard. Nothing too difficult. I had wanted to use him just for recruiting the men and for the weapons procurement. But if I can't have Coebus to lead the Op, then I'll ask Niek.

We agree to meet.

MAY 2003: ZURICH, SWITZERLAND

The *Baur au Lac* hotel, on the city shore of Lake Zurich, screams 'Money!' *Jawohl, Mein Herr.* Dollars. Pounds. Euros. *Schweizer Franken. Bitte schön…* This is our RV.

The inside glitz is upstaged by the sumptuous gardens. The landscape designer had aimed for 'Garden of Eden'. He hasn't fallen short. It's lunchtime.

I sit outside in the sun. All around me are slim, blonde, toned, tucked and tanned trophy wives, drinking white-wine spritzers with their Caesar Salads.

Through thick bush, I spot Niek. He's seeking me out, squinting in the bright light. He's in khaki trousers, neutral plaid shirt, boots. Over his shirt he wears one of those sleeveless khaki drill war-correspondent waistcoats. In some places just wearing one of those things will get you shot. He looks like a movie actor who's stumbled onto the wrong set.

Niek joins me, orders a beer, then takes out an enormous mobile phone to make a call. He adjusts the electric toothbrush-like antenna so that it is vertical. I can feel the X-Ray trophies gawping. They're thinking as one: what kind of man has kept a phone like that these last 20 years? An electric brick… Has he just stepped out of a time machine?

I wish Niek wasn't doing this. The phone is not a mobile. This is an Iridium handheld satellite phone. Latest kit.

When he finishes, I tell him, 'I don't think this is the best spot for us.'

'Agreed,' he says, draining his beer in three gulps.

I lead him to a jetty on Lake Zurich. We board one of those 50-foot tourist/commuter boats: the MV *Brunhilde*. No one is following us. The boat is almost empty. It putters off. We stand on deck, eyeing the billions of pounds' worth of real estate that litter the sapphire-ringed shoreline.

I watch Niek glare hungrily at the mansions and yachts.

He's been soldiering all his life. He's developed a kamikaze disregard for his own safety. After this meeting he's on his way back to more war-torn rainforest, in Liberia. That was where the other party to his both-ways satellite phone call had been hiding. There the rebel force Liberians United for Democracy and Development (LURD) are trying to depose another rank tyrant. President Charles Taylor.

I know about Taylor and Liberia because I only just got out of Monrovia alive, back in '89. I had been working for the then Finance Minister to President Doe – one Emmanuel Shaw. He, Jonathan (an ex-Mossad pilot) and I had to escape in Shaw's old Beechcraft Baron light twin.

We only just made it off the ground, small-arms fire helping us pedal faster down the crappy single paved runway of the James Spriggs-Payne Airfield, in the heart of Monrovia.

The three of us barely flew out one end of the shanty crap city, as Taylor machine gunned his way into the other. The firing at us came from the Presidential Guard. Meant to be Shaw's bodyguard, they were in fact his would-be jailers. Doe trusted only two blacks: Black Magic and Black Label. Doe was famously executed: on the beach, by chainsaw.

The ex-Mossad crowd, sixty or so Israelis who were meant to be Doe's bodyguard, not surprisingly ran away. Doe wasn't worth an African Alamo ending. This close protection team sped off in style.

The Israeli bodyguard team had all made so much money illegally trading diamonds (mostly walked in from SL) that, when the balloon went up, they could zoom around the corner to safe Conakry, all in their polished Sunseeker speed yachts. But all of that's another story.

On the *Brunhilde*, I brief Niek on the EG coup plan. I ask him to lead the troops. I make it clear that I want him to be my commander on the ground.

You hire the men, you buy the kit, you own the plan, I tell him. Just so long as I like the plan too. I know from before that these South Africans must feel that they are running their own little show ... that at least they are running their own little show. '*Moenie sy gat krap nie.*' 'Never stand in another man's shadow.'

There are two golden rules we're going to follow, I explain. This Op is against the heads: not the way we've worked before. This Op is exotic.

I tell Niek the rules. Number one: men and weapons shall only ever meet right at the last minute, and for the least time. In this case, that will be when we are on our way in to Equatorial Guinea. The longer they are kept apart, then the more easily deniable is the op. That's the old Provo rule and they know what they're doing by now, to be sure, to be sure. The Boyos. Number two: Severo Moto has to be with me, and with the men, when – finally – we are both armed and on the wing. If we're caught without Moto then we're the bad ass mercenaries. They – whoever they are – will throw away the key. But if we are caught with Moto, then we're the close protection team of a senior statesman going home to make an election happen.

Angels.

Niek takes the job. No surprise.

We both agree our top priority. A recce. Put men on the ground. I have to find out if the horrific tales I am told about EG are really true. The Boss tells me. Moto tells me. The web tells me. But *I* must tell me. Is this guy, President Obiang, really as bad as he is painted? I need my own eyes and ears, but I am too toxic. It is too early for Niek to go. We need others.

Once on the ground our agents can seek out deals and projects. We've used this MO before. We plant them in the target country to set up businesses. Then we can move in people, goods, money. In and out.

Setting up the right businesses in Africa takes you to the right people. It's what we called Bongonomics, in dubious honour of the late and unlamented leader of Gabon, President Omar Bongo. African politicians love foreign investors. Get to the politicians and you quickly get to the top *hombre*. Once you're with the number one, then the treasure box flies open.

Niek has the right men for that job. We agree to send them in straight away. We both remember the old tag: 'The only good cover is real cover.'

Remember that one, girls.

Niek has already come up with a plan for the coup. He will speak to his friend Sekou Conneh, the head of LURD. Niek is sure that our offer will be grabbed. If we bung the rebel leader some cash, he'll provide 200 of his LURD fighters – with their weapons and ammo – for our op.

Getting these fighters into EG from Liberia would be my task. I'm a sailor, of sorts. I know that I can pick up a small coastal cargo ship in the Baltic, something like 20,000 tons, for £800,000 or so. With the EU chopping and changing shipping regs, cargo ships are going cheap. I am sure I can pick up a ship for less than a million. I'll sail her to Southampton. Pick up kit and stores. Then I'll sail her down.

Around the corner. Left at the lights. To Liberia.

I'll close the shore at night, at an agreed safe spot, then ferry Niek and the 200 men and weapons aboard. We'll ferry using the half-dozen rigid-hulled inflatable boats (RHIBs) that we'll need on board anyway. For the beach landing.

Getting Moto onto the MV *Princess Maud* is a slight problem. He is worth too much to be allowed to wander around in a Liberian jungle war. I hit on the idea of parachuting him into the sea just before we pick up the troops.

A child can do it. It's 100 per cent safe. Almost no training needed. The UK MoD let their civilian staff do it as a perk. Or used to. For his parachute jump, Severo will fly with Crause out of the Canaries. This is not a customary airline.

We will then sail directly to EG's capital, Malabo, on Bioko Island: just over 1,000 nautical miles south-east of Liberia: at eight knots, six days' steaming.

Our men inside EG will be waiting for us at an agreed beach landing spot. They will provide the vehicles. By then they will have the local knowledge to transport our commando raid to the palace in Malabo. And to the other targets: the KPs.

The *Princess Maud* will then act as our fire base. Naval Gunfire Support (NGS) with four 82mm mortars and two 23mms on board, she will be a floating battery. A match for anything. She will be able to give massive fire support if, God forbid, it is needed. She will also give us a five-star E&E plan.

On the sun-kissed waters of Lake Zurich, this is what Niek and I agree. This is Plan A.

Niek's next step will be to get together with the head of LURD to agree terms, and then with him and me, to shake hands ... and pay. We cannot but laugh for the joy of plotting such a wonderful piece of Grade A, Plan A derring-do. In such a bountiful bourgeois picture-postcard setting.

Days later, Niek calls me. He's in the jungle. He's hard to hear, talking on that Iridium satellite phone of his, but the LURD leader, Sekou

Conneh, has leapt at our offer. No surprise. A goodwill bung of $20,000 will kick things off. Niek has set up an RV for the three of us, in a fortnight. All I have to do is get the money from the Boss. Turn up.

The Boss loves Plan A. At our weekly meeting he promises the loot. Seven days later, another meeting: no loot. I know he's loaded. What's $20,000 plus travel to a man with his money? He'll have it for me next day. Then the day after that. So, the day before I fly to Conakry, capital of the Guinea Republic (not to be confused with Equatorial Guinea), I still don't have the $20,000.

I phone one of the other backers. 'I'm being fucked around,' I tell him. 'I'm supposed to be sorting out LURD tomorrow, but I haven't got the cash.'

Two minutes later I get a call from the Boss.

'What are you doing? Going behind my back?' he hisses.

Get off the bloody phone, then, I say to myself. I understand what he means but I don't care. I just want the money. The money I have been promised every day for the last fortnight. I have a mountain to climb. He tells me to meet him at an appointed location. My mind is ablaze. He's been winding me up to get a move on, then – when I come up with a firm plan – he and his money melt away.

What is he playing at? Does he want to go ahead with this thing or not? Am I being set up? Who's pulling the Boss's strings? Or am I fucking this thing up? Have I done something to make him lose faith in me?

Or maybe he's just following his golden rule. The golden rule of the super-rich: never use your own money – use someone else's. 'OPM', the fat cats call it. Other People's Money.

I arrive at the appointed location. The Boss's chauffeur is there to meet me. I've been told that this big fat lump is ex-SAS. He is, kind of. He's ex-21 SAS, the TA part-timers. But the Territorial Army SAS, 21 and 23 SAS Regiments, and the Regular Army SAS, 22 SAS Regiment, are from different planets. That isn't the point anyway. With this guy's weight of lard he wouldn't last an hour on Selection – 21 or 22.

Fatty holds out to me a thick brown envelope, tugged from inside his tight jacket. He cranes his neck around. Conspiratorial, seeking out spies.

'That's for your trip… Watch yourself with that much cash on you,' he mutters.

'Do please fuck off,' I want to say, but keep it to myself.

MAY · 2003: ZURICH, SWITZERLAND

Thirty-six hours later, I'm in the rainforest of the Guinea Republic, very close to the borders with Sierra Leone and Liberia. I'm with Niek and the Liberian rebel chief, Sekou Conneh.

Rainforest rain rattles down all around us. Dawn in the High Veldt.

We discuss the deal, with no mention of the target. I hand the LURD leader the envelope. He counts the notes, his face lighting up. In this neck of the wet woods, $20,000 is a war winner.

The 200 men and their weapons are on stand-by, Sekou Conneh tells me. As soon as he gets the lump sum – the next and major instalment of $500,000 – the men and equipment will be released, for training under Niek, and thence to execute Plan A. The pay and rations of those men, along with compensation scales for injury and death, are down to us. The amounts are agreed and noted, between Niek and Sekou. Or will be.

I get back to the UK. I learn that other elements of Plan A are firming up. My contacts have sourced vessels for sale in the Baltic. The right ships at the right prices. Pals in the Special Boat Service (SBS) have directed me to the best RHIBs and outboard motors for this kind of op. I pencil orders with suppliers.

I've been down to my local B&Q in Southampton. I'm putting together a costing for our software kit lists. In this game, software has nothing to do with computers. Software means all kit, minus weapons, ammo and any other undeniably war-fighting stores. It's rations, webbing, clothing, cooking gear, water containers, tents, medical supplies, defence stores, axes, spades, picks, ropes, machetes… A list without end.

At the same time I'm making contact with air crew, sailors, suppliers. All the people that I will shortly put on stand-by. Of course none of these contacts knows what I'm up to. Not yet.

But Plan A is ready. The Boss has agreed to my wheeze to parachute Severo, but I have to jump with him. That's fine. Water jumps are fun. I look forward to telling Severo – in flight – that he will be leaving the aircraft before it lands. How badly does he want to free his people?

All I need now is the lump sum, then it's RED ON… GREEN ON… GO GO GO!

CHAPTER SIX

MAY 1993: SOYO ANGOLA

For the next five days the lives of our South Africans hung by a thread. UNITA's attacks crashed onto the Boers one after another. Like storm waves onto a wall. At some point, in the end, the wall will give. The fighting flooded closer to the inner South African trenches, and became fiercer. Grenade range. Then hand to hand. Each attack was perilously fought backward, then outward. Lost FAA trenches were counter-attacked, retaken.

Those of the South Africans who had joined for grim battle (there were a few addicts) had found what they sought. Day by day the thread held. At each day's end, it still held. By luck, skill and courage.

Crazy things happened. An FAA boy soldier, undergoing instruction on the PKM machine gun, accidentally fired a burst into a tree top 200 metres away. He and his South African instructor cheered when they saw a UNITA sniper fall out.

One of several white ex-*Koevoet*★ Namibians, who were among the South Africans, felt a terrific blow on the shoulder while firing his PKM. He looked to find that his muzzle had been split open – peeled

★Koevoet, the South West Africa Police Counter-Insurgency Unit, which operated in what is now Namibia during the Border Wars 1966–89. *Koevoet* in Afrikaans also means crowbar: an allusion to their mission of prying insurgents from the local population.

back, like a banana. An incoming bullet had precisely hit the centre of his muzzle, as he fired.

A South African, standing in his trench, saw a grenade come flying in. He caught it and threw it back as if it was a one-day cricket match, like in a schoolboy's war comic. Each of the first few nights of the battle saw frantic salvage work aboard the LCT. Its critical, sea-soaked cargo had to be brought into the battle: ammo, mortars, tanks. The swell, and the surf it caused, died down. With improvised cables, passed around the ragged shoreline palms, the LCT had been more or less secured, half in and half out of the water. But still broached against the beach.

Salvage parties worked through the night. They rummaged the salty debris and formed a human chain up the beach, to haul away their prizes. As with the Mi-17 helicopter lifeline, the priority was always the same: ammo.

Praise the Lord and pass the ammunition!

The second priority was the 82mm mortars on board, and their bombs. Meanwhile, on the main tank deck, wave-harried, the South African mechanics struggled to start the first of the two tanks.

On D Day Plus 3, Steven Mason was hit by a rifle bullet in the forearm: Steven – the South African commander who had led the beach recce for the heli attack on Soyo. He came out on an Mi-17 casevac flight with Dom, another wounded South African.

Dom had fired an RPG-7 with a seawater-damaged rocket. The first stage had fired, but the rocket had stayed attached to the launcher. The second stage had therefore fired straight into his face. I went to see them both as soon as they came in. They were to be flown to Windhoek by Crause, a ten-hour flight in his twin-engine Cessna Night Rider, with two refuellings. Eighty per cent of the flight was over UNITA territory. We prayed that our luck would hold. That there would not be a death as a result of the long casevac. That we would not lose an aircraft.

The medic, a friend of both men, was busy telling Dom how ugly he had always been, so not to worry – now that his face looked like the inside of a Big Mac.

'Hard enough for you, Steven?' I could not stop myself from asking.

On the *Bangala*, before setting off on his recce mission, Steven had pissed me off. Telling me how the op would be a piece of piss, UNITA a walk-over. Hardly fair that we were to use ball and not blank.

Steven forced a grin. 'What a fuck-up, eh?'

Steven and Dom had news for me. There were 3,000 of UNITA's finest on Soyo. They had been waiting for the attack. UNITA orders were to hold Soyo, at any cost.

The helicopter assault had achieved tactical local surprise, even though strategic surprise had been well and truly lost. A sea assault had been the expected option. Also expected had been clear warning immediately prior to the attack taking place. This UNITA had not been given.

Surprise, therefore, had been achieved. Kind of.

Steven and Dom had no evidence, but were sure that South African soldiers were fighting on the UNITA side. They deduced this because of the determined way that UNITA were fighting, and because of the stories from questioned prisoners.

There's another twist: the presence of Moroccan troops, Moroccan Special Forces. This sums up the lunacy of what was going on in Angola. Barrel Boyz' mischief.

Oil companies were funding the MPLA, by paying to drill and exploit oil reserves off the coast of Soyo.

At the same time, the US was financing and supporting the rebel force UNITA against the MPLA. The French obviously realised that, if UNITA won the civil war, then the US – by dint of supporting UNITA – would have control of oil production in Angola. To ensure they didn't lose out in the event of a UNITA victory, the French had supplied UNITA with Moroccan soldiers.

In West Africa, oil is everything.

The French intelligence service Direction Générale de la Sécurité Extérieure (DGSE) has a saying about the CIA: '*Toute chose sale vous pouvez faire, nous pouvons faire plus sale.*' 'Any dirty thing you can do, we can do dirtier.'

This time there was some proof. French and Arabic soccer magazines, and music cassettes and cassette players, had been found in more than one overrun UNITA position. Dom, who knew UNITA well, said it was impossible for these to belong to UNITA troops. They wouldn't want such things, even if they could buy them.

Steven and Dom also told me about the FAA commander, Colonel Pepe. Convinced that some boy soldiers were inflicting gunshot wounds on themselves to escape fighting, Pepe had an answer. He would walk among those wounded and awaiting casevac by Mi-17. Any of his boy soldiers whose wounds looked self-inflicted, he shot dead.

Much to his amusement, Dom had seen apparently badly hurt boys suddenly jump up and run back to their positions, as Pepe loomed into view. Dom was like Pepe.

On D+3, one of the South Africans was killed.

Willy Erasmus died instantly from a burst of machine-gun fire. There was a good side to this. He had died instantly. Not because of our slow casevac to Windhoek.

Violent death wasn't new to me. So why was I so shocked?

It dawned on me. These men were not doing this for their country. They were not doing this as Tony and I were – in order to defend their property and livelihood. They were being wounded, being killed – in Willy's case – purely for money.

The money was not enough for some.

Coebus sent 20 men out. To be flown home. They didn't want to go on fighting. So Coebus didn't want them. Meanwhile, Tony announced that the pay and bonuses of the 20 now departing would be added to the bonus total, and then distributed as a further increase for the rest. Tony had already upped the bonus.

He, too, had been taken aback by what these men were doing. Just for money.

Crause and two other pilots, Werner and Johan, were flying non-stop. Back and forth, and always over UNITA-held territory. They had two Beechcraft Baron 58s and the Cessna Night Rider: all twin piston-engine propeller light aircraft. They flew replacement men up, together with any vital stores, and wounded men down.

In addition, Crause lent an unlikely hand by getting together the FAA Antonov An-12 cargo flyers in Luanda. One of the early nights, D+4, they flew their old cargo planes over Soyo, rolling bombs off the rear tailgate, Crause shoving.

The sky was overcast. Bombs were dropped by rough calculations and Global Positioning System (GPS), trying to make sure that they did not hit our men. They could see the flashes of the bombs going off through the cloud cover. Crause was sure that this was a help. A morale booster, at least.

When he arrived at Soyo, to pick up Steven and Dom, Crause told a

92

strange tale. A well-known SADF officer, known to many of the men, had been killed in a car crash outside Pretoria. This officer, held in high regard by the South African Special Forces, was the son of a general. Except, it seemed, there had been no car crash. The story making its crawl around the bars of Pretoria and Jo'burg was that this man had been killed fighting for UNITA. At Soyo.

Joaquim David, Tony and I slaved over those five days. A ghastly routine of begging, pleading, scrounging, bullying, checking and loading held us in trance. Stores. Supplies. Logistics. Fuel. Ammo, and more ammo. It was the only thing to do. Every minute there was a sense of the needs of the fighting men in Soyo. Their lives hung on a logistical thread. Only we three could keep the thread strong. Then, in the middle of the morning of the sixth day, D+5, I had news for Tony and Joaquim.

'We'll win.'

'What the fuck are you talking about, Simon?'

'We're winning. It's going to work.'

'Fuck off!'

'No – Tony, please,' said Joaquim, frowning at me. 'Why do you say this? Please do not make jokes!'

'Look!' I pointed. 'That Mi-17 crew, where I've just come from, what do you see?'

'Don't play games, Simon. What are you talking about?' asked Tony.

'You remember how pathetic, but how typical, it was that the Angolans could give their air crew a bloody great helicopter to fly, but no flying overalls? How we used to laugh at them – flying in their ragtag civvies... I'm sorry, Joaquim!'

'Is OK, Simon. No problem,' said Joaquim.

Tony stared at the crew who were today – for the first time – wearing overalls.

I carried on: 'I've been talking to them. I asked them why they had been flying in civvies but had now put their overalls on.

'The pilot speaks French as badly as I do – that's how we could talk.'

'What's the reason?'

'They wore civvies before because the chances of being shot down were so great that they expected to have to escape on foot after a crash. The civvy clothes might help, so they can pretend to be civilians themselves!'

'Makes sense. So...'

MAY 1993: SOYO ANGOLA...

'So, today is the first day they feel safe enough to wear their uniform overalls. They think we are winning.'

At that moment, as if on cue, a signaller appeared with a message from Coebus. Last night they had got one of the tanks on the LCT started and offloaded. It had done some useful work that morning. Furthermore, there had been a small, but noticeable, slackening in the determination with which the UNITA attacks of that night had been pressed home.

A PC-9 rocketed over the shacks, then shot upward over the town – executing a V roll as it went. Another safe return from a CAS sortie over Soyo.

'V roll! He thinks we're winning too.'

'Or he met a new girl last night, and that was for her.'

'I do wish that they would not feel they have to beat us up every single time they land,' said Joaquim.

Each day survived by Coebus and his band of heroes was its own victory. Although still a far-off mirage, an overall triumph, in the end, now seemed just possible.

Logistics were the weak point. As always, logistics were the key point.

In the plan, the LCT was to be the logistics linchpin. The *Bangala* was to be the back-up. Without those two assets, the resupply burden fell upon the Mi-17s. But these were the only Mi-17s in Angola. Don't forget, the war between the MPLA and UNITA was nationwide. Angola is twice the size of France, with no road or rail network. These Mi-17s were being called for by every commander in the war: a war that the MPLA were losing.

Then there was the question of security at our base, Cabinda International Airport. Our security.

Each day that passed without an attack on Cabinda itself was a huge relief. UNITA had an ally in Cabinda who could have attacked us at any time: Front for the Liberation of the Enclave of Cabinda (FLEC), the local guerrilla force, demanding independence from Angola.

If they hit us hard at Cabinda, they'd strangle our supply line to the Soyo battle front. They could destroy the air support that gave us our all-important edge. Yet, despite this threat, the FAA chiefs at Cabinda didn't put a guard on the planes at night. Or on us. Or on anything else.

Despite these shortcomings, that now-uniformed Mi-17 crew had proven to be a true tell-tale. From that day, the tide turned. Slowly

UNITA's ebb had begun. At a meeting with Coebus, it was agreed that he should go onto the attack whenever he could.

Taking the fight to UNITA made sense. However, the casualties among the South Africans grew because attack exposed the men more. Which was how Smith was killed. An Englishman, and one of Coebus's three platoon commanders, Smith had fought in the British Army's Parachute Regiment, the Rhodesian Army Fire Force and the SADF Special Forces unit known as the 'Recces'. He was noted for a laconic humour and professionalism.

That day, he had led his platoon on a counter-attack. The UNITA withdrawal was a trick. Smith's platoon hit an ambush. He was hit twice in the chest. He knew he was dying. As he died, he said to his sergeants that they must not let his death put off any of the young ones, and their enthusiasm for this, their chosen line of work.

Gradually UNITA's fight drained out of them ... then all but disappeared. Logistics again. UNITA's logistical chain – from their headquarters in Huambo, in the centre of Angola – some 600 miles away – all the way to Soyo, in the extreme north-west – on foot – proved their undoing. They couldn't get weapons, ammo and supplies there as well as we could from Cabinda. Their casualties had a long walk to anything like a doctor.

Having achieved a miracle for them, the MPLA paid us in full, and on time. Then they made us a proposal. We'd helped them win the Battle of Soyo. Now could we help them seize the rest of the country from UNITA?

Could we win the war? Could we finish the war?

CHAPTER SEVEN

JULY 2003: THE EG COUP

Plan A: GO GO ... STOP!

The Boss loves it. He has the money to make it go ahead. He just doesn't have the money today. Or he doesn't choose to have it today.

Why not?

He assures me that the money is coming through. Any day now. He's been saying this for weeks. I'm getting twitchy. What's he playing at?

The key elements of Plan A – to invade Equatorial Guinea from the sea – are in place. LURD, the Liberian rebels, and their weapons, are on stand-by. The gnarly old South African dogs of war are on stand-by. The purchase of the cargo ship and the RHIBs is on stand-by. Everything is flashing amber. We just need a green light.

And enough greenbacks to make it all happen.

I warn the Boss that his GO STOP GO STOP is steering us into rocky seas. The operation is in danger of smashing into a reef. The longer we wait, the more likely that we will be compromised.

Mercenaries gossip. Soldiers network. Shady crooks. Dodgy businesses. Spooks.

They owe a policeman a favour, or they'll be nicked.

It's likely that rumours of an op are already leaking to intelligence agencies. To the major oil companies. Maybe even to Obiang himself. Each has the money and the power to kill the op. Or to ambush us. Kill us.

97

If Plan A is going to succeed, we need the elements of speed and surprise. We need to move fast now, to avoid springing too many leaks. We need to move fast now to ensure that unfriendly agencies, who have guessed about the operation, don't have time to stop it.

This is what won the day in Angola. In Sierra Leone. Speed and surprise are our most vital weapons. This is what I've been at pains to explain to the Boss. From the get-go.

I explain it again. I need the money. *Now*.

I have a black book of specialists who are crucial to this operation. Sailors, soldiers, pilots, suppliers. I can't hire any of them until the money is in the bank. Yet if I wait until the money's in the bank, I'm then facing a checklist, stretching to pages, that will take man-days to work through. More delay, more leaks.

The worst of this is that we have men on the ground in Equatorial Guinea. If the operation is leaking, you can be sure the information will eventually find its way to EG intelligence. Any moment, our men could be captured, tortured, killed. The operation sunk.

I had wanted to go into EG for the recce myself. But I know my arrival could have triggered an alarm. By all accounts, Obiang has survived/repelled/foiled about a dozen coups. If a coup-conscious secret state like EG spots my name on an inbound pax manifest, they'll surely act.

We have a bunch of black EO mercenaries, from our Angolan and Sierra Leone adventures, who come originally from São Tomé. This is the island republic some 300 nautical miles south-west of the coast of EG's Bioko Island. These men had been originally recruited by the SADF to fight against the MPLA Angolans in the Border Wars.

Then the SADF dumped them. Disbanded many units. They discarded men who'd fought a war for them. They callously stripped these men of their source of living, and their pensions. Then EO recruited these tough São Tomé fighters, along with the other 32 'Buffalo' Battalion men.

Since then, some of them had also become businessmen. Now Niek and I have recruited them as spies. These men have been able to slip into EG unnoticed. They have the right skin colour. The right dialect. The right backgrounds. The right businesses.

By now one of the men has been in there for more than a month.

His reports are frightening. Obiang wants to outshine the nastiness of his predecessor. Francisco Macías Nguema's brutal rule came to an end when his nephew Obiang murdered him in 1979.

Four years earlier, Uncle Francisco had plumbed depravity's deepest depths. The venue: a Malabo soccer stadium. The occasion: the execution of 150 alleged enemies. The twist: Francisco had a soundtrack to the executions, playing over the stadium loudspeakers: Mary Hopkins's hit 'Those Were the Days'.

My sources tell me that such dark days are far from over in EG. People are being tortured and killed. People are vanishing. Being imprisoned without charge. Disappearing into the prison system. No free speech. Movement is prohibited: you can't go from one village to the next without bribing the police officer and a priest.

Obiang has his party piece. He allegedly eats the flesh of murdered rivals. A senior police commissioner had been buried without his testicles or his brain.

Such are the stories.

Obiang's is a rank tyranny. Ousting him is the right thing to do.

All the time, the Boss's monthly burn rate is going up. He has to pay for Niek. For my costs. For the guys in EG. The EG businesses themselves.

All the time I'm trimming costs. Short cuts here, favours there. There's a simple solution: one big fat cheque for £1 million. That would kick off the whole thing. I know he can raise this money. If he's had a change of heart he needs to tell me.

'If you want to kill this Op,' I urge him, 'do it now.'

'Simon, the money is coming. I promise you, the money is coming any day now.'

Then comes dramatic news. A development no one could have seen coming.

Liberia is being ripped apart by her civil war, which has been going on these last six years now. Then, in June 2003, the barbaric despot Charles Taylor flees to Nigeria. Suddenly the US starts taking a keen interest in mineral-rich, ruler-free Liberia.

On 26 July 2003, President George W. Bush orders American warships to blockade the coast of Liberia. He orders LURD rebels to sign up for peace. Bush and his CIA spooks no doubt sniff some sort of diamond deal with a new regime.

JULY · 2003 : · THE · EG · COUP . . .

There's oil offshore of Liberia.

Cue the Barrel Boyz.

In West Africa, it's all about oil … but then everything is about oil, full stop.

Sailing my little Scandinavian coastal steamer, the *Princess Maud*, to the Liberian coast to pick up 200 armed men doesn't now seem like a good idea. Being a gung-ho derring-do dog of war is one thing. Tangling with the United States fucking Navy is another.

Under the Argus eye of a USN boarding party, the story – that my 200 LURD troops were on an educational enviro-tourist cruise – might not stand up.

Plan A is scrapped. We don't care. We're used to plans going tits up. Another plan at least as cunning is taking shape.

Our São Tomé boys – those already in EG – have enjoyed good luck. Their joint ventures have been snapped up by the EG government. Already they are working at ministerial level.

Niek du Toit is posing as the real power and money behind these schemes. He's made several trips to EG now. He has met and spoken with Obiang. This now forms the basis for Plan B, as follows: we will establish a Forming Up Place (FUP) in the DRC. We have picked the Kilo Moto region in the north of the country. The DRC is the size of Europe. Ungovernable. Kilo Moto is brimful of gold.

We have a deal, to pay off the local warlord. In return he provides use of his grand metalled landing strip, some accommodation and a rifle range. And his promise not to kill us.

Plan B is to fly our 80 men from South Africa into Maseru, in Kilo Moto. Their cover? Security for our gold mining and gold trading in that region. By D Day those activities will be genuine.

Only real cover is good cover. So, did you remember that one, girls?

We have chartered two Russian planes – an Ilyushin 76 (Il-76) and an Antonov An-12. This charter has been organised for me – out of the icy depths of the old Eastern Bloc – by a potty and antique German friend of EO, and of mine: one Gerhard Merz. Gerhard is Benny Hill doing a German accent. He's a convicted gun runner, but very funny. Very good at it. 'Zer baby bottles,' he calls a shipment.

Niek has based Gerhard, with the aircraft and crews, in Malabo International. He's squared this with the EG authorities. They love it. As far as they are concerned, the planes are an essential part of Niek's business operations, all of which are, of course, JVs with VVIP locals.

The Boss's monthly burn rate has just doubled.

Plan B. Niek tells Obiang that his company, Triple Option Ltd, is making him a goodwill gift: four top-of-the-range Toyota Land Cruisers. The President, Niek tells me, loves new toys, loves gifts. (Try it. The unsolicited gift is hugely potent in African culture.)

He will come to the airport to receive his Land Cruisers, to wallow in the moment. Niek tells Obiang to let him know what colours he'd like them.

As the aircraft bearing gifts draws up, Niek will be beside Obiang. The Il-76 will indeed be carrying four Land Cruisers. It will be our Trojan horse carrying 70 armed men. The vehicles and the weapons will have been picked up at Entebbe, Uganda, then flown to Maseru, Kilo Moto, the FUP. Once there, they will be married up to the men flown up from South Africa. Test firing and last-minute rehearsals will be carried out.

At the last minute, Severo Moto will be flown to the FUP in a biz jet from Europe. Men, weapons and Moto will only be together hours before we take off, for H Hour, D Day. Malabo.

'We are not a customary airline.' 'Beware Afrikaners bearing gifts.'

Arriving at Malabo International, the Il-76 will land, then taxi over to the Presidential party. The Toyotas will come roaring out, ready to shoot. Niek will grab the President. Niek's São Tomé team will overpower the Presidential security.

We will place Obiang under arrest. We will escort Moto to the palace. Plan B is breathtaking in its simplicity. There's an added satisfaction in knowing that Obiang will have been undone by his own greed.

The Boss loves Plan B. He swears the big money for it to go ahead is coming. Those dollars have to cover the pay of the main party, the weapons and ammo, and the Toyotas. The Boss reveals alarming news. News that cranks up the suspense further. News that banishes any doubts I had harboured about his dedication to the plot.

He has heard, from his EG sources – neatly cross-referencing his US ones – that President Obiang is terminally ill. If he dies, then whoever takes over might be less easily wobbled. There are rumours, the Boss tells me, that Obiang is about to hand over power to his eldest son, California-living, wild playboy Teodorino.

JULY · 2003: · THE · EG · COUP . . .

Teodorino, not forgetting the terrible curse of the twin skulls, is a wannabe rap star with an international reputation as a hothead and spendthrift. In one weekend in Cape Town in 2003, he purchased two Bentleys – an Arnage T and a Mulliner – to the tune of £1.1 million. Then he splashed out on a Lamborghini Murcielago and two luxury homes worth £3.7 million.

Teodorino's largesse is not what concerns his enemies. They are scared by his tendency to open fire in nightclubs – and at meetings – whenever things don't go his way. Mostly he shoots at the ceiling. Not always.

One thing seems certain. If Teodorino is made President, then the EG Army will mutiny. Our Op will be dead in the water.

As the Boss puts it: 'Simon, we need your coup yesterday.' I comfort myself that he, at last, shares my sense of urgency. But where's his fucking money?

The money doesn't come.

Then, just as Plan B would have come together, had we been paid the money, it all falls apart. The Il–76 and crew leave Malabo. The Il–76, one of the cornerstones of Plan B, has fucked off. Just like that. No notice. No warning.

The Il–76 had a straightforward cover story for being in Malabo. It was a part of Niek's business in EG, Triple Option. The company had an air-freight JV that the place badly needed. However, to pull off that cover story, the aircraft needed to be busy. It needed to be flying in and out of Malabo regularly. Otherwise Obiang's people would smell a rat.

Now I find out that Niek and Gerhard have failed to come up with work to keep the jet busy. They have hit West African paperwork difficulties. Excuses for bribes, in other words.

I find out that the Il–76 crew have been on a low basic wage, topped up by a bonus for each hour flying. The crew has been stranded, idle, for week after week, earning a pittance.

So they have fuelled up and fucked off. I am furious.

Why hadn't Niek and Gerhard kept them busy? Or at least struck a deal that would have made it worth their while to stay on at Malabo? Why had I not been warned that there was a problem?

Niek explains. He thought the Boss would have stumped up the big money by now. He thought we'd be 'in' weeks ago. He and Gerhard should have seen the problem on their radar. Dealt with it. They are being paid to do a job.

But, as Niek points out, every mishap can be traced back to one singular failing on the part of one person. Why is the Boss not coming up with the big money?

'Look, I've made up my mind,' I tell the Boss at our next powwow. He gives me his hangdog look. He knows of my difficulties, but I can pull this off. 'I'm gonna look for other investors… You can have a veto on them, that's OK … but we sure as hell can't go on like this.'

The Boss thinks about something. On this he knows that he hasn't got a leg to stand on.

'Who do you have in mind?'

'I've just the man.'

I first met Mark Thatcher in 1997.

My family had just moved to Cape Town. Days after arriving, I'm approached by a pal of Thatcher's, our very own Frank Thomas, who has connections to Margaret Thatcher.

Thomas tells me his chums in South African National Intelligence are nervous about my turning up in their country. They are agog. What am I up to? Executive Outcomes casts a long shadow. I must meet his boss. I do that. I've nothing to hide. SA NI agree.

Then Thomas introduces me to my new neighbour, Mark Thatcher, only son of the former British Prime Minister, Margaret. Mark thinks that the SAS walk on water. Because I'd gone even further and won through in Angola and Sierra Leone – in two private wars – he treats me like I'm a star.

Mark bombards me with invites. Social and business events. I think he's lonely. He doesn't seem to have many friends. So he's seized upon me. Simon Mann, MT's new best friend. I mean, we move to SA in late November, and four weeks later we're all round at his place for Christmas dinner, meeting Mum and Dad!

As I know, Maggie shares her son's fondness for the SAS. They had made the difference for her. Gone the extra. More than once. She had for them too. She takes a shine to me. Over the years, whenever we have dinner, I'm always sat next to her. Maggie's Cape Town favourite.

Other than that of Nelson Mandela, our house is the only Cape home she visits, for lunch or dinner. Amanda and I even go on a game lodge holiday with Margaret, Denis, Mark and his wife, Diane. A long weekend. Endlessly long. I had warned Amanda, but she wasn't having it. 'Oh no, Pilot. I'm not missing going on holiday with the most famous living Briton. Are you crazy?' You have been warned.

Soon I am to find out where meeting up with a former Prime Minister can take you. In London I become friendly with one of Lady Thatcher's former advisers. His name is David Hart and, despite his former political allegiance to Maggie, he is close to Jonathan Powell, Tony Blair's Chief of Staff at 10 Downing Street.

Hart – another Old Etonian – went spectacularly bust in the 1970s while speculating in London property. On hearing of his bankruptcy, his mother hired a butler for him. Sent him round to cheer the boy up.

His main rise to fame and power came about by smuggling papers from the cellar archives of the Kremlin. Hart's standing with Maggie was that of superstar. Or of an SAS man. Even so, that did not stop them from having fiery rows.

Oddly (or so it seems at the time), I first met Hart through my eldest son, Peter, then 22. He and his friend Charlie, Hart's son, had decided their fathers must meet. They set up a blind-date lunch for their two dads at the Ritz in Piccadilly.

We eat where David Hart holds court, Cohiba Esplendidos and all, in the alcove just off the main dining room. The one immediately right, then right again, as you walk in. So tucked away, went the argument, that it was a separate room to the main dining room. So Hart could suck and puff his expensive Cuban smoke.

Serendipitously or not (but now I think not), this lunch date happens in February 2002. We hit it off. Meetings, lunches, dinners follow – while David brings me into his network. I check him out. Very improbably, he is indeed the Big Man that his boasts say that he is.

David is close to Number 10. He is close to those who matter in Israel. His father was a Jew, his mother not. But he thinks of himself as a radical free-thinking Jew. Among other things, he knows Frank Thomas, the Cape Town spook so keen to have me shake hands with SA NI.

But Hart, I find, is a man who wields extraordinary behind-the-scenes power.

In the US, he has links with the neo-conservatives. Prominent among these is Richard Perle, a political adviser and lobbyist who worked for the Reagan administration. Perle had earned himself the dubious moniker 'The Prince of Darkness'. He is one of the neo-cons openly pushing for a US invasion of Iraq. Perle is not alone. Among others in Hart's Stateside circle are Donald Rumsfeld, Secretary of Defense; his deputy Paul Wolfowitz; Phil Condit, the Chairman and CEO of Boeing.

One day, David tells me, he was sitting with Rumsfeld in his Pentagon office. They talk about the need to invade Iraq, as soon as Afghanistan is subdued. Israel comes up. They debate, for a while, the same old arguments. Then Rumsfeld waves a hand towards the window. Potomac River. White House.

'On the other hand, David,' he observes, 'who needs Israel ... when you have all this?'

Hart is an ambassador for invasion. He tells me he's not paid by the neo-cons or by any government. That he likes it this way. He's unaccountable. Deniable. His kickback comes when big companies win contracts, for war or peace. David is on a percentage with God knows who.

Hart, freelance invasion ambassador, flies me to the south of France for lunch with Perle, Prince of Darkness. The lunch feels weird. I know well enough that Perle is checking me out. Taking a read-out.

A week or so later David invites me to a party where I meet Perle, members of Mossad, my old Russian tutor from Sandhurst Chris Donnelly, now working for NATO, and Sir Graham 'Jock' Stirrup, then UK Deputy Chief of Defence Staff, responsible for buying equipment for the Armed Forces. The jungle drums beat hard. The talk is of 'how' and 'when' we invade Iraq. Not if.

David tells me he needs my help. He is writing papers on Iraq and the desired downfall of Saddam Hussein. These papers are going to Jonathan Powell, Chief of Staff at 10 Downing Street. Powell, in turn, is passing them on to his boss, Prime Minister Blair.

What David wants are the ideas of someone like me.

'Why me?' I ask.

'You're ex-SAS.'

'Like many others – a hundred of them – here in London – and most of those better qualified than me.'

'True, Simon. But they haven't fought private-venture campaigns as you have – and won them – in Angola and Sierra Leone. We need outside-the-box thinking.'

Of course, I'm flattered. Who wouldn't be? I also want to do anything I can to make the invasion happen. There is no question in my mind: Saddam is a war criminal. He's a mass murderer. He's a despotic madman who needs to be brought down. A bully that needs to be fought. Fast. Not having a go against a Saddam is like not having a go against a street mugging. Only the distance is greater.

While I work up outside-the-box invasion ruses, I regularly meet David.

Of course, we argue through the pros and cons of an invasion.

Oil. Yummy contracts. Jolly good fun for the Barrel Boyz. Bush junior seeking the scalp that Bush senior failed to take. Saudi is going cold on the West. If Iran grows punchy, then what better new place to have as a forward operating base than Iraq?

I want to know what other reasons we have to risk the lives of our soldiers.

I fear the Born Again factor. Bush and Blair, God's avenging angels. Bible-bashing. I need to know: how much of this invasion plan is down to Born Again mumbo-jumbo?

'Well … yes … too much,' David says. He takes a big suck of Cohiba smoke, blows slowly out.

This worries me.

One day I ask David straight: 'We knew Saddam was a bad ass long before 9/11. So … is payback for 9/11 what this is really about?'

'Afghanistan isn't enough,' says David. 'The last people to attack the US had two nuclear bombs dropped on them. If you attack Uncle Sam, revenge will be total. Mega. Afghanistan went well. Now they need more. Bigger.'

At that stage, the issue is one of *casus belli*. Is there enough to justify invasion? I am sure that, if I was an Iraqi, I would pray that someone in the West would have the balls to help us get out from under. Topple the tyrant.

I am equally sure, and say so to David, that trying to bamboozle, or josh along, the Ordinary Joes of the US, or UK, is unnecessary, dangerous and wrong. There is no need to bullshit. I tell David that Saddam's alleged possession of Weapons of Mass Destruction is a red

106

herring. There's no need for us to use them as argument. In any case, if he has them now, then he had them before 11 September.

So why didn't we invade before?

If the British and the Americans look at the crimes of Saddam's regime, they will see it is right that we go in. How many people does a tyrant have to kill or torture before you can take him on?

English Common Law is clear enough on that topic: tyranny is assault. To fight against assault is good. To fight to help someone who is being assaulted is good.

Arguing the toss like that isn't my job, even if it does make for good lunchtime argument. My job – by way of *casus belli* – is to come up with schemes of derring-do that will kick things off in a fitting manner.

'Raising the Flag' is one of my schemes, 'Q Ships' another. The idea behind both is to trigger a chain of events. Raising the Flag involves the thousands-strong body of Iraqis in exile, of which I meet Jalal al-Hashim. The intro comes from Perle via Hart. We get on. He is the CIA/neo-con/White House first choice for leader of a liberated Iraq. We meet in his large and shadowy apartment in the swanky St Germain district of Paris, just behind the Institut de France. The rooms have an Edwardian scale and grandeur. So does the furniture and the decoration. There are many silver-framed black-and-white photos, with signatures. The old King of Iraq and his family. It is the classic *Grand Émigré*. More loyal in absentia than ever they were *in situ*.

The idea is that Executive Outcomes would be reborn under a new name. We would train up his men, then accompany them into action. We'd take over an Iraqi city that was well clear of Baghdad but well within the zone of air supremacy of allied air forces, operating from well outside Iraq. Saddam would then have a horrible choice: come after us and risk being annihilated from the air, or leave flying the flag of rebellion. Saddam would have to tolerate the presence of a foreign force in his own land.

Q Ships means buying an old cargo ship in the Far East, then sailing her round to Karachi. There she would pick up genuine – and genuinely nasty – nuclear weapons-grade fuel or other bomb parts. From Karachi the ship would sail for Basra. En route – in the Persian Gulf – she would be stopped and searched by the Saudi Navy. As the Saudi boat closed, the Q Ship would bounce and burn the Saudis. The international outrage from all directions would be deafening.

The Q Ship – once in Basra – and once word of her deeds and cargo had been cunningly leaked – would be loathed far and wide: an attack on Basra to take her would be justified, and war would begin. Of course, my plan is not to actually kill any Saudi sailors. Just to make sure that the world believes we have.

By May 2002, David tells me he's discussed both plans in face-to-face meetings with Tony Blair and Jonathan Powell. They like certain elements, dislike others. David asks me to continue to work on these options, but to explore others. It is clear that they're going in.

I'm irritated. I tell David that he and Blair are not taking this seriously enough. They need to move on from casually kicking about ad hoc plans. If they're going to risk the lives of British soldiers, they need to prepare properly. If they go in half-cocked, our soldiers will get killed.

'That's what soldiers are for, isn't it?' counters David.

Irritation turns to fury. I tell David he has no idea how much it hurts when one of your men is killed or wounded. The guilt. The fear that you hadn't been diligent enough. It is the first of many screaming matches.

That August in 2002, David and I fly to Israel. We waltz through the bedlam of Ben Gurion Security. I find myself at the King David Hotel, on the edge of Jerusalem's old city. I'm in a lavish three-room suite. David is across the hall, alone in four.

For this trip, David Hart has warned me about talking to my old friends. They are *peaceniks* now. Out of favour with the people we will be with.

I can't be bothered to tell Hart that anyone acquainted with war is a *peacenik*. That war is the last resort, only to be put on the menu when a justifiable objective (like survival) can be achieved by no other means.

I remember dear Nicholas Elliot too (another *peacenik* and spy), and his adventures in Israel. The funny story of the time when Nicholas had been sent to the desert dressed up as an Israeli Army Intelligence Captain. He was there on behalf of MI6 in order to make a trade. He was to hand over a copy of the entire Egyptian Order of Battle. The Israelis were to allow Nicholas to ask a few choice questions of a captured Egyptian General.

On the way to the front, Nicholas talked of the importance of the correct handling of information before it becomes usable Intelligence. His host, an Israeli General, stopped the jeep and waved at the desert.

'Don't tell me that, Nicholas, this bloody place is meant to be flowing with milk and honey ... apparently it does: for three weeks of the year ... but that was when Moses' scouts were here...'

On the way back from the interview they stopped for a swim, stripping naked.

'My God, Nicholas ... I'm impressed ... your service is thorough!' said the General, seeing that Nicholas was circumcised, and thinking this was all part of his cover.

David Hart and I begin our mission

We're driven to Mossad HQ. There we meet two government ministers and three directors of Mossad, two retired, the other – Meir Dagan – appointed a week earlier. David introduces me as ex-Special Forces. As if Mossad don't know. I'm the man who can kick things off in Iraq. The new Mossad chief is dismissive. Rude.

'No, no, that is not how you must do this. You must go in big. A full-scale invasion is the only option.'

We argue the toss. Then the head of Mossad puts us straight on another matter.

'Unfortunately, you have chosen the wrong country. You should really be invading Iran. But anyway, you've chosen Iraq and now you've made too much noise. You have to do it now. Two things. If you don't do it now, you will look ridiculous. If you don't win, you will look ridiculous.'

Then the Pentagon's news filters all the way down the chain to the likes of me: '*Casus belli* is no longer an issue. We're going to invade Iraq anyway, and for whatever reason. We're going, and we're going HEAVY.'

The US and UK invade Iraq in March 2003. I'm convinced they're doing the right thing. Heavy is the best way, and they're going for the right reasons. Tyrants and tyranny are not OK. My father George had been a pacifist at Cambridge in the 1930s. But the spectre of Hitler's tyranny left him with no choice but to join up and fight in World War II. Grandfather Pop had gone into the Great War in the same way. The Kaiser could be as big a shit as he liked, a tyrant – until he invaded Belgium. Abuse of power equals bully. Bully means: 'You've gotta fight.'

JULY · 2003: · THE · EG · COUP . . .

I had been ready to put my arse on the line to fight Saddam's tyranny. I would have gone on the ground for Raising the Flag. I would have gone to sea for Q Ships. I had loved the feeling of plotting with David – the endeavour, the risk – maybe action just around the corner.

For me, though, the 2003 Iraqi campaign is over. No job for Mann.

Later, David Hart wants me to do a highly paid job, in post-invasion Iraq (as do a couple of other people), but I have other fish to fry. My own ARC. I ask David if he wants to be an investor in the EG coup. No, he doesn't.

To ensure our coup happens, I decide to go to a man who is a likely investor. I target my new best friend, Mark Thatcher. One sunny southern winter's day, we go for a walk on Table Mountain. The unique flat-topped rock is like a natural city wall protecting Cape Town. One local legend calls Table Mountain the slain dragon of the sea. I tell Mark that Table Mountain's name is echoed in that of the constellation Mensa, Latin for 'table'. The Mensa constellation can be seen in the Southern Hemisphere around this time of year – August – just below Orion. Of course, he knows I haven't walked him up here to talk of star stuff. He knows very well that I'm up to something, so now I tell him all about the EG plot. I ask if he'd be interested in investing.

No surprise.

He nearly bites my hand off, but Mark makes one thing clear that day on Table Mountain. Not only does he want to share the spoils of our EG adventure. He wants to play an active role in our op, and in whatever comes next. To be an officer.

I'm not surprised by his enthusiasm. Mark is a habitually naughty boy. He loves the craic. However, I can see that this mission offers much more to him. He can become 'one of the boys'. SAS. EO. That's where Mark wants to be. Sure, he can gain influence, and power, in an oil-rich country. He can win the approval of his mother – as well – but, I tell him, first you have to meet the Boss.

At the meeting, Thatcher talks about his love of boys' own adventure. He buys into our plot. Just as I knew he would. He puts up $300,000. He wants protection, though. He is high profile, under scrutiny.

We agree to help Thatcher stay super-secure. He will not put his money in through a Logo Logistics shareholders' agreement, like everyone else. Thatcher's money is to come in via a false joint venture with Crause Steyl (our old Executive Outcomes pilot) and his company, Africa Air Ambulance.

Two days after the meeting with the Boss, Thatcher asks to meet me. We are to have another lunch together that day. But first he wants a chat.

Mark speaks about our proposed Plan C: how it involves the use of an old oilfield support vessel – the MV *Cape Endurance* – that can take a Mi-17 support helicopter on the aft work-deck. Some of the South Africans would be landed on Bioko Island – site of the capital, Malabo – by air, while the main party would go ashore by RHIB support boats.

The plan is similar to that which worked to such good effect in Soyo. I had asked Mark, an experienced helicopter pilot, if it would be possible to operate an Mi-17 off the aft deck. He had been worried about the 'air recycling' effect.

Then he brought in his own helicopter team to advise. He even came with me to look over the vessel in question, while she was making ready, still tied alongside, at the Cape Town waterfront.

At the same time, Mark and I were also looking over the FV *Madeline* in dear old Haut Bay Harbour. I still have my Republic of Haut Bay passport somewhere. It was just a joke. But it was one that didn't amuse the Zim authorities when they found it in my kit.

The *Madeline* was being made ready to sail to EG by Peter Bush, a Cape Town fisherman friend of mine. She was one of Niek's EG businesses. She was also Niek's E&E vessel. Who knows? I wondered. She might end up the E&E vessel for everyone. And of course, she would be available to help with whatever other options came up.

Mark, better than I, can see the highways and by-ways for making money out of post-op EG, as well as the pitfalls. I tell him about my big worry. I fear the Boss's greed is spiralling out of control. In truth, I'm every bit as worried about Mark's. Then I see that Thatcher has a different outlook to the Boss on the benefits of Moto's gaining power in EG. His is closer to mine.

We can change EG. We can make EG into an African Singapore, or a Dubai. EG must have an infrastructure. Basic utilities, running water, schools, a university, proper hospitals. We look at what Dubai has achieved and how. Like EG, Dubai has oil. But, smartly, it has ruthlessly nurtured other industries: tourism, financial services, real estate.

These sectors now earn more revenue for Dubai than oil. EG could be the seed point from which everything could change in the basket-case region of West Africa. Thatcher is determined to play a major role in post-coup EG. He's planning to centre himself on Malabo.

Depending on how the Boss behaves, I may have to do the same. I'm determined to see this through. I'm not doing all this so that the current corrupt regime is replaced by another. I worry that this outlook may leave us isolated.

There are many powerful agencies and people who don't want democracy in oil-rich, diamond-studded West Africa. Political and economic stability is simply not in the interests of big oil or big business. Therefore, it's not in the interests of the world's major governments.

Democracy and stability would mean trade regulations. Transparency. The G8 nations would find themselves dealing with an African version of OPEC. It is cheaper, more straightforward, to deal with corrupt dictators. Or rebel groups desperate for money. I know only too well how oil and diamond companies thrived when Angola had been kept in a state of civil war.

Both the MPLA and UNITA had been desperate for money to fund their armed struggles. The MPLA sold oil concessions – behind closed doors – to companies from the richest countries in the world.

EG is the third-largest oil supplier in Africa. The world powers – who need this oil – will do anything to prevent this coup taking place. Unless it's their coup.

If we don't get on with it, then someone is going to stop us. Fuck us up.

Chapter eight

1993: THE ANGOLAN WAR

25–30 MAY 1993: HOBACHERE BUSH CAMP, ETOSHA NATIONAL PARK, NAMIBIA. LONG: 16.9403; LAT: -18.8076.

With Soyo done and dusted, the Angolans wanted to talk about what was to happen next, even more than we did. A meeting was agreed.

We flew to Windhoek International, Namibia. The RV itself came straight out of Wilbur Smith. Secrecy was as necessary as speed. We flew onward by light aircraft – from Eros Airport, Windhoek – to a place called Hobachere, north and west of the Etosha Pans and the National Park.

Flying into Hobachere were EO's four principals: Eeban Barlow, Coebus, Tony Buckingham and me. With us were Crause – the Red Baron – and Amanda, love of my life and great lover of the bush ... not to say the craic too.

It's real bush there, but pretty: thick and dry, in strange-shaped rocky hills, or *kopjes*. If you don't know the airstrip, it's hard to spot, even with GPS. Once it's spotted, then first you beat up the camp, so they'll send a wagon for you. The 20-minute walk can make you Special of the Day.

Then – second – you beat up the strip itself, very low and fast. That's because there is often game on it. They need to be scared off. Buck like to graze the edge of the strip. That way they have better fields of view around them, and more time to flee. They are always on the menu. Spotting predators in time is the name of the game.

The Angolans flew in clandestinely, from Luanda, refuelling at Benguela. Joaquim David was one, General Luiz Faceira the other. Faceira had been our FAA general at Soyo, with us in Cabinda. Amanda straight away christened him 'General Savile Row' since, out of combats, he looked so strangely dressed.

Also from Angola came JD's bodyguard, dubbed 'the Leopard' by Amanda, so feline and predatory was his face, the more so because of the stripes of his tribal scars.

Our finely worked-up proposal for the MPLA was twofold: land and air. Coebus presented. Land first. He told the MPLA generals that to win the war they needed a brigade of 2,000 men. That, he told them, in a war like Angola's, is the smallest force that can safely work on its own. Take on pretty much anything. That brigade would be formed of three battalions.

The first and spearhead battalion would mostly be made up of EO South Africans, soldiers in armoured BMP-3 Russian Armoured Personnel Carriers (APCs). 'BMP' is short for *Boyevaya Mashina Pekhoty*, Fighting Vehicle of the Infantry, known by the South Africans as *Die Verwoesters*, the Destroyers. They will need 18 weeks to train the other two battalions, each of 600-plus Angolan soldiers. The annual price of Coebus's land plan will be just under $30 million.

His proposals were accepted, in full and for immediate action. It was an acceptance that underlined just how badly the war was going for the MPLA government. Or it underlined just how ill prepared the MPLA had been.

Unlike UNITA. The Boy Scouts. Be Prepared. Ever Ready.

My air proposals were also accepted. But with a phased delivery programme, as expected.

So, from June 1993, we were hard at it, putting those proposals into effect. By September the EO battalion was ready. It had deployed to Saurimo, the capital of Lunda Sul province. The two Lunda provinces, Lunda Sul and Lunda Norte, in the north-east corner of Angola, are the biggest diamond source (by value) in the country. Just as Angola is the biggest diamond source in the world.

The strike brigade then slowly formed around that spearhead battalion. Offensive operations began. All UNITA woes were by now the result of EO action. Or so UNITA radios were busy telling one another.

A UNITA jeep accidentally turning over was brought about by the South Africans. To UNITA fighters, the South Africans' durability and courage, throughout the Border Wars, and then again at Soyo, had gained mythical status. They knew them too well, were audibly scared.

Our strike brigade made a concerted attack on Cacola, an important UNITA HQ and a diamond centre. The force had engaged hard-core UNITA units and beaten them. A telling victory. Other than Soyo, it was UNITA's first defeat in a major-units set-piece battle.

With Soyo won, and our great plans now fast going ahead – those by which we hoped to win the Angolan war outright – Tony and I worked from our smart new London offices at 535 King's Road, Chelsea. With the offices came a brand-new Bentley Mulsanne Turbo Nutter Bastard, with chauffeur. We bought them all for cash. I was hardly ever there, but it was great fun when I was.

Michael Grunberg ran the place. Clever, able. An accountant and a management consultant. We had needed someone, or we would have fallen into chaos. Michael was ideal; right for the job. He was an old family friend. Jewish. He'd watch my back for unscrupulous – unfair – money movements. Our yuppie offices were full of snazzy secretaries. Part-time models. Friends of Michael.

One day, a model bleeped my phone.

'There is a Nicholas Blackwell calling for you Simon, Nicholas Blackwell of Franklins.'

I shifted awkwardly in my leather exec chair, turbo nutter wanker. 'That *the* Franklins? Stockbrokers to the great and the good?'

'That's what he says,' she said drily.

Blackwell was the Senior Partner at Franklins. I had some family connections with him but I hadn't seen or spoken to him in years. So – much as I loved him – why the sudden call?

'Nicholas?'

'Hello, Simon. Your secretary … she as lovely as she sounds?'

'Yes. Thanks.'

'Ha ha! Jolly good. Jolly good.

'Listen, old chap. Edward Lipman asked me to call you. He wants you to ring him, so he can get you over for a drink. I don't know why he can't call you himself, but he doesn't know you, and it's obviously important. I have no idea what it's about; none at all. Can you do that for me, old chap?'

'Course, Nicholas. Where do I call him?'

'Oh – well, he's the main man at MBC Minerals. Call their London HQ.'

'Will do. Thanks, Nicholas.'

'Thanks. Bye.'

'Bye.'

Edward Lipman, son of Laurence.

The Lipman mineral dynasty. My mother and father were both great friends of Laurence.

What could his son, Edward, want with me? Apart from anything else, the family link was strong enough for him to have got in touch with me directly without fagging someone as high up the food chain as Nicholas Blackwell.

When I rang, Edward was a cheery and hail fellow. He had a mouthful of cherry stones. Wah wah pedal to the floor.

Money will buy you only so much.

We set up for a drink at his house in London, the following Thursday at six thirty. Just as he was about to say goodbye I told him that, since we must be going to talk about Africa, I would bring my partner and friend, Tony Buckingham, if that was all right. Except, my tone said, if it wasn't all right, then I wasn't coming. TANGO SIERRA. Tough shit.

He wasn't thrilled, but he agreed.

So round we both went. The house was smart but quite modest, in an affluent part of the city. Mrs L and Mr L both looked as though they had been blown up by bicycle pumps. As we arrived, she greeted us like long-lost explorers.

Then, with lots of cherry stones, and wah wah, she asked what we would like to drink. The two of them went into a knockabout: pouring drinks, fetching ice. They asked after my mother and father, who they knew so well, of course, and how super they were.

Then we were told how bloody badly their damn horse had run that afternoon, in the 3.30 at Newmarket.

Tony, of course, was loving this. Plenty of ammo. Family and class insights galore. He'd rip the piss out of me later. As if the Lipmans weren't enough, I was choking on the chintzes.

1993 : THE ANGOLAN WAR . . .

Edward paused, checking with himself that he'd played all the family calling cards. He needn't have worried: he'd played most of them twice. Mrs L vanished.

Edward took a draft of his gin and tonic. He was looking at me all the time. Wishing Tony anywhere else.

'Now, Simon, Angola.'

'Angola.' I agreed.

'We – that is … well, we have a business idea to put to both of you … a *quid pro quo*, if you like …

'We know you're helping the MPLA. We know about what happened at Soyo. What we want to know now, though, is this…

'How much would it cost, to make you, you two, and all your men, go away? To get out of Angola altogether? How much would that cost? …You know: to buy you out?'

Edward fidgeted.

Tony and I glanced at one another. Disbelief. A silence lengthened in that prissy, over-baked sitting room.

Edward waved his bucket-sized gin and tonic: 'Of course – one feels sorry for all the people caught in the war: but … well … this is business …'

Silence again. Edward gave Tony a quick look. So Tony spoke: 'Ask Simon, Edward. He'll tell you.'

Edward looked at me.

'The MPLA are the government of Angola. They were freely and fairly elected, under International Supervision. What UNITA are doing is thuggery, banditry, murder. UNITA attacked us. Devon Oil and Gas. Our Soyo Joint Exploration Venture.

'The MPLA are our friends, and our partners, Edward … now they are our Brothers-In-Arms as well. Our flag is nailed to the MPLA mast.'

Edward was shocked. We were shocked. There was nothing more to say.

Tony and I put down our untouched buckets on the dinky side tables. We said our goodbyes. The air that greeted me outside felt fresh. I needed it. The offer was an insult. Without a word to one another, we walked.

We'd just seen a show of strength. For God's sake. The phone call from the Senior Partner of Franklins. Blackwell knew what was behind the meeting damn well. But, even if he didn't, it's part of the MBC/Lipman warning. They're telling us: watch out! We can fag the Senior Partner of Franklins to act as our bloody secretary. We are the big time. Big hitters.

If you don't take our offer then watch out.

Why buy us out of Angola? We knew why.

At that time, UNITA controlled Angola's mineral production.

The way MBC saw it, if the MPLA won the civil war, and gained control over all Angola's mineral mines, then they would be in trouble. Their highly profitable, and strategically all important, power play in Angola would be over.

Lose control of Angola and the whole of MBC's control of the world market, always tenuous, could start to slip.

So what does Edward Lipman come up with? Ah, yes! Cheap at twice the price. Buy out these two arseholes helping the MPLA. Just do a deal: buy them out.

What if they say no? Ah. Well. Then – unfortunately – having given them every chance – and, after all, the MPLA are Marxist Leninist Moscow-backed bastards – then we'll just have to – you know – well, and don't worry – we have an outfit (no link to us, of course), who has an outfit, who know some people, who will – er – take care of, er, Mr B – and, er, Mr M – and all their works: rest assured.

This is business.

We slunk wordlessly into a pub in Shepherd's Market and ordered a large brandy each. Tony took a large mouthful and looked at me in horror. 'Shit – Simon. We've just turned down a blank-cheque deal from one of the most powerful companies in the world! I mean, to them, "If you can't buy them out, take them out" is a fucking company motto.'

I took a swig of my firewater. I knew Tony was right. My mind revved.

'But what can we do? What should I have said, Tony?'

Tony smiled at me. 'You said the right thing. There's nothing else we can do. You were one hundred per cent.'

Tony took another mouthful. Spoke again. 'We're committed now ... but what kind of fucking mercenaries are we? We should be taking our cheques and headin' for the high hills.'

'No, we have to crack on. Try to become too powerful for them to touch, but quickly: "Damn the torpedoes, full speed ahead". MBC are not the only ones gunning for us now. That's our only option against them all.'

'Well said, Tony. I'll get us another glass of this firewater. Then let's drink to it.'

Brothers-In-Arms.

Throughout 1993 and early '94, I spent most of my time in Luanda. Amanda was now technically 'living with me', at 36 Portobello Road. I paid. But she did the house up – brilliantly, beautifully. No Colefax and Fowler there.

My being away was tough on Amanda, but she had known what she was getting into. She knew that I had to see this Angolan conflict through. To a speedy victory, we both hoped. To peace.

To that end, Crause and I had been busy putting together an unusual air force. By late 1993, we had set up a support-helicopter wing of Mi-17s, with South African pilots, that was attached to the EO spearhead battalion. We had also bought two Beechcraft King Air Super 200 turboprops and two Boeing 727-100 airliners.

The two Boeings and one of the King Airs supported EO, always with one eye on the critical casevac issue (casevac being distinct from medevac, medical evacuation). The other King Air, call-sign Papa Whisky, was our spy plane.

The South African defence contractor Denel, without knowing the purpose, installed a day-and-night digital imagery capture system. A bunch of SIGINT (signals intelligence) devices were also on board. Papa Whisky's SIGINT and ELINT (electronic intelligence) role was to help us gather intelligence on the enemy by intercepting radio signals and other electronic radiation.

I too flew Papa Whisky sorties, partly to check how the systems were working, partly to cheer up the mixed South African and Angolan crews. It was hard graft, and dull, but also frightening.

A detailed effort had gone into assessing the risk of a hit by a SAM. All precautions had been taken. But the thought was always present, as we sat there for hours on end, day after day, at between 15,000 and 20,000 feet, photographing.

Throughout every one of these sorties, there was a nasty sensation around the arse. The bottom of the spine. A nasty fear … slithering sometimes around the gut. The nasty thought that UNITA might have bought a Strela-3 SAM. Something that would deal with our altitude and blow us out of our grid-search flying pattern.

After each sortie, the imagery was downloaded onto a Local Area Network (LAN) of Apple Macs. These were located next to General João de Matos's office, at FAA HQ. Here the imagery was enlarged, processed, enhanced, interpreted, managed, stored. Carefully, it was compared with previous imagery of the same area.

Information was gathered from as many sources as possible, then was all ground through the Intelligence Management System. Mainly it was Papa Whisky's imagery and SIGINT that formed the hard core of usable intelligence: Combat Intelligence.

One thing we were all sure of: Papa Whisky was effective. It found targets.

More importantly, in a war like this, UNITA hated Papa Whisky. To UNITA, the machine had supernatural powers. They believed it could see things way beyond what was technologically possible. Papa Whisky's mythological status suited us fine. It seemed to bring us supernatural luck.

The Papa Whisky digital imagery, combined with a long SIGINT operation, in the HF and VHF bandwidths, led to a breakthrough. The intelligence staff (South African, with Angolans under training) believed that they had pinpointed a UNITA TAC HQ. Or, at the very least, some sort of replenishment depot.

That night, we strapped two 250-kilogram iron bombs onto the wings of one of the EO-owned and flown L39 jet trainers. Our most experienced South African pilot, Pien, strapped himself into the craft. By flying at night, using Night Vision Goggles (NVGs), he would achieve surprise. He would be safe from any air defence. And he was going to hurl those great bruiser bombs straight at the target.

I'd flown with Pien on these night sorties before, back-seating for him because the cockpit lighting was not set up for NVGs. The back-seater used a lumo-stick – tucked up the sleeve of his flying suit – to read his instruments. He would call out to Pien what Pien wanted to know. Pien had no instrument lit, because the lights would dazzle the NVGs. It sounds hairy. It was hairy.

Crause wanted to fly Papa Whisky. To watch and film. There was competition to fly on that sortie. All seats taken, standing room only, so I stood down and waited for news at HQ.

News didn't come. They had taken off late, the air base ops room told me. I returned to my hotel room at the Tivoli. I tried to sleep. Instead I fought with my elbows. And my over-active imagination. At 0300, attackers burst into my room. Pien, Crause and all the rest were in high spirits. They flatly refused to tell me what had happened. Instead, they took me to the FAA HQ Ops and INT centre.

They called together the various FAA watchkeepers and duty officers. Then they set up their video. The bluest of blue movies could not have had a keener audience. They switched the tape on. Papa Whisky's normal GPS and avionics video feeds came up. The image contrast intensified. I could make out the light grey, dark grey of terrain.

I could see an insignificant-looking cross-track in the centre of the screen. We watched for a while. Then – *bam!* – the whole screen just turned white. Then it flicked, flickered, strobed, shone white and more white. It was as if the very continent of Africa had atomised.

The audience cheered.

Pien yelled, 'Simon, honestly, man! The whole fucking place blew up – it was awesome.'

Crause, who had been at 15,000 feet, 12,000 feet above ground level, told the same story. His eyes were wide. He could never have imagined anything like it. *Lekke.*

The next morning at 11 I was back in FAA HQ. I had a scheduled meeting with Joaquim David and General João de Matos. They wanted to know if I still wanted to go ahead with the next step of my air plan. It was a vital step, but one that had made the two of them baulk.

Our best chance of bringing this war to an end – of bringing about peace – was by threatening a massive use of force. Overwhelming firepower. We needed to convince UNITA that they were surely doomed to defeat.

We needed to show them that we had the money, the power, the weaponry, to blow them away. Literally. I was aiming for what would later be coined a 'shock and awe' blitz. I wanted to give UNITA a shock that would bring this thing to an end. Once and for all.

There was one way open to us to make this happen. The purchase of some fuck-off bombs from another country. I researched the market.

The answer was a Russian fuel-air bomb, the 500-kilogram ODAB 500. These produce a wider, more intense and longer-lasting blast wave than condensed explosives. Put bluntly, they do more damage. They are like a poor man's tactical nuke, without radiation or fall-out.

Other than political.

One reason for this plan, that I would not be dwelling on, was that far too many top brass, in FAA and MPLA, wanted the war to carry on. Just like UNITA. They made money, or they did not want the pressures of peace – schools, hospitals, civil rights.

One FAA general, I had on good authority, was busy making a packet by flying diesel out of Luanda and into a UNITA-run diamond mine. Diamond mines need plenty of diesel. These guys were bandits and *garimpeiros* (seekers of gold or precious stones) first, generals and politicians a poor second.

I wanted a knock-out punch that would fry the venal bastards…

Now I had to persuade JD and DM – who were not of the warmongers' bunch – to put up the money so that we could buy the ODAB 500s.

Last night's fireworks must only help my cause.

The HQ building was still in a state of excitement. Not everyone had seen the video yet. The Reconnaissance Interpretation Cell (RIC) was doing a fine trade. I went into DM's large, dark office. JD was already there. The Angolans were both very pleased. They had seen the video.

Many times over, they laughed.

I went for the jugular. In that case, buy the ODABs!

My two friends were straight away serious. No, they were not buyers.

I laid into them. The ODABs could end this war… Why? … JD held up his hand for me to stop.

'Simon, listen. How is it in English? "You are preaching to the converts" – yes?'

I nodded, confused.

'Your friend, and mine also, Tony, is a businessman. Very much a businessman. We, João de Matos and myself, have been unable to persuade the President to release funds to Tony – or rather through Tony – as payment for the ODABs.'

DM took up the slack: 'The problem is this: you will not be able to persuade the Russians to sell them to us. Apart from anything else, you see, we owe the Russians hundreds of millions. The President thinks we will just lose the money, to the Russians ... or to Tony.'

JD again: 'Much as João and I want the ODAB 500s, and much as we agree with you about their importance, Simon, we think the President is probably right.'

'Can I speak to the President?' I tried. 'Could that help in any way?'

They both shook their heads glumly.

'Are you sure, Joaquim? General? Have you really given it your best shot?'

JD could read how disappointed I was. Kindly, both his hands made that very Luandan gesture: 'I'd like to help, but I can't.' As ever, it was made with a sorry smile.

I cursed. My heart sank. This was not the first rebuff. Not a big surprise. But a huge disappointment.

I'm a soldier. This war needs winning.

War hurts.

I would have to risk my Plan B. And ... a big argument with Tony. Assuming DM and JD would accept it first, that was.

'OK. Will you help me if I try a different way?'

They looked at each other. DM smiled and shrugged. He and JD were two of the very few top brass really keen to finish this war. Others seemed keen to keep it going. Keen to milk more money out of it.

'My plan is this,' I began. 'You know these things have to be bought government to government. You understand that?'

They nodded.

'OK,' I continued. 'What if that is how the deal is structured? You – Angola – only pay out cash on delivery to you, here, in Angola. How about that?'

They looked confused.

'Tony and I will put up the money, up front. We'll buy the ODABs.'

JD and DM eyed me. Eyed each other.

'You serious?' asked DM, with eyes that said: 'Please say you're serious!'

'Serious,' I nodded.

They went away. I waited. And waited.

Then the news came. The ODAB purchase could start. I would have all the paperwork and support I needed. Sovereign state to sovereign state. EUCs (the all-important End User Certificates, required for any kosher arms deal). Letters of Commission from the President. Embassy help. Anything.

Then, in London, my least predictable hurdle. I would have to work hard to push businessman Tony into such an unbusinesslike deal. I explained to him that half the money at risk would be mine. That helped. To my amazement, he said yes. Tony, too, wanted an end to the bloodshed. He asked me again, 'What kind of fucking mercenaries are we?' Which was fair enough. Cuddly ones?

I knew who I had to talk to next. I had already arranged for a legitimate arms-dealing friend, Nick Potter, to act as the wheeler dealer. He, in turn, already had a Moscow Mr Fix-It, whom Amanda was later to pitilessly label 'Giorgio Armani'. How he loved those shades.

Next I needed the heavy muscle, to open the right doors for Nick. What the Russians call 'roof'. My man for that was an Israeli, David Kimche. He, I knew, was busy in Moscow. He wielded power there, both in his person and by dint of his Russian associates. I had met David through Nicholas Elliott, one of the great British spooks of the 20th century. Elliott went to Eton, where he became friends with my father and my uncle. He was the son of Claude Elliott, a renowned headmaster at the school and a great mountaineer. Claude was the man behind Mallory's ill-fated Everest climb of 1924.

David Kimche had been Nicholas Elliott's opposite number in Mossad. He had also been Golda Meir's Personal Under Secretary on foreign affairs.

Being an intelligence officer, David had dug up facts on me. He knew, for example, that my mother's father, Marshall Clark, had been once busy in Palestine. In World War II, Marshall had been the Senior Engineer in the South African 6th Armoured Division.

Straight after the fighting in Italy was over, Marshall was given a new task: to reopen the Alexandria–Damascus railway line. Over several years he did so, and was awarded the CBE. The railway ran beyond Damascus, to Aleppo, and that too was reopened. Marshall had quite a job. Arabs and Israelis both wanted to blow the railway line. To tyro terrorists a railway line is a gift.

Today, the line is blocked in the Rosh Hanikra Grottoes that should link Israel with Lebanon. Instead, the Israel Defence Force has blown in enough of the tunnel to ensure that the line will never run again.

That Kimche knew all this was flattering and telling. Luckily, I too had been digging. When – back in '89 – I had fled Monrovia, with my protégé Emmanuel Shaw and the ex-Mossad pilot Jonathan, in Shaw's Beechcraft Baron, the Israeli 70-strong Praetorian Guard, assigned to President Samuel K. Doe – all ex this and that – had themselves fled.

The next-door safety, and better food, of Conakry (capital of Guinea Republic, an ex-French colony and therefore food-friendly) was where these careful men fled to. This escape they carried out in their speed yachts, paid for by their illegal diamond trading. Their hobby during years of supposedly looking after their pet despot.

David Kimche, I had found out, had been the Mossad desk officer responsible for the Doe bodyguard op, one of many ops in West Africa then under his aegis. Being David he made no bones about it. 'Oh God, what a disaster!' We laughed at my having crossed with one of his ops so long ago.

Since then, we had become friendly, talking at length, long distance, after Nicholas Elliott's sudden death. I arranged to meet David in London. Before the meeting, I took a three-page paper on the situation in Angola to his hotel. It told exactly how and why Tony and I were involved. What our objective was. I'd put several days' work into those three pages. I had only one chance. The nub of the argument was simple: help me buy the ODABs for Angola. You can help end a war.

We met for dinner. I was nervous. I sat down opposite David and he slipped an envelope across for me to pocket. It held my three-pager.

'Congratulations, Simon!'

'Why?'

'Your paper. It's excellent. If I was still on my old job, I would want to hire you.'

I blushed. From an ex-number two of Mossad, praise did not come higher.

'Will you help, though, David?'

'Your paper makes sense. The cause is just. Peace is what we all want. Nothing is worse than war. Nicholas would have helped you, and he would have told me to help you.'

David smiled at the thought: 'That's enough… Now let's eat and talk of other things: your beautiful Jewess, Amanda, for one. How is she? And how come you are not married yet, and not surrounded yet by little Jews?'

1993: THE ANGOLAN WAR . . .

With Nick and David in Moscow – the former in my full-time employ – all had seemed well. Nick's reports said as much. Then the project turned sour. Nick became defensive. David evasive. Nick asked me to come to Moscow, expecting success any day.

As soon as I got there, and received an update from Nick and Giorgio and David's associates, I knew success was a distant hope. Nothing more. I knew I'd made a big mistake. I should have been in Moscow from the start.

In Moscow I saw that no real progress had been made to secure the purchase of the ODABs. I went to work with Nick. We sat down and drew a Michelin 1:500,000 road map of ODAB release land. We had to lay it out as a map. That was the only way we were going to make sense of the Byzantine highways and byways of the Orthodox Apparat.

This was the only way to see what was what.

On our map each committee or organisation had to be marked up. The names and positions of the members had to be marked. Who was the titular decision maker? Who was the actual decision maker?

Once that circuitry was all drawn up, and carefully colour-coded, we moved on to the paperwork. Flow chart lines had to be drawn to show how the various documents, each with its own name, must move back and forth between the committees.

A signature here, a stamp there, approval by such and such committee over there. Further lines had to be drawn, also coloured, to show other factors. Inter-committee rivalries. Turf wars. Family relationships.

I began to wonder: how had it taken the West so long to win the Cold War? These people had tied themselves up in knots. It was a miracle that it was bicycles that came out of the back end of bicycle factories.

Nick and I had adventures. One particular document was only signed thanks to our visiting a military hospital. We strode up to the bedside of some old apparatchik colonel as if we owned the place. The old boy thought that a basket of fruit and a bottle of smuggled vodka were more than enough. He signed. I prayed that our hospital visit hadn't killed him.

Amanda visited. For that week I took an attic suite at the five-star Kempinski Hotel. It sported a big-budget movie view across the Moscow River, onto Red Square and its three cathedrals – Assumption, Annunciation and Archangel Michael.

Nick would climb out of our attic and onto the roof. Facing the Kremlin, he would cup his hands to his mouth and yell: 'Come on, you Reds!'

All this time our map was becoming more dense, more coloured, not less. Documents were clogged up in the mazes without escape, lost without their balls of string. Nothing was moving to its next step. Each tick in a box threw open more boxes. They each needed their tick. There was always a box within the box.

Our Moscow holiday was costing a fortune. Tony was becoming even more pissed off than I was. By now the thing had turned around. My failure was letting down the Angolans.

I suggested to Nick, who was staring at our Michelin ODAB release map in a glazed funk, that I try a new route. A new way out of the maze. I wanted to push buttons and pull levers that owed nothing to David or Nick.

Nick looked sick. Heresy.

What I had suggested could be a really bad idea. Moscow, in the summer of 1994, was packed with desperadoes, each of them desperate to sell their non-existent Mr Fix-It powers to any ignorant, dollar-rich, non-Russian-speaking Anglo-Saxon. It was the only business in town.

Unless you were an assassin. An inside-track Mafia. Or KGB.

'Nick. OK … look: here's the deal: ten days from now – if I don't think we have made real progress…' – my eyes drifted back to our Michelin map, despite my trying to force them away – '…then I'm going to try something else. OK? That's 12 July, and I'm noting the date.'

But on the seventh day it was Nick who hit the ball back to me. Try whatever you like, he cried. Once again we stared at our map. It was as though a will of the wisp was out there, always a step ahead, always doing just enough to thwart us.

We'd had enough. So had our livers.

Eventually it was agreed: Nick would keep his post as our dealer. But I would try my way, my contacts.

I telephoned Sparky in London. Would it be OK to talk to Maria and the General about a problem in Moscow? If Sparky needed to know more, then Tony could brief him in London. Sparky told me to carry on as I wished. He would take that briefing from Tony. Over three five-star courses.

Sparky was my old SAS boss. He had joint-venture partners in Moscow, Maria and the General, with whom I had enjoyed adventures in the past.

To understand my connection to the General, you need to understand the General's connection to Sparky. It goes back to the Cold War.

In my British Army days, during the Cold War, NATO had believed that the Red Army's Special Forces were the *Spetsnaz*. They had been rated good, but not that special. Only after the Soviet Empire collapsed had NATO found out how poor their INT had been. The real Special Forces of Russia, their equivalent of the US Delta or the British SAS, were the KGB's Alpha.

General Viktor Karpukhin, KGB, had been the commander of Alpha when, in August 1991, hard-line Communists launched a military coup against President Boris Yeltsin. These Kremlin hard-liners opposed the reform programmes being forced through by Yeltsin and Mikhail Gorbachev. They ordered Alpha into Moscow's White House Parliament Building: kill or capture Yeltsin!

The General went into the White House with his troops, then called the Kremlin hard-liners. He was there, he said, but to save Yeltsin. If they wanted Yeltsin, he said, they had to get him first.

Yeltsin went on, in 1993, to seize almost dictatorial power in Russia. That in turn made his old ally the General one of the country's most powerful men.

Following those events, the General had decided to set up a private security company. The new Russia was going to need plenty of private security. Besides, he wanted something better for his ex-Alphas than a state pension. The result was a new company, Alpha A.

New to the game, General Karpukhin sought a British partner. He chose Defence Systems Limited (DSL), an outfit with Sparky at its head. DSL had been founded by Alistair Morrison, 'Mogadishu' Morrison, ex-Scots Guards and ex-SAS, and also a good friend of mine.

Now DSL was run by Sparky, also ex-Scots Guards and ex-SAS. Sparky had been my boss in G Squadron 22 SAS, although he had left before the contact in which Richard Westmacott was killed. In fact, Sparky's father had been a wartime officer in the Scots Guards. He had been commanded by my father, then Officer Commanding Right Flank 1st Battalion Scots Guards.

When I told my father about this role reversal, all he said – quietly – was that he hoped the son was a better map reader than his father. This veiled warning turned out to be a good one because, on one famous occasion, Sparky made G Squadron very lost indeed: he'd misread the scale, and the vertical interval of the contour lines, on a map of a most unfriendly and mountainous piece of deeply frozen Norwegian island, Senja.

When I joined Devon Oil and Gas, I wanted to find business for Tony. I introduced him to pretty much everyone of influence I knew. One of those was Sparky, not least because I valued him so highly, as a soldier and as a friend. I had hoped that my old SAS boss's new Russian joint venture could throw up something interesting in oil and gas.

That's when the General, with the snow of Dzerzhinsky Square puddling off his boots on to the carpet, turned up at DOG's London office. The General was helping Tony win an oil exploration licence in Turkmenistan.

With the General, but lithe in her furs, came Maria, the interpreter. Stavros asked Maria what she used to do in the good old days of the Cold War.

In a gravel voice of ice and Stolichnaya, she answered, 'I – KGB – I – seductress.'

The General, Maria, Tony and I had made an unforgettable trip together. To Ashgabat, in Turkmenistan, an ex-Soviet splinter republic on the Caspian Sea. On the Silk Route. We set off in high hopes.

In the midst of a smelly slum tenement that the Turkmenis called a luxury hotel, we found out why the General knew the capital city of Ashgabat so well. It had been the forward operating base for Russian Special Forces into Afghanistan.

We drank terrible vodka. We laughed at the utter filth and corruption. But we secured no oil deal. That didn't stop us four becoming friends.

It was for that reason that I hadn't made contact with the General or Maria since I'd arrived in Moscow. It would be impossible to see them and not explain what I was up to.

I was sure the General would not settle for that. He had ways of finding out pretty much anything he wanted in Moscow. Well, now I needed his influence and his help. The question wasn't so much could he help, but would he help?

1993: THE ANGOLAN WAR...

I was asking a lot. The General was now my big hope.

I made the call. Maria's wonderful voice answered. We agreed to meet for tea at our hotel the following day.

I lost count of the number of tea pots we went through. Nick had been banned, although I spotted him snooping from behind an aspidistra, twice. Maria took careful notes of my account. I told her the full story, using the paper I had written for David Kimche as notes.

As we parted I couldn't stop myself from asking: 'Can you help, Maria?'

She looked at me smiling, but puzzled: 'Simon – we can help! But it is General will say will help.'

'Yes. Thanks. When will you be back to me?'

'Simon. Please. You – and little Scotch friend' – she rolled her eyes towards the aspidistra – 'must not leave *Moskva*. I will call – soon as can. Less than ten days.'

'OK. Great.'

'Well – you will have definite *yes*, or definite *no*. Also: you have been in great danger. You are in great danger. Please, do not terminate existing contacts. But put to sleep, yes?'

Four days later, Maria phoned me. She asked for another tea ceremony, this time at the Kempinski.

I was there on time, thrilled to see that the General was with Maria. He embraced me, Russian-style. It had been winter when we'd last met in Moscow. In a bearskin cap and a fur coat, he'd been enormous. Now in his summer coat there was less of him, but not by much.

We sat.

'Simon – please – General Viktor like you. You ... er ... impressed General in Ashgabat, in Turkmenistan – please explain situation in Angola – your position and Tony – your plan ... intention – why you want the ODAB.'

The General had chuckled at the Ashgabat and Turkmenistan mentions, to which I grinned. The Ashgabat epic had been fruitless, but had become something of a comic legend. But now I had to focus my energy: how well I spun this yarn could change the fate of many for the better.

The same arguments that I had rehearsed on David – and then on Maria last time – were used again. They had worked before. Even so –

the slow repetitions – as Maria translated for the General – made his very Russian mask all the more opaque. Were those arguments working now?

I knew that the MPLA were not much better than UNITA. But then it was not the MPLA who had restarted the war. UNITA had not been elected. For the poor people of Angola, it was only the MPLA who could play Hobbes's Leviathan. The MPLA had a mandate to enforce peace and stability.

Human rights, civil liberties, consensus government, gas and light: these would follow. If I could help shorten the war by one day, then I would have achieved something worthwhile.

I was proud of my job. I was sure that I was right. UNITA had sinned, and they had attacked Tony and me. If UNITA had big bad dragon friends, then Tony and I would fight them too.

Under the all-seeing gaze of the General, there was nowhere for any falsehood to hide. I could sit there and face their search because, although matters of rank, pride and money had all got me involved in this operation, taken together they now had less weight than my will to end this war.

I spoke. Maria translated. The General nodded. I was thankful for the effort I'd put into that three-page staff paper. My thoughts and arguments were clear, ordered. Then Maria's last paragraph had been delivered. We were done.

For ever – over teas and cakes – the General studied me, then spoke. Maria, the seductress, expertly started her interpretation before the General had stopped. 'The General asks – in principle – do you know how many Westerners have been killed in Moscow this year, so far?'

'Quite a few – bankers mostly.'

'Twenty-three to date.'

'Do you know how much danger you have been in? Of death? Or arrest, and a summary imprisonment?'

'Probably not.'

'Definitely not.' The General stopped, and with him Maria. An age passed. 'Yes. I will help you, Simon. I do not promise, but I will do my best.'

'Thank you, General Viktor. Thank you very much.'

'Several times you – and your friend, er … da – this Nick – you have thought you had the ODAB deal closed. Am I right?'

1993: THE ANGOLAN WAR...

'Yes!' I replied, surprised.

'Since you spoke to Maria, last week, we have made our enquiries. One...' – the General held up his index finger – '...of the reasons that I would like to help you is this: I do not like the ... tinkerings ... of foreigners in our affairs. They won the Cold War, but now they must not toy with us.'

'I don't understand...'

Maria stopped me. An elegant hand. The General hadn't finished. Maria's smile suggested that she was watering down his words.

She went on: 'The General says: your ODAB deal is being clandestinely blocked, here in Moscow, by a foreign power. The General says: this foreign power has no right to block, or to unblock, anything in *Moskva* – not one drainpipe. The General says...'

Maria broke off and spoke to the General in rapid Russian.

She shrugged, smiled, then dropped her voice: 'The General says: the Soviet Empire is broken – thank God – but Mother Russia is not – thank God. Mother Russia, he says, is her own power, always. It was ever so.'

I kept quiet. The General watched me and laughed. He spoke again, and Maria smiled. 'Simon, the General says you understand well – you studied us well under Peter Vigor at Sandhurst, 1971. You were his top pupil – Intake 50 – you won prize for Soviet Studies – *Niet*? Ha ha ha!'

I forced a laugh. The hairs pricked outwards on the back of my neck. For God's sake – they do their homework. And they didn't mind letting me know. I had to enjoy the joke. 'Come now, General! There's no need to show off! Ha ha ha.'

The General was serious again. 'The General says: he will help because he can see...' – Maria turned for clarification – '...and here he is agreeing with me, Simon, that you are sincere: you are determined to try to bring this war to an end mainly – mainly – because you want peace. Is that so?'

'Yes, Maria. General, yes.'

'A speedy end to that war is something the General also wishes to see, Simon. Despite your enemies, UNITA, and all their friends, he believes you can do it. He will help.'

The General closed off our Kempinski tea with a question: 'Simon – have you ever seen an ODAB 500 detonation?'

'No.'

'Well, you have waited in *Moskva* for two months, so far – am I right?'

'Yes, nearly two.'

'If you have to sit in *Moskva* for another six, it will be worth it!' He paused, then Maria translated again: 'I have seen the ODAB detonate, in Afghanistan. You are right: it can end the war.'

'I hope so. I hope we can end it.'

Maria said something to the General. He replied and Maria turned back to me: 'There must be no mention of us. None. You will still be in danger. Russia is a dangerous place. We – the government – are not fully in control. If you do get into trouble, then we will be trying to help, but you will not see us. Don't ask for us. Don't talk of us.'

'Thanks. I understand … but I have to brief Nick. Do you accept that?'

'Of course. Good luck in Angola. We would like to see that won. The MPLA were our … associates. Perhaps, when they win, they can pay Russia some of the money that they owe?'

'I'll ask,' I said, with a smile.

As we stood to part, the General, now frowning again, said farewell.

Maria turned to me with a kiss, and a whisper. 'Kimche is your friend – in principle – but, in practice, he must not go against his proxy masters in Langley … he has to betray you. He has no choice. Please, Simon, please, the CIA have bought many people here in Moscow … some are killers. You must use your skills … you must be careful as you work.'

I left the Kempinski and walked back to my shabby three-star, along the Moscow river, opposite the Kremlin. My route took me past the British Embassy, the building which had so infuriated the old comrades with its elegance, its pride of place.

I thought about the meeting. About this wild tale in which I was now a part. The General had made it clear who had been blocking the purchase – the CIA. How they were doing so was easy to see.

Why wasn't difficult either: the CIA – or the Barrel Boyz within – must want UNITA to win. Or for the war to go on and on. Naive though I was back then, I suffered few illusions on that score. With the Yanks pushing and pulling, it was no surprise that dear old David Kimche had run for cover. The only thing for Tony and me to do was to fight on.

Slowly our progress drew us closer to the place to which all roads led:

the Final Release Committee meeting at the state arms export bureau, then called *Rosvooruzhenie*, now *Rosoboronexport*.

This, Giorgio kept repeating, was the big hurdle. We only reached this far because all the other rules, committees, agencies and forms had shown Green Lights. Now the Committee would look at whether or not they should allow release to take place.

The Final Release Committee meeting would be held at *Rosvooruzhenie*'s offices, true enough, but the Chairman and two other members came from the Foreign Ministry. They would be ranking KGB, scarcely veiled.

On the day itself, I woke and dressed feeling calm.

I had reached the point where I knew I'd done my best. That was that. If this thing was going to work, then today it would start to do so. If it wasn't, then it wasn't.

Then today would be the day to go home and think again.

At breakfast I ran through everything with Nick and Giorgio. Nick and I both needed to put all thoughts of the General and Maria out of our minds. There could be no hint of our 'roof', if we really had any. We must play it straight. We must play to win, but straight.

We met in the Roz boardroom. Present: the Roz apparatchiks, the Angolan Ambassador to Moscow, his Military Attaché, the Admiral (or so he was introduced: – Navy – Foreign Ministry – KGB – anyone's guess), his interpreter and his two nodders.

The Admiral started by demanding to see the credentials of the Angolan Ambassador and his Military Attaché. He then asked who I was. I answered: an officer in the Armed Forces of Angola, brigadier general; an agent, specially commissioned by the President of Angola, to carry out this procurement; the man who will physically, himself, fly with the ODAB consignment, from Russia to Angola, to ensure safe delivery.

I handed the Admiral those papers. Copies were already in his file.

The Admiral sneered at them, sheet by sheet, then quizzed me: 'How do we know you not terrorist?'

'If I am a terrorist, then the Ambassador to Moscow and the President of Angola are lying.'

'How do we know you not bribe – not bribe Ambassador...?' – he nodded in that man's direction – '...not bribe President?'

The nodders nodded. I was stunned.

I had heard, from Nicholas Elliott, the joke that the title 'Comrade' was Russian for 'kaffir'. But this was embarrassing. Looking at the Ambassador and the Attaché, I could see that they were used to such insults. To such diplomatic outrages.

They were going to take no part in this exchange.

I tried: 'Admiral, please. Insulting the people of Angola, whom the President and Ambassador represent, is not going to help.'

I smiled my best, and least sincere, Old Etonian smile. 'The point, Admiral – surely – is that your colleagues, *Rosvooruzhenie*, and ourselves, have tried to pre-empt these objections: my flight to Angola is in your aircraft, paid for by Angola [not true: Tony and I were paying for it, as we were the bombs]; the air crew are yours, and the flight will be met, and checked, by your *Rosvooruzhenie* agent, their country manager, in Luanda [true].'

The nodders looked to the Admiral.

He focused on the file and started sifting, paper by paper, leaf by leaf: each, from his grimace, more worthless than the last.

He darted his stare at Nick: 'You! Arm dealer?'

'Yes, sir.'

'Glencoe Arms Limited? Your company?'

'Yes, sir.'

'Where is licence of British government – for Glencoe – for arm dealer?'

'There is no such licence, sir. Under British law no such licence can exist: if a company is within the laws of all parties, then it can trade, in arms or anything else. Nobody has a UK arms dealer licence.'

Nick frowned at one of the Roz apparatchiks.

The man timidly brought the Admiral's glare to the three sets of letters that endorsed what Nick had said. One set was from the Russian Embassy in London, one from the British Embassy in Moscow, and the third was from the chief of Roz itself. Each was separately written in Russian and English. Each had been attested and stamped by a notary.

The Admiral, however, wanted to see a licence, or a permission, from the UK. His bureaucratic mind could not imagine a world without such an explicit sheet of paper. He smiled unpleasantly. The nodders nodded. Then they too smiled unpleasantly.

This was it. I nudged Nick, for him to run out our last great gun. This was to fire our golden cannon ball – something we had planned, just in case we came to this point. A last shot.

Nick dished out new papers to everyone around the table: a letter, with translations, stamped by a notary, and with a very distinctive letterhead.

The letter said again what Nick and the other letters had said. It ended by stating that, therefore, there was no reason why the Glencoe-sponsored, government-to-government, Russia-to-Angola sale could not go ahead.

'Why not in file?'

'Just arrived this morning, sir,' lied Nick.

He waved a DHL delivery slip. In fact the delivery slip was for another paper – one sent purely to achieve a DHL delivery slip, dated that morning.

The Admiral looked carefully at the slip. We had tried to anticipate any nit-picking problem that could become a barrier, if such a barrier was what an opponent sought. We had not wanted this letter to be on file, unless it was needed.

The Admiral stared at the embossed notepaper, taking in the understated self-confidence.

'House of Lords. House of Lords. What is House of Lords?'

'I think Simon can best explain that, sir,' Nick replied brightly. Just as I'd feared.

Sweating, I placed my two elbows down on the table, hands and fingers held up straight, to form the two upper sides of a triangle.

'The British system of rule – and law – sir – is a pyramid…' I waited for the interpreter.

'At the very top of this pyramid…' I wiggled my top four fingertips, while staring at them. Seeking their meaning.

More interpretation.

'…is the House of Lords! The top!'

This was met by a big '*Da – Horoshiy!*', then its echoes from the nodders – as if what everyone really wanted was a lesson on the English constitution.

They wanted to know more and more about the two Houses of Parliament, the Crown, the Law, the Church, but always came back to the Lords.

Russians, better than anyone else, love a pyramid. The pyramid is what squashes us, the proletariat, the hoi polloi, those unlucky enough not to be a part of the party, the apparat: the vast 3D triangle of flesh-crushing stone above us.

Now I could see, horror of horrors, that the Admiral wanted to join that most exclusive club, the House of Lords. He was about to ask me to fix it for him. I was fearful.

Then what?

But – unsignalled – from that moment the meeting rolled downhill. It ended with smiles and handshakes all round. We should hear their decision the next day, we were told. To Giorgio's amazement.

Once we were outside, Nick could not help himself. He laid into me. Over one of our many shared bottles of wine, I had told Nick what I thought of hereditary power in general, and of the Devon Oil and Gas 'Unit Lord' – Viscount Fotherington – in particular.

I had talked endlessly to Tony Buckingham about having this peer on our payroll. I just couldn't see the point of it, even if it was Nicholas Elliott who had asked us to take him on, and even if that unquestionably meant that Fotherington had been or was some kind of spook.

Now we were getting our money's worth out of the Viscount: the headed notepaper had been all important. Absurdly, I smiled to myself about our old Unit Lord, Charles Greenock, back in 1 SG, British Army of the Rhine (BAOR). He who coined the term. His uselessness, as a soldier, had been without dispute. Like Fotherington. Then all had to be forgiven.

During a midnight swimming-pool party, high in the Bavarian Alps, Charles pushed a very cross and pompous brigadier into the pool. In his dinner jacket. Before the brigadier belly-flopped and swam, the wretched man had been trying to place all us party people under arrest. But that is another story.

Noon next day, Giorgio appeared in the hotel, shouting, 'Baobab, baobab.' This had become our slogan, for a successful delivery to Angola, a land of baobab trees. We could go. The Admiral, the Final Release Committee, had finally released: 20 ODAB 500s.

I called Maria to circumspectly give her our news, and thanks. We would settle up in London someday soon, I promised. That was because, as Angolans have it, '...*as pernes do cabra deve passar* ... the legs of the goat must pass.'

Back in Luanda, after a wild journey in our chartered Il-76, and with the ODABs just delivered, I met up with Stavros, in town on DOG business. We had a quick drink together in the dear old Tivoli, many times winner of that unusual award 'War Zone Hotel that Tries the Hardest'.

Stavros needed cheering up. I told him of our Russian highlights. Stav the Greek, I knew, hated the Russians more than Poles do. What he liked best, however, was the description of the time when I had enough of Nick's determination to recruit all and sundry for MI6, and for his arms-dealing network.

I had explained to Nick: you are on our payroll. You have a job to do: buy the ODABs. No sideshows. Especially not the kind of sideshows that could easily get us shot.

Then it was time to celebrate. JD and DM picked us up from the Tivoli in a Toyota Land Cruiser that seemed several sizes up from the one that the poor people get. They took us to the best restaurant in town, the Barracuda. Very smart: five crossed hammer and sickles.

A bottle of vintage champagne popped straight away, and off we went. DM was beside himself with the success of my mission. JD, as ever, was courteous and slow, but he too was excited.

'Simon – João and myself – we say to you, "Sorry."'

'Why?'

'We thought that you couldn't do this – and we told you so. Tony the same. Well – now we have our ODABs – they are here. But I will tell you why we are so thankful ... why we are surprised.

'Firstly, UNITA, and UNITA's friends, are powerful. They have a long arm. We thought they would be sure to stop you in Moscow, to harm you, to kill you even.

'Secondly, there are people here – in the MPLA – people who are making money out of the war – they do not want the war to end.

'Thirdly, we, Angola ... we owe the Russians so much money! We never thought they would allow this deal, when we owe them hundreds of millions ... or so they say, with their crazy and not very Marxist-Leninist system...

'Fourthly, Russia, we know, is under pressure to stop arms proliferation.

'Lastly, 20 ODABs … is so small a deal. Nobody was to become rich by this … and that way it is so much harder to make the deal happen.

'João de Matos believes – and I agree – that these ODABs can tip the balance of this war such that UNITA will want to stop fighting…'

I replied, 'Well, we've done it… Next thing is to use them wisely.'

I looked both Angolans in the eye. An atrocity could be laid at my feet, if things went wrong. I prayed that the ODABs would not be used to commit some ghastly act against innocent civilians.

DM spoke. JD nodded and turned to me: 'Rest easy: what we plan for the ODABs is to twist their arm – yes – but with no bloodshed. You'll see.'

'Good. Because I am in your hands.'

They nodded.

I went on: 'In Moscow, as you know from all the delay, I had trouble…' – they nodded again – '…but, luckily, I had friends in Moscow – the right ones, it seems…'

'Surely.'

'…they warned me that I was in danger. Moscow is a perilous place just now. And that UNITA had friends. The biggest reason they wished to help us was because they did not care to have their business tampered with by a foreign power. In short, they said that the CIA, the US, were the friend of UNITA. They were trying to block me, in Moscow!'

I watched for the reaction of my two Angolan friends. Stavros, I knew, was watching too.

Neither showed his hand.

I continued: 'So … to what extent are the CIA still helping UNITA? Did the CIA help push UNITA back into war?'

A hush fell over our table, stark against the background buzz of the busy dining room. DM broke the spell, talking rapidly to JD. He looked knowingly around the high-ranking, big-bucks diners.

Some Barrel Boyz here, for sure.

He laughed.

JD nodded and spoke. 'João likes your question! But not in here. Not now. Let us enjoy dinner. Then we can go … there is a new nightclub – João's girlfriend will be there – and some of her friends.' JD paused. 'Your question will keep for a more private … a safer place. We will talk about it soon.'

The next day I lunched with Stavros, who was flying out that afternoon on the Sabena flight to Kinshasa, then Brussels.

'Don't, Stavros. No lectures, please,' I said.

'Simon – you're living very dangerously...'

'Stavros,' I interrupted, 'if you eat that prawn cocktail, you'll be living dangerously! In Angola ten million people have lived dangerously, in civil war, for 20 years, every fucking day. Now we're going to finish it. By winning it. End of discussion.'

A bottle of Mateus Rosé in an ice bucket appeared. I poured. Once the glasses were filled I noticed only a few chunks of cork floating in each. Things were looking up. I raised my glass.

'As Abthorpe would say, Stavros, here's how!'

Once the deadly dangerous Cocktail de Maresco had been eaten, Stavros asked me if I'd heard about a Mr Andy Smith – and the diamond-mining plans. I knew no details, but had been warned by Michael Grunberg, the clever, able accountant who we'd just appointed to run our London offices. I expected to be briefed the following week, back in London.

'Tony's met this guy Andy Smith – seems he's a mining hotshot. Apparently JD has asked Tony to come mining here, in Angola – Tony wants to do it – Smith wants to run it – wadda you gonna say?'

'I will say: how can we go mining before the war ends? Then again: if we can make money by securing concessions now, which we can flog off later, then, why not?'

Stavros considered, then said, 'I thought that's how you'd see it. Nothing wrong with that – and I won't lecture ya, OK? But maybe the goddam agency are our enemy, maybe not – BUT maybe one of the mineral traders is as well.'

'You and I have talked about it often enough, Stavros – but so what?'

'So what? So s'pose one of the mineral traders was there pushing UNITA, after the elections, with or without anyone else – so s'pose, OK...?'

'I'm s'posin', Stav.'

'Jeez – fuckin' limey faggot... So s'pose this: Tony and you, having fucked up their plans for a quick UNITA victory, or their plans for a long, slow war, now – and – FOR YOUR NEXT TRICK! – become mineral producers, as well. C'mon, buddy. They're gonna go abso-fucking-lutely ape-fucking-shit.'

I toyed with the cold water condensing on the outside of my wine glass. He had a point. And another one.

'An', Simon – I mean, sure, – Angola want people to go mining again – or will do, as soon as it's at all possible – so don't ya think that's one of the reasons they want you an' Tony to go a-mining', while things are still hot? So that then they can use your example as a stick to beat everyone else with.'

'Must be why Tony's calling it Branch Minerals, Stav: Branch – stick!'

'Jeezus, Simon!'

Of course, I knew Stavros was half right on both counts. Maybe better than half.

I grinned at Stavros. He understood that grin. Didn't like it.

'You know, Stav? You've just made mining more attractive to me.'

'Oh, fuck off, Simon! You and Tony are having a lovely time right now. You're doing a good job well, you're earning money, and you're winning. Hooray.

'But, buddy, one day, UNÍTA, or the Agency, or a mineral trader, or some sonofabitch an' a bachelor are gonna catch you out. You're gonna see that one interferin', over-reachin' limey is like a beetle 'neath their Cuban. Scrunch, pop… That'll be you.'

'Fancy a Marlboro, Stav?'

CHAPTER NINE

JANUARY 2004: EG COUP

Time is running out for us.

I had hoped that our putsch – Plan C, to down the ruling gangsters of Equatorial Guinea – might take place on Christmas Day 2003, when everyone was looking the other way. Instead, Christmas is crisis time for the coup.

Thatcher's money alone isn't enough. We're still short. We're always short. The Boss coughs up some more, but not enough. He tells me that the rest will come in a few days' time. I believe him. Why would he pay the first sum if the second wasn't coming? We start to stand-by the men. Again. Making payments here and there.

Then, when the money dries up, I have to stop. Again. This has happened over and over. GO STOP GO STOP buggers up everything. It pisses people off. I can't blame them.

Our Op leaks.

I should tell the Boss to fuck off. I know it, but I can't. I want the top of the mountain. I want to carry out this Op. In my head now is a Hollywood calendar: paper days, blowing away fast. We're like an aircraft in trouble now. We're low and slow. We're on a shoestring for cash. We can't get anything properly jacked up. We're in wild haste.

The leaks that we're uncovering make it ever more sure that other heavyweight players desperately want us to carry out this Op too. I don't know quite what's going on with the powers that be, but there are many signs. Too many. It's like trying to figure out the English weather: too many variables, too much rapid change.

So I scan my virtual instrument panel. I weigh up pros and cons. The Boss has always hinted at a US nod and wink. The US is certainly very interested in the affairs of oil-rich EG. They showed their hand years earlier with the BAT Systems fishery protection proposal.

Obiang considered the proposal – presented to him by a US company from Geddings, Texas. Then a strange story emerged that BAT was in fact a US-backed coup attempt. BAT was promptly aborted. My own information, from several sources, confirms this to be true.

A source of mine in Washington gleans a telling reaction about EG from a political appointee in the Pentagon. She described Obiang and EG as 'a multi-faceted fuck-up'. Any change that makes it less of a fuck-up would be good news. So long as it does not damage US interests. Or threaten US citizens.

I know that the US have been informed of our coup plot by South Africa. Also in that loop is MI6. On top of this, there is a battery of the UK's Great and Good supporting the coup, all lined up by the Boss. These are well-known people with connections to the highest levels of British politics, business, finance and intelligence. All in on it. All no doubt leaking.

Other nations are backing us, but more subtly. China is backing the coup. I have doubts about the Chinaman, brought into the game against my orders by a friend who I had asked – out of my desperation with cash flow – to find more backing.

The Chinaman, having paid his investment over, then turned out to be a selling agent for Chinese government armaments. All he wants to be sure of – he lies – is that the new Equatorial Guinea does not recognise Taiwan, and that EG buy their future kit from him. China's ambitions to have an African empire are well under way. EG will be grist to the mill.

South Africa is the issue, not least because South Africa is where we're based. I brought a spook, Frank Thomas, into the coup plot quite early. I paid him, and he took the money: $10,000. Frank has several jobs. He has been to Nigeria for me, to find out how they will jump when the coup goes down. Whatever is best for their own pockets, is the not surprising answer to that question.

Frank will go back to Nigeria when the coup happens, to make sure they stay on-side. After that he is earmarked to ride shotgun to those EG locals who will be running security and anti-corruption in the new interim government – that's the one I'm about to put in power. I hope. I need someone rooting out all post-coup corruption.

Frank is one of my pairs of eyes and ears – my snout – within South African National Intelligence. (They also have MI – Military Intelligence – but it is under NI that our little caper falls.) I need someone who really knows what's going on in NI. Someone who can lobby within it if necessary. Someone who is not one of the Afrikaners.

That someone is Frank.

But I'm not the only one with snouts inside NI. Niek and his white South Africans all have their contacts in the echelons of government spooks. All in all, therefore, I know what is going on in NI. They know about us. They know about the coup. Niek has shown me SA NI intercepts of his telephone conversations with his wife Belinda and my phone calls to Amanda. NI have more than enough INT to stop us, or to shop us, if that is what they want to do.

I am in and out of Jo'burg and Cape Town International airports all the time. When in South Africa, I either stay with Mark Thatcher in Cape Town, or at the Sandton Towers in Jo'burg. Everyone knows that.

NI know me. They know my friends. Usual suspects. Known associates. If NI want this coup to cancel, they can pass that message to me as quickly and as easily as opening a packet of *biltong*. They don't. That is good news, because it puts South Africa into the same box as Spain: co-conspirators, but passive, their handiwork clandestine, deniable. South Africa are there for the same reason as Spain: oil. Barrel Boyz. South Africa are the African Empire builders in this century. How the tables turn.

You see: Niek has told me how clever he has been. A Jo'burg-quoted security company had signed a deal with President Obiang 12 months before. The security company was to supply a personal bodyguard for Obiang, military and security training for EG Special Forces, and help with fisheries and farming. And if that strikes you as an odd mix – farming? – then you don't know how South African empire-building works. The Afrikaans word 'Boer' means 'farmer'. Like in the *Iliad*, every one of them is a farmer first.

This deal was worth $30,000,000, to be financed by a loan to the government of EG, secured against EG oil revenue. The security company in question is well known to be an NI front company. It was set up as such in the first place. So this deal has NI written all over it.

Niek finds out that the security contract has stalled. It's dead in the water. As it has been since it was signed a year ago.

What Niek tells me is that he has negotiated with President Obiang, that Triple Option, our company, will become the agent and project manager for the contract. Cleverer yet, Niek has persuaded the security company and the bank – the original players in the deal – to let Triple Option take over as the management agent. For a percentage. I congratulate Niek on his financial cunning. But he doesn't know my fears. I fear that Niek has sold the coup down the river. I convince myself this is the case because if we hadn't surely we'd have all been arrested by know, or told to bin the project. In my mind, I grow convinced that Niek has struck a deal with NI. If such a deal has been struck, it will come to fruition after the coup is successful. After we are in EG.

What an opportunity for NI!

They get a piggy-back ride into a successful coup plot. At no risk. At no cost. If it fails, then it wasn't their coup. It was ours. No money trail to them. No fingerprints. Brilliant. But that's OK, by me. Because that's what it takes to get the job done.

What is not OK is if Niek is smooth-talking me. I am going along with what he tells me because it suits me to do so. The op has got to go ahead. It is being mounted from South Africa. I need NI. For now.

Forewarned is forearmed, I tell myself. If needed, I'll sort out Niek and the bloody South Africans later – when we're set up in EG, when Moto is boss. My plate will be full then. But isn't that how the West was won?

I remember when I joined 22 SAS. You had to quickly pick up what was what. They don't tell you. The idea that you must do whatever it is necessary to do in order to get the job done burns in the core of SAS soldiers. When they say 'whatever', they mean it.

Swallowing a betrayal, and carrying on along the path, in the company of known enemies, joshing them along in friendship, fearing their dagger in your back every step, is just par for the course. Part of the job. If you haven't got a sense of humour, don't join.

My other fear with Niek — founded or unfounded — is that he is running the project as a gravy train. My fear is that he's spinning it out for as long as he can. Milking it for all it's worth. We are spending a lot of cash up in EG. Genuine businesses are being built, he tells me. Niek owns them, or as good as. What if Niek has taken the stance of some of the South African soldiers in the run-up to Soyo? Could his primary motivation be to keep the cash rolling in for as long as possible? What if he has no plans to carry out the op itself?

Then things get murkier. A top-secret report falls into our hands. I have to react to it because others know about it. The report has been hacked off the computer of a commercial intelligence officer. The report is intended for SA NI as well as for the clients of the officer actually paying for it: Big Oil, the Barrel Boyz. It gives well-informed details of our plot, although it isn't sure whether our target is São Tomé or EG. Then I get confirmation from other sources. Sources external to the coup. Copies of this document have been sent to the CIA and to MI6.

We have a crisis meeting: first with Mark Thatcher at his home.

Mark is annoying me. All he wants to do is hold long and tiresome meetings about how investors and coupsters will work together post-coup. The divvy-up. The Bight of Benin Company is planned. The BBC. The London Docklands Development Corporation is seen as a model of how to plough through red tape. The legislation around the BBC is to copy that of the Docklands scheme. Business will take no prisoners.

Then Crause flies me and my PA Anthony down to George, the small city on South Africa's south coast, where Niek is. We fly in my Aerostar 600 — tail number N90676 — the Porsche 911 of the skies. We laugh. I love to fly with Crause. It's like the old days. The stakes feel much higher, though. It isn't just our own lives we're fooling around with now.

To everyone's surprise — except mine — Niek is not fazed by the report. Carry on up the river, he says. It's as I suspected. We are the troops of NI now. Or so thinks Niek. So think NI.

Any one of the intelligence agencies — of the US, UK, Spain, South Africa, China — could act against us at any moment. Perhaps they're waiting. It's a trap. Giving us enough rope. Maybe they plan to catch us in the act. Keeps it neat. Clear-cut.

Or perhaps they will allow us to carry out this coup.

Perhaps it's something they've dearly wanted to happen for some time. Of course, they couldn't possibly sanction such an act. They can't do it. But they could sit back and let some other mugs do it for them. Let some mercenaries take the risks. Do the dirty work. Then stroll in after for the rewards.

What is crystal clear, however, is that we are short of money. We are short of time. Our security is blown. Everything is going wrong. Is it worth carrying on? Or do I cut my losses now and bail out? Am I charging headlong into an ambush?

If it goes wrong, what will happen to Amanda?

What will happen to me? Jail and a slow death, or execution?

I know I should walk.

Amanda is telling me to drop it, even though she had been in favour: what reasons do I have to carry on? What reasons did I have in the first place? I'd been flattered that the Boss had sought me out. I wanted the craic. This is something to live for.

I genuinely want to knock a world-class bully like Obiang off his perch. OK, but what am I doing? Bodyguard to Severo: an elected man going home.

At what point does this become a crime? If I'm walking down the street and your house is on fire, should I refuse to do anything about it until the fire brigade arrives? You wouldn't mind paying. When I've used my men and kit to do the job? Just because I put out your fire doesn't mean I want the fire brigade abolished. This might sound simplistic but, in my experience, when it comes to the crunch, the international fire brigade – in the form of the UN – doesn't attend certain fires.

In Angola and Sierra Leone, it was clear who the bad guys were. It was clear who was suffering as a result. In each case, what was needed was for someone to go and give the bad guys a smacking. Really, it is an act of self-defence.

You don't have to be a crusader, trying to change the world. You don't have to stand up for what's right. You just have to deal with what's wrong. Bullying. Tyranny. That's all.

For all these reasons, on New Year's Day 2004 I commit myself to the Equatorial Guinea coup. I'm soldiering on.

I'm fucked if I'm going to let the Boss down.

CHAPTER TEN

MARCH 1995: FREETOWN SIERRA LEONE

Tony and I stood in the lobby of the Mammy Yoko Hotel, Freetown, Sierra Leone.

Dressed in our tropical best khaki drill, we waited for Ian Campbell, collecting us to meet the President. Ian had been the country manager for Sierra Leone, for Selection Trust, the old colonial diamond company. Their Sierra Leone diamond concession had been the whole country. Campbell knew every MP, every Minister, every Paramount Chief.

He was a Paramount Chief. Half the people who mattered in SL had been beneficiaries of Selection Trust one way or another. Many of those had been chosen to become beneficiaries by Campbell.

After Angola, Sierra Leone felt pleasantly backward, relaxed. The strange English patois of the natives was fun. Instead of 'Good morning', they said, 'How de body?' They expected back: 'De body fine.'

Boasting the best natural harbour on the coast of West Africa, Sierra Leone became a British colony in 1787. After that, it had acted as the main base for the Royal Navy's 19th-century war against slavery, from Angola northward. The Navy took many liberated slaves from their ships to the Sierra Leone capital – hence its name, Freetown. To me, Freetown is forever linked to Abthorpe in *Sword of Honour*. Here Guy Crouchback, Waugh's hero, is unjustly accused of killing his friend, Abthorpe, by means of smuggled whisky. Abthorpe lies sick, in the same hospital as the wounded, unrepentant Richie Hook. Fresh coconut on his bedside table.

I think of Moscow and the ODABs. The military hospital and my old Russian apparatchik colonel. His signature on the scruffy form that Nick held out. Clipped to the back of a hospital millboard. I hoped we hadn't killed the old boy.

Ian drew up in a large 4x4, with driver.

As we struggled through the town centre, we passed the Freedom Tree. It's an enormous cotton tree and, Ian told us, has an enormous history. The RN had no choice, often enough, other than to offload freed slaves in Freetown. The Freedom Tree became a clearing house. The freed and their relatives would search for one another. Here people would wait and hope.

Ian asked if, before we left Sierra Leone, we'd like to see the old Barracoons. It was in these barracks-style buildings that slaves were held before transportation. That was until 1833, when the British outlawed all slavery in their colonies.

The 4x4 swung out of the traffic noise and bustle. It careered towards an old colonial courtyard, open on one side of four. This open side was fenced by iron palings. Here, too, was a sentry box, a barricade and an entrance way. This was the first layer of an onion of security which, at its centre, held *El Presidente*.

The uniforms and AK-47s, the shouting, the saluting, were all spoiled by one thing: too many soldiers wearing shades, mostly of reflective glass.

For a Guardsman like me, a soldier in dark glasses is not really a soldier at all. This is a dangerous thought for an old Africa Hand like me. But I could not help but see these men as fake. Their guns, however, were real.

We moved on through the layers of security. Protocol. The sham grew.

'Tony,' I whispered, 'these boys have been watching too many movies!'

That was it: the Presidential paraphernalia was copied from a Hollywood banana republic military dictator. They were aping a Western cultural stereotype of a corrupt and violent African plutocracy. There was no need.

'This is how they think they ought to look.' Tony stifled a laugh. He had felt it too.

'Let's hope they haven't read *Black Mischief*!' he laughed.

'White man ... yum yum...'

Campbell looked daggers at us both, hissed us to quiet.

Protocol seated us in a smelly, stuffy waiting room, not lately cleaned. I leaned back. I tried to enter a dream state – a time-machine coma – to pass what might be hours. Days.

'Well?' I quizzed the backs of my eyelids. 'What am I doing here?'

It was six months since I'd shouted 'Baobab, baobab!' to Giorgio and Nick. Our Il-76 cargo plane carrying the 20 ODAB 500s had landed in Angola. That was August 1994. My elation at delivering the monster bombs had evaporated as the rubber squeaked on Cabo Ledo's massive concrete.

All I felt was unease.

João de Matos gave me his word. He would keep bloodshed to a minimum, he promised. How could he guarantee that? We've all seen how military intelligence can get it wrong. How schools and factories and villages can be targeted by mistake. For all our work and training, the system was wide open to abuse. Or stupidity.

We knew only too well how heartless rebels can use the *povos* as their cover. Their own people as shields. If a single ODAB were used badly, then the consequences would be apocalyptic. Like setting off a small nuclear bomb. Bought and paid for by yours truly.

Then – by November 1994 – UNITA had signed a ceasefire. It was an agreement that marked the effective end of the Angolan war. Victory to the MPLA. Never again was there a repeat of the 1993 scenario, whereby UNITA might achieve a military victory.

Desperate with worry, I needed to know: how had the ODABs achieved this? How, at a stroke, did these bombs put an end to a 20-year civil war, that had cost half a million lives? I had feared the worst. I had feared that my ODABs – despite all our best efforts, and despite all their promises – had done their worst. Killed hundreds. Thousands?

I found that the FAA had dropped an ODAB close to the UNITA capital, Huambo, a city just west of central Angola. The biggest single coming together of UNITA CIVPOP. The weapon had unleashed a scorching tornado from hell.

Then I learned that the weapon had been dropped only after public announcements. Learned about the where and when. It had been

1995: SIERRA LEONE . . .

dropped as a warning. And it was the only one of those bloody things dropped in anger. The fuel-air-mix dragon ODAB had duly shocked and awed.

UNITA: cowed and broken. The bomb had hurt nobody.

Phew.

Fighting did go on after that time. A low-intensity conflict. Armed banditry. This ongoing thuggery continued to make miserable the lives of Angola's *povos*. But it suited the many inside and outside Angola who still wanted some kind of war – any kind – to carry on.

They managed to keep it smouldering until 2002, for their pockets. Then the FAA – or their proxies – finally caught and killed the UNITA leader: my old enemy General Dr Comrade Jonas Savimbi.

Nevertheless, the 1994 ceasefire secured by the ODAB bombs ended the war proper. UNITA never again came close to a victory over the MPLA. Crucially, the Clinton presidency then ceased US support for UNITA, proclaiming them bandits.

The UN wrote to de Matos about his use of the ODABs – to thank him for his humanity and his restraint. I was shown that letter.

Earlier, in '95, I'd been in Jo'burg, where I'd met two old UNITA generals. They had not known who I was. Those generals were forthright: the ODABs had brought the war to a halt. The Executive Outcomes intervention at Soyo, and then countrywide, in 1993, had saved the MPLA, they said. EO, the spy plane, the constant attrition against their air resupply: all had made the war tougher and tougher. But, once the ODAB 500s had been demonstrated, that was the end.

I had seen FAA and UN reports. They all said the same. I felt vindicated. So did Tony and Coebus. Come what may, we could all truthfully say that we'd helped bring about a victory, the ending of a war: an end that, without us, would not have come so fast; might not have come at all.

So, I thought, sitting in the President's stuffy waiting room, up there in Freetown, that's one for the Game Book: 'Helped Shorten and Win Civil War in Angola!'

I wound the tape back to the very start of that adventure: to that day in Tony's office in January 1993 when we learned of UNITA's attack on Soyo. I remembered just how far off my dream of life with Amanda had been back then.

Above left: My maternal grandfather, Brigadier William Marshall Clark, serving with the South African Division in Italy in World War II.

Above right: Captain Frank Mann, Scots Guards in World War I. According to the magazine caption, at the time of this drawing he had recently been wounded for the second time.

Below: The Manns at the family estate, Thelveton, in 1929. Second from the left is my grandfather, Frank. The boy third from left is my father. Fourth from left is my great grandfather, Sir Edward Mann, the 1st Baronet. All the guns are by Purdey.

Above left: Captain Frank Mann, Scots Guards World War I.

Above right: Major George Mann, Scots Guards World War II. He looks too young for his rank and decorations.

Below: Lord's Cricket Ground, June 1949, England v New Zealand.

Left to right: The late Queen Mother, my grandfather 'Pop', King George VI and Daddy shaking hands. The man on the far right is Len Hutton, a future England captain.

My portrait, taken by Lenare in 1975. I was ordered to go to him by my mother, who had heard that he was about to retire.

Back seat in
a Red Arrow
Hawk, 1994.

Above: Competing in the 1997 Peking to Paris motor race. The Aston Martin DB 5 – car 79 – with its Skipper, Tony Buckingham. Somewhere behind is Everest, seen from the Chinese side. That evening, at this altitude, Tony's Cohiba Esplendidos cigar laid him out flat.

Below: Car 79 reaches Paris.

From left to right: Tim Spicer, Tony Buckingham, me and Michael Grunberg. A PMC line up: Sandline and Aegis, Executive Outcomes, New Century.

On Tony's yacht, 1995: I'm at the wheel, Tony Buckingham's arm round my shoulder, while Andy Smith hangs onto the backstay. Andy died shortly afterwards in an air crash in Entebbe.

Above: Amanda and me in the South of France, 1996

Below: Amanda out shooting in the November of my pardon and return home, 2009.

Above: Taken by Amanda in 1993 at Hobachere game camp, Namibia, the evening before the Angolan top brass flew in. We went for a long walk and the pump-action shotgun was an unused precaution against a pride of lions known to be around. UNITA were also possibly around.

Below: A King Air fit for a King. A Beechcraft King Air 200 chartered by Crause Steyl to fly Severo Moto into Malabo, the night of the attempted Coup d'État.

Above left: Lady Thatcher, Mark Thatcher and me, looking for game in 2002.

Above right: Mark Thatcher in one of the Shamwari Landrovers. In Shona, *Shamwari* means comrade.

Below: Amanda and me on the same Thatcher holiday.

Above left: President Obiang of Equatorial Guinea.   © *Getty Images*

Above right: Severo Moto. The man who would have headed the Interim Government, had the attempted Coup d'Etat been successful.   © *Getty Images*

Below left: A cartoon of me in *Private Eye*, shortly after my release.

Below right: On trial in Equatorial Guinea, 2008, I had just been sentenced to 35 years.   © *Getty Images*

Above: The Blues & Royals cavalry officer behind the wedding couple is Captain Jack Mann, my second son, 2011.

Below left: Captain Peter Mann, 1st Btn Scots Guards, on operations in Afghanistan. Peter's my eldest son and this was his second tour.

Below right: Captain Jack Mann, Blues & Royals, on operations in Afghanistan. Jack also had a tour in Iraq.

Above: On my release, November 2009.
Front row, left to right: Arthur, Freddy, Bess, Lilly, Sophie. *Back row left to right*: Peter, Amanda, me, Jack.

Below: Sophie's wedding: Jack, Lilly, Amanda, Will & Arthur, Sophie, me and Bess, Freddy, Peter. Summer 2011

Inset: Freddy at Inchmery, while I was 'away'. An unlucky sea bass, freshly caught. I couldn't look at photos like this when I was in prison; they hurt too much.

What obstacles had there been! Each one had appeared unassailable: money, Jewishness, my eight-year-old vasectomy.

Soyo had solved the first of these – the dragon Soyo's hoard of gold – and a skilful surgeon the third. The vasectomy had been an act of self-preservation during my not-so-good second marriage.

Now the business of making babies had to be juggled around the moon's phases, my trips to Africa and other unfathomable things.

Then we tackled the Jew issue. I agreed to convert. I did so on the understanding that this was for child raising. Not religious conviction. I thought there little difference between being an atheist Christian (of which, in my father's family, I was at least the third generation) or an atheist Jew. Amanda, an Orthodox Jewess, decided to accompany me through my learning. This helped us both.

After we'd learned plenty – all of it fascinating and a lot of fun – Amanda found out how rigid Judaism really is. She also found out that a child of a Jewish mother is, in Judaic law, a Jew. We came through it stronger, but Amanda asked me not to convert. I was happy not to do so.

Maybe our Jerusalem holidays' dinner together – kosher and vegetarian and, for God's sake, teetotal – helped us to make up our minds. Away had gone the final unassailable obstacle. Now all was sweetness and light. We would have children, we hoped, and live happily ever after.

Nearby chit-chat brought me sharply back to the Freetown waiting room. Campbell was talking with one of the protocol aides. Tony faked sleep. He had his own way of dealing with the wait. And with Campbell.

So, what was I doing in Freetown? I was diamond mining. That's what I was doing. And wading into another civil war. Maybe.

The Angolans had wanted to restart diamond mining in their country. DM, some other generals and JD had all pressed Tony to form a joint venture with them. Power men of the moment. The country needed activity. Opportunity was there. Tony and our crew were the proven achievers.

If one Western company made a start, others would follow. Others could be made to follow. If we went in and mined diamonds, other concession holders could no longer point to the *force majeure* clauses in their concession agreements. They could no longer use the ongoing war and banditry as an excuse.

Tony had been enthusiastic. To him, a diamond concession and an oil concession must be the same. You win one, then sell it. Or you farm it out. Or you pull in punters. Then Andy Smith had passed by Tony's grasp. Smith was a mining expert – especially diamonds, especially Angola.

Everything had come together: Tony and I had the money now. Coebus, and some of the other South Africans, would come in. The accountant, Michael Grunberg, had given the project his thumbs-up. Making money from Angolan diamonds would be a piece of piss.

My belief in Tony as a businessman, and in Michael's judgment in money matters, was absolute. I had thought that the war must end first. Then the war met the ODAB.

Suddenly, without really making the decision – or so it felt to me – we were miners. We were real miners too: paying out large sums of money, for concessions and for exploration.

Smith was in charge, but neither Tony nor Michael would tell him no. Within months Branch Minerals had concessions, or concessions designate, in Angola, Uganda, Kenya, Tanzania, South Africa. The diamond concessions were all in Angola. The rest of the concessions – across Africa – were for gold.

Then everything changed. The new way forward, they told me, was to bring in outside investment. The only feasible way to do that was through a Stock Exchange listing. Diamond concessions were not like oil concessions. Not at all.

Then it was explained to me that, in order to list a diamond-mining company, that company must have hard rock concessions. Crucially, these concessions could not all be in one unstable country. Like Angola. But two unstable countries would do.

Suddenly, I found myself in a place I didn't know, didn't like. We had concessions to mine gold all over Africa. We had concessions to mine diamonds only in Angola. But that wasn't enough to get the Stock Market listing.

The choice put to me became straightforward: we either go on pouring money into finding new diamond concessions outside of Angola, or we must stop, writing off all the investment so far. It scared me. I had to think of Amanda. Our child. All my children. Our future.

Tony and Michael had a different point of view. Neither had dependent children. Both were businessmen. They played and won, or lost, then played again. For them, this was just another game. For me, this was the only game. I'd poured everything into this. Branch Minerals had to work.

The next question had been: where do we find a hard rock diamond concession? Going cheap ... but not in Angola?

Answer: nowhere – except Sierra Leone, where there is a good one. That nobody wants.

Question: how come nobody wants it?

Answer: because, in SL there is a peculiarly nasty little war going on.

Therein lay the opportunity. If Tony and I could introduce SL's President to Executive Outcomes, then, maybe, EO could win the war for the President. We'd done it in Angola.

Why couldn't we do it again?

Then Branch Minerals could make a fair bid for the diamond concession. This had all been hammered out by Andy Smith, Michael, Tony and I, but with a lot of head shaking and cigar sucking from Stavros. Smith had then placed the last necessary piece on the table.

Ian Campbell, his friend and partner. With him as Branch Minerals' manager everything should work out. If he couldn't win the Koidu Kimberlite concession, nobody could.

So it was decided: we'd hire Campbell on a short-term contract. We'd send him to SL to carry out a business and political reconnaissance. At the same time, EO would clandestinely send three black agents, unbeknown to Ian. Their mission: to conduct the military reconnaissance of the SL war. The SL Strategic Situation.

Nobody needed telling the full horror of the atrocities carried out in SL by the Revolutionary United Front (RUF). Atrocities which were to win them worldwide condemnation. Nobody needed to tell me how Liberian boy rebels waged their sort of war (and most of the RUF were Liberian boy rebels). I'd been in Liberia in 1989 when Charles Taylor had taken the capital, Monrovia, and later killed President Doe. On that occasion, I had only just escaped a similar fate. But not before I had seen some truly terrible things. The recce, therefore, was to assess whether an EO force could defeat the RUF.

Ian's recce went well. He, of course, had relished the role of would-be saviour. Now the stage was set for the SL President to meet Tony and me. That's how we wound up in this waiting room.

1 9 9 5 : S I E R R A L E O N E . . .

Whispering grew. Someone came in, then went out. Someone else came in, waved his hands. An as yet unused door opened. At last, we were being ushered in.

But as we stepped into the President's office, there was muddle. His long desk, longer than Tony's in London, took up too much of the space. As soon as we entered the room, we were on top of the desk. On top of each other. Slapstick followed. We jockeyed for seats. After one false start, an aide waved me into the extreme right-hand chair, at the end of the row. To my left was Campbell. Then Tony was placed in the centre. The aides and the senior protocol officer fumbled about on the other side of Tony.

Having been the first to sit, I watched President Strasser. Slouched in his leather executive swivelling chair, sizing us up.

Valentine Strasser, 26 years old, was 'De Captain' and 'De Main Man'. Rarely was he called 'General', although that was now his rank. To call the President 'De Captain' or 'De Main Man' was not to insult him. Nobody in Sierra Leone insulted the President. Not in public. Not anywhere else. Strasser had been smoking. There was a large glass ashtray on the desk. The air held a mix of smells: distant curry, the sour tang of tropical carpet, the exhaust of an unmaintained air conditioner and tobacco smoke. I watched Strasser. His eyes looked a little wild, unfocused: yes – I had it – and the smell of *dakka*.

De Main Man was Boomin'.

With everyone in their appointed seat, Campbell went into his party piece. Tony interrupted or endorsed for emphasis. Twice I chipped in. I had to strain to hear what Strasser said, he spoke so softly.

Behind the President was a large photograph of himself. In the portrait, as in the flesh, he was wearing tropical disruptive-pattern combats, with British-style general's rank. Bright-red military-style collar tabs. A Hollywood African dictator.

Above the window, and to the right of it, the air conditioner rattled and banged, gamely competing with the noisy ceiling fan. The din made Strasser's words even harder to make out.

Below one end of the air conditioner, a quarter-full bucket caught a steady flow of drips. This meeting, I knew, was but one step in a dance of time: meetings, protocol and negotiation. This was not where or how real decisions and plans would be made.

De Main Man's gesticulations were growing grander, his eyes wilder. I hoped that this meant he was happy.

It was his desk that held my attention; it was covered in knick-knacks. Immediately in front of the President, a large doodled blotter. To his right hand, the telephone collection. Two of these were old-style, black, with rotating diallers. Others modern, coloured, push-button. Beyond the telephones, so out of reach, sat a desktop computer and a laptop.

I could lean forward slightly. Both computer screens were dead. The phones were not connected. In front of Strasser, beyond the blotter, was an old-fashioned glass pen tray, holding inkwells long dried up. Laid upon the tray, a plastic pink feather of the sort that holds a ballpoint pen at one end.

Beyond the tray, and therefore in pride of place, sailed a wooden model of an Arab *dhow* ... a memento of Arab West Africa slaving, maybe? To Strasser's left hand, other needs were satisfied. A Rolodex sat surrounded by a group of photo frames. Of these, I could only see the backs.

To their side stood a ten-inch-high crucifix. Christ, his cross and the stand were each made from a different, exotic hardwood. All beautifully carved and polished.

From the left arm of the cross, Jesus's left, hung two brightly coloured bird feathers, the kind used in witchcraft. Below the feathers, on the desk, a bundle of four bones, next to two small animal-skin pouches. Beside the crucifix, close to the right arm, rested a shrunken human skull.

In West Africa, mumbo-jumbo magic is fact.

My eyes and Strasser's met. He smiled apologetically, then turned back to his point with Tony.

My tour nearly done, I went back to the desk. Between me and the crucifix were parked a small model of the Mi-24 gunship helicopter (NATO codename HIND). Just like the one that Strasser had parked outside the barracks. The one that his men were failing to use. Another model, of a British Aerospace Hawk fighter, in the colours of the Nigerian Air Force was next to it. With these stood a Dinky toy, a London red double-decker bus.

That evening, back at the Mammy Yoko, Tony and I entertained ourselves over dinner by playing Kim's Game. List everything you can remember off the desk. A pained Campbell looked on, hoping that the waiter was not one of Strasser's secret police.

The four-day visit, and our meetings with De Main Man, were, however, deemed a success. Others followed. Two of which introduced the EO seniors: Coebus and two others. Meanwhile EO's spies did their work.

I knew the basics about SL already. Sierra Leone, Lion Mountain, had been named by Portuguese or Spanish explorers. The hills above and behind Freetown, from the sea, can look like a lion lying on its front with its head up. From independence the consensus government, and what prosperity that Sierra Leone had achieved, did not flourish. The country went downhill to such a low point that, in April 1992, young Captain Strasser and his six 'boys' had staged a mutiny against their pay and conditions.

The mutiny had somehow become a Coup d'État. The new government – Captain Strasser and his boys – were often to be found in Freetown's many nightclubs. Needless to say, they struggled with government. Rebel Liberian marauding grew apace.

By April 1995, the situation was dire. The RUF guerrillas were led by former corporal Foday Sankoh, an army signaller by trade. According to our sources, Sankoh personally ordered his men to carry out mass rapes and amputations. He had led the RUF well enough to garner some Sierra Leone support, which, mixed in with the drug-crazed, war-shocked Liberian teenagers, could make it to the capital. The population of Freetown, who knew well the RUF's *modus operandi*, were beginning to panic.

We were keen to start. The problem was Strasser's inability to pay. Should we go ahead anyhow? Or should we cut and run? Tony called for a big powwow at the end of April, in the King's Road offices.

The meeting kicked off – or more accurately lit up – at 11. The models – the glamorous office girls hired by Michael – had been told to hold all calls. Tony and Stavros had Esplendidos burning, Michael and I Marlboros. Tony began: 'Right. We know what we are here for: do we go for it in SL or not? If yes, then it may be tougher than Soyo' – at this Coebus grinned – 'if no, then I never want to hear of the bloody place again.'

1 9 9 5 :   S I E R R A   L E O N E . . .

Tony asked Coebus to go first. Coebus predicted that EO – with 200 men and the right air support – could turn the war around. He stressed that this view applied only if we went in before the RUF entered Freetown: an event forecast for any day soon. If we are to go, Coebus said, it must be now.

Next Tony asked Stavros, who looked asleep. 'Why ask me, Tony? You and Simon will do what you want. You're both fucking crazy…'

Coebus interrupted: 'No, Stavros. This is a council of war. I want to hear what you think.'

'OK. You've won the Angolan war. I'm amazed. It's incredible – but there you are. You have made yourselves some powerful enemies, however – all those who backed UNITA, whether they pushed or helped UNITA back into war. They don't like you.'

Tony and I both knew what Stavros had to say, but he went on regardless: 'My advice is: the mining is a big mistake. "The first loss is the best loss": get out now and cut your losses, then retire.'

Tony turned to me.

I said my piece: 'Tony – I know how you feel, and I agree with you. I'm not going to bin the mining when we have so much at stake: we need SL.'

Tony looked round: 'Exactly. Coebus, can we do it? If we say go?'

Coebus laughed. 'Let's find out!'

'OK. Go it is.'

'OK, let's go… Now let's go to lunch!'

My heart beat fast. One part of me had wanted to go just for the craic. Another part felt that, as with Angola, if we could bring a terrible war to an end, then we should.

But the biggest part of me was simply hell bent on making this mining work. According to Smith, Michael and Tony, this was an essential step. Win the war in SL. Win the hard rock concession, the Koidu Kimberlite. Put the diamond company up for a Stock Exchange flotation.

Seven days later, one of our two Boeing 727-100s landed at Lungi International, Freetown, with 100 EO men on board. The day before the two Mi-17 support helicopters had arrived. One was green, Bokkie. One was still in UN white, Daisy.

On the flight up from Angola, the two machines and crews had been arrested only three times. They had also made good practice with the

EO in-flight refuelling system. Garage forecourt hand pumps: Jet A-1 from standard 35-gallon oil drums into the internal passenger compartment's extra fuel tank.

The Boeing flight had left Jo'burg at 0300. On board were Coebus and I, plus many other of the EO old guard. Nobody wanted to miss this.

We refuelled in Luanda, without the Angolans being aware of our mission. We refuelled again in Abidjan, the Ivory Coast. Tony and Nick Potter had flown down from London to Abidjan to join the flight.

I found that I had to reassure Nick Potter. He and Tony had painted Abidjan bright red the night before. Both had 'A One' hangovers. As soon as we met, Nick took me to one side: was it possible to catch HIV/Aids from a blow job in the shower?

This was one of the easiest ways to catch it, I said. Normally viscous saliva dilutes in the water, thus becoming less viscous, and thus very much more mobile, more likely to go through the pores of the skin membrane and into the blood circulatory system.

Nick's hung-over grimace was so pathetic that I spared him. He must take care. Too strong a flow of water, with his little prick, and he could drown the poor girl.

When we reached Lungi, we got looks from the UN, and then from the Nigerian Air Force contingent – part of ECOMOG (Economic Community of West African States Monitoring Group). Neither were in on our deal.

I looked round as we offloaded.

Another 100 of our men would arrive the next day. Coebus and I were putting into practice a lesson we had learnt at Soyo.

With these kinds of operations, security is the nightmare. The way to win is to do things as quickly as possible. It is much harder for the authorities to stop you once you are all in place. A *fait accompli*. You have to move faster than those reacting to you. Faster than the leak. Faster than the rumour.

Within a day, everyone, at my insistence, had been enrolled into the Sierra Leone Armed Forces. This was a demotion for Tony and me, since here we were colonels, down from the dizzy heights of brigadier generals back in Angola. We had arrived not one day too soon. The RUF were at the gates, and already lobbing mortars into the city's pathetic defences. We heard the enemy's bombs stonking in while we were unloading the 727, out on the runway at Lungi Airport.

Coebus and his men went to work quickly. The following day the first 100 men and the two M-17s were in action. They had with them SL's Mi-24 gunship, now flown by South African pilots. A weapon of mass fright if nothing else.

We had bought a twin-engine Cessna for the INT role. We kitted it out with SIGINT VHF and HF antennae and scanners, plus, on the ground, the same Apple system that we had in Angola. Working in tandem with signal-intercepting equipment on the ground, we rapidly built a SIGINT picture.

Some of the ground kit was ours, other items came from a local and friendly source in Freetown. A building with a large flagpole outside it. Sankoh, chief of the RUF, was an ex-signaller. But he loved to chat, and he loved for his commanders to chat back. That was how he fucked up.

This put us a step ahead, gave EO an edge. We often knew the RUF's next move before their own soldiers knew it. Their signalling was not as good as they thought it was, so there were times when their radio orders came from us.

Two months after EO moved in, having been often back and forth, I was again in Freetown. The progress against the RUF had been remarkable. I flew on one of the night-time Bird Dog missions that had brought so much success. As soon as it was fully dark, Bokkie or Daisy would go hunting.

The helicopter would fly a grid search given to them by the Intelligence Cell. The search pattern would have been carefully chosen using all information available. Some of the best intelligence came from the network of tribal hunters. This had Chief Norman as its boss. One of the stars of the show, he was later, disgracefully, killed. But that's another story... Their information would be cross-referenced with the signal intercepts and the radio direction-finding.

On the night I flew, the machine was Bokkie. We wore combat webbing – full fighting order – and carried AKs. 'Just in case we get shot down, Squiffy.'

Nick's joke. Only here it isn't a joke.

The recce technique was crude. An EO officer hung out of the side door (Simon Witherspoon, in this case) leaning against a harness clipped to the aircraft. He wore earphones, helmet and throat-mike, so as to direct the pilots. He had on a pair of NVGs, Image Intensifiers.

The helicopter flew at about 5,000 feet, so could scarcely be heard on the ground.

The RUF, it turned out, were creatures of habit. At night, they gathered in little groups to cook and chat. The little groups gathered around their leader ... and so on up their formation.

Their cooking fires stood out clearly with the NVGs. The pattern they made on the ground was distinctive and readable. Different from villages, farms or groups of hunters. The EO officer, when directly over what he thought to be the RUF commander's HQ, would shout on the intercom for the pilots to 'mark' that position on their handheld GPS.

Often that information acted as fine-tuning: confirmation of intelligence that had been ground out of the other sources. EO would then plan and execute an attack: at first light next morning. These attacks used Bokkie and Daisy and the Mi-24. Mortar teams were flown in. Using GPS for precision, the mortars would then stonk the RUF HQs.

The guerrilla insurgents now found themselves at the receiving end of real guerrillas, Afrikaner Kommandos, whose idea of hit-and-run had, at its core, a deadly hit.

From intercepted traffic, the RUF could be heard falling to pieces. At one point, Sankoh and his commanders were being shot up so hard and so often that they were sure there were 2,000 EO troops fighting them. Not our 200. This rotating EO unit needed intense and constant support away from the battlefront: ammo, food, water, fuel. An entire support system had to be in place – working like clockwork – to feed and water the voracious war dragon.

At this point, EO had two operations in progress: Angola and Sierra Leone. There were close to 2,000, which of course included an EO padre, to take care of the religious needs of the South Africans. *Die Kerk*. Crause and I had organised all the aircraft into one company, first called Capricorn, then Ibis. There were 18 aircraft of nine types and over 60 air crew.

Ibis had just the one weekly flight. But, when I entered Jo'burg International's Departures and looked up at the huge information board, it moved my heart to see the Ibis Air weekly Boeing 727 flight up there. BA ... SAA ... Virgin ... Ibis Air: Luanda–Freetown.

The Ibis flight would leave Jo'burg early each Tuesday. It flew to Luanda, refuelled, then flew to Lungi, Freetown. The crew would overnight, then return the next day, to get back to Jo'burg on Wednesday evening.

Our single weekly Ibis Air round trip had unusual features. There were never any women, except the air hostesses. The passengers were all young or middle-aged. Never kids, never old people. Whether black or white, every passenger looked unusually fit. Their luggage – rucksacks, kitbags, never a suitcase – was often dark green, rarely any other colour. The flight was always completely full. (Not surprisingly since it was rotating the whole of EO's courses and leave programme – for 1,800 men).

In the hustle and bustle of Jo'burg International, nobody noticed. Besides, Ibis was official. No longer could Crause say: 'Simon – this is not a customary airline' – meaning that we don't go through Customs. No longer could Crause say: 'When are these pilots going to realise: a radio – on an aeroplane – is a luxury item?', referring to a pilot he had just sacked for obeying Namibian ATC's radio message – that he should fly to the capital, Windhoek, for inspection, thus delaying his Ibis mission to Luanda.

Because Ibis was now official – above board – we got our men in and out smoothly. It proved a crucial logistical factor in EO gaining the upper hand. Our air hostesses were a crucial factor too. They weren't paid, but the trolley was their own: they kept all their takings. They saw some rough sights, those girls.

At that time Nick Van den Berg – the EO Commander in Angola – remarked to me that, if every chancer in the bars and nightclubs of Jo'burg and Pretoria who said that he was EO was really EO, then we were a truly formidable force.

In SL, within two months of arrival, EO had taken the hinterland: Freetown could breathe again. We moved out to the provinces, to prevent the RUF from regrouping.

The day came when EO entered Koidu. A strategically important town. Home of the Koidu Kimberlite, a famous hard rock diamond mine – and the concession that Branch Minerals sought. The town was deserted. As all towns were, following a visit from the RUF.

Vultures flopped and flapped in the streets, and on the rooftops. In the roads were corpses without heads, skulls without bodies. The hard rock mine was secure. But, as yet, Sierra Leone wasn't. We battled on.

After six months, EO had the RUF beaten. They were holed up, the diehards, in small towns in the far reaches of the country, on its borders with Guinea and Liberia. A political halt was called to the operational plan to hit them there. It was thought that, for Sierra Leone to stay on good terms with those neighbours, it would be a good idea not to dispatch RUF remnants their way.

Nobody wanted the RUF.

But the problem was money. Once the RUF had been put on the run, EO had cut down to only 100 men, plus the air assets. This still cost $400,000 per month. Strasser was yet to pay one single dollar.

Tony and I had kept up a barrage of demands and threats, trying to secure some payment. Any payment. Fifty-fifty, all of this debt was our own money. Desperate, Tony called another meeting.

This wampum powwow was to be held in the garden of the Mammy Yoko, a location that was thought to be secure from any eavesdropping once sentries had been posted. Crause and I had flown up from Jo'burg.

Neither of us thought it possible to cut costs further, without an accident. Everything and anything to do with Sierra Leone had been chopped squared. More cuts – of the air wing at least – were likely to end in a crash. A crash was something that we had miraculously avoided, despite so much hard operational flying.

My view was that we must find a way to make SL pay something, or we cut and run. If that meant an end to the whole mining plan, then so be it. We had done our best, won another war, and ended it. But now I had to think money.

When Crause and I arrived, I spotted Michael at the bar and joined him. Then I saw Tony in the distance and waved. He was deep in talk with the hotel's American owner-manager.

'Where's Stavros?' I asked Michael.

Puzzled, he replied. 'Hasn't Tony told you? Stavros has gone.'

I was stunned. Tony had not told me. Nor had Stav.

When I spoke to Tony later, alone, he didn't want to talk about it. He just looked at me, hard. 'He had enough rope. He hanged himself. They all do.'

The words stuck in my head. They chilled me. Would *I* hang myself?

The powwow, when it eventually came together, was tiresome – an anti-climax. The monthly cost of the operation had been pared right down. Any more cutting back would be dangerous for the men on the ground.

Tony publicly gave me a flea in my ear for authorising a Boeing 727 to scramble from Jo'burg, fly up to Freetown, collect a medical case, then fly back. The medevac had cost £70,000. I didn't argue. We moved on. Everyone knew what had happened: a black EO soldier had contracted cerebral malaria and the medevac saved his life.

Michael gave everyone the result of his digging. There was no secret stash of money from which Strasser and Sierra Leone could pay. When they said they had none, they had none.

Nor could they raise any.

Strasser was barely recognised as a President by the international community. Possible lenders to the country still thought the RUF a political risk. Even if Strasser granted Branch Minerals a concession for the Koidu Kimberlite, the next day it would be worthless. No Stock Exchange due diligence and compliance committee would accept such a document.

It all came down to whether Tony and I would go on paying out $400,000 per month. That was what everyone had known before the meeting started. I'd already given Tony my view. I knew that one day soon he'd just say 'fuck it' and pull the plug.

The man suffering most was Ian Campbell. It was not just self-interest and ego. Ian had wedded himself to the interests of the people of Sierra Leone a long time before we had come along. He really did want Sierra Leone to stay free of the RUF, and to flourish.

With the RUF beaten, and the Branch Minerals bid for the Koidu Kimberlite well received, Campbell, Paramount Chief, was riding high. His nightmare was to be told one day: 'Sorry, Ian! It's all over. We're off. Thanks.'

I felt sorry for him at the powwow.

Ian could hardly argue with the logic of what was being said. But it was breaking his heart. By lunchtime Tony called the meeting over. No decision had been made, but the likely outcome was clear enough. With Tony and me owed the $4 million we had spent to date, and this going up by $400,000 per month, who could argue?

After a long walk on the beach – mostly unpestered, thanks to my protection money paid to the beach's chief urchin – I went down to the bar at 7.30. Dinner was to be at 8. It would be bigger and noisier than normal. A wake for our dream. The sadder for being so near, yet so far.

Shortly after Tony had joined the group at the bar, I saw Campbell furiously signalling to me from the doorway that led out to the swimming pool. I strolled over.

Campbell, who had looked close to tears all day, now looked as if he had been puffing on Strasser's *dakka*.

'Simon – we can't talk here – too dangerous – get Tony – get him now – I have to talk to you both – don't let the others see – get him out – go round through the lobby – then come round on the outside – I'll meet ye at the table over there!'

I hesitated. Had Ian lost it?

'Simon, please – it's vital I talk to you and Tony tonight. I know there'll be a piss-up at dinner. I've got to talk to you now.'

The old man was frantic. It seemed like the least I could do. But I feared an explosion from Tony. I went back to the bar, whispered in Tony's ear and took him quietly round through the lobby.

'What the fuck does he want, Simon? If it was his fucking money, he wouldn't be paying out like we are.'

'Come on, Tony. Let's talk to him. Humour him. He's really upset.'

Ian sat us down at the isolated table. Then, with a theatrical craning of the neck, he looked around for eavesdroppers.

'Tony, Simon. I've just come from the President…'

I tried to jog him along: 'Ian, spit it out. Let's hear it!'

Ian gulped for air, then gushed: 'The President will stand down – he'll announce it immediately – *if* a new President can be elected – in proper, free and fair elections.'

We were stunned. We stared at Ian. He stared wildly back. If this was for real, then it changed everything. If we could hold out. Carry on paying for EO for another few months. Keep the RUF at bay. Ensure these elections did happen. Then we'd be in another, much happier, ball game.

A new, internationally recognised President could raise money and grant kosher mining licences. With Campbell plugging away, surely the Koidu Kimberlite could be ours? Our bid was as good as anyone else's. The goal of a Stock Exchange-listed Branch Minerals diamond company might yet be reached.

Ian's announcement had been a bombshell, just as his pitch had been pure panto.

So Executive Outcomes stayed in Sierra Leone, to the huge relief of the entire population. Tony and I went on paying. Elections did take place, under UN supervision.

But the real security, without which no election would have been possible, was EO. At one point the UN had to be rescued by Daisy. A UN-manned polling station, attacked and besieged by RUF, called for help.

The end result of the election was the inauguration of President Ahmad Tejan Kabbah, with full international recognition, *de facto* and *de jure*, and the UN stamp of 'free' and 'fair'.

Strasser went so quietly that nobody saw him go. We helped him with the money that he needed. He went to study at a university in the north of England; nobody knew what. Cap'n Strasser, De Main Man, had turned out to be De Main Hero.

It wasn't long before Kabbah told EO we had to go. This came as no surprise. By this time, the same thing had happened in Angola. When President Dos Santos had met Clinton in the White House – the meeting when the MPLA became OK, and UNITA not OK – it had been made clear that EO should have our contract ended and be sent home.

We had moles at this meeting – one in each camp. These sources both told us that Dos Santos had spoken up on EO's behalf. He had made it clear to Clinton that EO had been legally enrolled as FAA troops. That we'd left no cupboards, or villages, stuffed full of skeletons…

'No incident.'

Dos Santos, of course, agreed to the US demand to send us home. In the event, the MPLA spun out EO's departure as long as they reasonably could.

It was as well that Angola had spun out the EO contract as it did. Otherwise, the money needed to pay for the operations in Sierra Leone, through to the elections and beyond, would not have been there. The country would have sunk down into the pit the RUF had dug for it.

President Kabbah, 64 at the time of his election in March 1996, had spent most of his working life as a UN apparatchik. What that really meant, God alone knew – self-administration? My direct experiences of the UN in action in Angola and in Sierra Leone had left me with a dim view.

This CV of Kabbah's was a two-sided coin. On the one side it was a weakness. Kabbah was inexperienced with the real world. With dealing with a bunch of psychopaths and torturers like the RUF. On the other side it was a strength. Sierra Leone needed help badly. Kabbah knew how to make the help machine pay out. He, and some of his advisers, knew that the only thing keeping the RUF in their distant box was the threat of EO.

Kabbah therefore introduced two important measures. He asked for, and got, a 30-man EO close protection team. And he allowed a security company to be incorporated in Sierra Leone, which would be EO run and manned, but would sail under a different flag. He also started, slowly, to pay off the mounting EO debt. And to get the debt itself on the books, properly recognised.

Kabbah also made it clear that, all things being equal, Campbell and Branch Minerals should be given a friendly hearing when they submitted their Koidu Kimberlite application for a production licence.

I juggled being in London with Amanda with trying to make Ibis and my Angolan projects work. I found my friendship with Tony coming under strain. We saw little of each other. When we did speak, often we were nit-picking. I felt in my gut that something was wrong with our business: with Andy Smith and the mining.

Tony and Michael never refused Smith's ever-growing calls for money, men, machines. At the same time, I felt my Angolan projects – the source of our revenue – squeezed and squeezed again. It was torture.

One afternoon, while sitting at a desk in my room at the Tivoli in Luanda, the phone rang. As I reached for it I was struck by a thought. Luanda now felt like home. My actual home in Portobello Road felt like a small hotel that I went to for brief holidays.

I picked up the receiver. Michael. It was always Michael Grunberg these days, never Tony. I couldn't remember when Tony last phoned me. Last came to Luanda.

'Hi, Michael. Luanda customer services speaking. How can I help you?' I asked, with sing-song insincerity.

'Simon – hi. Tony asked me to call you straight away: Andy Smith has been killed, and his wife. We don't know what happened exactly. I'm flying to Entebbe right now. They were in a light plane – just taken off – headed for the concession. I'll keep you posted…'

I was stunned. I knew Smith quite well. I hadn't liked him.

Andy and his wife, flown by a local pilot, had taken off from Entebbe. They were headed for the concession in the north-east corner of Uganda, near the borders with Sudan and Kenya. Hemingway Africa. This had been Smith's favourite concession. That had annoyed me: the concessions were held to make money; not for safari.

The area of the concession was unspoilt and beautiful. The mining exploration camp had been described to me as the best mining exploration camp, without any mining or exploration, ever seen. My spy for this titbit had been a hugely experienced South African mining consultant.

The aircraft, a single-piston-engine Piper, had taken off from Entebbe overweight, as per Andy's habit. Branch Minerals had often used the same company, same aircraft, same pilot. All the company, aircraft and pilot paperwork was in order. Five minutes into the flight, the pilot had radioed a loss of power. Apparently he decided to try to ditch in one of the creeks leading off the main lake, Lake Victoria.

It then seemed as if he had changed his mind and tried for a forced landing. He hit a power line. Crashed into the ground. Caught fire. The fuel tanks were full. Andy's wife was a non-swimmer and hated water. Possibly that had caused the fatal change of mind. All three occupants were killed.

Everyone was shocked. Then Michael asked me if I would take over from Smith with all the Angolan mining applications and projects. I was ready for this. I had no wish to take them over, but I had no choice. Who else was going to do it? It was my money being spent.

By good luck, over the previous few months I had made a new friend, Mario Von Haff. This had come about through Ibis Air, since Mario was the king of civil aviation in Angola. Mario had met Smith. When I told Mario our bad news, he looked thoughtful. He then volunteered to help, for an interest, also volunteering his cousin, Gaspar Cardosa. Here my luck doubled. Two better-placed, more helpful Luanda operators it would have been impossible to find.

The three of us went to work. Mario was hugely connected and powerful. Gaspar was a real worker, never defeated by too much paper or too tiresome a bureaucratic procedure: two of Luanda's specialities.

First we adjusted Smith's Angola applications. Amazingly there wasn't a Kimberlite hard rock application. The whole point of Sierra Leone was to get a second hard rock concession, when Smith had failed to properly apply for a first.

Then we set in train the necessary steps to secure the concessions – especially the new applications for the all-important hard rock kimberlites at Luo, in Lunda Norte.

Once these activities were moving forward, I flew to London.

I arrived early at the King's Road offices. I spoke to one of the models, Clare. She had been friends with Stavros. I gently asked her why he'd gone.

She looked at me in surprise, then glanced around. 'No reason really, Simon. Tony was tired of him, that's all.'

Clare had Stavros's forwarding card and gave me a copy. She and the other models were in shock over Smith and his wife. So polite, so charming, a gentleman, they said. I nodded and clucked. So much expense, I thought.

Once Tony had arrived, he, Michael and I sat in his office. I could see that Tony was truly shocked.

'Tell him,' he ordered. Then I noticed: Tony wasn't just shocked, he was embarrassed. So was Michael.

'Simon – Andy was a crook.'

Amazingly, Andy's Apple Mac PowerBook had partially survived the impact and fire. Michael got some hackers to dump off some 70 per cent of Smith's Word and Excel data files. Some strange and interesting correspondence had come to light, the foremost being Andy's letter of resignation from Branch Minerals. This was odd, when so many of Smith's expensive little green shoots were supposedly about to blossom forth.

This had triggered the suspicious instincts of Tony and Michael. They conducted a forensic audit of all Smith's affairs and transactions. To say Smith was a crook was to understate. He was a thief, a fraudster, a con. Michael and Tony were ready for my first question. No, there was nothing on Smith that cast any kind of a shadow over Ian Campbell. Not only that: Campbell's reaction had been such a blizzard of shocked righteousness that he couldn't have staged it.

A civil lawsuit against Smith's estate was being considered. But it seemed that Andy had been spending as fast as he was stealing. Tony then went into Churchillian mode, his Esplendido fully alight.

Branch Minerals would soldier on, notwithstanding the setback.

But I had to pass on my news. I'd done some detective work too.

'You remember how Andy said he was this big Angola diamond expert? And yet how odd it was that he actually spent less time in Angola than he did swanning around those Hemingway camps of his?'

Tony and Michael looked worried. They did remember. They had noticed.

'Well – there is another Andy Smith!'

'What?'

'What do you mean?'

'There is a real Angolan diamond expert – the Andy Smith who everyone knows. He is alive and well and living in Cape Town. Tony – when you did your checking-out of Andy Smith, the feedback you had from Angola referred to the Cape Town Andy Smith, not our one!'

'So who the fuck was our Andy Smith?'

'He must have been another Andy Smith – and used the coincidence to help his scam – maybe – I don't know – unless he was a plant from the start...'

'A plant?'

'Well, if our numerous enemies wanted to have a smack at us, they could hardly have done better – although that just seems too far-fetched ... impossible.'

'Jesus.'

'Now listen – there's one more thing. I don't know how seriously to take this – I'm just passing it on to you. I'm not advising in any sense, OK?'

'Sure, Simon – go on.'

'It turns out a couple of the Ibis boys know the Uganda flying scene really well. You know what a small world it is in Africa, among the pilots.'

'And how...'

''xactly. So they've spoken to one or two people who are plugged. The word is: there's a suspicion of sabotage. It could have been murder. Now, there's no evidence, I know. There won't be. Light plane crash is a common cause of death among African mining exploration companies, and that's a fact... So don't read too much into this. It's just ... well, let's all be careful.'

'Are you saying Andy Smith was murdered?'

'No. I am not saying that. But be careful, that's all. It may have been an accident. I think it was.'

We sat and thought about it. The whole Executive Outcomes and Branch Minerals empire was too stretched and vulnerable. Tony sucked, then blew: the two-stroke Cohiba engine.

'Come on, chaps – let's get the Bentley and go and have lunch somewhere decent!'

Two days later, I was in the King's Road offices, readying to fly down to Jo'burg on the late BA flight, BA 057, that night. Of course, the models had to arrange a car for me: chauffeur and Bentley were busy.

The telephone rang. It was Calvin, one of the best of the Soyo originals, now country manager for Branch Minerals in Angola.

'Simon. We've got shit. I'm in Luanda. The three okes doing the gold exploration in Cabinda: they're missing. Three days now. I'm going up to Cabinda tomorrow. You'd better come here, to Luanda, as fast as you can. The Angolans are being as much use as an ashtray on a motorcycle – as usual. Hopefully I'll sort it, but – well, if they're hostages – if they've been kidnapped by guerrillas or bandits ... then we've got big shit.'

CHAPTER ELEVEN

2004: THE EG COUP

The Spanish election is upon us. The Boss and other investors have at last come up with some money. We can take a low-budget shot. A low-budget, no-fucking-time, long fucking shot. We are going to carry out a coup.

Yet we have no weapons. No men. Everyone has been stood down since before Christmas. Our foot soldiers are not happy. Dicking people around. GO STOP GO STOP has pissed off everyone. But we're ready to take our chances. This is it now.

Niek rejects Plan C – the oilfield support vessel with an Mi-17 support heli flying off the work-deck. He wants to hit Malabo by air only. Just like Soyo: the Afrikaners don't like going in by sea. They don't think 'sea'.

We work up a number of options. Finally we cobble together Plan D at the last minute. Roll the dice.

Plan D spans Africa. The shitholes most crucial to Plan D are also among the most unstable and notorious of the entire continent. Zimbabwe and the DRC.

We will source our weapons for Plan D in Zim. Niek has done business there before. Next: transport.

Niek du Toit still has the Antonov An-12 cargo plane in Malabo, despite the flight of the Il-76. The An-12 is known as the *Herkski* because it's the Russian equivalent of the C-130 Hercules. Less effective, but much simpler and much cheaper. The plan is for the An-12 to fly down from Malabo to Harare. There it will pick up the weapons and the ammo from our suppliers, the government-sponsored Zimbabwe Defence Industries (ZDI).

I shall be on hand in Harare to make sure that the deal goes through smoothly. The *Herkski* will then fly weapons and ammo (plus me) to Kolwezi – a copper-mining airstrip in the southern DRC.

Here Niek is friendly with the Katanga rebels. Niek and I meet them, to do the deal. They will secure the airstrip in return for 18,000 rounds of ammo, AK 7.62mm short. Meanwhile, our South African mercenaries will be flown in to Ndola, where they will refuel. That leg will be flown by the three DC3s.

They will wait at Ndola, for the signal to carry on to Kolwezi. The signal will be given as soon as the strip has been called in 'Secure'. That call will come from one of our old hands, Simon Witherspoon. Up there with the Katanga rebels. Dodging the Interahamwe: murderous Rwandan fighters, drafted in as mercenaries by DRC President Laurent Kabila to fight these Katangese.

The *Herkski* will off-load at Kolwezi. Our men and hardware will marry up. The men can de-box, unwrap, de-grease, clean, oil and test-fire their weapons. They can sort out their kit, share out loads, make ready. Meanwhile the *Herkski* must return to Ndola, to refuel once more. There's no fuel at Kolwezi.

Next, the *Herkski* flies back to Kolwezi. Picks up the men and weapons. We fly into Malabo Airport, EG. It's D Day. It's H Hour. At least this means we are sticking to one of the Golden Rules, as I laid down to Niek at the outset. Men and weapons will only travel together for the last leg: the flight into EG.

Once we get to Malabo, Niek and his team will be waiting for us. They'll have secured Malabo Airport. By stealth. Force, if necessary. They'll have vehicles and drivers ready. They'll take our sub-units to the Key Point targets – the palace, the police station, the army barracks, the bank, the TV and radio station.

The plan is crippled by our lack of dosh.

We haven't got the right aircraft. The only reason we had the An-12 in EG in the first place was to act as a run-about between the island capital, Malabo, and EG's mainland, where the other capital, Bata, lies about 150 miles to the south-south-east.

We're rushing, sure, but here's how broke we are. For the first leg of Plan D, we're sending the *Herkski* north-east – in the wrong direction – to Douala, in Cameroon. We're refuelling in Douala because it's cheaper than in EG. The *Herkski* will then fly south to Harare.

We've chopped great chunks out of the plan. Essential elements. We're rushing. The Boss says it'll be fine. His man in EG says it's so rotten there that we could go in and change the regime with eight men.

My professional instincts are wincing. There's so much we don't control. The key step is for these Katangese rebels to secure the Kolwezi airstrip, but that will be out of our hands.

We don't even know for sure whether or not the *Herkski* can take off from Kolwezi. Some experts – who know the strip, and the performance of the aircraft – say 'No Problem'. Others are not sure. There is even disagreement as to how long the usable runway is. The strip is dirt. It's complex enough at the best of times: pax weights, kit weights, fuel weights, available runway distance, surface, gradient, altitude ASL, air temperature, wind direction and speed ... balls of the pilot...

And we don't even know yet if they'll grant permission for the *Herkski* to refuel in Ndola.

We're sending someone round to bribe the airport officials, with one of the heads of the Katangese rebels.

Then all we can do is hope.

Severo Moto will be based in the Canaries along with Crause Steyl and his Beechcraft King Air 200. Steyl will fly Moto out of there and into Malabo, via Bamako, the capital of Mali, where Crause will refuel. In Bamako, he'll await his GO GO GO signal. Crause is to time Moto's arrival for half an hour after our touchdown in EG. Seat of our pants, wing and a prayer.

At my last meeting with the Boss, before Plan D's execution, I am at last told why he's so blasé about Obiang's defences. He tells me there is to be no fighting at Malabo Airport. Behind the scenes, he has plans of his own. He has set up a separate coup. A palace coup.

Anthony and Mark in South Africa, and the Boss in London, will know what is happening in Harare because we will be in comms with them by mobile phones, voice or texts. But, in any case, I am to signal the Boss when I am finally gear-up and en route from Harare to Malabo.

I will do that on my Iridium satellite phone from the 727 flight deck. We know that works because we have done it often before. As a back-up, we can pass a message to Pretoria by the *Herkski*'s HF SELCAL radio set. Anthony will then pass the codeword to the Boss.

Once he has that signal, then he will send a message to his man inside the palace in Malabo. The plotters inside the palace will then take action. They have the weapons and the support on hand to seize the President, along with any security who stay loyal. They are overthrowing Obiang in his own bedroom. Plan X.

The Boss and I are the only people outside of the palace who are aware of Plan X. I ask him for the names of the plotters within the palace. He refuses to tell me: for their protection. That information will only be supplied to me after I land in EG, along with two other lists: Goodies, Baddies. The palace coup will only be triggered when the Boss is certain that I'm on my way to Malabo, and so is the new interim President, Severo Moto.

Once we get to the palace, the coup should have taken place. A *fait accompli*!

This puts my mind one click easier.

Even so, we may yet meet resistance at Malabo Airport. We still may have to fight.

There's more real and present danger though: the Boss could be bullshitting me. His plan can go wrong. We could yet be flying into an ambush.

And Plan D is still a shonky, cobbled-together recipe, with or without help inside Obiang's palace. Anything can happen.

With just days to go until Plan D, I meet with Mark Thatcher.

In the event of things going wrong in EG, I want Thatcher to come and rescue those of us still uncaptured. I explain to him how he can do this. I have a selection of EG coordinates, radio frequencies, dates and times. All in code.

If it goes wrong, I can relay a time and a place to Thatcher on a pre-agreed radio frequency. Thatcher is a helicopter pilot and a sailor. He can get to the appointed location by chopper or boat, at the appointed time, and pluck us to safety.

But the E&E plan is also a warning to Thatcher. This isn't a game. I'm telling him: if you want to step back, then now's the time to do so.

It's a chance for him to say: 'Stop! I'm an investor … but that's all I am.'

I need Thatcher to decide. Thatcher has the money, and the political connections – in Zimbabwe, South Africa and the UK – to help me, if collared. I need Thatcher to look me in the eye. Tell me what he'll do if it all goes tits up for my team and me.

Will he do all he can for us? Or will he deny us?

The E&E plan is the test.

Thatcher picks up his pencil. He dutifully notes down all of the information as I have in my notebook. He promises he'll help his great friend Simon Mann any way he can, if things go awry. We even shake hands on it. If nothing else, Mark loves to play the officer and gentleman. 'My word is my bond…', etc.

Big time.

We check in to Harare's Cresta Motel. I keep in touch with the other players around the African continent by means of Pay As You Go mobile phones. Every moment I expect the CIO to come crashing through the door.

We have to juggle between Pien, our flight ops coordinator; Simon Witherspoon, with the Katanga rebels in Kolwezi; Niek in Malabo; Gerhard Merz, with the *Herkski*. My PA Anthony is in contact with the South African mercenaries, preparing to fly out of Wonderboom Airport, Pretoria. At the same time, we have to keep others in the picture. Steyl in the Canary Isles. Those in London. Thatcher in Jo'burg.

I get word from Niek on his satellite phone in Malabo. The An-12 has left Malabo on time: for Douala, in Cameroon.

Meantime, I'm trying to get through to Witherspoon in Kolwezi. That's where the Katanga rebels have promised to seize the all-important landing strip. First, they're smuggling Witherspoon into the country. He's taking a massive risk going in there at all.

The DRC is in the grip of a savage and very haphazard civil war. Another one. The Interahamwe would flay him alive. Once there, Simon's got to wait … then: rebels attack. Their payback – ammo. That lands with me in the An-12, on their seized Kolwezi airstrip.

Time passes.

I'm growing concerned about the An-12. It should have landed in Douala. Yet there's no news. I get back in touch with Niek. Why haven't I heard from them? It's now I discover Major Fuck-Up Number One. Niek has sent Merz off in the *Herkski* without a satellite phone. And with very little cash.

Niek's sitting in Malabo with four satellite phones and a bag of cash. What the hell's he doing? How is Merz supposed to get in touch with us if something goes wrong? He may be in Cameroon. He may not. We may never know.

Merz is supposed to let me know when the An-12 leaves Cameroon. Maybe he can still find a way to do this. That will be my cue to be taken to Harare International, to check out the weapons. I will be taken by our ZDI contact, Captain Brodie.

There I will meet up with the An-12, Merz and the crew. Load up. Take off for Kolwezi. That's the plan.

With no word from Merz, I make a decision. I decide not to go to Harare International to wait for them. I want to spend as little time as possible with the weapons in Harare, for obvious reasons. Merz will have to find a way to contact me when they land at Harare, or Brodie will tell me. I can then drive to the airport.

Meanwhile, word from Kolwezi. Witherspoon is at the airstrip. No government forces in sight. Now he just needs to get the rebels ready. When we take off from Harare, I shall send the password. Witherspoon's cue.

Word from Anthony, in Cape Town. The soldiers are on the planes. They have clearance to take off for Ndola. Pien has bribed everyone in sight. There's an elaborate *maskirovka*: they are on their way to do a mining security job up in the north-east of the DRC. The famous Kilo Moto. Solid with gold.

The old Plan B has become Plan D.

They need to fly now. I give them the signal to take off. At least that part of the plan is going smoothly. Once they refuel in Ndola, the South Africans must wait there.

Wait for my Green Light – to fly on to Kolwezi next.

No word from Kolwezi. I need to know from Witherspoon if the rebels are present, armed and ready. I'm trying not to shout. I don't want to shout. Mugabe's Gestapo are never far away.

Me: 'Have you seen our friends yet?'

Witherspoon: 'There's a few here. Not many. They don't seem to know what's going on.'

Me: 'Well, you'd best fucking tell them then. Try to find out where the rest of them are.'

Word from Kolwezi. Witherspoon's voice strained, faint, his satellite-phone signal weak.

Me: 'Have our friends arrived?'

Witherspoon: 'There's just a handful. They don't seem to know we're coming.'

I struggle to sound calm. To remain in code. Inside I'm freaking out.

Me: 'But our friends should be there by now. Where are they?'

Witherspoon: 'No one seems to know. They might still come.'

I hang up. We don't even have the weapons on board the *Herkski* yet. Witherspoon is right. This is Africa. They might still come.

Three hours later. The An-12 should have landed at Harare International an hour ago. I haven't heard a word from Merz. I call our contact within ZDI. I ask Captain Brodie if he can find out if the An-12 has landed at Harare. He says he'll call back.

I'm starting to panic. I decide to take a gamble. The An-12 was supposed to refuel in Douala, Cameroon. I need to call the control tower there. Find out if the An-12 arrived or departed. I spend an age being put through to this and that Cameroon airport worker.

As I'm put on hold for the fiftieth time, another phone rings. It's Brodie. The An-12 hasn't landed at Harare. They've had no word in the tower. Brodie reminds me of the time window.

This sale is over the counter, not under the counter, but Commercial-In-Confidence. Get it? We have been told that the weapons have to be loaded into the plane's hold before 0500.

It's now almost ZERO FOUR BUFFALO (0400 HRS). Where the fuck is Merz?

Word from Witherspoon, Kolwezi.

Me: 'Have our friends arrived?'

Witherspoon: 'Our friends have not arrived. Repeat. Not arrived. There's just a few of our friends here. It just isn't gonna happen to night. Maybe we can risk it with what we've got? There's no government troops.'

179

Me: 'All right. Stand by. Don't leave. Call me every hour, on the hour, OK?'

The An-12 must have been delayed. If it comes to Harare, we can still make this happen. I call Niek. He has the contacts with the Katanga rebels. I tell him to get to work.

Suddenly, it's 0445. Our hotel room is like a steam room. Except the steam is the smoke from a hundred Marlboro reds. I'm seized suddenly by an unnatural exhaustion. I look at Charles. He calls it. 'Come on, Simon,' he says. 'You know what to do.'

I do know. Put the dog down. Plan D goes to Plan Heaven.

My skin feels raw. Like it's been scoured with a Brillo pad. I'm not going to bed until I know what's happened to Merz and the *Herkski*. I won't sleep until I find out. I'm worried about them. I'm worried about Witherspoon. I'm worried about me. I'm also fucking furious. Top priority is getting Simon Witherspoon out. He doesn't know how. Nor do we.

Charles and I get radical. I phone Coebus in bed in Jo'burg. He has no idea of what's afoot. Nothing about the putsch.

He and Calvin have an emerald mine up on the DRC border, Zambia side. Coebus tells me Calvin is at the mine. He'll put him on stand-by, with no idea of what he's standing by for. Coebus doesn't want to know either – not on this phone line.

'Go well, eh?'

Charles and I pore over my trusty Michelin 1:500,000 road map. We measure the bush that Simon has to cover. His best way out may be to leg it to the mine. Then he and Calvin can be *boschbefocked*★ together.

It's after 0700. Word from Merz. Where the fuck have you been?

They're in Mbuji Mayi, in the Democratic Republic of Congo, a serious shithole. Flying out to Ndola, if they can bribe a clearance. They have too little money, so they can't get home.

What the fuck happened to you?

When they landed to refuel at Douala, the An-12 broke its nose-wheel. It's a design weakness. The crew somehow tracked down another *Herkski* crew. They made a deal for the parts, and that cleaned them out of cash. They jacked up the plane on the runway and changed the nose gear, which took hours.

★Delirium induced by too much time alone in the bush.

As they took off again, they ran into overflight clearance problems. Somewhere over the Congo, the An-12 was ordered to land at Mbuji Mayi. The officials there required a bribe to let it leave. They didn't have more money.

Well done, Niek. Had he sent Merz off with a satellite phone and a few thousand dollars, Plan D could have won through.

Later, with not much fuel on board, and after God knows what bribery and corruption, Merz and crew take off for nearby Ndola. They know we have landing clearances there. And that's where they're now stranded. Penniless. They can't get home. There's nothing else for it. I drive to Harare Airport, meet Pien and the Hawker, then tell him to fly us north, back to bloody Ndola.

Simon Witherspoon, by this stage, has saved himself a hike in the bush. He had sweet-talked his rebel hosts and thumbed a lift down to the border, then south.

The South Africans, meanwhile, had landed at Ndola the previous lunchtime. They refuelled, then waited for my signal to fly on to Kolwezi. As I was gleefully told when I made it back to South Africa, the most comic scene of the whole exercise had been the sight of three DC-3s sitting all afternoon on the apron of Ndola International, stuffed with 70 former EO soldiers and their kit.

Farnborough Airshow. The Royal Tournament. Covert? For God's sake!

Then they'd flown home.

2000 ZULU, 25 FEBRUARY 2004: THE INTERCONTINENTAL HOTEL, JOHANNESBURG INTERNATIONAL AIRPORT.

An unusual meeting is taking place. It's the night of our return from failure. From Ndola. Sat at a long wooden table in the garden, lit by gusting flare pots, are the top team. Charles West, Simon Witherspoon, and others. Merz and the An-12, meanwhile, after receiving cash and a bollocking – both from me – have flown back north to Malabo and Niek – the latter having had the cheek to tick me off for binning the Op.

Here too is Sir Mark Thatcher. He's staying at the hotel. His natural caution has been unable to overcome his desire to be truly part of the gang. He's the reason why we're meeting at the hotel. Tonight I'm flying back to Heathrow from here, to see the Boss. The Op needs more money. Fast.

In London, I meet with the Boss and other investors. By now I know that Amanda is pregnant with our fourth child. She and the children are off to Méribel to ski. The hotshot investors don't even feign interest in my war story, the death of Plan D. All they want to know is: are we pushing ahead with another go? To hell with the skiing. To hell with the new baby.

'Jolly good, and all that, Simon... Congratulations! But you are still going ahead as planned, aren't you?'

I want better than that from the Boss, but I don't get it. What's it going to take for me to get that smile? No. No, I do not want a fucking cigar.

The meeting confirms that the Spanish aren't just privy to our plans. They are a part of our plans. The Boss tells me that, days earlier, the Spanish sent two warships on a show-the-flag cruise down to EG. In reality, the ships had been dispatched in support of our Op. The Spanish wanted them there as back-up. In case we needed it.

But he doesn't want this. He doesn't want the promised 3,000 *Guardia Civil* either. He fears that his post-Coup power and authority will be undermined by Spanish muscle.

Anyway, he wanted to do without those Spanish Men O' War. What he did next floored me. His network fed Obiang a story, via a Spanish official, who is a spy for Obiang. On the Obiang payroll. The spy was told that the Spanish warships had been sent as part of a coup plot.

The well was poisoned.

Obiang swallowed it. He openly accused the Spanish of aiding and abetting a coup. The Spanish, rattled, turned the ships around.

For our next tilt at Obiang – Plan E – the Boss comes up with only $200,000. We need another $600,000 – at least. He asks me if I can find more. I've already ploughed $500,000 into the project. My answer is no. The money belongs to Amanda and the children. I have gone too far already.

The Boss offers me a deal. If I put more money into the coup now, then all of my investment thus far – new and old – will no longer be treated as project finance. Instead, every penny of mine ploughed into these operations will be treated as a personal loan.

One of the other investors says he will underwrite this personal loan deal. If the Boss owes me the money, then the money shall be repaid. The debt shall be honoured.

The Boss is desperate for this Op to happen. So desperate that he appears to be growing careless. He offers to use his murky sources. An aircraft. Weapons. He makes the phone calls. Then it becomes clear: these options won't work. Not within our timeframe.

Shortly after the meeting, the Boss and I talk alone. He looks me in the eye. 'Simon ... I don't want you and Niek getting into something that you can't handle.'

He's gotta be kidding. Like getting shot?

I stare back. Now is his chance. If he wants out, he can say so.

If he wants to tell me that he will do nothing to help any of us – if things go wrong – now he can. We'll be on our own.

'You're behind us all the way, aren't you...? If things go wrong, I mean...'

'All the way.'

We shake hands, then hug each other.

'See you in Malabo.'

'Malabo.'

CHAPTER TWELVE

AFRICA: 1997

535 had by now been joined by Tim Spicer, an old Scots Guards friend of mine. Tim had been dying of boredom in the City. Banking. Tony and I rescued him. Tim had two nicknames in the Scots Guards, *Schmeisser* (after the old *Wehrmacht* sub-machine gun) and Tactical Tim.

Tongue in cheek, they tell plenty about Tim.

He knew of the pressure I was under. He knew about the huge amount of money – half of it mine – that Tony and Michael, all of them, had to keep throwing at the mining: that or throw in the towel.

Our mining had been all in one basket, Branch Minerals. Then we took out the diamond plays and assigned them to a Vancouver Stock Exchange-quoted vehicle called Carson Gold. Carson Gold was given a name change, DiamondWorks (DMW), and the company's stock exchange was switched to the more posh Toronto market. Our Luanda friends – brought up staunch Marxist Leninists – were bamboozled by these financial shenanigans. They found them hard to understand. Same here.

Shortly after Andy Smith's death, Tony asked me if I'd become DMW's COOA (Chief Operating Officer Africa). I didn't want to. But I knew that, to make any money out of all this mining, DiamondWorks had to work.

Raising the money, winning the concessions, bringing it all together: this was a beginning, not an end. Tony spelled it out for the team – Tony, Michael, Tim Spicer and me. It was best for everyone if I took on the role of COOA DMW. So I did.

With no training or qualifications, I was suddenly the Boss. The boss of what? On day one, I became the boss of a $20-million budget, and the two main hard rock diamond concessions, Luo (Angola) and Koidu (Sierra Leone), our geologist plus Ian Campbell, assorted workers, assorted machinery. There was no company infrastructure. There were no offices. Most of the key posts were empty.

I fell back on my army training. I sat down and wrote an appreciation. Not a good one, I knew, but it triggered the right thinking. I had to get the two mines built and working or DMW would die. All the time, it was a scramble to find enough money to keep going. The Angola EO contract was finished. Sierra Leone still weren't paying up. More and more capital was going to money heaven.

Always, yet more capital was poured into the other mining projects – Uganda, Tanzania, the gold mines in Angola; yet more into the alluvial diamond concession, Yetwene just north of our Luo area.

Always, our clients – the Angolan MPLA war machine – were being short changed. They knew it too.

They knew it, but had to keep my Op going.

That was because of the goal we scored. Using a paid spy, we found out the exact details of an An-12 cargo flight from South Africa to the still-fighting Savimbi die-hards. We intercepted the flight, in one of our three L-39 fighters, and forced it down into Luanda.

The cargo of weapons was put on show. The crew were given huge jail sentences. Months later, our spy ended up shot – in Miami – through loose talk on his part. The trick was that this incident – we made sure that rumour had it – was put down to the MPLA having a proper border surveillance and intercept capability. Ha Ha.

But – for many months – Savimbi resupply flights ended. One hundred per cent.

We tied in the scoring of that goal with a cheaper way of waging war. Through my flying training, I had learned how the worldwide civil aviation NOTAM system worked. Notices to Airmen.

I asked João de Matos to order his civil aviation authority to post an until–further NOTAM on the international database. Warning that anyone flying into Angolan airspace without proper permissions was liable to interceptions.

The Angolans were surprised at how well this worked. They hadn't realised that even dodgy old An-12 *Herkskis* have owners, bank loans, insurers. A flight that goes against NOTAM can mean invalid insurance. Very worried owners.

Mining was not my natural neck of the woods. Tony came down to Jo'burg to see me. I knew that Tim Spicer was running our next big op: Papua New Guinea (PNG). And doing my old job. Key link man between Tony, the South Africans and the customer government.

The PNG government had sought outside help. They went to Sparky and Co., who thought it too much like Guns For Hire for their brand name. So they had passed it on to us. For commission.

The PNG island of Bougainville (for the great French sailor and explorer) had been overrun by separatist guerrillas. They had killed policemen and soldiers, as well as civilians. They ran the island.

Not surprisingly, the PNG government could not allow a violent and illegal secession *de facto*; their sovereignty was at stake. As if guerrillas were to overrun the Channel Islands, then declare independence.

Desire to return Bougainville to the PNG fold was important for another reason: money. The island is solid copper, and home to one of the biggest copper mines in the world.

The plan was that an EO team, with specialised kit, would train up then lead a strike force of the PNG Armed Forces in a mission to bring Bougainville into line. In the meantime, Tim Spicer became such a close confidante of the Prime Minister Sir Julius Chan that he made him his senior defence adviser.

Well done, Tim.

The difficulty was that this love affair put out of joint the nose of the old adviser, a PNG national, Jerry Singirok who also happened to be the Commander of the Armed Forces. So out of joint was Singirok, that he locked up all the South Africans. And Tim Spicer. And the Prime Minister. The General staged a Coup d'État. The fallout from this was widespread.

We failed to make a great deal of money. Not least because we had arranged share options such that, at our call, we could take over the copper mining company that held the Bougainville concession.

Later, Tony and Tim were to fall out badly. Tim was to go on to set up Aegis, later to become the main Private Military Company (PMC) in post-invasion Iraq. But that was later. Tim was to have further adventures from within the Buckingham stable before he bolted.

When Tony came to see me in Jo'burg, the PNG op was getting started. I told Tony that I should be doing it, not Tim. He asked me to carry on with the mining. His argument was that, while it would be better if I did PNG, nobody else on the team could do DiamondWorks. It was the team pension fund. I may have been 50/50 with Tony, but he was the father figure. I agreed.

In the meantime, I had been stretching my brain about our mining strategy. The DMW money was sure to run out, so we would have to go back to the market to beg for more. That begging would be met with scorn. Unless we had defied all the doubters and nay sayers by bringing the mines into production. The Koidu, in Sierra Leone. The famous Luo Mine, in Lunda Norte, Angola. On the Chicapa river. Tributary of the Kasai. The tail of Conrad's Congo River dragon.

Tall order. Here were two mines in what were very recent war zones. Zero infrastructure. Luo is over 1,000 miles from Jo'burg; Koidu, in Sierra Leone, four times that.

We attacked it with all we had: me and my crew of about 100 full-time employees, and some 200 local part-time workers. Sure enough, we ran out of money. But thanks to this amazing bunch of people, we were able to go back to investors and raise more.

That was because the Koidu Kimberlite in Sierra Leone, and the Luo mine in Angola, had been successfully brought into production – on time and on budget.

One of Andy Smith's wilder applications had been for gold-exploration licences deep in the Cabinda rainforest. There had been an old Portuguese hard rock mine up there. This, Smith said, was a sure sign. (Something that I now know to be bullshit. More likely a sure sign that the old mine failed.)

EO veteran Calvin had been our man in Angola. After all the usual labyrinthine negotiations, arrangements and bribery, Calvin sent in a three-man team to make an exploration for alluvial gold. Not the old mine.

The three men – two ex-EO plus one crazy Yugoslav mining

engineer – oversaw the work. They were sub-contractors to Branch Minerals, not employees. Local hired labour (not slaves) did the digging.

They delved out 1 x 1 x 1 metre pits, according to a sampling plan. The miners then processed the gravel over a portable sluice box, tilted, watered and covered in artificial turf to catch the gold. According to the Cape Town Assay Laboratory which was testing the samples, it had been going extraordinarily well.

Then the three men vanished.

Calvin had known he must pay a security fee – or tax – or deposit – or squeeze – to keep the guerrillas at bay. The guerrillas in Cabinda were FLEC. FLEC had been quiet since the November 2004 ODAB ceasefire. FLEC were still there, nevertheless.

What had gone wrong was typical. So typical that Calvin blamed himself. Under the agreement to mine in Cabinda, Branch Minerals had been obliged to joint venture with a local company. This outfit had mysteriously popped up on the Ministry of Mines concession map, from nowhere, after the Branch Minerals applications had been made. Calvin had been paying protection money to the boss of that company. He was the brother of the Governor of Cabinda. The far-off cousin, more likely. Nonetheless, he was well known. It turned out that this man had been trousering the protection money. Keeping it for himself. So no protection. *Nada*.

Calvin called me in London. 'If they've been kidnapped by guerrillas or bandits … then we've got big shit…'

Days later, Calvin and I met in Luanda. The Tivoli.

Calvin was beside himself with worry. Also anger. I bought the beer, then dinner, as he told me about the three kidnapped men. The man in charge was an old Yugoslav miner, Tadek. With him, one of the original Soyo crew, Jannie de Beer. The third miner was a black EO trooper, Rusty. Calvin had to do everything and anything, for Jannie. Yet again I was taken aback by the iron loyalty of these Afrikaners.

The other two? 'Well, Simon, maybe … when we get Jannie out, eh?'

On hearing about their disappearance, Calvin had immediately travelled to Cabinda. What a nightmare. Officialdom were in denial: it was as if the three hostages had never existed. Our partners in Luanda could do nothing. The official line was: the Angolan government do not approve of the paying of ransoms for kidnapped mining personnel.

AFRICA: 1997...AFRICA: 1997...

With the Angolan security forces toothless – especially in the outpost enclave of Cabinda – we must somehow sort this out ourselves.

But how?

Calvin and I made a decision. I should cover Luanda and Cabinda itself, meaning official Cabinda. I had connections there, influence, since the battle for Soyo. Surely I could make something happen. In the meantime, Calvin would try to worm his way into the FLEC hierarchy. If FLEC is behind this, then we need to start making connections to senior members.

That we had heard nothing from FLEC was not a good sign.

Not long after that, Calvin and I met again, this time in Jo'burg. I confirmed what Calvin had suspected. Despite my connections in Cabinda and Luanda, I could make nothing happen. All I'd encountered was arse covering. Shoulder shrugging.

We were left with one option – to open a dialogue with FLEC. If they weren't the kidnappers, they'd know who were. So: I had to track down someone – anyone – connected to FLEC.

FLEC had reps in Brazzaville and in Kinshasa, and something in Paris. I got Paris. Days after Calvin's arrival in Brazzaville, he was arrested. Acting suspiciously. Hanging about with undesirables. In fact, the security services of Brazzaville were aware of Calvin's mission. He had briefed them. He had paid them off. So why had they arrested him?

To get Calvin released, Tony sent a new DOG recruit to Brazzaville. Mark Cullen (MC) was the former British Ambassador to Mozambique, and ex-MI6. He arrived a few days later on our HS 748 turbo prop private jet (ex-RAF Queen's Flight – going cheap) with three crew members.

The arrival of MC fuelled the Brazzaville Police. Within a day, MC and his entourage were also arrested and the aircraft impounded. Full marks, Chief Inspector. Police took their passports, placed them under arrest, but let them remain in their hotel, under armed guard. 'Tennis arrest', the models called it. As days drifted by, their incarceration in a five-star hotel gave me a fresh headache. A load of money.

Then, after two weeks of this, Calvin, MC and the crew were released. The UK Foreign Office had stepped in: arresting ambassadors, even ex-spook ambassadors, simply isn't on.

Again I met Calvin – again in Jo'burg.

Calvin told me why they'd been arrested. He had paid the bent police too much. The Brazzaville security services decided, if Calvin's visit to Brazzaville was this important, then they could extract more money. When MC turned up with aircraft and crew, then it must be Christmas.

Meantime, Calvin and I had come to the same conclusion: FLEC existed, but FLEC did not exist. Our sources weren't wrong about FLEC having people in Paris, Brazzaville and Kinshasa. And probably in other places too. They were taxi drivers and such like who, along with scratching out a living by any means that came to hand, claimed, if it looked like a good move, to be FLEC officials.

They were FLEC. They weren't FLEC. Money in it. No money in it.

However Calvin's Brazzaville odyssey hadn't been a complete waste of time and money.

Before his 'tennis arrest', Calvin had met some tough operators in Brazzaville. Gangsters. These men claimed that they could find out – for sure – which village head was holding our three hostages. They asked to be go-betweens.

I sent Calvin back to Brazzaville to explore this new route. Of course, the go-betweens would need to be paid. Of course the whole thing had Fucking Dangerous written all over it.

Days later, the men told Calvin they'd made contact with the village head. He was, and was not, a FLEC field commander. He had demanded $10 million per hostage. I burst out laughing. I told Calvin to go back and talk some sense into them.

After days of haggling, the village head and the go-betweens settled for a payment of $600,000: two hundred grand a scalp.

That pushed the cost of our ten-week hostage nightmare to over $1 million. There was only one place this money could come from. Mine and Tony's pockets. I had spoken to Amanda because it was her money too. She instantly said we must pay. Tony asked me if we really had to pay but he knew as I did: there was no other option. For us to mount a hostage rescue into Cabinda was too much. What else could we do? We paid.

We scrambled the money together, then talked it out of my bank in Monaco. We had to get a letter out of the Foreign Office, one which underwrote our account of the story, and said that the purpose of so much loose change was to save these three lives.

AFRICA: 1997...AFRICA: 1997...

We flew the money under guard to Calvin. Bravely, Calvin then made a truly desperate, worse-than-Hollywood 4x4 journey through torrential rain, in tracks swollen to rivers, expecting at any moment to be robbed and killed. Sitting on top of $600,000 in cash.

Calvin returned with the three hostages. Just. They were in bad shape. We arranged a get-together in Jo'burg. They had been tied to a tree the whole time. They were fed scraps and drinks that villagers dropped off for them when they felt like it. The village that had captured and held them didn't care, said the hostages. A ransom or three corpses. So what?

On the evening of our reception party, Rusty, the black trooper, broke down in tears to me, saying thank you. He told how his village captors had said that, while his bosses might pay a ransom for the two whites, they'd never pay for a black. After a while he had believed them.

Shortly after the drama of the three hostages, Calvin and I spent an evening together in Luanda, swapping yarns. It turned out that Calvin and his wife, Mary, had both been operators in London for the notorious CCB.

The CCB had been a government-sponsored hit squad during the Apartheid era. They had carried out illegal operations – including murders – under the authority of Defence Minister Magnus Malan. In London, the CCB had tasked Calvin and Mary to sabotage the ANC.

Then Calvin and Mary were only pretending to be man and wife, as part of their cover. They had lived in London. I told him how I too used to live in the same area of London. With a lovely Scots girl called Susan.

How times change, I laughed: I could remember Susan and I going to the enormous Free Nelson Mandela pop concert at Wembley stadium, just down the road. We had laughed when a West Indian next to us in the crowd had turned round and asked, 'So when's this Nelson bloke coming on, then?'

Calvin looked sadly at his beer, then took a swig.

'Jeez, Simon, we were fucked over by that concert, eh?'

I was puzzled. Calvin thought. Then he spun the yarn.

'We thought we could make money, something we were always being told we should do, as well as disrupt that concert, which was obviously a big money raiser for the ANC. We thought we could achieve both missions by flooding the market with forged tickets.'

'How did you go about doing that?'

'We made the right connections, with the East End gangsters. The tickets, you may remember, Simon, were very high quality: hard to forge. Jeez! We paid out £30,000 – that's a farm, eh? – to have the printing plates made. The forgeries would have been perfect replicas. Perfect.'

Calvin went quiet again.

'What happened?' I prompted.

'We never saw them again. Those bastards. We never saw them, the money, the plates, the tickets: ZERO. They took us for such a ride.'

I didn't try to disguise my delight at this outcome. I loved the story – just as I hated the idea of their Afrikaner thuggery going on back there in Blighty.

We drank a couple more beers and told a few more stories that night. But there was one thing Calvin said that shook me. In a pause, Calvin frowned, then spoke.

'We weren't meant to free those three, the three hostages.'

'What do you mean?'

'Well – think about it. If you take hostages for money you set the thing up to get the money. You keep your assets healthy. You keep them alive.'

'So what, Calvin? I mean – so what are you saying?'

'I dunno. It bugs me. I can't put my finger on it exactly, Simon.' Calvin looked up at me. His frown sterner, worried.

'Naah – look, Simon. I dunno. I've thought about this. You know – CCB, and all that shit – you start thinking that everything's a conspiracy, because you yourself do nothing but conspire! Know what I mean?'

'I can see that – sure. Maybe you become paranoid. But maybe you need to be paranoid.'

''xactly, Simon. Now: these hostages. I can't put my finger on any one thing – but I tell you this: I have a feeling that the real plan was that those guys should die, should never have been rescued: that somebody paid that village head to take them, and make it look like a kidnap. If those hostages meant a big fat pay day, then the villagers would have been looking after them really well. The men would be no value to them dead.'

'Who would want to do that, Calvin? What would be the point?'

'Come on, Simon. Who wants us to fuck up, here, in Angola? Fuck up things with our operations, our employees, with the locals, our partners, the ministries, the government? Who?'

'You mean a big bad mining company who wished the names of EO and Branch had never been? Never been near Angola, at least?'

''xactly, Simon. 'xactly.'

Calvin was far too tough, too highly trained, too experienced to say what he had said accidentally, unguardedly, without meaning to say what he had said. Calvin's bothersome worry, upon which he had been unable to put his finger, was more than that.

Or he wouldn't have mentioned it.

I didn't want to inherit Stav's mantle as the Grim Prophet in Chief. But I decided I must at least tell Tony and Michael of Calvin's observations.

Tony was bullish: 'But what difference does it really make? If we found out that Andy Smith was murdered, and this kidnapping an organised attack on us, then ... so what? What are we going to do? Stop? Go home? Nope... Damn the torpedoes.'

SEPTEMBER 1997

I knew my life was at one of those major crossroads. Take this turn. Or that. You don't know where either will lead. All you know is that they are going to be very different.

Meanwhile, Tony and I had entered the Peking to Paris motor car rally. We would be one of 94 classic and vintage cars. 33 days' driving, 14,000 kilometres: China – Inner Mongolia – Tibet – Nepal – India – Pakistan – Iran – Turkey – Greece – Italy – Austria – Germany – Paris. Then home. In time, I hoped, for the birth of our new baby. Our number two.

Of course, Tony and I had been better friends eight months earlier when we'd submitted our entry. That was before we were really pissing one another off. Since then, things had become more tense. This would be a test. This was our 40 days and 40 nights in the desert. This could break us up. Forever.

Instead, when we crawled into Paris, the only breakdowns had been mechanical. Our Aston Martin DB 5 (Bond's car, in fact) had survived: four deserts, the highest rally checkpoint ever (the Tango La, Tibet, 17,000 feet) in the Himalayas, river fordings, mobs of thousands, Pakistani truck drivers, oily Customs and Immigration.

Lahsa. Kathmandu. Delhi. Lahore. Quetta. Esfahan. Tehran. Istanbul. Thessalonika. Patras. Ancona. Rimini.

Searing heat, freezing bloody cold, passes closed by rockfall, a crash, several engine failures. Perversely, our friendship had thrived – the endless shift driving brought us together. Short of sleep, revolting hotel rooms, food so bad we would sit out in the car park while I brewed up our compo rations.

One day – back in China – I carelessly spun the car on a greasy bend. Tony wasn't kind. I got out: 'You fucking drive.' He showed me his technique. We drove another ten minutes. He spun the car. I said nothing. He said nothing. The car shook with gagged laughter. The car – like us – grew ragged, smelly, knackered. Like us, our Aston was quickly stripped of status. Stripped of ego. Stripped of its brash, shiny exterior.

When Amanda saw it creep into the Place de la Concorde on 18 October, 1997, she cried. 'Oh my God, what have you done to that beautiful car?' She remembered the car from three months previously: immaculate, gorgeous, ready to be shipped to Beijing.

The rally helped us to find our friendship again. We stopped acting like arseholes. We got on. I started to remember what great company Tony could be and why I loved him like a father.

Better still, I got home in time for Lilly's birth.

Next, as COOA DMW, I bade farewell to Angola. Then Sierra Leone. I decided to say goodbye personally to the DMW crew at the Koidu mine, and to the Koidu Mayor, his clients and the admen. Tomorrow: England.

The day before, I said my goodbye to President Kabbah. It had been tense, my meetings with Kabbah always were. But this one more so. I had been briefed that Kabbah had decided to scrap the last EO remnant in SL: the 30-man Presidential bodyguard team.

Kabbah had been persuaded to save the money and expunge the memory of EO – perhaps so that the little children of Sierra Leone could be fed a more palatable, patriotic, version of their recent history.

As I flew in Bokkie from Freetown to Koidu, I asked myself if I would tell the Mayor and the people the news that the last of EO were leaving for good. Months earlier, when the news had spread that Kabbah was to pull out the bulk of the EO force, this Mayor and his townspeople had tried to put together money in order that they could pay for the whole of EO to stay on.

AFRICA: 1997...AFRICA: 1997...

The people had been frantic. Their fear was a return to lawlessness and of the barbaric RUF. For them, EO was Hobbes' Leviathan – security.

As Bokkie settled into a cloud of dust blown up by her rotors, I decided to duck telling the Mayor that Kabbah was sending the last of EO home. Incredibly, I knew that those 30 men, seen as an icon of EO, had been enough to deter the RUF.

A day earlier, as politely as possible, I had told Kabbah of the folly of his decision. I warned him that, if the RUF were sure that EO had really gone, then they would be back in Freetown in a hundred days.

Back home, in Cape Town – *Kaapstad*, the boys would say – I watched with horror as the RUF rolled towards the sea. Freetown. I had been wrong about 100 days. They were there, but in 98.

Kabbah had flown. The shit.

CHAPTER THIRTEEN

MARCH 2004: ZIMBABWE

My knees are wet in the sand.

My hands are steel-cuffed behind me. The cuffs wrench my shoulders back, my neck and head forward.

I smell the river water. I can smell my death, even though I don't believe in it.

They say they're going to shoot me...

'Are you afraid?' 'Are you brave?' 'How tough are you?' 'Do you think you are tougher than a black man?' 'Do you think you are better because you are white?' 'Who knows where you are?' 'How long will it be before anyone misses you?' 'What can they do to help you – here in Zimbabwe?' 'Are you ready to die?' 'Would you like us to kill you – or shall we wound you ... leave you for the crocodiles to finish you off?'

I guess that even if they do shoot me I still won't believe it.

'Please kill me first – don't leave me to the crocodiles...' I say it, but to myself. Not to them.

Am I scared?

Yes.

Click. Click.

They laugh.

They order me to stand up, then kick me and pull me up. They chuck me back into the car. I'm slow and awkward so they laugh, then curse.

197

MARCH · 2004 · ZIMBABWE...

I'm not as tough as a black man. My hands behind my back make any movement hard. They need another drink. They're bored now – and tired. Danger.

The car is turned around. Cack-handed. A small victory.

I remember how I was once trained that – with Africans – if you are their prisoner, then the big thing is to be strong for 24 hours. After that they'll start to like you. But maybe I read that.

My mind clutches at another straw: the Boss. If anyone has the experience, the knowledge, the African clout, the money, to help us – it is him. This is his show anyway, even if he isn't here.

He'll help me. Mark Thatcher...? The same.

We bump back up the sandy track, climbing slightly, the river behind us.

The rain is lighter now. Our car finds a shabeen. By the light of one oil lamp I can just make out the shapes of wrecked humans sprawling around the stoop. They couldn't care about anything – just shuffling out of the way of the bullies.

After my guards and driver all have a swig from their new-bought bottle in a brown-paper bag, we set off. The car smells vile. Stale sweat and rank liquor.

My arms and shoulders cramp. When I shift to ease them, I get a dig in the ribs with a 9mm.

An argument breaks out. They are speaking *Shona*. Are they arguing about killing me? The driver rules. It's his car. He wins. Our course becomes less erratic. There is somewhere we are headed towards ... then we come to it. Halt.

A poorly lit house... No, it's a police station.

Sunday night, but it's business as usual. We're in the Sunningdale Police Post, a notice tells me. A crowd of arrests are being written up. A cartoon notice on the wall hooks my eye: it's a poster from the United Nations Refugee Agency, the UNHCR.

Beatings Are NOT to be a Part of Police Work.

In the corner nearest the cartoon, a boy is being kicked and beaten by two khaki-uniformed officers.

I'm roughly forced to sit on the floor. My handcuffs are unclasped. I'm told to hand over my boots, socks and belt, and watch. All my other stuff has already been taken. Stupidly I think about Brodie's $20,000.

MARCH · 2004 : · ZIMBABWE . . .

My cuffs back on, I watch from the wooden-board floor. My drunken captors and the proud khaki-clad owners of this wooden Good Old Days cop shop painstakingly write my goods down in their property book. Then they fill out the sergeant's desk book.

Dixon of Dock Green. Gone wrong.

Two men in civvies haul in a third. In tatters. They come through a back door. Throw their quarry into a small cell to one side. The two men won't look at me – which is odd because all the others – officers and civilians – look at nothing else. They pull open a steel locker. From there they take out two strips of what look like the off-cuts of lorry fan belt, each about two feet long.

The strips are just right for beating some poor bastard to death. The young man they just hauled in lies on his back, holding up his legs and bare feet. The two plainclothes men take turns to lash into his soles with their fan belts.

Screams. The door is left open. For me.

Other prisoners come to carry the crying man out through the same back door. The plainclothes men follow, at last giving me a telling look as they go. Their clothes – jeans and leather jackets – are new but of poor quality. Like their government.

After half an hour of the man's screams and cries ringing in my memory, the pair come back for me. The soles of my feet tingle. They drag me up – one aside – their hands under each armpit – then run me out of the back door.

Are all policemen drunk on a Sunday night? I can smell hooch again.

Outside is dark. Even the dim light inside the police station blinds me to the night. There are a few weak yellow streetlights dotted around here or there, but I can't see.

My feet are bare but they run me – shouting – across rough ground until I smash into a rock, then fall. They kick. One holds my shoulder down while the other strikes me in the face.

'You're not tough, Mann... Tomorrow you'll see. We are tough. Tomorrow you must tell us the truth.'

A uniformed police officer opens the steel door of a low, square blockhouse, 20 yards behind the police station. The goons take off my handcuffs and shove me inside. The door slams behind me. Outside they laugh as they shut the padlock.

There is no light in the blockhouse. Faint yellow light from a streetlamp slips in through a small, rectangular opening, high on the wall opposite the door.

I stand still by the door. My eyes and ears strain. There are people in the blockhouse. Quite a few. It's a 'tank': a police holding cell. A voice comes from my right.

'Here – there's a place here.'

I look – see nothing – but take a small step, kicking someone on the leg. Slowly I feel my way to where I think the voice has come from. Slowly my eyes are seeing.

I lie down between two men. One is unconscious, the other the voice. Something sticky wet runs over the filthy concrete floor. With some wriggling, space is made for me. So I lie in it.

In my shock and shame I think I won't sleep. I can't. Then, when I'm fast asleep, come shouts: 'Mann, Mann, wake up! *Handei!* Come here!'

In a daze I go to the door, frantic not to kick my fellows. A torch scores my sight.

'You better tell the truth. We're gonna see how tough you are.'

Every 30 or 40 minutes they come for me. I've no watch, but I'm sure. It goes on through the night. On one of these calls, two of them take me out. They beat me up, punching and pushing me to the ground, then kicking me.

Again they threaten me with beatings, again telling me to tell the truth later that day.

The light of first morning as a prisoner creeps into the tank. I now see what I should have guessed – that the wet on the floor is blood, now dried and sticky. The man on one side of my space has grubby bandages around his head that have failed to do their job.

There's no need for me to ask him how he has been beaten. I feel humiliated, but in a good way – humble: I am one of these men now. My instinct tells me that last night was how it is: I'm one of them. We'll look after one another as best we can.

The thought is a lifeline, because I have to fight against the need to bash my head against the wall. The thought of the pain that I am about to bring upon Amanda and the children is too much to shoulder. Then there is the pain of what my life will now be like, maybe for the rest of it.

Suddenly comes the sound of singing. It is not an African sound, but men in strict unison. A European sound. The man next to me answers my surprise: it is the police shift change. The officers coming on duty sing the Zimbabwe National Anthem. Of course they do.

Next there is a kind of tarts' beauty parade. We go outside into a pig-fence dog run. CID officers look us over – to see if anyone they fancy has been pulled during the night.

We stand or sit outside in the dirt while this unpleasant-looking bunch of about half a dozen men ogle us from the other side of the fence. They all look thuggish: more leather jackets. They look as if they have money.

They have money because they take bribes, same as everyone else in Zimbabwe. What is the point of any post in Zimbabwe, if not for bribes? The salary is going to feed nobody.

There is nothing to drink or eat for me. Others have had food brought by their family. One man tries to give me food. The officers scream at him not to.

Back inside our shit tank.

The latrine is a hole in concrete, in the corner. It doesn't flush. There's no paper. Piss and shit cover the concrete. The stench is terrible. My stomach has turned to a runny porridge. I badly add to the stench.

Slowly – one by one – most of my overnight companions go. Where or exactly how, I don't know.

I must try to escape. I know from my training that a principle of escape is that it will only get harder.

Escape. The one door is padlocked on the outside. The hinges are on the outside. The small opening in the wall, the one that lets in all the light, is small, heavily barred. High up.

Outside there is the wire-mesh dog run, except that the mesh also covers the sky. There is no way out of the run other than the gate. Whenever we are in the run we are heavily guarded.

All the time a thought careers around my head: the rest of my life will be spent as a prisoner of Mugabe. Hard labour. I try not to think of the pain that I'm going to cause Amanda and Freddy, but can't. There are the two lovely little girls, Lilly and Bess, and the child unborn, that Amanda had told me of days before. Made in Cape Town that Christmas. Made with love.

Within the maelstrom of sorrow and anger that swirl around my thoughts and feelings – Amanda, home, the children – I have two clear priorities. First, I must give Niek du Toit and the others with him in EG a chance to escape. That means time: 24 hours. Then, second, I must do the best I can to protect the other 69 men. They must also have been arrested last night.

Niek has an aircraft with him, the An-12 that let us down so badly on Plan D, a fishing boat, the FV *Rosalyn*, and a couple of rubber boats. He must have word of what has happened to us.

The team back in South Africa must have realised we'd been arrested when we lost comms with them. Niek and crew should have had time to get away. Niek has friends in São Tomé. They could escape to there.

At mid-morning a strange-looking white man with crutches and one leg comes in. He's a crook, for sure. Likely a stool pigeon.

Ten minutes after he comes in, an officer comes to take his crutches. The man shouts and screams but the crutches go. Now he has to crawl and hop around in the filth.

I learn that my space in the tank is all-important. How thankful I must be to the kind man of last night. The two corners on the same wall as the door are the best spaces. The corner diametrically opposite the door has the latrine built into it, while the one on the far side, opposite the door, is too close to the latrine's mess.

The corner closest to the door has the door right on it, so is liable to see aggro in the night. That is where I will end up in all the tanks. I am the aggro.

I see that everyone wears their clothes inside out. Later I find out that this is their way of trying to keep their clothes clean, the outers at least. They don't have others.

When they are taken from the tank, they frantically strip, pull their shirts and trousers back the right way, then slip into them once more.

My lack of food and water, the sleep deprivation, never knowing the time, the beatings – the beating demos upon others – are all part of the pre-interrogation softening-up process. I don't need SAS Combat Survival training to tell me that.

It is torture, by any modern definition. I know that from my time as a soldier in Northern Ireland. Tactical questioning, sensory deprivation – African style.

The man with crutches tells me that, if I agree to pay to get him out – that is, pay US$3,000 back to the company that has accused him of theft – he will pay off the station sergeant. I will walk.

I never find out if such an escape could work.

A uniform comes to the tank, takes me out and handcuffs me. He leads me to a small and bare wooden shed, smelling of creosote, in which I have to kneel.

Without ado, two CIO beat me up with punches and kicks. I try to cover the bits that would hurt the most. It comes as a shock, but I know that they're pulling their punches. If they want to really hurt me, then they could. Their questions are as poor as their kicking, so I stick to our cover story. We were on our way to provide security at a gold mine in Kilo Moto in the northern DRC.

I ask over and over to see a lawyer. They laugh at me: 'This is Zimbabwe! If we get you a lawyer, then he's our lawyer. You can't escape us with lawyers.'

They don't believe the DRC story – not one word. Strangely, though, their questioning stays around the DRC. How often have I been there? When was I there last? Who were my contacts there?

'Tomorrow you will tell us the truth, Mann. Think about what will happen if you don't.'

'Tomorrow I want a lawyer.'

'Forget it, Mann. Think about what we've said.'

I think about it, sitting on the filthy concrete. Why were they so limp-wristed? My one small hope is that there has been a muddle between ZDI and their chiefs. That this would be sorted out. We would be set free. That hope had started small, then shrank. By the second night it is gone.

I watch as the tank fills up with that night's shift of grubby wrongdoers. I'm an old sweat now, with my own corner space by the door. My fellow prisoners are cheerful and friendly.

That night my diarrhoea, my shock of capture, lack of food and water, and sleep deprivation all make me dizzy. I cannot not sleep but, whenever I do, there they are:

'Mann! Mann! Get up! Come here! Quickly. Quickly. Come to the door. *Handei! Handei!*'

This happens every half-hour or so. Sometimes they make me go right out and into the dog run. Other times I go to the door and that is all. When they take me into the run, they kick and punch me.

One time I go out and they order me to do press-ups. When I ask the time they laugh. They keep harping on skin colour. Are you as tough as a black? Are whites better than blacks? How do you like being a prisoner with Africans? Do black people bother you? Do you think blacks smell? Do you think you smell better than blacks?

Sometime morning comes. The Anthem is sung with gusto, then we parade in the dog run, to see if CID want any of us strays. There is no food or water for me. Most of my fellows have visitors who give them food. Everyone seems very poor, and so is their food. When any of them try to give me food they are shouted at.

The next shout for me will signal the next beating – the next load of questions. Niek has had his chance by now. If he has not escaped already, then he too is a prisoner. Now I must try to help the 69 with me. They, I believe, are already undergoing questioning with violence. Torture.

Finally, they come to take me to questioning, and not just to wake me. On the way, two goons take over from the two uniforms that took me out of the tank and handcuffed me.

'Tell the truth today, Mann – or we'll kill you…' And so on. They're tedious. Unoriginal.

In the smelly little garden shed a new shift is on, and the stakes are higher. In fact, three new shifts are on, so the shed is crammed full. They push me in. A small space is clear for me on the floor, in the middle. I sit: hands cuffed, barefoot, unshaven, stinking, beaten up and scared. My stomach is water, and has been for two days now.

There must have been 12 men around me. There's something comic: so many squashed into this shed, all so purposeful, each with his notebook and pencil. I sense that there are different agencies here, not all with the same agenda: probably army, police CID and CIO.

What's wanted, and why, is put to me loud and clear. My crew in South Africa have all been arrested. They've been given the chance to turn state's evidence. They've all taken it. They are talking as hard and as fast as they can.

My 69 men, being held in Zimbabwe, are being questioned vigorously. Some are talking, others not. It's up to me: I can tell them the truth, or they can beat it out of me. And they can beat it out of the men with me.

MARCH · 2004 : · ZIMBABWE...

For form's sake we go around the houses yet again – about my need for a lawyer. I ask. They refuse. Despite everything, I know enough to know that without a lawyer, this is duress. Worthless as evidence in a fair trial.

I also know enough that, around here, fair trials are UN Red List endangered. Like the wide-mouthed toad.

That's for another day. I have a higher priority: my 69 men held here in Zimbabwe. If I tell these goons the story, there will be no need to torture them.

I tell them about Plan E: our mission to oust Obiang and replace him with Severo Moto.

Then we go round and round. They try to catch me out. They become angry, and then, when they think they have caught me out, violent. We go round and round small details. Each of the dozen or so men squashed into that little hut needs his shout. Most of those men don't speak English well. The services present – CIO, police, army – show off to one another.

Suddenly the questioning stops. Thinking that I'm going back to the holding tank, I'm surprised to be put into a car. Once again I squash into the back seat between gun-toting heavies.

I miss my friends from the tank. I need not have. We soon arrive at another tank, just as bad. With the exact same characters.

My routine doesn't change: the denial of food, water, sleep. The swap, from one police holding tank to another – I realise – is because they are hiding me from the outside world. Thus far I am deniable. They can do what they like with me.

Kill me.

The next day is like the one before: I think that I am to be questioned. The Anthem and dog-run beauty parade are no different. All morning I wait – to be beaten up, then questioned again, while instead they just keep coming every 30 minutes to wake me. Some of them look as tired as I feel.

By now I am thinking again, how am I going to survive this? I think of the Vietnam combat survival stories: US pilots in $1,000 flying suits suddenly at the bottom of a Third World shit heap.

Floreat Etona? Floreat! Florebit!

My mind plays a trick on me. 'You want to speak to so and so? Then phone them, dummy...' I say to myself.

Then: 'No phone. Dummy.'

After two that afternoon, they do come for me again. They surprise me once more by driving me to Manyame Air Base, the military side of Harare International Airport, and our Boeing 727. Here scurry different uniforms, and more plainclothes men, in all directions.

In the chaos I am sat next to our flight engineer. Five minutes later a heavyweight CIO officer sees us talking. The man throws a fit, shouting and screaming and lashing out at underlings. But I have heard from him what I fear: the other whites, Simon Witherspoon, Charles, Lyle, and others, the hardcore ex-EO guys, are having a really rough time.

He has seen one of them being held out of a second-floor window by his ankles. Screaming.

They take me to a room and we start going around and around again – just as we had the day before.

'Why are you torturing the men who were with me?' I ask the man that I had identified as the senior CIO officer. The others shut up while he stares at me.

'Why are we going round and round like this? I've told you the story plainly enough. What more do you think you're going to get out of the others? I'm the senior guy here. Ask me.'

'Will you write out what you told me yesterday? If you'll do that I'll stop what is happening to the others. You can have a Coke, and something to eat as well.'

'Sure – I'll write it out … but do you give me your word … about the others, I mean?'

'You have my word.' His English is perfect, with a slight Zim accent. Stupidly, that makes me trust him, although, as things turn out, I'm right: his word is good. The savagery against the others stops from that point.

With a can of Coke (I've never had better), I sit down and write a bald account of the coup plot. As I finish each sheet, the CIO officer, whose *nom de guerre* is Guava, speed-reads it, grunts, then hands it to one of his men, for photocopying in another room nearby.

These are the old Parachute Regiment ops offices – not changed since the days of the Rhodesian War, when their Fire Force would have been there – when they weren't firing. (The legendary Fire Force helicopter-led counter-insurgency units were first deployed in

Zimbabwe, at that time Rhodesia, in January 1974, to trap and eliminate ZANLA and ZIPRA guerrillas in lightning strikes. Fire Force relied on covert intelligence on the ground to react quickly to enemy ambushes or attacks on farms.)

Later they drive me to yet another police station, Heathfield, and its holding tank. I eat a hamburger and drink another Coke as reward for my efforts. While the writing has been going on so has more questioning. Evasion is pointless. With the others telling all to the SA Police, they already have everything. Now they want it from me.

Whenever I partly tell them something, they know there is more. They want it. When they have all of it, they know that too. They're ticking off what's in front of them already.

CIO officer Guava has all my personal stuff: phone, laptop, notebook, my loose-leaf A4 notebook. He is searching. I thank God that I have used a security program. In Jo'burg I deleted large amounts off my laptop in a secure manner. The program double-overwrote the deleted text. I did it the night before flying up to Zim, two days before my arrest. I had been expecting trouble.

I wished I'd done more.

Guava looks through my loose-leaf notebook – in which is my address book.

'Mark Thatcher – he's in here, Mann. Was he involved in the coup?'

'No.'

'Why is he in your address book then?'

'He's a friend.'

'Only that? No business between you?'

'No. He's a friend – that's all.'

'Are you sure about that?'

'I'm sure.'

'You're lying, Mann.'

He shuts the notebook and walks off. He does not look worried. He knows.

I am lying. I hope to get away with it because Thatcher, although an officer within the Op, does have better cover than anyone else. That cover had been set up precisely because of his high profile – his vulnerability to low-flying shit.

This vulnerability is mostly brought about by his extreme toxicity. It's a toxicity that – in his determination to be *l'enfant le plus terrible* – he does his best to broadcast.

If anyone can pull us out of this Zim mess, it is Mark. He has the connections, to the top and the near top, and the leverage, the money. He has money for them. They'll listen.

Therefore keeping Mark clear of the wreckage is a worthwhile goal. The Boss will make sure Mark does his best for us. The Boss understands leverage.

Next morning there is the same long and frightening wait, but I am getting used to that. They come for me at midday, surprising me yet again.

'You're going on a trip, Mann. How's your French?' asks a goon.

My heart sinks. My arse goes sixpence, half-crown. That must mean Equatorial Guinea, even if they do speak Spanish. Fuck.

My kit and I are bundled into a new but tiny car, a Far East brand that I have never seen before. We drive to Harare International Departures and park outside.

I watch others, free others, going about their travels. I sit in the back, squashed between two goons, filthy in my handcuffs, with leg-irons on and bare feet bruised.

We sit and sit. Other CIO men come and go, all busy on their mobiles.

I can't shake off my fear: I know that if I am taken to EG I will die. They'll put me in a pot and cook me. The goon tells me that the EG President's jet is parked on the other side of Departures. That my reservation is confirmed … e-check-in.

The agony goes on, and then on some more. I watch Guava talk to one of his men. They stand on the pavement not far from our parked car, the windows open because of the heat. My stink. As I guess.

I overhear Guava: '…something's gone wrong. It isn't going to happen today… Take him to the 727 anyway…'

I don't know what that means. I hope that as much as possible is going wrong. We drive again, but this time back to Manyame Air Base. To my Boeing 727, on the other side of the runway from the terminal buildings.

Once there, the diminutive owner/driver of our small car – very bright, very black and very well dressed – points back over to the terminals. I see it and swallow. The President's snazzy private jet.

MARCH · 2004: · ZIMBABWE...

'Looks like you're in luck,' he smiles. 'You're not flying – not today at least – but we've got plenty of other things for you to do – don't worry.'

Still barefoot, still handcuffed and leg-ironed, I am taken over to my 727 then led up the rear stairway and into the aircraft. The familiar racket of the auxiliary power unit howls away. The hold doors are open and a team of Zim Parachute Regiment soldiers are unloading our gear out onto the concrete ramp.

All around the passenger compartment are the bits and pieces of our planning: fast-food packages, some eaten others smelling, lie on the floor. The small kitbags that had been the allowed baggage of each man are still in the now open overhead lockers.

They take me towards the cockpit. There are 15 men in a clump, sitting and perched around the forward-most seats, larger than the rest and Club configured so that the front two rows face one another. One man has a full-size video camera on his shoulder, while others also have cameras and tape recorders. On the floor are my two suitcases.

We start to go through my kit. Every item is logged and filmed. I am asked: 'What is this for? Why are you carrying it?'

A competent-looking Warrant Officer Class One, wearing Zim SAS wings (ha ha ha), is running the show. A show is what it is. I'm asked about the floor mat in my suitcase. I joke: 'I'm over 50 – I shouldn't be lying around on floors!'

'Then you shouldn't be running around doing shit like this, then, should you?' comes the Warrant Officer's reply. I won't be lying on anything other than floors now.

He grabs my Michelin 1:500,000 road map of Africa, and points to Malabo.

'Ha! That's proof of where you were going, Mann.'

'I've told you where I was going ... and look! Here's a map of bloody Paris...'

The money that had been in my silver aluminium pilot's case is gone, of course – US$220,000. The Warrant Officer and the CIO goons are not impressed when I show them another part of the Africa road map. Carefully but casually marked to show our spoof Congo destination. Proof of our cover story. No marks on EG.

At last that ordeal is over. It feels like a rape of me – going through that stuff. It's humiliating – but humiliation, I know, will now be my every day.

They take me down the stairs, then onto the ramp for what's next. Once again I am carefully filmed as I describe all the kit coming out of the aircraft holds: combat webbing, boots, uniforms, a field trauma medical set-up, a sack of first field dressings, radios, loud hailers, torches … a rubber inflatable boat.

Like me, the boat is deflated, but it makes me smile: it isn't ours. It must have been loaded by mistake, back at Wonderboom Airport. One more fuck-up.

Finally, they let me relax. I smoke a cigarette under the wing, out of the sun. Anywhere else the concrete is too hot for my bare soles.

The smart little car owner, who seems to be in charge, or maybe is Guava's number two, looks at me, smiling. 'Why have you got police blue lights and loud hailers, Mann?'

'Because we would have used those to get people out of the way, off the streets.'

'You know, having met you – and having been through what you were carrying – and why you were carrying it – I'm now quite sure that any coup organised by Captain Simon Mann would be a very gentlemanly affair – very politely done… Yes! You see! Mann's coup would have been gentlemanly…'

'So why don't you let me go and do it, then?'

The Warrant Officer and I laugh. Even so, he meant it to be a compliment. Little does he know. I turn to the Warrant Officer.

Guava's number two has asked him: 'Would you go on something like this? A coup – organised by Simon Mann – a coup like this one?'

'Yes, yes, I would… If the pay was right.'

This is idle chat. Nothing is going to get me out of the pile of shit that I am in. My life is over. I've messed up everything for Amanda and for the children. I feel sick.

That night – the night of the Op – the night that I was arrested – I thought that I might die – but in EG, in a firefight. I had known that we were compromised. How could we not be compromised? When two NI agencies had given us explicit green lights, and when God knows how many other NI agencies knew some or all of what was about to happen?

I had braced myself for the worst, which I imagined to be death or wounding. I had even made practical plans for the worst. I'd loaded handguns as our weapons of last resort. An Executive Outcomes golden rule, back in the days of our Angola and Sierra Leone Ops: nobody must be taken a prisoner by blacks.

The EO men all used to carry a last-resort hand grenade. If capture could be no longer staved off, then they planned to blow their own heads off.

Death had been my worst-case downside. The trouble is, I realise now that my being a prisoner is far worse for Amanda and the children to cope with. And for me too. Fucking hell.

But I'm not going to try to explain the real story to these Zim CIO and Army officers. They aren't that interested. Zim had been an enthusiastic seller of arms, without paperwork. We had been welcomed as buyers. Where the arms were going was not their concern.

Niek and I had promised them intelligence, about the DRC and about the Katanga rebels, things that – because of their President's stake in the Congo diamonds racket – the CIO badly needed.

They had stopped the sale and arrested us, the buyers, because someone had blown the whistle on us, telling Zim. At that point Zim had no choice but to turn against us.

Who?

As I am handed another ready-lit cigarette, still chatting to my captors, I take time to enjoy the design of my purchase: the Boeing 727-100, tail number N4610. It's the first time I've seen the aircraft in daylight. Even now, I feel this strange love of flight. I have since a child... I stare, and stare again. In the bright sun I see that the brand-new white paintwork, near the tail fin, has covered but not hidden the logo of the previous owner: 'UNITED STATES AIR FORCE'.

Shit.

That evening they take me to yet another police holding tank, the one at Greendale, another Harare suburb, with another misplaced name of somewhere leafy. Somewhere pleasant and law-abiding. When I arrive the tank is already crowded. As time passes, more and more of les misérables get thrown in. It is a Thursday night, so the week's action must be warming up. Friday night will be worse.

A white man joins us, greatly overweight. A Boerer, or something like one. Not long after he first comes we are let out into the wire-mesh dog run outside that tank. His wife has brought food, so I watch him tear into hamburger and chips. He knows about me.

He says that I should hope to be taken to Chikurubi Maximum Security, because once there I will be safe. I wish that I were there already. I know that Bob's Gestapo can do whatever they like with me while I'm in the tanks. I might disappear any time. Croc feed. Mugabe likes to be called the African Hitler, so Gestapo is just how the CIO want it. In this reign of terror, it is the job of the CIO to be terrifying.

Back inside, the crowding is bad. Every inch of the filthy floor is taken up by body. Then I am taken outside again. They push and punch me. Sit me down. Kick me. I can't understand what's happening. Since I'd told them the truth, this thuggery had stopped.

Once the kicking ends, they make me sit still. They are back to their taunts about how tough a white man is compared with a black. They ask me how I feel about being next to blacks in the tank. Living with them.

They're upset that the colour of the men I'm with doesn't bother me.

The men in there are each worth a hundred of any of these arseholes – and that has nothing to do with skin colour.

By the time they shove me back into the tank, it is dark. There's no light in there. The stink is dreadful. I push people away, to win back my place, and squeeze down. The white guy is shaking. I can feel him next to me.

After 20 minutes of his shaking growing stronger he bursts. 'I can't make it. I can't stand this. I need space. God – God! Please, help me… I can't stand this…'

I try to talk to him, to calm him, but I can hear the panic flood up – swamping what is left of his strength. I try to help him by saying that we have to treat it as a joke. The worse it gets, the more we must laugh at it. Bad? Pah! This isn't bad…

It was the old army game. Cold? You're cold? But this is nothing… I remember when it was so cold that…

That game goes down badly. His panic floods ever higher. Just then one of the street boys, one that this big fat white had been cursing earlier, calls out.

'Simon, send him over here … over here I have some space for him.'

With a group effort the man is led over – through the crowded darkness − to where the street boy is. I don't know how much more space is really there, but at least he goes quiet. At least I am not the one having to deal with him.

Afrikaner, meet Rent Boy.

Lengthwise I cannot stretch out without laying my shins under or over someone else's. Crosswise I must lie on one side, squashed between two other men. We all have to lie like that, and we all have to lie on the same side, so that we stick together like spoons. When it becomes too painful, then we turn, but everyone in our row has to turn together.

One prisoner says that he had been one of the freight handlers out at Manyame Air Base: one of the ZDI gang there to help put our kit into the 727's hold. The guy is friendly. He chats. Then he spits it out: 'This government of ours − here in Zimbabwe − is shit … some of us are ready to fight it. Let me join you, then we can fight Mugabe.'

I don't want a war with this guy. A stool-pigeon? Others, I have already noticed, treat him with respect − or fear.

'Oh,' I say, 'so you want to be with us… Are you very strong? Let me feel your arm… Let me see if you are strong enough.'

That wins a laugh, out of the street kids at least. He shuts up.

Every 30 to 40 minutes, I'm woken and made to go outside. I don't have a watch, so have to guess the interval. Sometimes it seems short, others long. I don't know… Maybe it just feels short or long.

The difficulty is that each time I go out of the tank, I lose my space on the floor. When I come back there is a struggle just to get back my filthy sliver of floor space. Each time it is smaller.

At about 11 that night, I guess, I am woken again. Now I am scared. Outside are more than a dozen men and women, all in the British Army type of khaki service dress that is worn by the Zimbabwe National Army and the Zimbabwe Prison Service (ZPS). Army? ZPS? God knows who they are − but this is it.

I think that Mugabe has sent his so-called War Veterans along, to finish me off. They loathe the Brits. They are the Brown Shirts.

Most of the group carry before them a candle lantern. They stand still. Silent. In the middle is an old man, also in uniform, with a great row of medals. He is wearing the medals themselves, not just the ribbons. He carries no lantern but the two either side hold up theirs for him.

They make me sit down in front of this bizarre parade. There is a feeling of something ceremonial – religious – as if this is a ritual... A ritual killing?

I have no idea who they are, or what they want, while I fear the worst. There is something Ku Klux Klan about this.

I'm scared now.

After ten minutes, during which the old man only once comes forward, to look at me more closely, they leave. Once again I have to fight my way back inside. Elbows and knees win back my place. My relief at having not been executed is overshadowed by the fear that those same uniforms will be back.

I still don't know who they were.

The next morning I'm taken to the police station itself, where they put me back in handcuffs and leg-irons, then sit me on the floor. They keep me like that for something like an hour. I don't know why, because then they take me back to the tank.

As we walk back I notice that the man who asked if he could join my group – to fight against Mugabe – is chatting to two plainclothes police officers. They are surprised to see me clock them. After that he doesn't come back into the tank, so I am sure that he had been sent in as an *agent provocateur* – a poor agent.

It will not be the last time that the Zimbabwe security services prove themselves a waste of rations. More than once I will feel shame at being the prisoner of such cack-handed gaolers. Sometimes I am embarrassed by them.

This day is a long one. There's no interrogation. All the time I think there will be. The tank has emptied such that there are only half a dozen of us. The fat white man, now very quiet, is one.

My feet are still bare, and by now very dirty. I pace up and down. Every tenth time I do a length, I climb up onto the wall that retains the one, overflowing lavatory. That allows me to stretch, then pull myself up to look out of the high opening in the wall. From there I can see the 50 yards between the tank and the police station. I can see where cars drive in and out of the station's leafy car park.

A new BMW arrives. South African and with diplomatic plates. Right, I think, NI are busy. My two-timing friends. They will be hard at it. Hand-washing. Proving their innocence. Tut-tutting.

I pace up, then down. Little do I know what a world-girdling trek of paces lie ahead of me. From the wall opening and the door's peep-hole, I can work out direction and time, using the sun as compass and watch.

Luckily, I know how to do it. I laugh at myself. Such a Boy Scout. So how come I'm now in such an almighty fuck-up?

The day drags. I want to escape, but can see no way. Even at that early stage, the key thought about any escape has already struck me: how far can a ragged and shoeless white man go when everyone else is black?

Already I am frantically bored, yet I've only been a prisoner for five days. How am I going to cope with months? Years? My spirit sinks, withering and sickening inside me. *Inshallah*... Then maybe they'll kill me.

I can see a short row of huts. They are neat and homely, belonging to the police officers of that station. Each one is only one room, but the doors and windows, as well as their surrounding patch of earth, are well kept. A child crawls out of the hut I can see best, then starts to play in the sand. His mother fusses around, making ready a meal while also taking care of him.

I watch them. I might as well be a million miles away, watching through a telescope, so remote am I from any such life, such loveliness. I am a living dead.

Once it is early evening, the tank slowly fills up. We all dread the crowd sure to be thrown in with us: another night in that unlit stinking hole, unable to lie out, pressed in on all sides by tight bodies. The fat white man isn't the only one to feel the panic of claustrophobia, even if he is the one to show it.

Each time we see an officer, we beg that he run the water into the tank's lavatory cistern so that we can flush. Sometimes he does, although the relief only lasts until the next time somebody has a shit.

Of course, there's no paper. I long ago used my underpants, then chucked them. My hands are my only way, then cleaning them on whatever I can find: floor, wall, a piece of old cardboard.

We fear the worst for that night. We are right. The dread calls that I get all night long – 'Mann, Mann – wake up – outside – *Handei!* – come on – outside...' – are in fact a help: they give me a good reason to hang onto my spot of concrete by the door. Everyone knows that I will be out and in all night. It's them I'll be treading on.

The morning comes. One of my friends of the day before is taken off to the police station. He chanted and sang in the night. When I said how good the singing was the street boy next to me – my friend, Rent Boy – said: not singing, Simon, he's praying.

Half an hour later I too am taken to the station. It seems quiet, sleepy. It's sunny outside but not hot. We could be in England. I remember that it is Saturday. Then what Saturday meant: fishing with Freddy. I never would again.

At the front desk sits one of the CIO officers. Before him is stacked paper, some sheets of carbon paper and a large old-fashioned typewriter. There's something so quaint about it all that I smile, despite it being unquestionably aimed at my downfall.

I sit across from him, while he plonks away with two fingers, sometimes three. The quiet – and the comfort of a hard wooden seat – make me drowsy.

The fat white man is brought in from the tank. He's made to sit on the bench behind me. My CIO man casts one eye over him, makes no change to his face, then carries on with his hen-peck typing.

As I sit watching the old typewriter work, I can feel the fat white man over my right shoulder. I feel his rage coming up to the boil; with us, in the tank, it has been somehow kept on simmer.

'Excuse me, sir…' bubbles over the heavy South African accent, the 'sir' ridiculous, 'I need to see my Minister – the Right Honourable Mkube Mazazongo – Minister of Baboon Shit, or whatever – he will order my release – he…'

'Shut up.'

'No – you people…! You people, you don't understand – the Minister and I are par…'

'I said, "Shut up." So shut up … Sit on the floor!' says my man, with one long, cold stare.

The fat white man sits down on the floor, his bolt shot.

The typewriter clacks slowly along.

The white is taken away by two uniformed police. (I didn't see or hear of him again, so I guess he was made to trek back again … to Voortrekkerhoogte, maybe. He was lucky.)

The CIO man looks up – then he pushes a newspaper my way, turning it so that I can now see the front page. There's my Boeing 727-100, N4610, parked at Manyame Air Base, on the south side of Harare International.

MARCH · 2004: · ZIMBABWE...

'MERCENARIES TO BE HANGED,' says the banner headline. I glance at the semi-informed text, then look up at the CIO man. He is coolly watching my face.

'Don't worry – we're not going to kill you. We'll find you somewhere in the rural areas and keep you there ... maybe for a very long time ... maybe we'll find you a farm – yes – maybe a Section Six farm.'

He laughs. I try to smile. My throat is dry and scratchy. I can feel a coarse hemp rope around my neck.

(Then, I don't know it, but that feeling – 'maybe this all ends with a rope around my neck, and a long long drop' – coming with a nasty cold slither in my gut – is not to leave me for four long years: not until after my trial and sentencing in Equatorial Guinea, in 2008.)

After 40 or so minutes, all is ready. The CIO man gives me the papers that he has been so carefully typing. They come as no shock to me, just as what is to happen next comes as no shock. He has typed up my handwritten account of events, so now he will ask me to sign it. Then it will be a confession.

I read it through. The typing at least is accurate.

'Is that OK?' he asks.

'It's a copy of what I wrote ... but you know that I cannot sign this without a lawyer present.'

He looks at me, unworried. Then he stands and goes to a side office, from where he comes back with a decrepit old man, tall and stooping. He wears a tweed jacket, a V-neck pullover, a shirt and tie, and grey flannel trousers with turn-ups. His shoes are scuffed black lace-ups. Were he not black-skinned, he would have been a caricature: of an English public school Latin beak.

'Come with me,' orders the CIO man.

He leads the way down a corridor and I follow, while the Latin beak files along behind me. We go into a small room. There's a table in the middle with three chairs. I am pointed into a chair next to a double-door steel locker, painted grey, that fills the far-right corner, almost blocking the waist-high window.

'Sit there,' the beak is told, with a wave to the side opposite me. The CIO man is going to sit between us, and therefore at the head of the almost square table.

'You will sign, Mann,' he said. 'This is the Commissioner for Oaths –

MARCH · 2004 : · ZIMBABWE . . .

the Honourable Terence Mapfumo – and you will sign, in front of him.'

He walks out of the room, opening the door opposite that leads to another room, similar to ours, yet empty of both furniture and people. He turns right, out of my sight. I hear his footsteps, then a shout, a howl, another shout. A rush of feet come close, then into view. My singer friend of the night before flies into the room opposite, half thrown, half carried by two bruisers.

They hurl him to the ground, yelling at him. The noise is sudden and terrific. They kick him into place, all the time yelling. He goes down, then onto his back, arms by his sides, palms downward to the floor. His bare feet stick out of his frayed trouser bottoms, while he holds his legs straight and up at an angle of 30 degrees.

I watch. Horror.

My mind is stupid: why does he lie like that? So vulnerable. Over the coming years, I will see men take up that position many times. Like the singer did, on that sunny Greendale morning. I will learn that they hope, in that way, to make their beating less harsh. They hope to be just beaten. They hope to be thrashed that way.

Not killed.

My CIO man stands in the corridor, just to one side, watching me. The beak, beak-like, studies a sheet of typed paper on the table before him, as if the only nastiness is its poor syntax or grammar.

The two bruisers head for me, breathing hard. The first goes behind me, rattling open the doors of the steel locker, then smashing one door back into my chair. The second grabs my chair and forces it round halfway, then he grabs both sides of my head so that I am facing the steel locker.

They smell of sweat. Stale and fresh. Their breath carries their last night's alcohol. The locker is empty, except for a heap of half a dozen two- and three-foot strips of lorry fan belt, the same as I had seen used the first night.

Goon One takes a handful of the strips, while Goon Two holds my head. Goon One keeps them in his left hand, putting one into his right. I think how cheap leather jackets are *de rigueur* for Zimbabwe Bruisers, that Southern Hemisphere autumn fashion: these two have them, like every other goon thus far.

Next Goon Two holds my face, his stinking mouth close to my ear,

MARCH · 2004 : · ZIMBABWE . . .

talking shit about white men not being tough, while Goon One put his bruiser's face into mine, talking more shit, rubbing my neck and cheeks with the harsh V-shaped fan belt strip.

'You will sign, Mann,' the CIO man says. Then he orders the bruisers: 'Show our Englishman why he will sign!'

They let me go, then spin my chair round to face out of the door. As the bruisers move from me to the singer, his feet still offered upward, his eyes meet mine. Pain fills them. I don't need the message.

The beating starts, one bruiser for each of my singer's feet. He shouts and screams in his pain. I wish I could say that I try to grapple my handcuffed hands onto those of the torturing bastards, but I do not. A lesser pain fills me too, and shame.

'Are you going to sign, Mann?'

'Will you stop that if I do?'

'…but you must sign.'

I nod, then sign. The Latin beak looks pained, then rubber-stamps, witnesses, then stamps again. Months later, I am to learn that the beak is dead, of a cancer that he has fought and lost to. He died a few weeks after my signing ceremony.

At the time, I think his pained look is due to what is happening.

They take me back to the tank, calling out two prisoners as they push me in. There are about four left in the tank. I pace up and down, climbing and looking out across the 50 yards to the station at each length.

Soon I see two policemen walking either side of the two prisoners, while they carry the singer between them as though in a chair. They each have one arm under his armpits, their other hands under his legs, holding his knees up and keeping his scoured foot soles off the hot, harsh, red African grit.

They bring him into the tank. The singer's eyes accuse me. The two policemen look at me: 'This is your fault,' say all of their eyes. The two prisoners lay him down gently on the filthy floor. The singer shuts his eyes.

Rent Boy, who had just carried back the singer, turns to me. 'It isn't you, *Bwana*. What could you have done? We are all suffering now. It isn't you.'

I'm pretty sure the street kid is a rent boy – in the tank for hawking himself – but I don't know that. I don't ask. Why should I care? My whole world has reversed polarity.

So many things that mattered once don't any more.

Not long after that, I pace again. The singer looks asleep. I hope so. The street kid is also pacing. We have just shared a smuggled cigarette. There is not meant to be any smoking in the tank so, whenever they do smoke, which is often, they take off their shirts and whirl them around as fans. That way, if an officer comes in, there will be no lingering smoke.

Of course, this is just a matter of form. The contraband cigarette and lighter is smuggled in by the officer anyway, in return for one for himself.

I must learn.

'Look! Support Unit – they have come to take you, Simon. They will take you to Chikurubi now.'

I climb up beside him and look. I can see a dozen police, armed like soldiers, and three open pick-ups.

'How do you know they are Support Unit?'

'Brown boots … there is nobody else here for them, but you.' He answers my first question and my next. I ask anyway.

'Then … how do you know they will take me to Chikurubi – not somewhere else…?'

He laughs at my dark view. By now I understand that the police and Chikurubi, terrible though they may be, are safety. The Zimbabwe legal system is bad, but not as bad as their Gestapo.

'Because the Support Unit can only be here for you. They can only be taking you to Chikurubi…'

An hour later I am taken out of the tank, careful not to say any farewells in front of the officers. I am learning. My goodbyes are already said, except to the hurt singer. Still asleep.

The Support Unit men have the look and manner of crack troops. They will do whatever their masters order, but they bear me no grudge. When I ask, they tell me straight: Chikurubi.

Relief.

I am moving on to something else. It will be better. The nights in the tanks have been hell. The fear – that I am a CIO non-person – has been terrible. I was never sure that they were not going to pull out my fingernails, or put electrodes to my balls, or shoot me. Feed me to the crocs.

As we drive into the Chikurubi Max farm and complex, and then into the prison itself, I try to scan everything into my head for future use.

For my escape.

Going home – somehow, anyhow – by now feels like the wildest of dreams...

But – somehow – I've got to get there. Home. Escape.

CHAPTER FOURTEEN

CHIK MAX

Checking in to Chikurubi is surreal. Chik Max is the Harare Hilton. Our doors are open to all. The hardest and most secure prison in Africa. So they say.

I feel safer now. I'm out of the hands of the CIO and the police. I'm in the hands of the Zimbabwe Prison Service, the khaki-uniformed ZPS.

Chikurubi has an outside-of-Africa feel about it. The machine has discipline. There is a white man's machine-age brutality. Sparta. Echoes of efficiency. Checked in by Reception. Forms are filled. Property signed for.

Two freshly washed and ironed uniforms (khaki drill shirt and shorts – white is for convicted men), four clean blankets, a plastic plate and cup, a bar of soap and a roll of loo paper. Issued. Signed for.

A doctor gives me a quick medical.

I'm back in the army.

In leg-irons and handcuffs they escort me for the first of too many times up the two sets of stairs to 'A' Hall.

I pass the mess and stink of all the pigeon shit. They nest and coo in the roof. I pass by where the wild bees will hive. Then I go through a locked door and walk six paces: across the 'A' Hall exercise yard, under a steel-wire net in the sky; through another locked steel door; along three paces of passageway; past a steel-grille officers' cage; through another locked steel-grille door; then into a passage.

All around me there are faces. Super-black against their white drill shirts. All eyes stare at me…

Then duck away when I look back.

Cell Six. The door is unlocked, opens… I walk in. My crowd of escorts have halted outside, craning to see my resting place.

The heavy hardwood door slams behind me.

The escorting officer rattles the handle. Another rattles it again. To check. Silence … near silence … my ears adjust.

Stunning.

I'm entirely – absolutely – alone.

I have to communicate with Amanda. I must … or with someone on my side. Anyone.

But: no mobile phone, no room phone, no screen and keyboard, no pen or paper, no nothing. No room service.

What's happening? What are other people doing?

My Brothers-In-Arms, partners in crime, friends; they have money, they have contacts, they know Africa, they know the Zimbabwe top brass, they know Colonel Dube, Head of ZDI. They know how to operate in a zoo like this. Yes. They know how to operate in a zoo like this.

My cell is five feet wide and seven normal paces long. It's high, maybe 12 feet.

A single bare bulb lights the space. All day. All night. No light switch.

At the other end to the great door, well made in some African hardwood, there is a small air vent, six inches in height, a foot in length, covered in a fine mesh at both its cell and outer ends.

At that same end wall, starting at about seven feet above the floor, a gallery juts out a couple of feet proud of the wall. The gallery is wood and glass, to allow daylight into the cell.

To one side of the cell, against that far end, is a built-in concrete box with a steel lavatory bowl let into it. At above head height, there is a short rope attached to a cistern flushing arm. The cistern itself is built into a solid and painted hardboard box. I pull. A mighty flush of water falls down. Luxury.

Ceiling, walls and floor are bare concrete, greasy, filmed with dirt.

I can see where most people lay their blankets to sleep on the concrete by the mark on the floor: along one side, head next to the lavatory base. I throw my four down.

A voice carries to me, louder than those that I could just hear from 'A' Hall's exercise yard outside. Where is such a voice coming from?

The voice comes again, urgent.

A shade of light moves against the door. It catches my eye. I look to the skylight gallery. Two heads and shoulders are dark in silhouette. I see two black heads staring.

I raise a hand, one waves back, then they go. The skylight, I am to learn, is not there to let light in. It is a way for the watch-tower shift officers to keep an eye on 'A' Hall prisoners.

And an eye on their cage shift and yard shift comrades.

'A' Hall was built as a punishment block. Twenty cells along one long passage, I later learn. One shower and a *dhobi** sink are in the middle, by the officers' cage and the double entrance doors.

I must do something. Minutes drag. How am I going to cope with years?

I fold three of the four blankets longways: my mattress. The fourth will go on top. I see that my cell, built to keep a man in, is not keeping mosquitoes out. I worry about fleas, and lice. At least there is no malaria here. I think (wrongly): at 3,000 feet we must be too high for malarial mosquitoes.

Walk.

I walk up and down, up and down. With no map yet in mind, I start to walk.

Voices catch my ear ... not the same as the background ones from the yard, not the gallery either. I strain to hear.

I try to make out what is being said.

Afrikaans!

Slowly I put it together: all of the whites that were arrested at the same time as me are in these cells, along the single long passage of 'A' Hall.

I wait for a pause, then call out to one of them: 'It's me – Simon. Can you hear me?'

He can, and I can just hear him, but it is difficult. My gunfire-

*Military slang for clothes washing.

damaged hearing doesn't help. When there is any other noise going on, such as singing, 'churching' or praying (Gawd 'elp us), it is impossible.

The only way is to use Standard Army Voice Protocol, as if we are a radio net. 'Over and out' – and other standard words – make it workable. As with a radio net, we must assume that every word is being logged.

Good information comes from prison cells.

A surge in sound from the rest of 'A' Hall makes our radio net 'UNWORKABLE – OUT'. I hear doors being opened, held, then slammed shut.

What's happening? The door rattles and slams come closer.

My door flies open… Three officers, one of them a sergeant, and half a dozen black prisoners, all in white drill, all crouching close to the floor.

A sawn-off black plastic dustbin, so old that it is torn and frayed, holding white thick goo. *Sadza*. The staple diet of the *Shona* (and many other southern Africans), made from mealie meal: ground white maize corn and boiling water.

A second crappy dustbin holds stewed green grass.

I grab my plate and shove it at the prisoner running this whirlwind: slap, slap. Back it comes.

An old orange syrup bottle, Mazoe brand, filled with water, flies in.

Slam – my door crashes shut. Locks.

That was Norman, I learn later.

Not long after that – by the sounds – I come to the idea that everyone is being locked up. There is a hubbub of sound around that of the already too familiar slamming doors. More doors this time.

It makes me think of an old-fashioned railway carriage. Like the one I boarded, aged 12, at that two-track rural railway station, days before the results of the Eton Common Entrance exam.

A door to every compartment.

Slam. Shut.

'What if I fail, Daddy?'

There's no whistle toot.

We're not going anywhere.

The black population of 'A' Hall start to shout to one another. Our mercenary radio net is still 'UNWORKABLE – OUT'. It stays that way until the quiet of the next morning. At ten at night, that's it:

'Lights out, girls. No talking.'

Except that the lights stay always on. Except that there are no girls. The routine of a Chikurubi day, as I begin to learn it, goes like this:

0600: The cage officers' and watch-tower officers' shifts change. Eight-hour shifts.
0800: The yard officers' shift comes on. Unlock prisoners from their cells.
0800–1000: Breakfast – thin gruel – *bota* – appears.
1100–1200: Lunch – *sadza* – appears.
1200–1400 (or thereabouts): Prisoners are locked back up – for the officers' lunch break.
1400: The cage officers' and the watch-tower officers' shifts change.
1400–1600: Prisoners are unlocked again. Supper – *sadza* – appears.
1600: Head counts. Lock-up. Yard shift officers go home.
2200: No more talking or noise. Cage officers' and watch-tower officers' shifts change.

I don't know all that to start with, but it doesn't take long to find out.

Anyway, for the first two weeks we – that's the mercenaries – are kept locked up all of the time.

Each shift of officers coming on duty, parade, are inspected, then sing their stupid bloody national anthem: sometimes well, sometimes so badly that the sergeant taking the parade makes them sing it again.

Right under my cell.

White men make rude remarks – or shithouse noises – before, during or after the anthem. Not popular.

No prisoners black or white ever join in.

Over these first days in Chikurubi, the shock of capture is wearing off. I find my bearings.

A shower is my greatest prize, when it comes. Then they are allowed daily.

A mad chaos comes out of the blue when – without warning – we mercenaries have to sign in our other property – for me that's my suitcases and all their strange contents.

While that is happening, we meet our lawyers for the first time. This is done in a mob of all my 69 men, many prison guards, police CID and CIO.

The law is now to start its pantomime of justice. In Zimbabwe, the law is very British. To understand that, think of the plumbing of a house in which all the parts are there, and most of them work: pumps, tanks, pipes, cisterns, taps, plugs and drains. In Zimbabwe, all those parts are made in England, but the water that flows through the plumbing of the house is all filthy: don't bathe in it, let alone drink it. The law in Zimbabwe is corrupt from top to bottom, left to right.

I know my man, my Zimbabwean lawyer, as soon as I see him. Small, fancily dressed, very black, round and smiling. I nickname him the Croc.

What can I say? Days become weeks, then weeks months. Remand hearing follows hearing.

I hear from the Croc about EG. Niek and the others have been arrested. Gerhard Merz died while being interrogated. They are being mistreated. Their conditions are terrible. The news makes me feel sick. For them. For me, if I go there.

Letters and messages to Amanda get through. She replies.

Amanda, I am lovesick. I think of our love, of our love affair, of our love story. I want to write it, but that's selfish … but why not write it as a love letter to her?

Even if I never get out of prison, then that would be something for her, whatever happens in the rest of her life. A souvenir. Our children might gain something from it one day. At least they would know that the love from which they came had been strong and beautiful. That their births were willed with care, as well as by passion.

Amor vincit omnia.

I believe that now. I understand it now. Love is denied me now.

An armed robber has befriended me. We talk a lot. He's called Kaunda because he is fat – just like Kenneth Kaunda, the former President of Zambia – but his real name is Elisha. All the time he's weighing me up. One day he says that he and his friends have been watching me. I am different. They see that I am the boss. A great man.

I don't feel great. I know I'm not. I laugh it off.

'No,' he says, 'we know – we watch – you are not like these farmers. You think – you walk… We know…'

I laugh it off again.

'No, Simon – I mean it – we're serious – you are one of us – the armed robbers … we watch you – how you stand back to let an old poor man walk through a door before you … or in the queue at food time… You have respect for us, you see…'

It sounds like nothing but it means a lot. Then. Now.

Then Elisha backs off me. He has been warned not to be close to me. Security told him. They have spies everywhere. Security and the CIO are one.

We keep apart – but it doesn't work. A couple of weeks pass and Elisha is moved to a 'big section'. It is because of me. I see him three months later, but he is no longer Kaunda. Time in the big section has stripped the fat off him better than any stick-thin fashion lady's spa.

I have one book in my cell now, and Security will swap it for another of mine when I ask. And when they feel like it.

Security have at last agreed to let me lend books to others in 'A' Hall. That feels good, and has come about because of popular demand. It also means that I can have more of my books to hand. I'm learning to work the Chikurubi system.

I find that religious books are popular. I have a very good *History of the Jews* (by Paul Johnson) that everyone wants to read, especially the three *Madzibabas*, or priests, in the section. They want to study. They think that the Jews absolutely are the chosen people, so it must be worth knowing about them.

One of these *Madzibabas* has a regular supply of delicious crocodile *biltong*. I eat all he gives me, taking the chance of eating them, rather than them me. He's in for rape, having convinced a number of his female followers that their cure for being barren was to be fucked … by him.

Another *Madzibaba* is keen to read *Paradise Lost*. Having found that the way to read it is out loud, I loved it. Incredible sound … So, the *Madzibaba* takes it, after days of asking, then soon hands it back. He hadn't enjoyed it as much as the cover (a naked Eve) had lead him to hope.

That one is in for molesting two little girls of his congregation. Whether he did or not is a matter of Section debate. I have asked him to pray silently if he can, because he keeps on waking me in the middle of the night. His prayer sounds like a horror movie.

Noise, I am to find, is the true horror of prison. It doesn't stop inside. Every pin drop by every man can be heard. There is so much noise that everyone shouts. Coughs, farts, guards working their rifles, guard dogs, the cooking boilers. Prayer. Singing. Churching. Moans and cries of the sick.

Noise is bad, but I am already aware that any sentence, for any crime, is meaningless and wicked when it has been meted out by a ruling gang who are themselves guilty of terrible sins … genocide, for one.

Take away a man's freedom, or his life, then you and your set-up had better be squeaky clean.

But learning to work the Chikurubi system, however, isn't hard. Aged eight I had to deal with North Foreland prep school. Here, I'm an aristocrat in the prison hierarchy. The armed robbers are at the top of the heap – and for good reason. Blaggers.

'We are locked up for trying to knock off a bank, carrying a handgun… You are locked up for trying to knock off a country, carrying two tons of arms and ammo!'

I'm also rich. Cigarettes are the prison currency and, despite my smoking 20 a day, I have plenty to spend. A packet of 20 Madison cigarettes will get you married, to a prison 'wife'.

Two more will buy your divorce.

Everyone wants my *fodya*, my fags. I dish them out fairly. As many as I can. It is never enough. My fellow prisoners are not shy. They know how to ask.

'What do you think I am?' I joke. 'A fucking fag machine?'

One guy comes to me – a *povo*, very skinny and weak – with an escort, to interpret.

'*Shumba*, this man asks for your help. Perhaps you can help him. He has nothing – the rags that he was arrested in were taken by the police… When he is released he will need clothes, but he has none. It worries this man… All he will need is a shirt, a jacket, a pair of trousers, and a pair of tackies…'

Of course I will help.

'When is his release?'

The escort sucks, then frowns, hesitates. He turns to me. 'Fifteen years, *Shumba*… I'm sorry…'

The man doesn't look as if he'll last five. (He will die two years later.)

Quite a few men I do help. A system gets going whereby I tell my Zim lawyer, the Croc, who to pay. They, or someone, go to the Croc's offices. Sometimes it is a few hundred dollars, to help someone released to be resettled. Sometimes it is money for medicine, for a child or a sick mother.

I do this for officers as well as prisoners. I can't differentiate between the two as well as I should be able to. Chikurubi is such a sump of misery that you don't know where to start.

One place I could start was with the morning mug of tea. My cigarette wealth allows us to get regular hot water for tea. *Mvura pisa.* Hot water: the life-saver. This comes once in the morning and once in the afternoon, just before lock-up. A pack of 20 Madison pays for two weeks' supply. The essential item is a five-litre plastic fruit juice container used for carrying the water. These are precious and suitably decorated to the owner's taste.

I learn how to use a blanket as a way of wrapping up the container. A homemade thermos. I can make a cup of tea an hour after lock-up, but still drink it hot. That becomes important as we head for a cold winter. Harare lies 5,000 feet ASL. In winter it is cold, often below freezing. We are in one shirt and shorts. In the early days, that is all we have.

I learn how to use a strip of old blanket to wrap up my head. Not flattering, I imagine. But there's no mirror. Who cares?

But the idea of a love letter to Amanda – that tells the story of our love – remains a burr in my mind. Why not? I have some writing stuff. I have been using it to smuggle letters out already.

I start the letter. It grows fast. Then it grows in scope.

Then they take away all my papers, notebook and pencil. The letter is taken too. There are stories that I have smuggled letters outside. These have been bought and sold and are in the UK press. I wonder how the media could have got hold of them.

Things are going badly and getting worse. My faith in home's ability to do what has to be done is shrinking. I have heard nothing at all from those who could be helping me, the bosses in this coup – not a squeak, and not a squeak from them to Amanda, or my lawyers. I'm sure they are busy with something to get me out. They must be … surely? But what are they doing? Why not send a message?

Things had been looking good. Hush-hush talks. Buying our way out of Zim. We were working towards fines. Not custodial sentences. Haggling.

It's just a question of: 'How much?'

Then Thatcher pleads guilty in South Africa. To supplying a helicopter for the coup plot. Unwittingly, he says.

He needn't have done that. He would have won his case, had he fought it. Instead, Thatcher does a deal. To avoid a custodial sentence, he pleads guilty to breaking anti-mercenary legislation. He receives a $500,000 fine. And promptly flies back to the UK a free man. This, I'm told, infuriates Mugabe and his cronies. Stiffens their collective hard-on for me and the men. Now we must be made an example of. The white man won't make a mug out of Mug.

Thanks, Mark.

But all the time I am making decisions that are not in my best interests. I can fight the case in Zim, but to do so would be worse for the men. I will win, but the case might take five years, during which time everyone would be stuck.

At the same time, I hear things from the big sections, where the men are. For the first time, through the network of my fellow prisoners, I find out that all the men with me were fully aware of what the Op actually was before they left South Africa.

I want to try to write the love letter again, only the idea has grown. It's a book now, that will tell the whole story. It is for Amanda and the children. It will tell them who I was. What I did with my life.

It may even make them some money. They can sell it, if nothing else.

You see: I may be going to Equatorial Guinea any day. There I will be killed.

Here I may be killed. The prosecution are asking for the death penalty against me.

I'm sure that I can get the book done in here. I find that Chikurubi is like my prep school or Eton or the Army: its rules are not rigid. The rules can be bent; but not too far, or they snap.

If I write the book such that – to a casual passing prison officer – it looks like a piece of fiction, I may get away with it. If it looks like any kind of log, journal or memoir, then I won't.

Thinking about it, I will need more cover than that. How will I write my story without making it obviously mine? I can use what we used to call 'veiled speech'. Not a code really, just a thin cover.

I scribble. I start to write. I will go on writing that book for two and a half years – off and on – one way or another – over and over. The whole manuscript is to be taken off me twice more. In February 2007, the book – by then codenamed *Straw Hat* – will be smuggled out of Chikurubi, then flown to London.

Much of what you have already read in this book came out of Chikurubi, from *Straw Hat*.

This is *Straw Hat 2*.

SUNDAY, 26 SEPTEMBER 2004

Yesterday, a fourth child was born to Amanda and me. Arthur. That's a week after I was convicted, then sentenced to eight years' imprisonment and hard labour.

Shit. Treble shit.

Even Arthur's naming goes wrong. Amanda has asked me to come up with one, working from a shortlist we have agreed in our letters. She kept the names a secret from everyone … until they read it in the UK newspapers.

Some bastard had picked up his chosen name from what I had said in prison, or from my message through my lawyer, then sold the story.

Here in Chikurubi, five years' actual time is a magic number. More than that and a man should tell his wife that she is free to get on with her own life and enjoy it. Not wait.

Five years is when many men become prison homosexual.

Even if I get out of prison tomorrow, Amanda might not want me back. I wouldn't blame her. The hurt I've done her is horrible. I can hear her pain behind her jolly loving letters … her jolly loving notes really. She isn't a letter writer, that's for sure. But the notes are so wacky – they are so 'her'. They make me weep.

You see, *Straw Hat* – my book – is my way of saying sorry … my real way, I mean, because just saying it is no good. The book is my real voice of that time, even though it mostly isn't about that time.

Day to day – in my mind – I am moving through a hellish landscape. I may go to Equatorial Guinea, to be tortured and killed. It can happen any day, with no notice.

It will be: 'Mann – get your blankets! You're off.'

Sometimes I rack myself some more, by thinking of Amanda with someone else. But then, why should she not be?

All around the prison are my other 69 men. They all got two years or so, to my eight. I blame myself for their being here. I blame myself that we were unable to do the deals we thought we had done: plea bargains and fines, then go home.

I did what I could. I put their cause before mine in all the choices I made. It was the least I could do.

Facing their anguish, every one of the many times we were all in court, was too much to take. I faced it because … what choice did I have?

Then there was the epic row about the men's pay. Their first month's payment had been held up because Niek and I had decided to up it, at the last moment. Just before I left South Africa for the last time, I had told someone to pay it: $3,000 per man, I think it was … maybe more. He told me the next day – by which point I was in the Cresta Motel, Harare – that the payments had been made.

Except they hadn't. I don't know what happened. Now I'm powerless, in prison, but the men look to me for that money. There is no money in South Africa now. Everything has vanished. I sign over my Aerostar 600 as a way of raising cash, but even that goes wrong, with accusations that people stole the plane, then that they stole the engine and the avionics.

I'm a prisoner. A non-person. I can do nothing.

'How do you survive in prison?' is a FAQ. 'How do you not survive in prison?' would be more like it. If you break down – lie on the floor of your cell in tears, cry out – nobody will come.

There's no way they can help if they do come.

I have had to make myself stop thinking of Amanda and the children. I don't want photos of them. They are barred from my mind. It hurts more to let them in than to keep them out. Even so, the bar doesn't work.

In all my efforts to get free nothing works for me. All the time I am being fed garbage by lawyers, the only voice of the people who are trying to get me out. 'London' is how I call the team, so that they are not muddled with Amanda and home. Amanda is never 'London'. David Hart is 'London' and he brings in the lawyer, Ben Romney. When David gets sick, he leaves, so then my sister, Sarah, and brother, Edward, take over. Others come and go. My eldest son, Peter, does his heroic best. Amanda is always with 'London' but never within.

When I try to tell them what to do, they ignore me. They go their own way. I am the bad child. It is my stupidity that put me here. I am a Zombie – a dead person breathing. Just existing. Far far away.

I can do nothing. So I am nothing.

Then I find out that this is how it often happens. I find that everyone

I talk to has the same shit: their money, their children, their power to make things happen outside – all lost.

Amanda is no longer one of 'London'. I have to keep them apart – rightly or wrongly – because I hate 'London'. It will turn out that I am right. She hates them too.

I can't go on griping like that without telling the story. The trouble is that I am grateful to everyone who tries to help in any way. I thank them and I mean it. They're great. They don't have to help at all. This is my fault.

The only ones who should help don't.

The difficulty is that just because someone helps – and has my thanks – doesn't mean they do a good job, however much they may try. That doesn't mean they are trying to do me down … but they should listen to what I am asking.

The first big blow against my faith in 'London' comes when Maggie Victor asks me straight out, 'What are "London" playing at?' Maggie is my South African lawyer. She's senior. She's white, but did a load of work for the ANC when they were the enemy of Pretoria. She's a judge now, and a great lady. Here's how it goes one day inside Chikurubi, when I haven't been tried yet – only a couple of months after my arrest:

'Simon, I really want to help you, but I must understand what is happening in London – please tell me: what's going on?'

I stare at her – confused. We are not in the usual meeting place in Security. We've been sat at a table and two chairs in Reception, the desk where the guy runs paupers' burials, a busy post. So – for once – we can talk without the goons listening, or so I hope.

Maggie can see my muddle and misery about her question. My brain is in a panic. It scrambles to take on what this means. 'I must get home' is the only thought I can easily handle.

'I'm really sorry to say this – I know how it will hurt you – but I have to know, if I am to help. You must tell me: what is going on?'

All she sees is the same confusion, so she goes on.

'You see, "London" are indulging in armchair strategy. They are complacent to the degree of danger you are in … they lack any sense of urgency … they are not pressing the buttons they could press … I need to understand why. Do you see?'

I see little but churn up one thought. David Hart – he's in charge of getting me out, right? Maggie V nods.

'He's very close to some of my Brothers-In-Arms and their families … maybe they are his priority?'

I think about how Mark screwed up so badly. At just the wrong moment for us. He had been fine – out of South Africa. Then, with what looked like incredible stupidity, he returned. He was arrested.

Three South African prosecutors visited me in Chikurubi. They said that they would get me out, to South Africa, with an immunity to prosecution, if I would turn state's evidence against Mark. I refused.

(I won't forget those three. Two were classic old-school Boer police. There's the old South African joke: if you're looking for a criminal, then find a policeman. The third was young and very quick. Cape Coloured. A lawyer. The other two were the sort who pierce the skin at their wrists, so as to wear their Long Service Award cufflinks. They don't own any shirts with long sleeves.)

Mark pleaded guilty under the Foreign Military Assistance Act of 1998 (FMA) my Act, I called it (or the Face the Music Act) as it came into being because of EO.

I can't understand why Mark went back to South Africa. I can't understand why he pleaded guilty. To this day, the FMA hasn't been used successfully against anyone who pleaded not guilty, anyone who fought their case. Instead, having pleaded guilty, he paid a big fine. RSA RANDS 2,000,000. But why?

Whatever their reason was, the effect on all of us in Zim, and Niek and his men up in EG, was catastrophic. At that time, we were very near a deal. EG had not yet made headway with Mugabe and Co. But as soon as Mark pleaded guilty to supplying money which he knew would be used for mercenary activity, it was an admission of there having been a coup plot. The Zimbabwean Black Supremacists went crazy: demanding again the death sentence for all of us. Me especially.

Mark's return, arrest and plea – by accident or not – torpedoed – sank without trace! – any chance we had of a slap, a fine and a ticket home.

Back in the Chik Max paupers' burial area, Maggie and I kick the thing around some more, but neither of us knows. I am in no position to find out. Maggie looks more uptight, not less. Then I find out why.

'There's a group in South Africa – your friends – they agree with me that "London" are not helping you. These South African friends are offering to help you – they'll go all the way for you, Simon…'

My mind reels at the shock of what I am hearing. I must be quick:

at any moment this oasis – of our being able to talk – can be snatched from us.

'…but you must know that, if you let them help, then "London" will probably hand the job over. They'll stop helping.'

'Maggie, I'm grateful – thank them all please – but I cannot go against "London", Amanda, my family … it's impossible.'

Then there's a letter that I write to David Hart, asking him to please try and get the lawyers all working together. The lawyers had all asked me to do this. I get a letter back: they are working together, and if you don't like the way I am helping you, then I will stop. Fucking hell.

All my life I've wondered about that saying 'There's nothing colder than charity.' I mean: if you need charity, then how can it feel cold, when you get it? Right? Wrong.

Now I know what that saying means.

Then comes the first helicopter deal, Helicopter One. My Zim lawyer is going to London to meet them. At last he is about to really become my lawyer. He tells me that the Zim government are desperate for some helicopter parts. They can't get them because of sanctions.

My crowd in London can get them for sure, so I tell the Croc. Then I write a secret note that I get to 'London' by my other lawyer, an ace. I tell it to him through the steel mesh in security, the place I usually see lawyers. He takes it down and reads it back.

My message is that this helicopter deal is the way to get me out. I beg them. I know 'London' get that message and understand it. Then – little Boy Scout – I say that, if they can't do it, then I will understand. But, in that case, they must *tell* me that they are not doing it. I have other routes – just as good as 'London', if not better. I can switch 'on' my other routes.

I hear nothing back. Security is everything. Then, much later, when it is all too late – I find that 'London' did exactly the worst they could have done: they decided that they couldn't do a sanctions-busting deal; but they didn't tell me that they couldn't do a sanctions-busting deal. They torpedoed me.

Then – later yet – 'London' try to do a helicopter deal – Helicopter Two – but it fucks up. So why didn't they do the first one, when everyone was hot to go?

But 'Escape' is the name of the game.

When we all meet, when there is a court appearance, we talk about what to do in the likely event of our being shipped to EG. We know what happened to Gerhard Merz. We know what is happening to Niek.

We know by now how to undo and open our handcuffs.

They will fly us together. We run through what we will do. Some of us may be killed but we will overpower the aircraft. No question. Then what? We will not be welcome anywhere. Fly into EG, I suggest. I am only half joking.

Then I have to be serious. There is an escape being put together by the South Africans but I *veto* it. A full-on heli assault of Chikurubi. Even if it works, we would end up killing many of the officers. I tell the South Africans that I will barricade myself in my cell rather than be a part of such an escape. These prison officers are not our enemies. If we end up bringing about their deaths, then it is murder. Thus far, we have done nothing wrong. The EG Coup *didn't* happen. And, if it had, it was to be bloodless.

As time goes on I know that 'London' are screwing up. The job of getting me home is being handled badly. Right. But Cell 6 is not the place from which to sort out something like that. Even from Cell 6 I can see: the job isn't simple.

I try to think how to help. How can I guide 'London' to help me better? I remember a success: how I won the diamond concessions in Angola. No small victory. No easy job.

'London' need a Country Manager. Someone who will come to Zim once every six weeks. He will check on who is doing what and will cross-check the information through his own circuits, not the same as those of our Mr Fixits, the lawyers, and the other Zimbos attached to our cause.

I write to 'London' and tell them, but nothing happens. They don't even reply. Then – like a miracle, out of the blue – Mike Christie visits me. How he does it, I don't know. But I see him for an hour each day in the Security meeting place, almost unbothered by goons listening. Three days.

This is a miracle. Visitors who are not lawyers can only meet inmates in terrible cubicles with filthy plate glass, so you can't see, and broken telephone handsets, so you can't talk.

Mike Christie is an old guy, and my great friend. Tiny, chain-smoking Marlboros, wealthy, successful, always cheery. He is a South African of Greek extraction. We worked together on the Yetwene diamond mine, in Lunda Norte, Angola, and became friends. Then we both invested and worked together on a gold-exploration prospect in Guyana, South America, once British Guiana – where Conan Doyle was inspired to write *The Lost World* and where Sir Walter Raleigh went in search of El Dorado.

We didn't find gold – not in economic quantity – but we had a wild adventure, and passed our S Level exams in high-altitude mountainous jungle logistics, by porter and chopper.

Anyway, back in Chik Max – and in the course of our wonderful chats – Mike tells me that he is ready to spend the next 18 months of his life helping to get me out of prison. He won't charge me. He'll come up to Zimbabwe from Cape Town once a month.

Bingo! I have someone who can be the person to pull together what's happening between 'London' and here. Mike is the perfect man for the job in every way, but mostly because he has done this shit – all over Africa – many times before. He knows how to make them love him.

Mike Christie knows how 'the legs of the goat must pass'. Mike will make sure that they do. As we talk, in my last meeting with him, the door behind me opens, pushing against my chair. A shaven, shiny, black-skinned head shoves half round the door, at chair height.

'*Shumba*, excuse me, give me your water, please,' the head, Ringo, hisses in a stage whisper. From under my chair I take my favourite five-litre plastic container. It is filled with drinking water.

Mike carries on where we were at, a slight frown furrowing his always creased sunburned brow. Much of his head, in fact, due to baldness. A little later, we are rushing. We need to run through all our plans before they call, 'Time, *Shumba*! *Handei*!' What is Mike to say to 'London'? What priorities?

'*Shumba, mvura ino pisa!*' whispers Ringo from floor level behind me, the door again pushed open.

I half turn, take the scalding hot container and shove it beneath my chair. '*Detenda*, Ringo.' Thanks.

Mike's frown is back amongst the creases. He breaks off our stuff.

'What the hell is going on?'

'Don't worry … it's my hot water … You know, for tea.'

'Yes, yes … but before, you gave water to that man! I thought that water was the big problem … that you don't get water in your section – what is it? – in FB1!'

SIMON MANN

'Water is a problem … That's why I had to give him some … to heat up … except it's a swap: my good cold water for his good hot…'

Mike's frown was growing, but we had vital matters to deal with.

'Look, Mike – it's too complicated … leave it! Please.'

So we carried on.

Then Mike went to London, together with a letter from me explaining what he was to do. Guess what? 'London' don't just switch Mike off, they piss him off. He tells me about it in his last letter. He had cancer once before, then made himself better. When he visited me he hadn't looked great. When he offered to spend 18 months getting me out they were his last, and he knew it. A year later he dies.

What amazes me is that I don't tell 'London' to bugger off.

My lawyer came into the circus on the say-so of David Hart. Things are going so badly that I want to see him.

Then a fellow inmate – an educated guy called Wicknell – tells me that the Croc is far more of a crook than I think he is. Wicknell's stories are terrible. I don't know if they are true or not, but by this time my view of the world is grey. I must at least pass a warning to my London lawyer.

Having sent a request to my London lawyer that he visit me, sent through the Croc because by now I have no other way, I eventually get a reply. The Croc tells me through the steel grille in Security's office. 'He says he'll only come and visit you when there's something that's important enough to make a visit worthwhile.'

I'm without words, and without breath for a minute or two. No wonder the Croc looks nervous.

I construe what my London lawyer has said into English. At best he's telling me that he thinks I'm an idiot. At worst … at worst doesn't bear thinking about.

I'm a prisoner. There's plenty of time to think.

Chikurubi Sunday afternoons are for sleep. Like outside Sunday afternoons. It's dead. Halfway through one of these afternoons, Security come into the section. They want me. A senior prison officer (SPO) training up to be a padre looks twitchy. He won't tell me why I am suddenly popular. The SPO doesn't like me. He knows I don't believe any of his mumbo-jumbo. Once, I'd asked him why he didn't find a proper job. As well as being a lay preacher, he fills his spare time being a prosecutor when there is a prison trial. One of those where you lose remission.

Full of the love of Christ is this one.

None of that tells me why he is now so nervy, silent to my questions. What's up, Doc? I am off somewhere? Blighty? Fantasy Island (EG)? Santa's head shed – up in Lapland?

I wait outside Security.

Then there's a man in front of me… It can't be… Charlie Wake. As I live and breathe.

He is one of my oldest and best friends – from 14, at Eton – and has three beautiful sisters – Diana, Caroline and Sarah. His mother, Julia, and father, Sir Hereward Wake, were like second parents to me, on lovely school holidays without end. Our fathers had been great friends, also at Eton, and then during the war.

Charlie is here on a daring mission to help me. Amanda and my family know nothing of it. He's with Colonel Miala, the CIO man in charge of my case, and Señor José Olo Obono, the Attorney General of Equatorial Guinea, with his interpreter. The latter had been heavy-handed with his scent.

A deal had been put to the Croc, and through him to 'London'. If I give all the information that I could give – and hand over the documents that Equatorial Guinea think we have – the contract between Severo Moto and me – and the bank statements – then they will make no extradition request against me.

When my time is up in Zimbabwe, then I will go free.

This Sunday-afternoon meeting is happening in late 2005. I've been in custody now for 21 months. By now my Earliest Date of Release (EDR), with good behaviour and so on, is 11 May 2007.

They tell me again that the offer has already been put to the Croc and 'London'. 'London' and the Croc do not know it is being put to me now, directly.

By this time, it is almost two years since our arrest. My Brothers-In-Arms have failed to send me so much as a postcard. They have made no effort to help the men, or their families. No share of legal fees. No postcard to Amanda.

I am ready to put the boot in.

The deal is placed on the table once more.

'You bet.'

I ask Charlie to take that message home. Then, a few days later, when I see the Croc – who is amazed by the news of my Sunday visitors – I send the same message through him. No one gets back to me.

I am losing everything. Keeping me inside, and trying to get me out, is costing a fortune. Amanda and the children also have to eat, live, go to school. Inchmery – our home – has to be kept standing. Worst of all is the ruinous civil action being brought against me in the UK by President Obiang. It's costing millions – but if it is lost, then all will be lost.

Nobody asks me if we should start this UK case, or do a runner. I would have run. Hidden the assets. Never, ever, would I have got into such a lawyers' jamboree. The bill for that case alone is to be over £3 million. Still not won. Until I sort it.

A month or so later, I write to my sister, Sarah, and Amanda: the 'Sitting Duck' letter. I have it in front of me now. If you let me sit here until May '07 – my estimated earliest release date – without a deal having been done, says the letter, then I will be a sitting duck.

No answer.

Why should I worry?

Mainly I walk now.

I can walk home. If I walk from here – Chik Max – to Cape Town, then I will free myself. I work out the distance, from the differences in latitude. Cape Town is 33 degrees south, Harare is 17. Sixteen degrees' difference at 60 nautical miles per degree equals 960 nautical miles. Give or take.

Then I time my speeds: up and down the 'A' Hall yard. Up and down my cell. I log my time walking. I log my miles for each day.

Then I walk to Cape Town. But I'm still in Chik.

So I walk back.

I'm still here. Still walking. Up down. Up down. Except for food, showers, shits, writing and sleep.

Walking and barring thoughts of Amanda and the children are how I push time. My friends inside, Lucky and Zeb, have told me how: 'You think too much, *Shumba*. Don't think too much – you won't make it…'

'How can thinking ever be bad?' I ask.

'Not that thinking … You know what we mean! Thinking about outside … *pamwe* … you must make the inside of the prison – and all of us prisoners – your life, your home. That's it.'

It is true.

It's hard, but that's how you do push time. After about two years, I get the hang of it.

Shumba is my name now. In *Shona* it means 'lion'. It is an honour to be called that – the lion is king – and it is fun: the powers that be hate my having that prison name. By the powers that be, I mean the real powers – the CIO – the top. The officer in charge (OIC) also calls me *Shumba*, but then he doesn't like the real powers that be either.

When officers walk past my cell, they sometimes shout out to *Shumba*, so I squeak back, 'Meeeow.'

I bond with the inmates too.

Poor Zeb. He's been in here five years without a trial. He's a 'Notorious' – an armed carjacker – so that makes prison without trial OK.

Then his wife is killed in a car crash. We all feel bad for him. We say so.

Then we hear that the car was his. Then we hear that his best friend was driving the car … then that the friend was drunk … then that the friend had been fucking his wife. We don't know what to say.

Zeb and I run these days. We're all in section FB 1 together (FBI, we joke). I was moved out of 'A' Hall because FB 1 is the most secure. It's the old Death Row. We run laps round the yard for 30 minutes a day, slowly building it up. The yard is only 25 metres square, so we run ten laps one way, then ten t'other.

We're fanatics. We run as soon as we're unlocked. We don't care if there's no food or water or electricity. It's a way of stamping ourselves on the shitty set-up we're in. It's fun. It's two fingers up at Mugabe and Co., and his troops, who come in to see me twice a day.

More guards than the Queen, I laugh at them.

Running hasn't stopped my walking. Just more miles per day.

The troops are there because the Zim Army think that they own me too. They don't trust the CIO or the ZPS. All these stakeholders in me only care because they think there is some money to be made out of me.

I never fail to tell the ZPS that the Army don't trust them.

Lucky and I run what we call the 'travel agency'. This is our name for the process of softening up, then bribing, chosen prison officers. Then they are hooked onto the payroll. Then they will help our trafficking. Our smuggling. Maybe an escape…

The 'travel agency' is part of the *Shumba* Group. This group pride themselves on being the very worst of everything. It started when we noticed that the phosphor heads of Lion-brand matches, an export of Zambia, either didn't strike or flew off the stick if they did. 'Lion' is *shumba* – and so the *Shumba* brand. If someone sings in their cell badly enough – annoyingly enough – we ask them to sign up to the *Shumba* label. If a cooker – a prison cook – is useless enough, then he may be asked for his recipe, for the *Shumba*-brand foodstuffs division.

One time, a new batch of Pakistani matches, Khyber Pass brand, came in. They were so bad that the executives of *Shumba* quickly negotiated a corporate merger.

When someone's clothes fall apart, then they are from the *Shumba* autumn collection. It happens more and more because Zimbabwe is running out of everything.

You get the idea.

Security try to kill the *Shumba* brand.

One day we are making tea leaves by opening old tea bags and spreading the used leaves in the blasting tropical sun. By this means, I was making sure that everyone in the section had a mug of tea every night. It was vile, *Shumba*-brand tea, but a little better than nothing.

My guard, the army guard, were handing over. They swapped monthly. There must have been 20 in the yard. The old and the new palace guards. Changing the guard at *Shumba*'s palace.

'What are you doing?' they ask. Friendly. We tell them. Lots of *Shumba*-brand jokes.

Next morning Security are in my cell.

'Where's the tea?'

I show my bags. Not that tea. The other tea. Something about brandy. They take everything.

Days later, we find out. '*Shumba* brand' had become '*Shumba* brandy'. Mann was concocting brandy – hooch – out of old tea leaves. Clever Boy Scout.

My mind is playing tricks on me. I see moments that I guess were once real, although maybe not. For example: I have just put fuel in my motorbike, at a motorway service station, on my way up the M3 from home to London. I have paid, and I am walking back towards the bike. The sun is out, but rain has just stopped.

I look at the bike and can see it, bright and shiny but in exaggerated detail. The image super-clear. The resolution high. I look at the ground, then my boots. I feel sick. Something is wrong.

I can see every drop of water on the black stones of the tarmac, grains of sand between the stones, the stitches on my boot. I look up – in my mind's eye – to escape the detail. I look at the trees – bright green – a hundred yards from the service station – but I can see each leaf waving in the English breeze... At home are Amanda and the children. I'll see them this evening...

'But his soul was mad. Being alone in the wilderness, it had looked within itself and, by Heavens I tell you, it had gone mad.'

It's evening now in Chikurubi. We're locked up. I think of Conrad's words as I write this book. *Heart of Darkness* lies beside me.

I start to walk up and down my cell. Seven paces.

Why should I worry?

CHAPTER FIFTEEN

CHRISTMAS DAY 2005

Christmas Days in prison are worse than any other day. They mark the passage of another whole year of my life … going … gone. Christmas Day is even worse than Amanda's birthday, or the children's.

According to my lawyer, I should be sitting at home. And have been there this past week. I look round my cell. It is my home, but that isn't what he meant.

'London' have screwed up at least two other deals that I know of. I don't understand why. Or how. I never will.

So sure have I been that I am homeward bound for this Christmas that I've given up smoking. There is no way I can go home to Amanda a smoker.

When I know I'm not going home, I want to smoke. But the effort has been huge. I look at my chart. Each day marked with the fags smoked. Somehow, I harden up. I don't smoke again. I'm a mountaineer, not a smoker. In my mind, at least. I have to be.

I still need loads of *fodya* to pay the staff – my butler, Agrippa. I share him with Wicknell, who insists on calling him our butler.

Agrippa is a wonder. Young and built like a tank. He is a ball of energy. He has gone homosexual, but that bothers Wicknell more than it does me. That is why he is in our section. To keep him away from boys.

Our butler is serving 94 years for armed robbery. He had owned up to one so that the police would stop beating him. He had no lawyer, so the cops dumped all of their other outstanding armed robbery cases onto him.

I try to tell him that I do not need my shirts and shorts washed, starched and pressed every day. But I am his only hope of escape. That's how desperate Agrippa is.

If I am your best hope of escape, then you are truly in the shit, I tell him.

He grins. 'No, *Shumba*, you will be free soon.'

In Chikurubi, not only is no food ever too rotten to eat: optimism is something on another plane to that of those who are *pamwe*, outside.

Chik Max gets odder and odder. They have sent three boys into our section so that they might be less often sodomised. They found out that the boys are too young to be here in Chik anyway. They should be in a young offenders' prison.

That there is a guy just come into our section for homosexuality – in fact with these same three boys – bothers nobody. Then the OIC, Makoro – meaning 'dug-out canoe' – comes to see us. He's CIO and a prat but he's OK. He is in our section to talk to these boys. He talks to them in *Shona*, at length.

Reon, or Rocky as he's known, listens and shakes his head. As soon as Makoro has gone, I ask Reon, what's the joke?

'He was telling the boys how they will go to a young offenders' prison as soon as possible – three to four weeks. Meanwhile, they are safe in this section. In their futures they must not again commit the sin of sodomy. Then he gave them a lecture about the immorality, as well as the risk of HIV AIDS. So then – get this – he tells them that, if they have any more trouble of that sort then – if all else fails – they should talk to us – the white men! We'll sort it out! They can trust the white men!'

Amazing.

Why should I worry? What are they doing out there?

Soon after that, we get a new OIC, Mudzamiri. He is a sport. Although not so much a sport as would allow me to escape.

One man in the section isn't pleased. The reason he's still in prison is that, having been told to clean an officer's car, he drove off in it. This was in a normal security prison. The officer who owned the car was Mudzamiri.

He has a thing about clean cars. Just after he takes over at Chikurubi, a bag of *dagga* – weed – is stolen from his new car's glove box. This theft must be the work of the car-cleaning detail. To catch the thief, Mudzamiri puts some more *dagga* in the same place the next time the same detail are put to work.

Success. On their guard, this time, the escorting officers collar the thief. They beat him half to death at the time. Then they beat the other half that Sunday, when Mudzamiri has one of his mass public beatings of homosexuals out in the centre court.

We can't miss it there. If we did miss it, we can hear them screaming from anywhere in the prison. But beatings are not the big worry for us right now.

Water. We don't have any. Other than thirst, the knock-ons are dire. We are told that Chikurubi – with its 3,000 prisoners – can be smelled four kilometres downwind.

I'm all right because – as with anything – money talks. I'm *Shumba*. In this case, cigarettes talk. Our hot water for tea and coffee keeps coming. Cost: one packet of 20 Madison every two weeks, or something like that. They'd taught me: don't pay the same sum. Don't pay when due. Make the *povos* sweat. Stay on top.

I offer, and have offered many times, both directly and through my lawyer, and through my family, to drill a new borehole. Fix the water problem. Dig a well.

My offer is unconditional and without payback. The ZPS would love to accept, but the ZANU PF Commissars go crazy: Mann cannot be seen to be helping because it makes it look as if the authorities can't cope.

The authorities can't cope.

Many days, 20 men die in Chikurubi. The count of the day's dead is never less than five. As soon as the weather grows cold, or there's no water, or there's diarrhoea, or we have a maize crisis … the count goes up.

It isn't simple. About one in three men here is HIV-positive. There's a TB epidemic – that's fed by the overcrowding and the endless passing around of the little *mudzanga*, or roll-ups, smoked by the *povos*.

Then there's the diet.

Then they die.

Of course the poor bastards die. Nobody gives a shit. The whole country is dying. We are at the very bottom of a very nasty shit heap. It's a bad feeling. Any day the infrastructure may seize up for good. Then we all die. Or there'll be a prison riot because we're starving and dying. Then they will come, shooting.

To the officers I say: 'The day you decide not to come in any more, remember to unlock us, please?'

They laugh: 'Ah, *Shumba*.'

I ask why they don't do something about Mugabe and Co. They shrug: ZANU PF won the war. They freed the country from the whites. From colonialism. To the victor the spoils. They must be allowed to serve out their time as heroes. One day, they'll all be gone. Then we can run what's left of our country better.

This is from a prison officer whose monthly take-home pay will buy him a litre of cooking oil.

I recall the time an EO white South African told a yard duty sergeant how pathetic Zimbabwe is, because they can't keep the lights on.

'How long has been South Africa run by blacks?' the sergeant asked. 'Ten years…'

'Twenty years, here in Zimbabwe. You wait another ten years of your black rule down south. Your lights will be going out.'

Light or no light, I've been burning the midnight oil. I've written a paper called 'Hurricane'. It is a true account of the coup plot. Wicknell and I plan to place it in a Zim newspaper, by way of pro-Mann propaganda. Everyone tells me how the media has painted me as some kind of blood-sucking, war-starting monster.

One guy – Henry – had his whole family in shock because I had given him my wool sweater. He was sick and freezing. They had refused to believe that a monster – who sucks the blood of African babies, and who goes around starting wars, and whose teeth are all filed to points – would do such a thing. But despite all this, their real shock was that he had worn it.

Henry never did give it back. Maybe he thought it was a gift. He's in prison for being a member of the political opposition party, MDC. Nothing more.

I have told Wicknell that Operation Hurricane must not go ahead without the nod from my sister Sarah back in London. Always, my wish is to be loyal to the chain of command. But I cannot risk a short circuit of whatever it is that they are doing. I have to believe in them. I have to believe what they're telling me.

That's why they make me so fucking angry.

Hurricane does not go ahead for that reason. My sister vetoes. God knows why… Why should I worry? What are they doing out there? My spirit is dying inside me, day by long day.

Wicknell begs me. He tells me how Zimbabwe works. He asks: 'Does your sister understand? In Africa the unsolicited gift is massively powerful. If one of us gives $20,000 to Mugabe for a birthday present, then it is a big deal. That person will be asked to lunch or something. He will be expected to make a request. He has earned that right … do you see, *Shumba*? … I mean – he may not get what he has asked for, but …'

Meanwhile, this book, *Straw Hat*, is slowly, painstakingly, getting written. The pages number hundreds. As a challenge, I am trying to write a good book.

Then it is stolen by Security. They destroy it.

So I start again. I've plenty of time. All I want is to have something written for Amanda and all the children. It may be the only thing that makes it home to England.

It may be the only way that I will ever again put bread on the table. They've done me a favour stealing it from me. It's all in my head anyway. Rewritten, it will be written better.

We have a saying here, a Chik Max maxim: 'Just when you think things can't possibly get worse … they get worse.'

The other one is as good: 'Hope for the best … expect the worst.'

JULY. MIDWINTER.

Sure enough, I hadn't thought things could get worse. Then, sure enough, they did.

But I am sick. At night, 5,000 feet ASL, it is freezing. Prison rules have changed. There are no more food parcels. I'm eating prison rations. *Sadza. Bota.*

I have diarrhoea. To me, like to most people, a runny stomach had meant a couple of days of holiday discomfort. Taking or not taking Imodium.

This is different. Weakened by the poor diet, the diarrhoea floors me. I've no strength. I feel as though I'm dying, and I don't mind much.

One evening, they come – when I'm at my lowest – and move me

251

again: 'A' Hall back to FB 1. These are the two max-max security sections, FB 1 the more so. Both are single-cell. Both have steel grids above them to foil attempted escape by helicopter.

I complain. I'm an old prisoner now. I hate change. I'd read about that (in Waugh's *Decline and Fall*). Now that is me. Like an old cat having to move house. Poor old *Shumba*.

In FB 1, next morning after we are unlocked, Hassan Banda takes one look at me.

'*Shumba, Shumba* – this is not you! Come – you are sick… We must make you better.'

So he does make me better. He knows. He nearly died in the last diarrhoea outbreak. It's easy to die here.

Hassan is a musician, in his fifties, and a soldier. He's South African, a Zulu and a Muslim – although he doesn't believe or practise. He is lucky not to have hanged. He knifed a man to death for fucking him over on a stolen-car deal. Luckily, there had been enough doubt to float an argument of self-defence.

His partner, Johnny, told me how he was a traditional musician. He needed backing. He told me that the steel jew's harp he played was best made from the steel rods used in reinforced concrete.

'What did they use then?' I asked.

Johnny looked blank.

'I mean, if this is traditional music, how did they make jew's harps? Before such steel came along?'

There must be an answer, I thought. Maybe soaked ironwood, which becomes incredibly hard.

Johnny understood now, frowning. 'Ah, *Shumba* … that I don't know.'

As a boy, Hassan Banda had joined *Umkhonto we Sizwe*, Spear of the Nation, the fighting part of the ANC. They shipped him off to Angola for training and war. That meant that we could swap Angolan war stories, even though our wars had been at different times – his in the 1980s, mine in the early 1990s. Same war. Just a long one.

As I grow stronger, and the weather kinder, Lucky and I begin running in earnest. Our target is a half marathon inside the yard. Hassan is timekeeper and lap counter. Sometimes the others sing and clap in their beautiful African way. Keeping us running.

One day, we go for it. We've worked it out. To run a half marathon, we must complete 850 laps. The yard sergeant tries to stop us. He is sure we are going to kill ourselves. He would be in the shit. We did it. The yard sergeant wasn't far off. Maybe we are obsessive, but we have nothing on our fellow inmates next door.

Next door – meaning over the 20-foot wall – through the steel-grid anti-helicopter top cover – is the next section, FA. They're religious, with competing churches in the same yard. The sound of badly sung hymns plagues us. All day, every day.

The mad-keen Christianity that is the norm in Africa angers me. I loathed religion before I came to prison. Everything about it in here strengthens that feeling.

'You really don't like it – when they're churching – do you, *Shumba*?'

'No, Lucky, I do not.'

'You know that they are the homosexuals, don't you?'

'All? How can that be?'

'Not all, *Shumba* – but most... And the worst – the most religious – they are the ones who organise the homosexuality, make it happen... You know what I am talking about, don't you?'

I do know. There is a whole racket to force young boys into sodomy. The religious make sure that the boys are pushed to the back of the food line. Then – once they are truly hungry – if they do as they are told, they get shunted higher up in the queue.

Then they get better food. Shunted some more.

It is a poor choice: die of starvation – or die of AIDS.

The prison officers connive in this food queue homosexual racket. In return, they get paid: a new blanket (in the days when there were new blankets) or a pair of trainers, or some *fodya*.

An ordinary guy off the street – if he has no money, and no pull – will be dead within five years of going inside Chikurubi. Since the sentences are long – and many men are here on framed charges – seeing and coping with tragedy is now my everyday life.

We are a black hole of misery.

Shumba has pastoral duties too.

I'm often asked what I think about things. Sometimes I am asked to be judge. I don't know which is worse: the Christian questions or the black magic ones. The latter, however, are more fun.

Our yards sergeant (a little Saturday afternoon drunk) tells me he doesn't believe in magic ... mermaids in the river, stealing clothes drying on the rocks and so on.

'Good.'

'And the bad things mean human blood, human sacrifice.'

'What? What bad things?'

'Surely *you* must know, *Shumba*? Things like flying baskets. These are true. They are woven from grass, you can fly around in them … but they are bad because of the need for the blood of people.'

'How do you know they are true?'

'Ah, *Shumba*, everyone knows that. There was a woman who fled her home. She flew from one end of Zimababwe to the other. Then she was found … alive … but – *NO BABY!* The baby was found in the middle of Zimbabwe, fallen out of the flying basket … so you see …'

Then Wicknell, well read and educated. He asks me about goldfish. After a while we come to the heart of the story. You can catch these goldfish in South Africa. They are worth about £25,000. About what a good VW minibus taxi costs. But you need a live boy as bait.

This is known to be true because a couple went to Jo'burg not long ago, with a boy, and came back with a VW minibus. No boy. There is a man in the section for murdering his son in the course of witchcraft. He claims that it was an accident, while chopping down a tree. I assume that this cannot be true: for the obvious reason, and because there are so many inside Chikurubi wrongly.

'No, *Shumba*, it is true.'

We talk about trees, and the forest in which sit the Chikurubi prison farm and the prisons.

'We will never chop down all the trees in the forest,' says the sergeant. A debate follows. In the end you will.

A young officer sits by the sergeant, on his upturned broken bucket. He looks at me. Then he speaks up. 'We Africans only chop down trees. Look at the whites! The first thing they do on a new farm is they start to plant trees.'

Zimbabwe is dying. That is true. But it is ZANU and Mug's fault, not the common man. It is not a fault inside the Africans' blood. I try to speak out, but the conversation is too political for the sergeant. He shuts us all up. Many times, I have to tell them that there is nothing wrong with the Africans. That they are as good and as bad as anyone else. They fear that they are a lesser sub-species.

'Where are our Beethovens, our Einsteins?' they ask.

Then the black magic becomes personal. A young owl is trapped beneath the helicopter grid one morning. As soon as we are unlocked, they kill it. I try to stop them but fail. The owl is haunted. It is bad.

Then I hear that I am a 'water soldier'. I ask what that means. It is powerful. It makes me dangerous. The story comes from that land of endless bloodshed and horror, the Congo. From the heart of darkness, therefore.

A water soldier is one who, as when a round is fired into water, is not harmed by the passage of a bullet. He cannot be shot.

FA – next door – do have their uses. Their Chik footballs fly onto our helicopter grid. We ask a passing watch-tower officer to go out on the grid and chuck them down. Simpler than making our own.

A Chik football is as good as any beachball. It is layered. Inside are three or four inflated rubber surgery gloves. These are held by having been placed inside a plastic shopping bag. The outer layer, which gives the ball its roundness, is a hand-made string net. The string is rolled from the stuff of mealie sacks. The sacks are carefully picked apart, then the threads are rolled into string.

Lucky and I hide the balls in the section's broom cupboard. It drives us crazy that, every time one of my guards – the army guards – sees a football, he has to start kicking it around the yard. Showing off.

A good football is prized by officers with sons. We traffic.

This broom cupboard is also Lucky's dead-letter box. This is where officers drop off and pick up contraband. Before they were banned from coming into the section, that is.

Early in my education – and the setting up of the 'travel agency' – Lucky had sized me up. Then he said, 'Tell me, *Shumba* – are you a good liar?'

'No.'

'I didn't think so. Don't worry, though. We'll lie for you.'

My education is an ongoing project for my friends. Just as, in return, I educate them with my books and our book club talk-ins. One guy at this time – in on a framed rape – wins his English O Level, thanks to my informal classes. I'm happy.

A month before his exam, he is moved out of our section for being too friendly with me. In fact, I think he is moved because I'd given him a pocket dictionary as a present. One of the officers whom I am also helping – illegally, and in a much bigger way – has grown jealous.

At this time I meet a man – black – who is in Chikurubi for an unusual offence. Even unusual by the standards of Zimbabwe, where the law defines good witchcraft (OK) and bad (against the law – go to prison).

This wretch had taken the name of his country and used it in vain: ZIMBABWE – 'Zero Intelligence Mainly Because All the Bloody Whites Emigrated'.

Colin, Norman and Lucky are my instructors in car theft – stealing and hi-jacking. I learn how to pop a car-door lock with a carefully cut-open tennis ball. I learn why – when I buy a new or second-hand car – the most important thing to do is be sure that I have all existing sets of keys.

They tell me of the car hire-purchase scam that they ran down in Jo'burg. Bribing the salesman and the insurance man are the key elements.

One day, Norman comes to me and asks to be taught about computers. This will be good, because the last guy I started teaching how to program bottled out. He was tipped off that Security were going to have a go at him, for being too close to the notorious *Shumba*.

He was an ex-general, and in deep shit with the CIO, for treason.

Norman and I start. After a few days – when it has become clear that computers are not Norman's cup of tea – Lucky drifts over to help out. We kick the thing around a bit. Then Lucky cuts to the grist: 'But, Norman, why do you want to know about computers?'

Norman looks round, then nods to the empty corner of the yard – the one where the sun is hottest at this hour and time of year. We quietly and separately go there – to do otherwise would attract others – then get to the truth.

Norman has a plan. Norman is another armed robber. Famous outside and in. He is even more of a 'Notorious' than Zeb and Lucky. Norman's nickname is 'the Refrigerator'. This is not because of his build – which is slight – but because he once stole an enormous refrigerated lorry, full of sides of beef. He drove the truck up to Lusaka, Zambia, and sold the beef. Then the truck.

Norman wants to know about computers because he wants to hack into the Police Vehicle Database. He wants to be able to flag a car on the electronic file as 'not stolen' when the police have flagged it 'stolen'.

Around this time the great suspicion that I am under leads to a backfire of the *Shumba* brand. I start making marks and calculations in the yard so that we can work out our Longitude and Latitude. I want to show the others how this works.

I already have makeshift sundials, using only the shadow of the helicopter grid. We can tell the time with such accuracy that officers and my guards often bring their friends into the section to show off *Shumba*, the talking clock.

Security assumes that I am up to something. Signals to London maybe. They make me stop. When I write about my barefoot astronomy to my poor boy – to Freddy – they bin the letter. Except they don't tell me they've binned it. I find out only because he will never get that letter.

One day, with the Croc in Security, I row with the Security lieutenant about another letter. This one had again been pulled without my knowledge, but I have found out.

I'm very angry.

The lieutenant says, 'Look, Mann – my orders are clear. I have to censor anything that I don't understand…'

'That should give you plenty of scope…'

All is well. Until the Croc gets the joke and starts laughing. The lieutenant's penny drops. The lieutenant does not enjoy my joke.

Security and my guards will not even allow me an electronic calculator. Plenty in here have one. All who are doing their Maths O Level. I tell them there is nothing that I can do on a calculator that I cannot do manually.

'What do you want to calculate, Mann?' they ask.

'Calculations,' I reply. Deadpan.

Luckily, I have made an old-fashioned slide rule from paper. I cut it out from an article in *Scientific American*, my favourite mag, along with *Vogue* and *Tatler*. For some reason Security allow those three. Although they keep on snipping out photos of girls that they think are too sexy.

A few times, after they have done that, I accuse them of encouraging homosexuality. What do they want us to do? Ogle the pictures of men? I say this is something they shouldn't be doing, when there is such a serious problem in this prison.

'Is there a homosexuality problem, Mann? How do you know?'

'Well, maybe we're just imagining it then – the officer in charge and me…'

But these guys are so Chinese/ZANU PF-brainwashed that, if the party line says there is no such problem, then no such problem there is.

Even if it is falling in on their heads.

At that time, a US supporter, the tenacious and wonderfully named

Street Brewer, sends out *Vanity Fair* to me. It reports how Tim Spicer and his company have just achieved the incredible feat of winning the USA contract to manage all the Iraq PMCs on Uncle Sam's ticket.

Of course, Security get their scissors out and obliterate the piece. Not least because I have an honorary mention. Equally, of course, Security fail to cut out the contents trailer for the article, so I can read what's happened anyway.

I cheer for Tim about this. For me, it is a moment of escape. It's my side scoring … somehow. I'm happy for him, and glad that, when I was asked, I sent my postal thumbs-up for Tim's election to White's. God knows if that made it through Chik Security. God knows if that made it through White's sceptics. Either way, he's a member now.

How strange it is. My exercise routine is everything to me. It allows me to hold my head up … to myself, if that can make sense. Sometimes it becomes really odd. One year – sure that I am going to be out in time for skiing the following February – I religiously start my best pre-ski exercise. The one where you sit against the wall as if there is a chair, but there isn't one. Very good for the upper thigh. The downhill racer muscles, as I had once raced. Of course, I'm not free that February, nor for many more. I don't ski. But it doesn't matter. I'm still strengthening those muscles. Something is happening.

Back in the real world, I love the men in my section. And they love me. We have to love one another because that is the way we do what has to be done.

Escape death. Survive. Get out.

Of course, like anything positive in this shithole, love is doomed.

'In Chik, just when you think things can't get any worse…'

Slowly but surely there is trouble brewing in FB 1. There is my lot. There are the neutrals. And then there is Valentine. The trouble is jealousy. Valentine thinks that if he can engineer the departure of my gang, then he would be top dog.

My best friend. Therefore, kept. *Fodya*. Food. Coffee. Money. Freedom.

The other problem is Security. I am the most exciting toy they have ever had.

We don't help ourselves either. A chance eavesdrop tells us that a particularly stupid yard sergeant thinks that I am about to be rescued by helicopter. Valentine 'helps' by telling Security that there might be truth in the rumour.

We play a prank. We start a ruse. Helicopters. We start to build one, a small toy. Then we talk about it, as if it's a real helicopter. We do so covertly – but loudly enough to ensure we are overheard.

A wind-up helicopter…

The joke works. It backfires. Our section comes under scrutiny. Security has a hard-on for us. At the same time, Valentine catches us making an electric kettle out of some wires and a razor blade. All contraband.

Next – unknown to us – he works out that men in the section are washing the clothes of officers. The 'travel agency' in action. They're not just washing the uniforms. There is a tailor's shop at work. Security's nightmare. Prisoners in prison officers' uniforms.

Valentine shops everyone.

As Reon/Rocky had so prophetically warned me: 'We all love one another in the section… We love the guards too … but that's because we have to… You see, in Chikurubi, all those who aren't spies want to be spies… They'll love you, and you'll love them – but that won't stop their betrayal… It won't be the spy's true story that fucks you, it will be his lie.'

We try to beat off the shit storm that follows. Then we try to keep small the harm done. But Lucky and Co. are arrogant. Valentine wins.

My whole crew are broken up. Dispersed all over the prison. It's a wipe-out. For Valentine it is a Pyrrhic victory. He too has to leave the section. He winds up murdered – still in prison – over a homosexual love affair.

Valentine is the one who laughs most at the notes I write in the margins of my books. He's the one most worried when he hears me talking to myself, as I pace my seven paces up, seven paces down … hour after hour … night after night.

They used to laugh at me bashing the mozzies – the lawyers, I call them – as I paced up and down. A pair of shorts over my shoulder or in my hand as my fly swat. *Bang! Bang!*

'You bastard motherfucking lawyer … take that. Don't you know this is a No Fly Zone?'

Not long after that, Lucky is out – having fixed a dodgy 'bail on appeal' ruling.

But Norman the Refrigerator suffers the worst. He has been a true friend to me. He has helped me out, often – and often when there was no gain to him.

Norman is HIV-positive. We all try to help. I campaign to have him signed up with a UK charity run by friends of Amanda: the Ark Foundation. They try to get anti-retrovirals into places that don't give them to their HIV people. Of course – that isn't allowed in Mugabe's Workers' Paradise.

A month after the FB 1 explosion, I'm passing through the Maxi Gate (with my standard ten-man escort, bayonets fixed: me in leg-irons, and two pairs of handcuffs, one pair for my two hands, the other pair round one wrist of mine and that of a Security sergeant) when I see Norman. He only just recognises me. I've failed to recognise him. He's thin and drawn, his head lolling. The two men carrying him do so with ease.

One month later, Norman is dead.

He dies because of the FB 1 explosion. He dies because of our helicopter. I didn't know that a small downgrade of diet could kill an HIV man so fast. Once transferred back to the madness of a big section, his diet fell over. Norman follows. It's all wrong. Norman could be alive.

Zimbabwe learns what is happening to their Refrigerator. Even so, food parcels are denied him. An appeal, to spend his last few days at home, is turned down.

It scares us all to see how brutal this gangster regime is. But for me – in the abstract – I am grateful to see tyranny at work. Tyranny squashes peoples whole.

But you can't become a tyrant on your own. It's a pact. Tyranny is a pyramid, and the pyramid is made of petty tyrants.

Beneath, the *povos*. Us.

I see that people ruled by tyranny are helpless to get out from under. Tyrants prosper, unless an outside force comes in.

My friend Wicknell – well educated and bright – will tell me a load of shit against ZANU PF one afternoon. The next morning I laugh at the unfree and unfair election results. 'Oh no,' he says. 'Don't you dare criticise ZANU! I'll report you to my uncle.'

Amazed, I ask him about what he had said yesterday. No, the election is free and fair. The Party says so.

Tyranny is many pacts with the devil. *Quid pro quo.* I'll believe whatever the Party says. I'll do whatever the Party tells me to do. In return, the Party will feed and clothe me. Put me above my peers. Everyone in the pyramid makes that Faustian bargain.

Every little tyrant in the pyramid lives by those rules. All the way up to the tyrant at the top. In prison I read Simon Schama's series of books *A History of Britain* (wonderfully and lovingly sent by my North Foreland Court buddy Tim Robarts). I am deeply struck by the English people's struggle to win their freedom, which Schama describes as 'the English Epic'.

In prison I think about how hard it is to win, with no outside help. How precious it is. How essential. How easily lost. How tyranny can take away freedom in different guises. Different ways.

It isn't that I have any great revelations in gaol. But I do find myself seeing things more clearly. Prioritising better.

The automaton Security officers act as programmed by the Party machine. They anger me. Sometimes I am rude to an officer. He says, 'But, *Shumba*, I'm just doing what I'm told... What can I do?'

'Walk out of here. Keep walking. Go to your village out in the rural areas ... but on the way – as soon as you can – take off that uniform. Burn it...'

Sometimes I try to explain how, especially at the Nuremberg Trials, it had been firmly established that there is no such thing as collective guilt. Each guard, each officer, each whatever is guilty for what he does. Under orders. Not under orders.

One sergeant, when we are talking about the cruelty of the prison, and of his government, and of his tyrannical party, ZANU PF, says to me that Chikurubi is a white man's prison. Africans, he says, didn't build Chikurubi. That is true. Chikurubi Maximum Confusion was built to a British Maximum Security Prison design, by an Australian contractor, for Ian's Smith UDI regime. They too were at war with their own people.

Chik has a gallows room and a guillotine room, with a coffin-making workshop handy next door. All these are just down the passage from FB 1, where I live, because it used to be Death Row. These days Zimbabwean hangings are all carried out at Harare Central, although two condemned men have been in FB 1 with me, before Valentine's explosion.

The sergeant is saying that Africans didn't build Chikurubi. Couldn't physically build it even if they wanted to. But wouldn't anyway. It is a white man's prison because it is carefully and methodically put together in order to inflict a structured and disciplined disembowelment of the human spirit.

Africans may do terrible things to one another, but in the heat of the moment. They'll chop a head off, or an arm, in hot blood. But long-term custodial imprisonment is not a part of their culture. They'll build a kraal of thorns to keep you in – for a while – maybe starve you – a bit – but not a Chikurubi.

As I tell them, when they say to me how uncivilised Africa is, that it was Europe, who in living memory, suffered World Wars I and II. Hitler. Stalin. How civilised is that?

The same sergeant, another day, out of the blue asks me, 'So, *Shumba*, all this Jesus Christ, and the Lord God Almighty … all this religion … is this something you believe in? Or is it just more rubbish left behind for us…? By the white man?'

'Just more rubbish,' I said. That was an easy one.

The Valentine FB 1 explosion comes at a bad time for me. I'm finding it harder to do my exercises and to run, because of my hernia. The thing is dangerous and needs an operation. I know that, if my gut becomes stuck outside the stomach wall, then I have only 24 hours to live. That isn't enough time to get you to surgery. Not in one of Mugabe's prisons.

One day, one of my hot water men charges into FB 1.

'*Shumba* … it's all over … you are going home …'

'Why?'

'There has been a coup in Guinea. The government is changed. You will be free.'

I start to cry. I sit on the floor of my cell, where I never ever sit, my back against the wall. Tears fall. My shoulders shake. I haven't admitted to myself before now how badly I want to be free.

Hours pass, then days. Waiting for news. It comes: there was a coup – in Guinea Republic. Wrong Guinea.

By now my visitors – the Croc, the British Consul (I'm on my third by now. They are all excellent) – know not to ask me how I am.

How do you think?

But prison officers asking me that question cannot be answered in the same way. Not because I don't dare be rude to them. On the contrary. *Shumba* can be as rude as he likes. He's worth too much money – to Mugabe – for an officer to hit him.

FB 1 now has four prisoners in it: three new ones and me. The three have all been chosen for being half-brained and non-English-speaking. They are there to sweep the yard. To do my *dhobi*. To do the things a white man mustn't do.

I complain to one of my best officers, one whom I have helped with money for his journalism studies. 'These guys in here, X, ... none of them can speak English.' (I must not name X. He's still there. He asked for more help the other day. But I can't help any of them just now. When I make some money, yes.)

'Ah, they can hardly speak *Shona, Shamwari.*'

But they are *Shona*, not Matabele. They are not Ndebele speakers. They are the village idiots, as they used to say – or shout – back at dear old Sandhurst.

One of the Security sergeants puts Magneto into FB 1. He takes out one of the village idiots. Even so FB 1 is now solitary confinement in all but detail.

I start to water the weeds that live between the concrete slabs. It starts as a joke, but then everyone joins in. One of the plants is milk nettle. Medicinal, so they say.

There are 14 plants of enough stature to count. More little ones.

I am alert to going crazy. I think. The plant business might be a sign, but I know that I am fine. Just before the FB 1 explosion, Valentine himself had become upset. He could hear me in my cell. Talking to myself. Pacing.

It's true, but that too is fine.

I found myself doing it, became worried, but then decided that it felt better that way ... so it must be fine.

I'm sure that I'm fit and mentally sound, even though the fear that I may go mad is real. I think about it often. Every time that I pass myself mentally fit and fine, I think of the comedy patient, in a straitjacket, in a mental hospital. He's Napoleon. He would tell you, if asked, that he – Napoleon – is mentally fit and fine too.

So, OK, ya.

I do talk to myself. All the time. I like myself. Sometimes my jokes are funny. I mean: I know I'm doing it. I've got to talk to someone. If only to cope with my ongoing anger for 'London'. When I get a letter from them, I know it will take me a week to get over it.

In the old days in FB 1, we used to have some very high-quality singing, led by Hassan Banda. African. Or Jazz.

When everyone left the section, after Valentine, I missed it terribly. Friday night was always a big singing night. Especially the last Friday of the month, when the officers had been paid their pittance. Their voices and complex intertwining African harmonies were wonderful. Fugue-like.

A couple of weeks after Magneto comes to FB 1, he tells me how much he misses the singing too.

'Well – Magneto … sing then!'

'But I can't sing, *Shumba*…'

I don't believe him. An African who cannot sing beautifully? They are born and raised to it … but it is true. Magneto can't sing. He asks me to sing. Magneto is vital to my sanity. I know that I feed him cigarettes, water, tea, food… Anything to keep Magneto happy, and in FB 1.

But sing?

I sing.

He asks for the repertoire again. Then again. The next night. The next. So now – most nights – I sing for Magneto. I don't know how many songs. 'Once a Jolly Swagman', 'A Bicycle Made for Two', 'My Rhubarb Refuses to Rise', 'What Shall We Do With a Drunken Sailor', 'Daisy Bell (A Bicycle Made for Two)', 'The Eton Boating Song', 'Swing Low, Sweet Chariot', 'The British Grenadier', 'Early One Morning', 'Sigh No More, Ladies, Sigh No More' (from *Much Ado About Nothing*), 'Rule Britannia' (with most words replaced by 'pom-poms'), 'Jerusalem'.

Magneto's favourite?

> *'Daisy, Daisy, give me your answer do.*
> *I'm half-crazy all for the love of you.*
> *It won't be a stylish marriage.*
> *I can't afford a carriage.*
> *But you'll look sweet upon the seat*
> *Of a bicycle made for two.'*

Maybe he likes it so much because it is short. We never ask the village idiots what they want, or what they think. One of them – a self-confessed child rapist – wasn't up to much thinking. He was the one I had to order to use a container when he was delousing his blankets in the sun.

The Croc and I work on a letter from me to the UK government and the European Commission. It sets out my situation. It begs that they should stop my extradition to EG.

I will be killed.

This letter is smuggled back and forth between me and the Croc as we draft it. It is moderate. Careful. The fair copy goes out.

'London' block it. They will not even allow the British Consul in Harare, Sarah Mannell, to see a copy. Not even if she sits and reads it in the Croc's office, then hands it back to him.

But why should I worry?

'London' are refusing me an advocate (barrister). They are blocking my letter to my own government. They don't explain these actions. They just happen. They screwed up the helicopter deal. They stonewalled Charlie Wake and his deal. Then Mike Christie.

Then they do the same when Wicknell gets out. They won't even see him. All along, I know they are acting in my best interests. The torture of not knowing what they are doing, and not understanding what they are trying to do, is too much...

I pace seven paces up. Seven paces down. Talking to 'London' in my cell. Cursing them.

Sometimes in Chikurubi, I forget that I have not committed a crime at all. I begin to think of myself as my fellows do: as a law-breaker. I forget to ask, whose law? By what right? By whose mandate?

There isn't a man inside Chikurubi who is more criminal than the government who had put him here.

Even if you say that to overthrow a murderous tyrant is illegal, or ethically wrong, I hadn't done so.

Intent is not an attempt.

Anyway ... where's my victim? Raped? Robbed? Defrauded? Hurt?

A little later, I am hugely relieved to find that My Honourable Friends among the UK Law Lords agree with me. Nine Law Lords agree that no offence was actually committed, whatever the intent. Of course, that the Law Lords find in this way doesn't help in the slightest. Even in the UK, all that happens is that EG lodge a new appeal.

Even more costly.

Then I get an email – brought in by the Croc – along with my others. Missed by Chik's censorship.

Two misses. It's incredible. I'm being censored by 'London' and the Croc.

As if the CIO Security censorship weren't enough of a head-fuck.

The email is from a woman named Miss Wilna Lubbe. She tells

how she has tried, but failed, to get through to me before. This time it works, because the email is short and vague. The 'From:' is someone unknown, some South African prisoner welfare charity. The email asks me to make contact.

When I see Wilna's name, my heart leaps: she is the old EO attorney. A message from her is as clearly from Coebus, Michael and Tony Buckingham as if they themselves had all signed it. At last, I think. My old friends are doing something out there. I knew they would be. I just hadn't seen anything yet.

By luck, one of Lucky's best 'travel agency' customers is around, and mad to travel. He has just been made a sergeant, but Security hate him. They know he is a rotten apple. I give him the codename 'Uncle Keith'. I write a note and give it to Uncle Keith to email to Wilna. He has to go to a Harare Internet café. I coach him.

Slowly, dangerously, through emails back and forth, a plan comes about. Uncle Keith will travel to South Africa, meet Wilna in Pretoria, then travel south to meet Mike Christie in Cape Town. (Mike was, in fact, already dead. I didn't know.) Sure enough, an escape plan is taking shape. With a little more money, I know I can make it work.

Uncle Keith wants to do a 'ringer'. He will get hold of an exact replica of the OIC's car. On the night – a wet one – Uncle Keith's 'ringer' will be identical to the OIC's car – in every detail.

We drive out. Guards salute.

Piece of piss.

It takes months but Uncle Keith makes this epic journey to South Africa. He meets Wilna, but obviously not Mike. His escape plan shuffles forward until, one day, I get a smuggled letter tossed into my cell.

My hair stands on end.

I read and reread. Over and over. Wilna (and therefore Michael, Coebus and Tony Buckingham) are begging me to sign a letter of instruction to their lawyer in London. I know of this lawyer because Michael had achieved great things with him in the old days.

They have a deal in place with the EG authorities that will get me out, in exchange for my cooperation and information.

I cannot believe the words in front of my face. This letter is not one from a hysterical or ill-informed source. The letter goes on. It begs me to do as they say because, they fear, unless I do so, there will not be a happy ending. They don't spell out 'Mann to EG'. They don't have to.

An answer is urgently required. They have given me a draft of words that will legally oblige my London lawyer to do as he is told by the lawyer instructed by Michael and Tony Buckingham. Uncle Keith whispers to me, dangerously, in terrible English. I have to do this *now*.

My head is in my hands. I can't bear it. Where is Amanda? I need her. My whole instinct and training is to stick with the chain of command. To be loyal. I could go this route, as they ask, and fuck up whatever it is that 'London' are doing ... are about to pull off. Whatever it is that they are so sure will work.

I stick to it. I am loyal. I write, but not the words they want. I tell them to work with my sister. I write to her telling her that she must work with them.

I hear nothing. Weeks pass. Nothing. Then a letter comes from my sister, who has spoken to Michael Grunberg. This lawyer has a poor reputation, she says. I curse, 'For what? For being effective?' In any case, she cannot see that what is on offer is worth pursuing.

Everything is fine her way, she says.

So ... why should I worry?

Not long after that, Uncle Keith left the ZPS, disgusted with my lack of adventure. He had wanted me to be his big meal ticket, knowing that, if he made my escape, then he would be rich.

Only three months later, I hear terrible news. Uncle Keith has been arrested in Harare. He was caught red-handed in a bank robbery, in the getaway car, with a Star 9mm in his waistband.

It takes another two months, and £200, but we get him bail so he can do a runner. This is Africa. A man can easily disappear. Then reappear as a new one.

Things in Chikurubi grow worse and worse. For me. For everyone. As they do throughout Zimbabwe.

Food parcels are again allowed for all. That is good, but expensive. The Croc's driver brings me a meal twice a week. The Croc brings another, and a small box of supplies, on his weekly visit. If he doesn't make a visit, then the driver stands in for him. The supplies are cigarettes (as money – I'm still not smoking but keeping Magneto and the other two supplied is no small matter) – and to pay for our water (cold and hot). Matches. Soap (laundry and body). Biros. Loo paper. Powdered milk. Coffee. Tea.

The *Shumba* café is still trading. Standards must be kept. The 'travel agency' is also trading.

The Croc brings magazines, letters, news. I have given up on books. I have many in Security. The Croc has many more at his home. I don't want to read any more.

I write and rewrite *Straw Hat*. Other than that – these days – I just walk: in my cell, or in the yard. I walk. But first thing in the morning I run. I try to run.

By now my hernia is bad. Every ten minutes or so, I have to lie down flat on my back. I push my gut back inside the ruptured stomach wall. I become good at this. The hernia is genetic: an inguinal hernia. The tubes where the balls drop through the stomach wall, when you are in the womb, make a weak spot.

I run. Not so far now. The hernia is bad. I have to make sure that my stomach and gut are empty at run time: 0830 or thereabouts.

I'm going a bit crackers. I know it.

Water from the tap is a memory. Although, with only four of us in the section, it is easier to keep our supply going. We get it brought in by means of my cigarette cash: our precious – vital – plastic containers are carried out, then back in, daily. Water of varying quality, from various sources.

Hot water – *mvura pisa* – still comes in twice a day – paid for by my *fodya* – in a prized and *Shumba*-branded five-litre plastic container. So tight is the water supply that the same container – but full of cold water – has to go out of the section. They're running so low.

Some days it comes from Chikurubi's own farm borehole (best); other days from the Egypt crocodile farm down the road; other days from the quarry (poor); other days from the Chikurubi cooking boilers (bad).

I am a water hoarder. I rarely have less than 200 litres stashed in containers in my cell. This has become an obsession. It started at an earlier time, when the section was full.

Somehow, during that time, I have become in charge of water, as if I was a young Scots Guards subaltern and these my men. My fellows are not good at self-discipline, or at pacing their use between the last supply and the likely next. In the end I treat them like recruits: lining them up twice a day, each with his allowed container in front of him. I walk along the line, issuing the ration, while warning each that he will get no more until the next water parade.

This ridiculous carry-on is liked by all. The other prisoners like that I deal with the village idiots, rather than they. The idiots like it because it allows them to take even less care with their water. The prison hierarchy look askance, then away – not liking it, but not caring that much. Thankful that the idiots are being cared for somehow.

Shumba is just about everything Security has been drilled to loathe.

Then there is the lice business. Being in single cells, it is possible – and desirable – to be lice free. I am lucky. I stay lice free for four years. When a man has lice, the only way to get rid of them is to lay out the blankets in the scorching African sun. One blanket at a time.

The lice cannot take the heat. They run for cover. There isn't any. They are easy to pick off the blanket. The trouble is that if the man delousing chucks the picked louse from his blanket onto the concrete, then the critter is still alive. If it is picked up on someone's shoe, then a new home, in another cell, inside another blanket, is possible.

The way to make sure that this does not happen is to place the picked louse in a container and flush it away with the next big flush. The best containers for this are small Vaseline jars. Their screw tops make sure there will be no escape. There are plenty of such jars. To my amazement, my fellows see Vaseline as a necessity. If they are rich, they rub their whole body with it once a day. I can see the difference. Their skin becomes shiny and sleek. They look good. Without it they look dull. There are times when I grow jealous of their skin. It seems much better adapted, tougher, as well as better-looking.

One day I have to tell one of the village idiots: don't hunt the lice off your blanket without using a container. He says, OK, *Shumba*, but carries on. I fetch him a Vaseline pot to use. Use it, I say. OK, *Shumba*, he says, but he carries on.

I lose it.

'You're an idiot! We'll all have lice because you're idle…'

'SPO, SPO … *Shumba* cannot tell me what to do like that … just because he is a white man, he cannot say what to do…'

The SPO in charge of us that day stirs sleepily on his seat, an upturned 25-litre container. Mine.

Magneto rushes into the fray. 'SPO, *Shumba* is right: the idiot must use a container…'

'Do you think I don't know about lice?' says the SPO. 'Magneto, *Shumba*, leave him alone…'

'Now as for you, Mazo … you know what is right. *Shumba* is right. Use a container.'

Food is scarce. There is at least one stretch of more than 24 hours each week when we get no food. We're only four, so I do my best with my supplies. God knows what is happening out in the big sections.

I fear that there will be a riot. If that happens, then they'll come in shooting.

'We're really suffering now, *Shumba*,' Magneto tells me.

'Travel agency' covers – mugs – served at the *Shumba* café are down. Each week. Security have made it an offence for officers – even SPOs – to visit FB 1. They lock the outer doors now. They sit on those keys now to the outer doors.

This sometimes means that breakfast – *bota* – is delayed. After starving myself because of the hernia – so that I can run – this is not good.

Café covers are down, but *Shumba*'s value is going up. The Security screw turns ever tighter on me. Because Mugabe is seeing how much fuel oil and cash he might get for me. Chikurubi, like Zimbabwe, is a sinking ship.

When I was first in FB 1, the officers could walk around outside our cells, even though they did not have the keys for our cell doors. It could be useful. Like when Lucky – King of the Blankets – would cry out from deep inside his bedding: '*Shumba*, I think I left my packet of Madison in your cell…'

Then I would know: I must give one to the officer, for Lucky. Which meant one for the officer too. Lucky hadn't had a packet of his own for weeks. He was always ahead of the ration I gave him.

But then – because the officers' pay has become worthless and the officers desperate – the rules change. Now, at the 1800 hrs lock-up, the whole section is locked off, as well as the cells. The officers have the keys to neither. All keys are held by the duty officer, in the armoury safe. This drastic step is taken in order to stop the trafficking.

Lucky's dead-letter box goes dead.

Thereafter, the trafficking has to go on when we are unlocked. A much more dangerous business. Everyone who isn't a spy wants to be a spy.

The fear of my going to EG has never once left me. Not since my arrest.

The fact that by now there are only us four in FB 1 speaks volumes. As my hostage value goes up – how much Mugabe will get Obiang to pay for me – so does my security.

Only selected officers and sergeants come into FB 1 now. Not even an SPO can come and visit without first going to Security. The screw turns. Many of the officers feel sorry for me, and say so.

'You have done your time, *Shumba*. You must not be sold now ... but you have been sold – there is fuel on the streets of Harare that is there to pay for you...'

At the same time, the wheels are falling off Chikurubi itself. Officers are not showing up for shifts. Officers disobey sergeants, to their faces. One watch-tower officer climbs down from his post midshift and goes home. Everyone laughs. But it isn't funny. My stomach is a deep pit of unease.

One night, I know that there are a total of five officers actually on duty. For 3,000 prisoners. There should be 35 on duty. If this place goes crazy one night, then the blood will be knee deep. My army guards, 100 men, are right outside. With the itchy trigger fingers of a scared elite.

The Croc has told me. And the CIO. And the British Consul. And the Army. If you go to EG, Obiang will put you in a pot. Cook you. Eat your balls. To boost his libido. Spread his terror. Now that fear grows. I think of my sister's promise, that I will never be sent to EG. Then I think of her other promise: that if I need an advocate (a barrister) for my extradition hearings, then I will have one. I do need one. Even the ZPS sergeants tell me that I need one. But I don't have one. All I have is messages that everything is under control. I know it isn't.

All the time, this fear of being extradited to EG is growing. One day, Magneto says to me that he has had a dream. That I am going soon. My hope is his hope because, if I am out, maybe I can get him out.

'Magneto, I may be going. But I fear it will be to EG... I can feel something...' – I look up and over the wall, looking east, to where the wall faces the outside – '...something is closing in on me ... out there.'

I think of my sister's promise. I will not go to EG.

I think of 'London's' track record.

Why should I worry?

Because I run I have to wash. For this I use water from a two-litre plastic lunch box. I stand in the vile black hole that is the shower. Black because the power is off. Black because light bulbs – these days – are as rare as water. There are no windows in FB 1. I share this hole with an unseen and uncounted number of mosquitoes buzzing around. My flannel – a sewn square from an old towel – I use to wipe on some water. That uses one third of the two litres. Next I soap with my hand, then use the towel again, with the unused two-thirds, to rinse off. It just works. When times are better I use a second two-litre lunch box as well, most of the second going to shaving.

I have a pair of running shorts – prison uniform shorts, but used only for running. I run shirtless. That cuts down on the *dhobi*. I am lazy about my *dhobi*, but Magneto is not.

Part of the point of running is my two fingers at Mugabe, and his piss-pot pyramid of petty tyrants. I can out-tough them – even the army who come and see me every day – when I am their prisoner. That's what my run says. They know it. *Shumba*, they say, how can you keep running? You've hernia … and no water … how do you wash?

Sometimes the soldiers bully me. Two bring in a bunch of comrades to show me off. One time, they come when we are locked up.

'If you come to see the monkey in the cage, bring peanuts,' I tell them. Another time, there are eight of them, from Parachute Regiment. I am running. They lounge against the wall, hands in pockets, eyeing me.

'These aren't real soldiers. They're fake,' I call out to the ZPS sergeant, sitting on an upturned bucket, next to where they prop up the wall. He frowns.

'These aren't real Paratroopers,' I call out on my next lap. 'Because real Paratroopers wouldn't lounge about with their hands in their pockets – *would they?*'

The jibe works. All take their hands out of their pockets. Then, hesitantly, four put theirs back in. All eye one another, for a lead. Taking orders from me must be wrong. Hands in pockets is wrong.

One of these four changes his mind. Out they come again.

Another stands with one in, one out. He puts the out back in. Then, the in out.

I laugh. Magneto looks away. Hides his grin. The ZPS sergeant and his two officers laugh openly. The army retreat. We don't see them back again that day.

When it turns out that the army had stopped my overdue hernia operation, I ask why.

'Security.'

'But you're the army … you're meant to be securing the whole fucking country' – Africans hate swearing – 'so how come you can't secure one sick white man inside a Harare hospital? …If you want to be a soldier, why don't you join a proper army?'

They love that. Coming from me especially.

Yet again I tell the ZPS sergeant, 'Remember – the army are here because they don't trust you – the ZPS.'

He knows it's true.

The funny thing is, so many of them want to join the British Army, as soon as they can. Their applications are in. Others – officers as well as men – want to be mercenaries. To some, I give the details of my friends' companies. Perhaps, I wonder, an escape can be engineered in this way?

Later, towards the end, when a bunch of them really piss me off, I let the ZPS OIC know about my recruiting office. I cannot identify the officers, or men, but this has to stop, I tell him.

Needless to say, the reaction to this is truly spectacular. Fireworks. CIO in and out. The lot.

Now the army come in and go out as if I have leprosy. They don't bother us any more.

Another time, when they again give 'security' as the reason for turning down one of my requests, I lose it.

'Security? Why don't you just shoot us all? Then there will be no security to worry about?'

Shumba, you see, never makes a complaint, only requests.

One day, an AK round is fired down into the yard. The jacket is brought to Hassan and me for inspection. The round had hit the helicopter grid, further amplifying the echo and roar in our concrete box.

'How much will that cost?' I ask the duty yard sergeant.

'Not much,' he says. 'How much does one bullet cost?'

'How much will that man be fined? I mean. How much will he have to pay for a negligent discharge?'

The sergeant stares blankly.

'He'll pay nothing, *Shumba*.'

'Two steel balls' becomes the key password and in-joke between Magneto and me. They (meaning everyone not a prisoner) would lose one and break the other.

There had been one time – early on, when the section was full – when I didn't understand very much about Chikurubi. Zeb and I had run. That day there was no water. No lights.

I stripped, walked outside, then bathed out of my bucket right in front of everyone else. The yard sergeant told me not to do it. I told him to stop me if he wanted to. How could we live without water? Without light?

Little did I know. By the end, no water and no light would be everyday.

The guys love my telling the prison to fuck off, but it is bravado. If they did, they would be beaten. Moved to a big section. Die. If I do it, nothing happens. Nobody dares touch me.

This is because I am the property of Mugabe, of the army, and of the CIO. I am valuable, because EG wants me. So do others. I am worth petrodollars.

Uncle Bertie, Uncle Keith's successor, tells me I have been bought and sold. Obiang wants me.

'*Shumba*, there is diesel fuel for sale on the streets of Harare. It is there as payment for you.'

Other officers tell me the same thing. They ask, 'Why on earth don't you have an advocate to run the case against extradition? Your lawyer is out of his depth with you.'

'Ask my sister!'

She has said don't worry. Everything is fine. She repeats: you don't need an advocate. You aren't going to EG. I know you're not.

I write. I beg.

Smuggled letters. Through-the-censors letters. It's no good. Everything is fine, she says. Everything is fine. Again. Again.

With my white trousers, made for me by Andrew the tailor for two packets of Madison – perfect, long white trousers with pockets – I sometimes wear scrubbed white pumps, a white T-shirt and a white jacket, from the same stuff as the trousers. I have a white sun hat. I must look like Lord Jim. All white. It is a way of giving two fingers to the system, I realise.

Despite our conditions, and no water, we are still well turned out, in laundered clothes. Fuck you.

When going to the section sergeant to ask for something, they call him *Mambo* – king. They go down in front of him on one knee. Clap their hand once. Respect.

When someone visits the section, we sit. Respect.

Magneto is 'the Sniper' because he sets up rat traps. He kills them, like a sniper. One night he and I kill 12 between us. Another time, when the water is on, we throw so many buckets down the yard drain, that we flood out the rats' nest below. We chase six or seven of them round the yard, until we have killed them all. In the big sections they eat rats. We never get to that point. Thanks to my rations.

At night the rats play football above my head. Along the large air vent that connects all the cells, and holds the long-dry lavatory systems. Or I hear them creeping down into my cell, looking for food, spreading disease, pissing. Leptospirosis from rat piss: a killer.

As well as being a murderer and an armed robber, Magneto is a tailor. He shows me how to sew, using home-made needles. No eye to them, just a hook at the point, like a cobbler's.

Magneto makes beautiful jungle hats for the female prison officers. They work upstairs from FB 1, where there are three women prisoners in their own section. He uses old green denim trousers. The brim of each hat is stitched many times, round and round. To stiffen the brim, he uses three layers of old-fashioned X-ray film, carefully cut out. His work looks like it was done by a machine.

All the girls want one of Magneto's hats, but they don't pay him. Next, we tell them that we are starting a new line – hand-made bras. The thing is, to get one of these, a hand-fitting session is needed. By me.

They laugh. Then one girl whips off her shirt.

'Go on then, measure me up!'

I blush. Dive for cover. Bluff called.

We do not have water any more, not out of the tap. Not for months. We forget what it's like to have a shower. Water from a tap. A loo that flushes (without a bucket).

Food is growing worse, and less. I do my best. At least Magneto's fed.

The lights are out more and more. Load shedding. Lines down. The prison stand-by generator is U/S. Or there's no fuel – not even EG fuel.

In FB 1, no lights is serious because there are no windows. When we're locked up at midday – as we are, lights or not – I cannot see my hand at arm's length. We are only out of our cells six hours a day at most.

Eighteen hours a day in pitch blackness. Walking becomes tricky. I count the seven paces, so that I won't walk into the ends. My hand I run down the wall. The lawyer squadrons – mosquitoes – feast.

Magneto shows me how to take an arm's length of loo paper, then split it in half, but lengthways. Taking the two lengths, you plait them.

275

When finished, the paper cord, hung straight up and down, will burn like a slow match. The men use it for cigarette lighting after lock-up. No more matches.

I use two. One at each end. They keep the mosquitoes away, I believe. They also give me a point to walk to. I can't write, though. That's a problem. When I can write, I sit on the concrete by the loo. The mozzies see this weakness as their chance of a lifetime. I have to take one of my big white shopping bags – brought in by the Croc – then split it out. I lay it on the dark-grey concrete floor. Put my feet on it.

This way – as I sit and write – I will see the lawyers, circling to bite my legs. I fight them off. The No Fly Zone must be kept clear.

In summer, Chik stifles. Bakes. In winter, Chik freezes. Chilly and damp. With a shudder, I remember the cold of our first winter. Shorts and a shirt. Nothing else.

Paper for writing on is a problem. I have to buy the exercise books (two packs of Madison per book: expensive). The books are smuggled into FB 1 from the big sections; the cigarettes out. At least I don't have to do as the *povos* do: make writing paper by layering and drying loo paper and *sadza*.

Perversely, there is no problem with the Croc bringing in biros. This is because Security – top to gloomy bottom – covet my blue Papermate Flexigrips. These are sent out to Zim by Sarah. Security can have them. So long as I get enough.

My EDR – 11 May 2007 – is coming closer. My painstaking chuff charts – countdown calendars – are clocking away the days. The weeks. The months. The years. My EDR is when I go home.

An extradition case against me, sought by EG, will be dealt with by then, the Croc tells me.

My second son, Jack, is about to go to war – in Iraq – with his regiment, the Blues and Royals. I can see him before he goes.

I ask the Croc: 'Are you sure I'm going home on my EDR?'

'Yes. I'd hate to come in here the day after your EDR ... tell you why you're still here...'

Surely he can't make that up? Surely I am going home.

One thing I had asked Sarah to promise me – one of three – is No More Disappointments. I tell her: I can take anything. Hang me. Just don't tell me I'm getting out of here, then I don't, again.

Surely I am going home?

Security will come and take *Straw Hat* again. They come. They take it all. The third time.

Wrong *Straw Hat*.

I knew they'd come for it, the arseholes. But the actual fair copy of *Straw Hat* I had already smuggled out of my cell and the section. My network had then hidden it. Inside my own suitcase, in the property store.

The Gestapo arrived.

'Where's your book, Mann?'

'Security need to vet it before you go.' (Never to be seen again, in other words. It wasn't.)

I kick up a huge fuss. The Croc will bring down fire and brimstone upon them and their first-born, I say. The Ambassador will hear about this atrocity. The White House. The UN. The Court of Human Rights… My huge fuss spent, I give them the plastic bag. I have it ready. Eight hundred pages of drafts, rewrites, repeats, unsorted in parts … a mess … Good luck, chaps!

The network then smuggle the real *Straw Hat* back to me. I lied to them. They thought that it had to go into my suitcase, so that I'd take it with me on my EDR. My suitcase wouldn't be searched. With luck.

Now I lie to my network again. I need the manuscript back for more changes. Back it comes. Why am I lying? Remember: everyone in Chikurubi wants to be a spy.

They'll love you. They'll betray you. They have to.

Once I have my exercise books back again, Uncle Bertie takes them out, stuffed down his trousers. I lie to him too. He knows nothing about the hiding, or the switch.

That afternoon, the manuscripts are in the Croc's office, carried by Bertie.

That night the Croc flies with them to London. The manuscript is given the treatment. Big Time. Not because 'London' values the book, but because 'London' is sure that I have convicted myself in the pages.

What happens next to that manuscript is another story, causing havoc between Amanda and 'London', who keep it from her.

It's three days before my EDR. I know that I'm not going home. I've looked forward to nothing else for more than three years. The Croc and my sister have not told me that I'm not going home. The Croc's promise – that I will go – stands. I'm going home. Never to EG.

But I know I'm not going home.

It's my shield.

I need to defend myself. One letter from 'London' during these days knocks me down for two weeks. The pain I'm in is an agony of frustration and despair. And fear. And more fear.

For me to tell Amanda that she is free would be wrong. Hopefully she has always been free. More free with me than without. Otherwise, what's the point? Even so, I have to tell her to carry on with her life. Have fun. She will know what I mean.

Writing that letter hurts. But I write it. I wrote one before. That hurt too.

I fear that she isn't there any more. I fear she is with another man.

Bang. Crash. *SHUMBA!*

Security take me to the OIC.

'There's been a mistake. Your EDR is today, Tuesday … not Thursday. Put him in khaki now … he must be in khaki before midday…'

My mind spins. Security take me to reception. A hullabaloo follows while khaki is dug out. Something is wrong. My EDR is right. The Croc has checked it. It's right. I know it's right. And why the fuss about khaki?

The Security sergeants swap. The one who now takes me back to my cell is the one who transferred Magneto into FB 1. Life-saver.

There are people around us in the passageway. This is very dangerous.

We're out of hearing… I beg him, plead with him: call the Croc, tell him what has happened. The EDR. Me into khaki. You must call him. Go into Harare yourself. Find him. Do what you have to do.

Back in the section, I don't know if my pleading has worked. Everything is wrong all afternoon. Everyone who comes into the section has a story: cookers, water carriers, shift-change officers.

'*Shumba* – you're going home.'

'*Shumba* – half of CIO are out there … for you!'

Then … what?

Days later I find out. Because of my message – delivered by the sergeant to the Croc – he had been able to thwart an EG and Mugabe plot to kidnap me.

In order for the plot to work, I had to no longer be a prisoner undergoing a sentence. Kidnap while on remand for extradition is OK. Kidnap while undergoing a custodial sentence is not.

That's Zim. Ridiculous. Thank God.

JANUARY 2008

Seven months after my EDR.

I'm still on remand, pending extradition to Equatorial Guinea. I have no date to count down to. No chuff chart.

I am really lost now.

I've served my sentence in Zim. I have this gnawing feeling that Mugabe is about to cash me in. I know that Obiang still wants me.

I'm desperate to escape.

Fuck the conditions. I have to be free. Extradition to EG means death.

An escape plan is taking shape. Uncle Bertie has been busy. He has recruited two other heroic officers to aid my escape. Uncle Bertie and I are making copies of the keys. Chubb, of course.

The door to my cell. The first door from the section to the officers' cage passageway. These are the two keys without which No Escape. The real ones live in the armoury with the duty officer.

Neither of us has done this before, even if it had been talked about on my SAS Combat Survival Course.

Our first shot is a farce. We try to copy using wax. The shonky, shanty town locksmith that Uncle Bertie goes to laughs. The second time, ten days later, we try with soap. Close, but no cigar. Another ten days and we try again.

We could open but we couldn't close. We need to be able to lock closed for the night rehearsal. Ten days later, I am sitting on my concrete bed. Uncle Bertie walks into the cell. He has come through both locks. Hallelujah! We have to be utterly silent. I hug him. I am in tears. We have keys.

The dangers of doing this, to Uncle Bertie especially, have been astronomic. If caught, he would be shot, after torture. I would get three years at least, if I was lucky. 'London' have paid Uncle Bertie the £300 for the key work. I am surprised. Maybe they've got it at last?

From that second door onward, and with the help of those other two officers, no more keys would be needed. Our plans beyond Chik Max are good, if vague.

Each of the officers wants US$200,000. Once operating costs are added in, the escape plan costs a million. The three boys, not unreasonably, need evidence of their money being ready – and available – before the escape happens.

The money is to enable them to set themselves up in South Africa. To buy new ID, a house, a small business. They are risking their lives. We will be on Mugabe's hit list for ever. They'll need that money for always having to look over their shoulders. To me it doesn't sound like enough, but to them it's a win on the football pools.

Fail: we are dead men.

Then the next step of the operation: Othello. One dark night, I'm going to walk out of Chik Max in prison officer's uniform, blacked up. Othello means I need theatrical greasepaint: easy to buy in London; hard and dangerous to buy in southern Africa.

I write another letter to be smuggled, for Sarah. The three plotting my escape with me – Uncle Bertie and his two friendly prison guards – need proof of funds. Some kind of underworld escrow account. We need her to pop round the corner to Covent Garden for my war paint.

Weeks pass. Uncle Bertie beats me up.

'You're going to die soon. You will go to EG. It's coming.'

Wait, I tell him. I have to trust 'London'. My fear is growing. I am losing my faith in 'London'. I begin to think they gave me the money for the op, as a sop. To keep us happy.

I worry that they have risked Uncle Bertie's life … for what?

They have let me get my hopes up. Why?

It can only be that my escape is coming by other means.

I hope that my escape is coming by other means.

The Croc sees me. He is worried. He tells me – frantic whispers in the passage outside Security – that the extradition appeal judgment is going wrong. My sister, he says, told him not to pass this to me. But he has to, he says.

Weeks pass. I pace my cell. Today, I tell Magneto – when he asks – why I look glum. I have this feeling: if I look over the walls of our box, I'll see the enemy closing in.

I pace my cell. I cannot deny my feelings. Escape. Faith in 'London'… I face myself: the time has come. If I am to live, then I have to screw down the top of my bottle again.

I must write to Uncle Bertie.

The lights are off. Mostly they are now. I've just told the officer, for his education, that Zimbabwe has wiped out 300,000 years of Man's achievement. No light. I climb up on the loo, open the cistern cover and stretch my arm deep into the ventilator shaft. Rat shit stinks. I take hold of the hidden cord. At the other end is the plastic instant coffee jar that holds my contraband — candles, cigarette lighters, bullshit notes, coded escape plans. I pull in the line. Taking out a candle, I spark the cigarette lighter. I sit down to write.

Drafts later, and still not happy, I try again. I go for it.

I keep thinking that 'London' has failed us. That is shocking to me. Not to Uncle Bertie. He's been warning for months that 'London' is full of shit.

Bought and sold. Diesel and petrol.

Forget 'London'. Let us go it alone. That is what I tell Uncle Bertie in this handwritten letter. To guarantee their money, post escape, I will stay with them, in South Africa. Their hostage.

The lights flicker ... the lights are on. How strange. They have been on so little. An omen?

They come on for me to sleep.

Tonight I can go to sleep feeling that I am moving on: for good or bad, we will make an escape.

Chapter Sixteen

WEDNESDAY NIGHT, 30 JANUARY 2008

I'm awake.

Afraid. Full of dread. Rats are here, in my cell, scuffling beside me. I can feel them. Nasty. Before I open my eyes. Before I throw off my best blanket – the one that covers head and body, a shield against the mosquitoes.

It is about 3 am.

Isn't it always about three when bad things happen? The graveyard watch. The secret police.

Isn't three in the morning the time we die?

They are in my cell, three of them, with a larger body of men pressing outside. Like bulls at a gate. This has been the nightmare of my days and nights; now it is here. I told Magneto they were coming. My prophecy.

They have come to take me away.

They? Mugabe's CIO, in my cell, to take me. The President's office, they call themselves, or the President's men. They wouldn't put Humpty together again. They wouldn't be able to read the instructions on the back of a tube of glue. Right. But they aren't to be laughed at. Many taken for questioning by them are never seen again. They tried to kidnap me out of prison last year but – by luck mostly – I foiled them. This time I have no chance. They are a black Gestapo, and proud of the epithet.

The CIO's mission is to kidnap me, steal me to Equatorial Guinea and hand me to Obiang. For God's sake – their last shot at this was a good enough clue. I have been told what my fate in EG will be by enough people to believe it. Once there I will be tortured, interrogated, shot. Then eaten.

'*Handei! Handei!* Let's go! Let's go! … Come on, Mann. Get up. Get dressed. Hurry up. You're going to Harare Central. Your time here is over.'

In Chikurubi, prison officers use your surname. It's a sign of respect, although I didn't know that at first.

'*Handei! Handei!* … *Schnell! Schneller!*'

My stunned mind catches up with me. I remember what I had been doing before I lay down on my blankets. I'd been working out my escape. One way or another, escape had been the tyrant of my thoughts since March 2004. Four years. I want to escape, sure; but not like this, not from Zim's Chik to EG's Black Beach. Out of Mug's frying pan into Obiang's pot.

Then I remember. Shit! The letter to Uncle Bertie is in the cell with me. It's in the coffee jar. Beside where my head sleeps.

If seized, the letter could lead the CIO to Uncle Bertie. He would be a dead man twice over if they caught him.

'*Handei! Handei!* Let's go! Let's go! … Come on, Mann. Get up. Get dressed. Hurry up. You're going to Harare Central. Your time here is over.'

'What the hell's going on? What do you want? You can't barge in here and move me without warning. Where's my lawyer? I'm not moving from here without him. Those are my instructions – from my lawyer – and the officer in charge knows that perfectly well.'

I stand up, naked, stepping out of my washed and lice-free blankets. It is high summer in Zim, roasting in my cell. Cell 2.

Faced with a stark-naked and angry white man, they have a look that gives me hope. Perhaps I can keep the letter from them. It is a pity that I don't have a hard-on to wag at them – to embarrass them further, these wannabe toughs. But not so tough about the sordid comedies of the day-to-day here in Chik Max. Not toughened to our shit stench. I can see their faces wrinkle at it.

Faking panic and anger, I repeat my mantra: 'Where's my lawyer? I'm not moving from here without him. Those are his instructions.'

As I bark this at them I take my blanket. I deliberately throw it to one side. I begin to pull on my threadbare khaki drill, clocking my kidnappers. I have never seen any of them before. But I know they are a mix of CIO and plainclothes police. All the plainclothes are new. That's a dead giveaway in Mugabe's shit-poor shithole.

My mind is racing. I have to hide the letter. To protect Uncle Bertie. That casually thrown blanket is now covering the plastic coffee jar in which I keep my contraband.

The CIO are now scooping my stuff into the worn but lovingly decorated cardboard box I keep in my cell. There goes my Penguin Classics *Iliad*, with me when I was arrested, still with me now. *Heart of Darkness* follows. I begin to get dressed, trying all the while to keep them away from the blanket.

I know that as soon as my cell is empty, and the routine opening of section FB 1 takes place, the officers in the cage will be in my cell, scavenging, filching anything they can find to sell. They will find the contraband. The letter.

I keep repeating my mantra: 'Not moving … my lawyer's instructions.'

They say theirs over and over: '*Handei! Handei!* … Let's go…'

My last chance. 'Magneto? You there?' I call out. Of course he's bloody well there, poor sod. There's no way he isn't there, next door in Cell 3.

'Here, *Shumba*,' he calls back, bravely, loudly.

'Ma one,' I say.

'Ma one,' Magneto comes back. Prison slang: a mixture of *Shona* and English. It means: 'Troubles? Oh yes, I have many ones.'

'Please – will you look after all my containers? You know that some of them must go back to our friend, Shambezi. But look after all my containers, will you?'

'OK, *Shumba*. I will take care of all your containers. I will.'

The goons are unhappy. They may not know 'Ma one'. They are trying to find some hidden meaning in what we said. They fail. They miss it. Instead, they hustle me to the officers' cage door and thence out of the section.

Goodbye home.

I hope Magneto has understood the urgency in my tone. He knows about the coffee jar, and its usual hiding place deep inside the ventilator shaft, the one that runs over our bogs. He knows I can only ever risk chucking the jar, anchored by its piece of string, rattling along the shaft like a ping-pong ball, when the officers' shifts change. I have to hide the stuff well in case our cells are searched. They are searched. They are rummaged. Hard. Often.

He knows what I mean. He knows the jar is out of its hiding place. He would have heard me moving it. He can hear me pick my nose in that cell.

As I'm bundled out, I think only of Magneto and Uncle Bertie. I hope to God I haven't cost them their lives.

At the Maxi Gate, I am the only white man among an even bigger crowd of goons. Maybe 20 in all. They look calm. Amused. By contrast, the ZPS men – another ten or so – are horrified. This – a kidnapping – is the one thing they always promised me would not happen.

I have always feared a kidnap most.

For form's sake, I have a go at Mashone, the OIC. I plead with him to telephone the Croc.

'Our exchange is closed, *Shumba*.' A lie.

'Then call him on your mobile.'

'No signal here, *Shumba*.' A lie.

He tells me he is sorry. He is clearly terrified. He knows that I am being kidnapped. This is the end for me.

They make me change into clothes from my suitcase. Jeans and the light-blue Ralph Lauren button-down shirt that I haven't seen for four years. Although I have worn nothing but prison white or prison khaki during that period, their familiarity gives me no pleasure. I call over the head man, a plainclothes police inspector but probably CIO as well.

'I demand to know what is happening to me. You know I have been told not to leave Chikurubi without my lawyer present.'

He measures his words. 'Mann, you have lost your appeal against extradition. Last night High Court Judge Patel found against you. We are taking you to Harare Central. Your lawyer will be there, and he will explain everything. You must come with us now. Quickly. No arguments.'

'And if I don't?'

'We will force you.'

'Then I want to make a complaint. You are using force to move me. I'm not going to start a fight…' – we both smile, while running our eyes over the massed heavies – '…but you are using force to move me. Were it not for your threat of force, I wouldn't move. Do you understand?'

'I understand, and your protest is noted: you are being moved by force.'

It is pantomime. I have to go through with it. I can't believe that 'London', the British government, the Croc and the rest will allow me to be kidnapped. Across half of Africa. To a messy death.

I have to register that fact. Make them understand. I am indeed being moved by force.

Only when I am dressed do they start to get rough. Handcuffs. Leg-irons. Another set of handcuffs fix me to an officer. I am an insect: wrapped up in a spider's web, ready for the larder. They manoeuvre me off the Maxi Gate loading ramp. They run me, pushing, pulling, punching, into the back of a waiting Grey Maria, its engine running.

The leg-irons burn me every step. That is not half of the pain. I am back where I was four years ago. Humiliated. Ashamed. Powerless. Disgusted with myself. I feel hostility, bullying, the misery of my first week in their hands.

Once inside the vehicle, I am fastened even more securely – the chain of my leg-irons passed behind the seat brace. My back is against the forward bulkhead, so I face aft. Troops, four of them, in full fighting order, AK-47s with bayonets fixed, climb into the back.

A CIO officer parks himself on either side of me. They mean business. I guess it is about 5.30 am when the wagon finally moves out. My predicament is as dark as the night. I am escaping from Chik, but not in the way I had wanted.

As the bus rolls out of the long driveway that serves the Chikurubi Prison Farm complex, I can see nothing about me. Nor do I want to be seen to be observant. I need to know where I am being taken, but if I'm too alert they will hood me and make me lie on the floor.

I have never before driven this route to Harare Central, but the place is as named – central. I know that downtown Harare is about 12 miles from here. But I wonder. No streetlamps, to cast their sickly yellow on to the gloom; no house lights; no traffic, even at that hour, if we really are heading towards Harare. Unless they are lying and we are not going there at all. The fear inside me begins to uncoil, its scales scraping cold in my gut.

The Grey Maria trundles along the dark road while the soldiers smoke and talk among themselves. The corporal, to whom I have often spoken before, chats in *Shona* on his mobile. Who to? The Croc?

I know these squaddies – visiting me twice a day all these years, checking that I haven't bribed the ZPS to let me escape. Zim squaddies!

Always asking how to join the British Army – as many of them do – or asking me for a mercenary job in Iraq or Afghan... Afghan, where my two boys are now – Peter and Jack – both captains in Guards regiments. Thank God they can't see this.

The two goons are silent. I recite my Chik mantra silently: 'Hope for the best, expect the worst.' Ninety per cent expectation. Ten per cent hope. I have been kidnapped. I am going to be smuggled to Equatorial Guinea. Murdered. Unless – my 10 per cent glimmer – the British government, the Croc or my family in London can somehow block that.

I am in this bus, heading for God knows where. How do I begin to set myself in order? Hope, fear, shame, self-disgust, rage – where do I start? And blame, too. How could 'London' have let this happen? How could my Brothers-In-Arms have let this happen?

Uncle Bertie was dead right all along. For God's sake.

I am aware of a faint glow pushing up on the horizon. I steal a look, trying not to make it obvious. Distant streetlights? A bush fire? It could be, but in my heart I know that it is dawn breaking and, with that, the dread in the pit of my stomach uncoils another inch or so.

If that is daybreak, then we are heading south-west. We have been since we left Chikurubi 40 minutes ago. We are not heading for Harare. Harare Central. Or Harare anywhere else. That makes it all the more likely that I am being taken to Equatorial Guinea.

I address my guards. 'I hope you two are being paid plenty of money for this.'

'What do you mean, Mann?'

'Your bosses are certainly being paid a lot of money for this. What you are doing is a crime. You'll pay for it in the end, you can bet on that. So, I hope you're being paid well – now.'

'You heard, Mann. Judge Patel, in the High Court, found against your extradition appeal last night. We are taking you to Harare Central. Your lawyer will be there. He will explain everything. We're just doing our jobs.'

'Just doing your jobs?' I laugh. How often have victims heard that mantra of tyranny?

'You have no right to extradite me until all my appeals are exhausted. The British Embassy has written to that effect. They've written to your Ministry of Justice and to the Ministries of Home and Foreign Affairs.

You're a bunch of lying thugs and you're not taking me to Harare Central at all.'

Ministry of Justice? For God's sake. You don't need to have read *1984* to laugh at that one.

Why am I bothering? I don't care any more. I feel bleak. I think of Amanda. I long for the love we once had. Maybe this change is better than nothing. Even the thought of being shot doesn't seem so bad. Better for Amanda and the children that I be dead. Not rotting away in prison.

'What do you mean, Mann? Why do you say we are not going to Central?'

I tell them I can see. The position of the rising sun. Our speed since leaving Chik. We must be by now about 30 miles due south of Harare. They look at each other.

'Ah, Mann, we were warned about you… *Shumba* – you are very dangerous.'

At this moment, *Shumba* feels as dangerous as Hello Kitty.

When we eventually pull up outside the guardroom of the Zimbabwe Army Military Police Depot, the bastards are still trying to tell me it is Harare Central.

'Put a hood on him!'

They have no hood, of course. They pull my threadbare old towel out of the pathetic cardboard box. Abducted with me from my cell, this they wrap around my head. They rough me up coming out of the bus.

With my hands behind my back, the hernia is forced further. They push me around. The leg-irons bite. I lose it. I pump up and down, shoulders working, ducking out of their grip, shaking the stupid towel off my face.

'You fucking arseholes…'

I should see it coming. I don't. The fist strikes. What am I doing?

They punch me. Shove me. Pull me. Handcuffs and leg-irons cut in with every move. The hernia is killing me. I beg them to at least cuff my hands in front of me, to ease the force.

'Here's your kit, Mann. Change.'

'What do you mean, "Change?" I am changed. You saw me getting dressed.'

They're at my old cardboard box again. Rifling through my suitcase.

'You look too well dressed, Mann,' smiles the goon-in-chief. 'You cannot look like this. I want you to put on something different.'

'Do you want me in something more … prisoner-like?'

His smile grows into a grin. 'Yes – more prisoner-like … exactly … but shorts…'

He holds up a pair of khaki drill shorts, tailor-made by Richard James of Savile Row, London W1. A long way from home.

'I'll wear them, then.'

'No. These look too good…'

'These?' I brandish a pair of crumpled lightweight khaki trousers. He eyes them.

'Better. But I want shorts.'

'Take these… Cut off the legs. These soldiers have their bayonets – use them.'

Changed now, I am put back into handcuffs, again fastened behind, and leg-irons. Unbelievable. They take me to a ghastly dungeon: small, dark, filthy. One small, high window, unglazed but heavily barred, lets in some light. I can feel the hernia push out again.

I don't understand. Why am I being treated like this? A prisoner for four years, I have never caused trouble, I tell them.

Push. Shove. Jab. Kick. Then the door slams shut. I'm on my own. I listen to the stupid fuckers, fiddling around with the cell's lock for what seems like hours. I want to see them all fried alive in rat's piss.

Then I remember. President Obiang has said he will eat me. But I love them all, really, the President included. My copy of *Introducing Psychology* – which followed my *Iliad* into the cardboard box earlier – explains that love of one's fellow men is one of the key characteristics to being a happy person.

This hernia is my constant companion. It was diagnosed as needing an immediate operation 18 months ago. I have had no treatment. The hernia pushes out of the intestinal sack more and more. You can reduce the pain and the protrusion yourself by kneading it back where it came from – lying on your back is best – as I have to do every ten minutes these days. But you need surgery eventually.

Now, with my hands pinned behind my back, I cannot stand up straight. The upper part of my body is forced into bad posture. It hurts. The fear of the hernia becoming trapped is ever present. That is an emergency. Unless an operation is carried out within a day, it will kill.

When the pain is too much, I start shouting. I keep shouting. My cries go unanswered. I lie there, on that filthy floor, on my side, wrists and ankles in irons, my hands and arms somehow stuck back and below my arse. Simon Mann, contortionist. For a time I despair. Then, as usual, despair gives way to something else. An awareness that nobody cares if I despair or not, so why bother? Now I feel more alone than ever before.

Not only have 'London' and the rest been wrong, now they don't even know where I am.

At some point, my captors come into the cell to rearrange me. Then they leave me, to play with myself again.

Out of nowhere: '*Shumba*! *Shumba*! It's me!'

A voice coming at me from above, urgent, hurried, slightly fearful. I look up at the foot-square barred opening. My cell is in darkness but at the opening, silhouetted against the bright light, I can make out an African head.

I can't see who it is. My mind starts to race. A trap? It wouldn't be the first time someone has tried to frame me. Set me up. It could be one of the soldiers that I know. Maybe one of the Commandos of the regiment that had last been guarding me in Chikurubi? I was friendly with some of them.

'It's me, *Shumba*. Thomas. You know me.'

'I can't see you in this light, Thomas.' And I really can't see his face. I can't place him. He must be balancing on something outside the window. The sill is about eight feet above the ground.

'It's OK, *Shumba*. I cannot help you in there… It's me. Thomas. You know me. I am a friend of Zeb…'

'Listen, Thomas – get hold of my lawyer. You know him. He will pay you. But you must get word to him of where I am. That's what you must do: tell the Croc where I am!'

He tells me it is OK.

Word of my whereabouts has reached the Croc. Zeb has already spoken to him. He knows how to talk to the Croc. So if the Croc knows where I am, so must 'London'. The British government – if they know where I am, surely they can put a stop to this? I line up my thoughts. The Croc must know. The thuggery can stop. The cavalry may be coming … but so may Christmas. I'm wrong. It's the old Chik maxim. When things are as bad as they can be, then you know: they are about to get worse.

That night is not a good one. But which has been? As the pounding hoofbeats of the cavalry grow faint, I can only see ahead my EG torture, and death.

I lie in the cell, in my own piss and shit, while squadrons of mosquitoes feast upon exotic blood.

Then – hard to face – another day. No better than the last. I am more in control of my body. With pain and effort I can just lie down or stand up, as long as I don't try too often. No mystery visitors at the window today.

In the afternoon I have a visit by a chief inspector, a torturing bastard if ever there was one. He has been responsible for my hardships from the first minute of my arrest.

'Ah, Mann. Now you are not so tough, are you?'

He has come to gloat.

'That's a fine new suit, Chief Inspector. And look at those new shoes … your shirt … your fancy tie. Don't tell me! Don't tell me that EG have paid … before you deliver me!'

During the second night of my stay in the Military Police Depot, soldiers come for me. Young, in a great hurry – they seem so frightened, so panicky, so jumpy – my apprehension dissolves behind hidden laughter.

There is the usual shoving and prodding as I am thrown up into an army truck. I help – anything to make it less painful – as I'm dragged along the filthy, torn rear deck. This is unlike anything that has happened.

A glim of hope.

More shouting. An oil lamp is lit. They place it in front of me, while six of the soldiers jostle. This gang scream and point their AKs at me. They're ready to use them.

I want to laugh. A mad laugh. To match this chaotic, wild scene. The truck, engine gunning, jolts off into the night. Our getaway truck. What is this glimmer of hope? This scene makes no sense at all – unless these soldiers are acting under the orders of General Solomon Mujuru. Am I being rescued, or aided in an escape?

General Mujuru is Mugabe's number two. Once Commander of the Zimbabwe National Army, he just about still is; his wife Joyce is Vice-President. He is the man who promised my sister that, whatever happens, I will never be taken to Equatorial Guinea.

Is it possible that…?

The truck lurches round a corner and knocks the lamp over, killing the flame. Puff. My tiny light of hope goes out. Ahead I see, lit by our headlights, an aircraft.

'*Handei! Handei!* Let's go! Let's go! Come on, Mann. Into the plane.'

My leg-irons make it hard to jump off the high tailgate. My hands are cuffed. I can't save myself. They shove me off.

I pick myself up off the deck. The hernia hurts. I try to push it back in. It won't go back. I need to lie down flat. Coax it in. I can't do that. The familiar charade follows.

I make the goon-in-chief own up. 'I am being moved by force. Under protest.' We both know our lines.

They shove me into the waiting aircraft, a twin-engined high-wing Casa C-212 200 Aviocar turbo prop. The Zim Defence Force use it for parachuting.

I've made plenty of military parachute jumps, but with a Zim chute? What if the rubber breaks? They're not planning to throw me out, are they?

They remove my handcuffs. Then, having run them through the crisscross web tapes of the jump seat behind me, they put them back on.

If we are going from Zim to EG, it will take days in this thing. An aviation adventure. Maybe a chance for me, Biggles, to escape.

As a trained pilot, I always enjoy the start-up/take-off sequence. But now, as we take to the air, I regret all the time and money spent struggling through my flying courses and exams. Amanda said I should do it; fulfil a lifelong dream.

Now, as I squint at the flight deck instruments, too far away to see the numbers, I regret the waste. How could I, stupidity and arrogance, be in love with a woman as wonderful as Amanda, then waste time not being with her?

It cannot be that we will make the journey to EG in this Casa. We've been flying 40 minutes. My time and distance computer has been spinning. Too many difficulties with fuel stops. Some of the countries en route are not on good terms with either Zim or EG. As if reading my mind, the Casa's engines change note and it begins its descent.

I pick up words from the goon chat: we are flying into Bulawayo. I'd always loved the name Bulawayo. I remember that it comes from the Sindebele word 'KoBulawayo': 'The place where they are all killed'.

Our last chance to refuel in Zimbabwe perhaps?

Now is my last chance for a goodbye para jump – without a parachute. 'Glory, glory…' I eye the door and handle. Measure the paces I need to make. Weigh up the goons. But ambition is greater than ability yet again, Mann, even if I am handcuffed to the jump seat.

Hallelujah!

I think yet again about Richard Westmacott, my great friend and SAS Brother-In-Arms, shot dead in Belfast. The battle he had with his parachuting. I must have thought of Richard every single day that I have been in Chikurubi.

It must be about 11 pm. Bulawayo Airport is dead. We wait and wait. I'm dying for a piss. Bursting. The whole hernia thing has upset my bladder. It's sore. I am cold in thin shirt and cut-off shorts.

When an An-12 lands, then taxis over, my police cadet and soldier escort show nerves. They think that this is my air cavalry. Attacking. I hope … but shit … no flashbangs… And, no … they are not my hostage release team. A little later an Air Zimbabwe Boeing 737-400 lands, taxis and parks up close to us.

The penny drops. This Casa was only ever meant to take me as far as Bulawayo. The bloody Boeing is Mug's own. Tonight it is mine. I will be flying out of Zimbabwe VVIP.

But not before my captors have another go at showing me how tough they are. The Casa has no step and, despite the fact that I am wearing leg-irons, they push me out of the side door. Free fall.

I am bundled into the back of a waiting car. A large man is already on the far side of the bench seat. As I am pushed into the middle, another large man squeezes in beside me. Pally. Five or six heavy large bags are hastily thrown on top of us.

With this cunning camouflage, the car rockets off. We drive 300 yards in a circle before they dump me at the foot of the 737's boarding steps. The point of this is beyond me. The airport is deserted. Nobody is watching.

The charade is proof, if proof were needed, that they are acting illegally. If this kidnap were legal, Mugabe would like nothing better than to parade me through Harare International Departures. In chains. Cameras rolling. There'd be a parade, a national holiday.

At some point during the Boeing flight, I wake. The plane is in darkness, apart from my ten-man escort and the crew. The latter are supposedly ignorant of what is going on. There was a ludicrous 'Welcome aboard' rigmarole when we embarked.

Flying over Africa at night is Europe upside down.

Instead of an overcast and darkened sky, there are, above, all the bright stars of the South. Rather than a carpet of man-made lights below, there is darkness. There are men, women and children down there, just the same, but they have no artificial lighting.

I read *Heart of Darkness* in Chikurubi, then *Lord Jim* as counterweight. Now I am flying over that darkness, not far from Joseph Conrad's great dragon, the Congo River. Even now I feel the same old rush of spirits inside me, caused by the wild lands below.

In my cardboard box, still with me, is my Penguin *Heart of Darkness*, marked up with highlights of interest to help write this book.

When I wake again, the instrument pilot in me tells me that we are in the latter stages of a descent and approach. At my elbow, the dozy lump of goon escort is asleep. I crane my neck around him. I try to catch glimpses of the city below. I peer through layers of cloud. As the aircraft banks to port, I look across the aisle and out of the windows on that side.

Sitting across the aisle from me is the CIO man running this part of the show. The goon-in-chief. He is scribbling away. His ballpoint pen catches my eye. It is light blue and flexible, with a click-button top. Papermate Flexigrip. Such pens are highly prized. How come this goon-in-chief has one of these pens? Maybe nothing, maybe everything. Did the Croc give him one? While they had a friendly chat. With brown envelope.

He notices me watching. Is that sympathy? Surely not.

But now we are descending into Malabo, the place I had planned to fly into – to take over – four years earlier. I'm here now. It has come to this. The last stop.

The plane banks again, this time to starboard, leaning into its descent. Below, I see many ships at anchor in the port, then a long spit of land that forms the outer breakwater. Luanda harbour; it looks just like Luanda harbour.

Odd that the intended target of the coup – Malabo – should so resemble the capital of Angola, my country. The very place where, in 1993, I became *Il Condottiero*, *El Mercenario*.

Idiot.

I look again, then again, more closely at the rising city. My heart leaps. I could kick myself. How could I not have seen where I am? It looks like Luanda because it bloody well is Luanda.

Dummy.

We must be stopping to refuel. I may have a chance. Halt this monster. Luanda is my home. Angola my country. Maybe there is something I can do. Maybe a friend can help.

So much for the heart of darkness. If this is Luanda, then the darkness that just stirred me, that rekindled a longing in me, must have been much further south than the Congo River. We must have been flying over the Angola–Zambia border. Over the basin of the Zambezi. Giant sable country, to a Shikari.

It makes sense that the Air Zim 737–400 should call in here. When we were planning the March 2004 coup – Plan E, the final attempt after I had aborted the first stab, Plan D – we had wanted to fly our ex-USAF Boeing 727-100 directly from Harare to Malabo.

Given our take-off weight (heavy: it included military equipment plus a 69-man force and crew) and Harare's height ASL – 5,000 feet – the aircraft would only just have had enough fuel for that range. Technically speaking, we didn't have enough fuel.

We didn't have the range; except that we did – because we were prepared to cut corners and bust regulations. We'd achieve the former by cruising on only two of the three engines, and the latter – well, that was incidental, an irrelevance since we were about to commit a private act of war anyway.

Given the high risk of bad weather at Malabo, especially in March, the whole thing was fraught with danger. The dreaded ITCZ would have been slap over the island.

Given that there was no Instrument Landing System, and that the runway might be unlit and unsecured, 'fraught with danger' becomes an understatement.

I wonder why I pressed on.

Once on the ground, I ask my escort – the dozy one, window side – why we have stopped in Luanda. His eyes widen. What does his village do without the village idiot?

'Mann – why do you think this is Luanda?'

'I lived here once,' I answer and pause. '…and because it says so.' I nod in the direction of the enormous lettering on the terminal building: *Quatro de Fevereiro* International, Luanda.

He still doesn't get what a dozy cunt he is. He is hurting me with these irons, hand and foot. Loving him is growing harder. Forgiveness is a taller and taller order.

If I could somehow cause a delay, or something that meant I had to be taken off the aircraft, I would demand that the Angolans throw me in their gaol. From there I might be able to escape. Jump over a wall. Diplomatic means. Legal means. Any means, for God's sake.

From where came this curious sense of comfort, in the familiarity of place? On arriving at the Zim Army Military Police Depot, before the flight, I had experienced a confusing sensation that I was home. Even after four years in the nick, I felt a reassuring institutional similarity between the Zimbabwe Army and the British.

Then, during the descent to Luanda Airport, I felt, if only briefly, like I was heading home. Now, I believe that it would be a good thing to end up in gaol here. I know about Angola. Its gaols. I am in real trouble if I want to go to one of them.

I pull myself together. If I am seeing gaol here as good news, then I am truly fucked. There is the one chance. Wicknell and I planned it. Maybe he had a warning of what was going on with this flight.

Maybe he did what he said he was going to do.

To mock me further, out of that same side window I catch sight of a shiny British Airways Boeing 767. Parked unassumingly on the tarmac, with DayGlo plastic cones placed at each corner. A wishful defence against the crazed Luanda ground crews. That looks like home.

Impossibly close. So out of reach.

This is it. Wicknell's chance to be a star. Then mine.

I ask to go to the heads. This takes the goons by surprise. They plot and plan, then bundle me aft. They unlock my handcuffs from behind my back. They relock them in front. They push me into the loo.

'I need a shit. Close the door! We don't want the hostesses seeing me having a shit, do we?'

'Shut up! Get on with it!' shouts the goon as he stands at the door, holding it open.

Pride long ago drained from me. I don't care.

Body pumps. Mind races. Running through our mad plan. Wicknell and I cooked it up, sitting on the floor back in good old FB 1. By this plan, there will be a 9mm handgun in among the stacked hand towels of the aircraft's rear head. The last time I'd been was just before take-off from Bulawayo. The goon on shithouse detail had blocked me from the hand towels that time.

I must try harder.

Months ago, back in Chik, Wicknell had promised: if he learns that I am being flown to EG, he will slip a 9mm handgun onto the aircraft, in among the hand towels in the aft head. He has the guns. He has the contacts. He knows all the security men airside at Harare International. His uncle is their boss. It is a straw. I'm clutching…

I finish my shit and wipe my arse, putting both handcuffed hands between my legs from the front. I stand up, rinse my hands in the micro sink. Goon eyes bore into me. I go for the towels. I make a meal of taking one. Clumsy me. I tug out others.

If I pull a 9-milly out of these towels, the wankers will die of shock. But I don't…

No gun. It was never there. No hope.

This is it. They will cuff me again. Hands behind my back, I can do *nada*. I spin … dive … reach for the starboard rear door. Opposite the head. First goon falls back to my lunge. Pass him.

Second goon runs at me, grasps my chest. I heave at him. Frantic. Reach that door handle.

Third goon hits.

In irons, my legs won't move right. I might make it. Reach that door. Pop it. Jump.

Flying sideways, back aft down the aisle. Fourth goon has hit. My wind all knocked out.

That's it.

They re-cuff me. Rougher now: punches, pummelling, kicks. They force me to my seat. The cabin steward looks on aghast.

'Go and tell the captain of this aircraft what you saw,' I yell at him. 'I demand to see him. Go. Go and do it.'

The wretched man looks terrified. The goons curse him but he goes to the flight deck nevertheless. He looks over his shoulder as he walks. When he comes back, the goon-in-chief fixes him with a look that would stop a buffalo.

But he lets him speak. He must feel he has to. The captain – I've seen him from behind – is white. We are sure to have friends in common, if nothing else. I stare at the steward's mouth, hoping for words to save me. Nervous, he speaks. The captain won't see me, he stutters. But I can give my message to him and he will pass it on to the captain, for sure.

'Tell him that this flight is illegal. My extradition has not been carried out correctly. You and the captain are committing a crime. This flight is illegal…'

I check myself. After all this, why do I still have such faith in the law?

'None of that! None of that!' shouts the goon-in-chief. 'Go! Go and tell the captain if you like. But this extradition is legal.'

Like hell it is. I've been kidnapped. I'm being smuggled. Trafficked.

Excitement over, the waiting starts. For what?

We have fuelled up, so what are we hanging around for? Not that I want to leave, but the delay brings me another glim of hope.

The Croc? 'London'? The British fucking government? Are they hot on my trail? This delay might be because they know that I am in Luanda. They are protesting to the Angolan government: I am being moved through their sovereign territory in a manner that breaks the terms of every fucking international fucking treaty ever pissed on.

I hope. Now, my only hope.

Luanda. In shackles, in Mug's stationary aircraft, at this Mad Max airport, I think of the other times I've sat here. Heady days some. Near-death others. I think of the times I have flown back-seat on combat sorties.

A figure I have not seen before peels out from Club Class. He makes his way for'ard, out of the aircraft. He is an Equatorial Guinean, I am sure. His clothes are smart, new. Black and red trousers, shirt and cap, Ferrari-branded. Flashy bastard. But no way is he Zimbo (even if that's the look they dream of). When he comes back, he is lighter. The air of the pilgrim who has paid so that the others may carry on with their journey.

He has not been called for earlier because the Zimbos – as I guess – are trying one of their pathetic money scams on the fuel … even with their sub-prime UN Red List extinct credit.

We take off – at last – from *Quatro de Fevereiro* International.

I peer out of the window, as best as the goon and my cuffs allow. Longing, I watch the early-morning landscape fall away. Sad farewell to blue remembered hills.

Minutes later, down there in the water-heavy clouds coils the great river. The dragon. Vast masses of water rushing forth, beyond the estuary, towards the river's deep ocean trench. Beyond me is my next stop. Last stop.

Destination: Treasure Island. Fantasy Island. Torture Island.

I think of all the many slaves shipped out from Luanda. Angola: jewel in the crown of the Portuguese empire. For centuries, slaves were the main export, mostly to Brazil. I've joined them now. I'm bought and sold. Dragged from pillar to post, chained hand and foot.

I sleep. Thankful to tiredness for smothering me.

Awake – how long? – my canoe has drifted into calm waters. Strange.

I think: if they are going to torture and kill me, I'll have to get through it. Except there will be no other side to get through to. Maybe they are after my help. My INT. They're welcome to it.

I hope they won't hang me. I'd rather be shot. If I am to be *plat du jour*, then why should I care what sauce?

Friends and foes alike back in Zim assured me that my execution – should I reach EG – was a dead cert. Obiang, my coupee, is reported to 'eat the brains and testicles of those he particularly dislikes'.

Bioko Island glides out from under the starboard wing. Shit.

Bright-green jungle green draped over the old volcano mountain. Jagged rainforest crags. Unspoilt. Climax. Primary. All around glittering bright-blue Atlantic Ocean, the Guinean Bight.

Wow. I still love flight.

I do love life. I think of how I do love Amanda. To love life you have to love someone else as well. Without a lover, then everything is blotting paper.

It blows my mind. Because, as we arrive, I get that same sense of relief that bemused me when I was first arrested. Four long years ago in Zim. It goes like this: now I'm really fucked – so let's leave off worrying. Not brave. Not unafraid… Just like I'd run out of the stuff.

After we land, I look out. There it is. The airport had been the first objective. The control tower. Terminal building. Key points. The 737 taxis past the normal parking spaces. I catch sight of an old, derelict An-12. Our *Herkski*. The very same one that I had chartered and based in EG all those years ago. The one that failed us so badly in the first coup attempt: Plan D.

Why do people hang on to these old crates? I wonder. I know the answer: they're idle. It's easier to watch them rot than it is to bulldoze them, scrap them.

Now, our old Cold War aircraft has a warm four-year overcoat. Bright-green rainforest moss. A prop from *Planet of the Apes*.

Mug's 737 comes to a standstill. We're a long way from the main buildings. Out on a distant taxiway, I watch army vehicles speed towards us, then surround the aircraft. Chilly.

Goons bully me down the aisle. No niceties. No farewells. My legs have grown bigger during the flight. I am in agony. Leg-irons: a steel noose around each swollen ankle.

I make my way slowly, painfully down the steps. At the bottom waits a neat, slim and well-dressed black man. He smiles, takes my arm and helps me towards a police Toyota Land Cruiser. Two soldiers stand by the wagon, with side arms only.

'If you help us, Señor Mann, I promise we will help you. Everything will be OK for you. You will see. But you must help us. If you help us, the President will do something for you.'

EG's Minister of Security, and the head of its prison service, General Manuel Ngema Mbo. He tells me who he is.

One of the soldiers holds open the rear door of the Toyota and ushers me in. They climb into the car, one beside me, the other at the wheel. The engine revs up. We drive off, the central vehicle in a heavily armed, speedy convoy of six.

Helping the EG crowd can mean only one thing: working against the Boss, Thatcher and the rest, my erstwhile Brothers-In-Arms. Nothing would give me more pleasure than undoing those men. They have broken their oaths to me. Oaths of armed brotherhood.

If I could help to nail them, then I could win yet. Maybe.

Off the back of the Toyota. They walk me into Black Beach prison. Dreaded place. My hernia hurts. I need to lie down. Get my gut back in. Everything hurts.

After the rumpus in Luanda, these Zim goons have made sure that my cuffs and leg-irons are clamped too tight. My body has rebelled. Now my flesh, swollen from the long flight, has puffed up. Flesh pushing against steel. Steel bites.

We walk through the prison yard. A crowd of black faces stare. Hundreds. I'm used to that, but these are new. The EG goons walk with me, so too the Zim. The General is beside me. Looking after me, I think.

That's a stupid thought, I tell myself.

Coming from the *1984*-like monolithic reinforced-concrete battleship blockhouse of Chik Max, as I am, Black Beach doesn't look like a prison. Two floors, whitewashed walls, red Spanish tiles on a pitched roof.

There's a steel door, leading into dark shade. More black faces. A shop, really just a stall, with a money tin and tall stacks of goods. Fags, match boxes, sardine tins, soap, sauces, football mags, pencils, razors, toothpaste, Laughing Cow, Gold Blend… It's Fortnum & Fucking Mason.

I look at the man manning this emporium. I stare. A woman. My Chikurubi-brainwashed brain goes into a flat spin. This cannot be.

I listen for screams as I walk. This is Black Beach. This is where the torture happens… Is this Club Med?

We go up two flights of stairs. Once inside, it looks like a prison after all: cells along the inner space, which is all open. The upper balcony that circles the building is cut off from the bottom by wire mesh. If you jump you won't fall.

Walk along the west side – I think it's west – and into – can it be? – Cell 6. My crowd of goons pile in. I sit on the bed. A bed with springs. A mattress. These are objects that for me have become myths from a fabled but Golden Age. Quickly I lie down on my back, then shove my hernia back in. General Manuel frowns.

He talks to the young officer, the one that drove me from the airport. He is the OIC, I will find out. The man goes over to the corner of the cell, turns on the shower, then the tap on the sink, then he flushes the loo.

I gasp.

I haven't seen water run out of a tap for months. I stare. The lights are on. If they go out, there is a foot-square steel-barred opening in the wall. I will never be without daytime light. I try to adjust to these wonders. The cell is the same length as in Zim (seven paces) but twice the width: ten feet instead of five.

For four years, I haven't seen my face. No mirrors. No photos. Nothing. I see a mirror over the sink. I stand, look at myself.

I grin. It's my own ugly mug. I laugh.

Four new plastic bags are pushed at me. I open them. Inside are brand-new uniforms, grey with white and grey stripes. New. It's Christmas. In Chikurubi, some prisoners have no uniforms at all. There are fights for uniforms. Here, I have already spotted, people wear civvies if they like, but they still get new uniforms.

I turn to the Zimbabwe goons. They are watching. They don't like this.

'You see! Here the water flows, electricity works, new uniforms … at least this is a country that works.'

'Shut up, Mann,' they say. Dopey.

Then I see what they are worrying about: the handcuffs and leg-irons are theirs. They are on their signature. They take them off. Heaven.

I change into one of the crisp new uniforms.

Then EG handcuffs and leg-irons are put on. Not a good moment. These are more modern than Zim's, and they are put on properly, so they are loose, but they are a bucket of cold water over my happiness. My executive suite has lost some charm.

But a bucket of ice water would not go amiss. The heat and wetness of the air are a too-hot sauna. There's no air moving.

A Chinese doctor checks me out. Nobody can tell him anything. Nobody speaks Chinese.

With the General is a young plainclothes cop: his interpreter. He wears with pride a badged jacket: INTERPOL.

'You must put me on malarial prophylactics… Please.' My request.

They don't.

Outside there is mayhem: everyone on the first floor, many of them, maybe four to each of twenty cells, are packing up and herding downstairs. If I hadn't worked out that this exodus was because of me, their looks would have told me.

Over the next few days, I keep going with the malaria thing. I know that this part of the world is rightly called the White Man's Grave. The Niger River, not far to the north, was only opened up to successful exploration after the discovery of quinine, and its anti-malaria capabilities.

In EG, there are strains of malaria that are cerebral and resistant to standard treatments. One of these strains can kill a healthy, fit man in 24 hours. As an Englishman born and bred, I have no resistance to malaria. Zero.

My executive suite is dirty. Cobwebs festoon the ceiling. They cover the high corners. From one of those, a fish-like CCTV eyeballs me. Smile – you're on telly.

My uniform is sweat-sodden. I drink from the bottled water. The General forbade me to drink from the tap. Teeth brushing OK. Drink not OK. The heat grabs at me, clutches me, hugs me close. I lie on the bed very still. It helps my hernia, and the stillness of it makes me less hot.

But I can't lie down. I must walk. I'm a walker. All I do is walk. I start walking, but the irons eat into my ankles. Sweat foams up. I'm alone. The door is locked. There is nobody to talk to. Even if there was, we would have no language. For the thousandth time I pray: if they're going to kill me, then let them do it by a bullet, not a rope.

Since my arrest in 2004 – four years ago – the thought that this story was going to end with my execution has always been there. Rarely at the front of my mind, but ever there, somewhere. Flitting about.

I think about being hanged. The minutes and seconds just before. I'm haunted by Orwell's description of an execution, in his essay *A Hanging*. I try to think of it in a way that I can cope with. Being hanged can't be worse than a really frightening downhill race, in which you are sure to fall over and break something badly.

Then, lights out.

It works. I've done that downhill. I can cope. Then … the big snake slithers inside my sick gut once more. I have to think it all through one more time.

Screwing back on tight the top of my bottle. Again.

I try to tell the panic to go away. Panic fingers are scrabbling at me, tugging, clawing. The heat and humidity and stuffiness are more than I can take. I fight for air. Night comes. I drift in and out of sleep. My poor body is being eaten by mosquitoes. If I don't know that by their many bites, then I would by the screaming air-attack whine of the deadly critters.

After four days and four long nights, my interrogation begins. They escort me to a courtroom, new built within the prison wire. The equatorial sun is frighteningly strong outside. The brightness blinds me. The courtroom was built for me to be tried in, they say. But I won't be tried there. It isn't big enough, they boast.

'Those were the days, my friends…'

I have company: Israeli Special Forces. They each carry a handgun, with spare mags around the waist, as well as a main weapon, each with his favourite: HK G3, M16, AK 74, MP5. All the main weapons are on a chest harness. Their clothes are a stunning mix of uniform and expensive sports civvies.

'*Shalom.*'

'*Shalom,*' one says, chewing back the first letters of the word into his mouth while the latter ones are still coming out.

My courtroom is bliss: six air conditioners blow an arctic wind across. The relief is great. I'm going to hate power cuts here. I'm given a Coke by one of the many goons, after General Manuel insists.

Along with the General, who met me at the airport, the EG Attorney General, José Olo Obono, is here. Business-like. I've met them both before: when they came to offer me the deal back in Chikurubi.

'Why am I in handcuffs and leg-irons 24 hours a day, every day? Please. They are making me sick.'

The interpreter, Miguel, looks pained.

'You must stay like this for the moment, *señor*,' says Obono.

I sense that he is boss here. I smile. I remember my Chikurubi rule: make a request, never a complaint.

I long for Chikurubi.

To go through the whole pantomime of interrogation, then trial – all over again – sickens me as badly as this heat. As badly as my hernia. As badly as the prickly heat rash, spreading from my handcuffs and now in my armpits and down my sides.

'The General told me that you will try and help me, if I help you. Well, I will do everything I can to help you, but we need an agreement, a legally binding agreement, that if I do help you then I will be released.'

'Mann. There will be no negotiation with you. We do not negotiate with terrorists. You are a terrorist.'

So why did you come and offer me a deal while I was in Chik? I said. To myself. Lips not moving. Obono is the Attorney General, and the man who hunted me down, took me to Chik and then brought me here. The Attorney General runs this prison. I am his prisoner.

General Manuel is the Minister of Security and the Head of Police. Miguel, my interpreter, is a petroleum expert, and a professor at the university. Few people speak English in EG. He has been roped in.

I've tried to get a negotiation going, and, as I have been trying to do each time, the General has come to my cell these last gasping-hot four days. I'll keep trying, but I can't push too hard.

All I can do is try to get it over to these men that the big-shot bosses in the plot are my out-and-out enemies. I will do anything to fuck them over because they are my Brothers-In-Arms who betrayed me. Four long years, still no postcard. They are my enemy.

Once they have that message – not too hard for me to project – then next I have to get over to them that I can do much more against those enemies as a free man than as their prisoner... Sure... Pigs might fly.

Our interrogation starts. It's old hat. The detail is tight. Question after question, then back over earlier answers. My interrogation will last three weeks, then there will be a trial.

Day 1, Day 2, Day 3… Each day the relief of the air conditioning in my courtroom is vast. In a break I turn to Miguel: 'What do you guys do for winter?'

'We fly to Spain.'

He isn't meant to be chatting with me. He answers quickly out of the side of his mouth.

I point out to the General that he is using mercenaries that look like Israeli Special Forces. Ironic, when they take so badly to my being one. 'Mann, why do you say these are Israeli, not Moroccan, Special Forces? They are Moroccans.'

'Sir, I can see an Israeli at 300 metres… It is the way they sling their rifles … and carrying a side arm as well as a main weapon says Special Forces… Anti-terrorist team. The SAS started it. I was in the SAS…'

Then the General notices how the Israelis creep forward during the interrogation. Courtroom bench by courtroom bench. He shoos them away.

Of course they want to hear this shit. Angola? Sierra Leone? They dream of doing what I've done. With me.

Then they are gone. I never see any of them again. It's a pity because I enjoyed watching them play the fool, with their clothing and weaponry: mix 'n' match, then accessorise. I know how bored they are. That kind of job is the pits.

Lunch the first day is one sandwich and a Coke, the second day two sandwiches, then the third a sandwich and a salad on a plastic plate. The General, I learn, owns Hotel *El Paraiso*.

The days roll on, while the lunches – slowly but surely – get bigger and better. My inquisitors are beginning to relax with me. The General has naps after lunch. I don't think Obono ever sleeps.

I sense tension between the two men. Obono and the General. Each morning when we start, Obono has a list of questions typed up on a sheet. We make sure that we have each of those well answered. I notice how these questions sometimes go down alleyways that seem out of keeping with Obono.

By this time Miguel is allowed to chat with me, so long as either Obono or the General can hear. Both have a decent grasp of English. One day, Obono goes to the loo. I ask the interpreter, 'Where does Señor Obono's list come from each day?'

Miguel smiles and turns to the General, who nods for him to go ahead with an answer.

'Simon, each evening – when Señor Obono and the General leave here – however late it is – they go to the President. They have to tell the President the answers to his questions of the night before, then he gives them new ones for the next day...'

By now we're working off my notebook, found by me in my suitcase, here in EG. Missed by the Zim clowns. That helps win their confidence. It also hugely helps me answer their questions about the nitty-gritty of four years ago.

Then – in the course of a careful search of my cell – by now I am an old hand – I find a cutting knife and a pair of heavy pliers. Good escape kit. Or planted? Or to be found in a search?

My best escape route, I believe, is more subtle.

I piss off the owners of the tools. I piss off the officers. I take my prizes to Obono and the General. Of course the General gives the officers a bollocking, but I get a wink from Miguel.

One night, when I get back to my cell, we find my bulb blown. The OIC – my escort that evening – puts me into another cell, over on the east side. A little later there is a power cut. I can see that it is a general outage by looking at the lights across the way. I know that the CCTV cameras work in the dark, and during power cuts, because before they caught me using a contraband razor blade to sharpen a pencil.

I'd spotted the razor blade on the stairs, on my way out to interrogation. I'm slow on the stairs because of my leg-irons. I marked the step. On the way back that evening, I saw the blade still there. I slipped on the stairs, went down onto my cuffed hands and palmed it.

Now it is a part of Miguel's job to make sure I have a supply of sharp pencils. They want me to make notes because that helps to jog my memory in our exhaustive search for clues.

That night – carefully – because of my hernia, the handcuffs, the leg-irons and the darkness – I climb onto the low tiled wall that divides the washing area from the rest of the cell. Slowly, I stand, craning to see, my eyes struggling to make out what is in front of me.

I can see the sea! I can see the sea!

My heart leaps with joy.

Seeing the sea is nothing next to the other good points about my new cell. The openings in the wall and the cell door have no old bits of mozzy net to block the air. Air moves. I am facing the sea and the breeze, when there is one. I feel it.

Below me is the yard. I can hear people having fun: playing football, talking. I can also hear their bloody chickens, this being an ex-Spanish colony.

Hard, in solitary confinement.

Next morning, I see the dawn. The sun puts on a great show for me. I feel so lucky. Whipping out my pencil, I mark the shadow of sunrise on the wall. I can pursue my amateur astronomy, my barefoot navigation, just as in Chikurubi.

I have malaria. I feel like shit, and the blood tests say the same. They treat me by locking me in the cell with a drip in my arm. If I scream nobody will come. The drip goes funny, so my arm swells up. I shout, but nothing happens.

For days I am all over the place. I wonder how Gerhard Merz really died. They told me it was his heart. In Zim, everyone had agreed that it was his heart because he had been denied his heart medicine while being questioned.

The prickly heat still spreads, grows worse.

The doctor is called in to see the General and Obono. He gets a massive rocket, but tells them he needs money. After that I get the Rolls-Royce treatment. I see that I am being treated with Artemesin, an anti-malarial wonder drug – a silver bullet that I had read about in *Scientific American* three years before, while in Chik.

I look at the Artemesin pack. There's no CE, 'Complies Europe', badge. The whole thing, except for the sticker saying 'Artemesin', is in Chinese. After that I get better quickly. One hundred per cent.

Slowly, and while the lunches become bigger and better, my ad hoc friendship with my captors grows. I have won trust. One of my requests is to take proper exercise. I tell them how I always exercised in Chikurubi, rain or shine.

They know that I exercise every morning as best I can, despite my handcuffs and leg-irons, and despite the malaria, prickly heat and bloody hernia. Press-ups, sit-ups, heaves, dumb-bells (in my case, a six-pack of 1.5-litre Ceiba water bottles). To my amazement, Obono comes back from a Madrid trip a few days later and gives me a French-made step exerciser that works on hydraulics.

This – of course – comes from the President, or with his blessing. By a miracle, my sister Sarah also gets me, at my request, a heart-rate monitor. This arrives with the UK Consul, who has braved local airlines from Lagos, Nigeria. Now I start to really exercise, even though the guards tell me I am loco. They are missing the point: part of the exercise routine is to tell them to fuck off. Look! I'm fitter and tougher than you, despite all this shit. It may be stupid, but something works. They do respect me. More importantly, I respect myself.

How I would so easily not do those exercises.

Two months pass. Tragedy strikes. The machine breaks and hydraulic fluid flies all over the now very clean cell floor. I cry. It's my lifeline.

I pull myself together. Even with my Chikurubi training, I can't make the step exerciser work… I think what I really want is a rowing machine.

Then I get it. The bottom of the barred opening in my cell door is tit height. If I hold on to that with my hands, I can bounce my body up and down. A rowing action. The Concept Zero rowing machine. I laugh at myself. It works, but it's hard to get my pulse up into Zone 3 and hold it there. Really hard. You see, I have a four-point-plan for keeping myself sane – my four-legged table, for living through every shitty day:

ONE – a strict daily routine
TWO – physical exercise every day
THREE – something creative every day
FOUR – logging of the first three

My routine means one day a week of real scrubbing. My cell is shiny clean. It also means a change-round, from day to night and back. This is all about shifting things around. I did it in Zim, where I made my blankets into British Army-style bed blocks. I became a fanatic: hoarding water and drinking an exactly prescribed amount, so my hoard would keep growing while I would keep my urine clear.

'Something creative every day' means writing – unless I am flying my airplane around. I should say my flight simulator. I made one by drawing an instrument panel, then writing out checklists and making up navigation charts, standard approaches, instrument approach plates and airfield diagrams. The charts are all unnamed, so can be anywhere in the world. I fly around in my aircraft – N90676 – and work the radio. To make it more fun, I do both sides of the radio, using – of course – the local accent of the peoples below.

That is fine, until one day the officers are all standing outside my cell laughing: the white man in Cell 11 has at last lost it.

Then they are sure. They catch me doing all the voices for the cast of strange people that I press-gang into a mad screenplay. It is fun for me. Double Dutch to them.

Meanwhile, there are serious matters afoot: escape!

My master plan – making the EG President let me go because I am trying so hard to help him – is failing. That's not because I'm not trying hard enough. That's because I don't know the intelligence that the Pres needs.

It goes like this. President Obiang and his men have worked out the truth. They deduced that there had to be a Plan X – a palace coup, or something like it.

The difficulty is, what the President needs is the IDs of the Plan X palace coupsters. My difficulty is, the Boss was clever enough not to give me those IDs. Lists, of the Goodies and the Baddies, were to be sent to me only once I was in Malabo. If I cannot come up with those names, then the Pres is not going to be happy. If he isn't happy, then I stay in Black Beach. Simple.

Snippets mean so much to my inquisitors. How did I know that Juan and 20 men were going to Israel for Close Protection training, back in November 2003? But I did. It's there, in my notebook. How did I know? they wonder. So few people knew at that time.

How could Severo locate the President as he had done from that Barcelona hotel suite. And how could we say that we could move the President (one time) to position him for the Op. It means that there was someone inside the President's circle plotting. Who? Is he there still, today?

Time, though, I have.

Slowly the thought comes to me that between March 2003 and March 2004 the Boss and I had many meetings. Many things happened. So, if I play back the tapes in my head of that year, then surely – like a lead scout – I will pick up the sign that I need in order to get on the trail of the IDs – those that the Pres wants.

I start. I play a part of my tape, and make notes, then notes of the notes. I play it again.

As I say, time I do have.

There was a meeting with the Boss when we were talking about getting into EG using a fishery protection contract as cover. Who else had been there? Amil Hammam, son of Rafiq.

The meeting had been odd. What had it really been about? Had Amil been checking me out? Yes, that fits the feeling I had. So, if he was checking me out … then he was a part of the team. The more I think about this, the more sure I become. This jungle 'ground sign' that I have picked up – Hawkeye, Boy Scout – leads somewhere that is worthwhile for Equatorial Guinea's intelligence agency. I make notes. I state my case.

Three weeks later, I am stating the same case. I have every day since I began. At every chance I have, poor Miguel has another earful. I know that if I cannot convince him, then I never will the others. Risking their anger, I go on and on. I am the dripping tap to out-drip all others.

Amil Hammam walks in. Under guard.

Hammam wears a pinstripe suit, New & Lingwood shirt, Ganes shoes. His heel tips ring with steel and confidence. The Hermes tie is crisp. A merchant banker, who closes one deal as the next opens.

They seat him at the end of our table. I am on his right. Miguel on mine. On Hammam's left, Obono. Then the General. I sit there in my stinking uniform and cuffs and leg-irons. I can't believe that they don't know that to question Hammam with me present is an inquisitor's no-no.

I can't believe that they fall for his asking to be questioned in English. As clear as day he speaks Spanish. Making them translate into English, through Miguel, is giving Hammam time. He crafts his answer.

The questions go on. After two hours he is under pressure. The Jermyn Street veneer is slipping. He went to public school, after all. What do you expect?

He leans back in his chair. Looks each one of us in the eye, takes an important breath, then launches his counter.

'I think it is time to tell you…'

Eye to eye.

'… that I am in fact … a double agent.'

Miguel and I look at each other. All I can think of is the joke: the wide-mouthed fly-eating toad (and you don't see very many of those around these days, do you?). I struggle.

I look at the Attorney General and the Chief of Security. They are looking at each other, amazed. Not laughing.

The days pass. Hammam's descent is rapid. He too is in a stinking uniform, but never handcuffs and leg-irons. He is failing, but he is not cracking. He is not coming up with the IDs of the plotters. The inquisition is failing, even though I am sure he's lying. I need the names. My ticket home – maybe.

I don't know that Hammam lived in EG, not now and not when I met him previously. I don't care. He is an enemy. They are all my enemies.

I ask the General if I can wear a wire. If they can leave me with Hammam, then he will tell me everything. All along he has tried to play the public school card: two white boys up against these stupid blacks. He is so far off. He makes me laugh. He makes me itch to hit him.

'The General is sorry, Simon,' says Miguel next day, 'but they do not have a wire for you to wear…'

Crazy.

Do I believe that, or not? I shouldn't, but I do. These guys are smart, but they have gaping holes in their logistics. But Miguel isn't finished.

'But, if you wish, they will permit you to question Hammam… You will do so with Detective Sergeant Rodriguez and me.'

This is my chance. I take it. Hammam is a jerk, and not all here (double agent, forsooth). But Hammam is my enemy, and – just maybe – my way home.

We start. We'll be in English throughout. Obono and the General by now trust Miguel and me.

'I am your friend, Amil … even if I don't sound like it. I am your friend because I'm going to help you get out of here … and the only way that'll happen is if you do as I have done: tell them the whole truth.

'You have said that you are a double agent. That means that you have worked for the coup against the President. It is an admission of guilt. What you have to do now is show the police here – me too – that – on balance – your efforts for the President against the plotters outweigh those for the plotters against the President.

'Guilty, or not guilty. Do you see that?

'Hammam, you don't get it. You're gonna be here for ever, unless you do as I say. Start helping them.

'OK, Amil, we're not getting anywhere like this. Let's start again. I want to get the background on you. Where were you born? What date?'

I ask him about the family home in London, the villa in the South of France. The family-owned yachts. What are they really for? What is the private jet really for? The stash of weapons at home? Specific Hammam dodgy deals and dealers. Amil is floored. He's trying to figure out how I know so much.

Then I get personal. His mum's darkest secret; his dad's weirdest kink. The strange thing is, an ex-girlfriend of mine once worked for Amil's father. She, of course, told me everything about the weird and wonderful Hammams.

I unsettle him. Rattle him. Catch him out. The family secrets cut deepest. I twist the knife.

The questioning goes on in a much more vindictive and vicious way and eventually he breaks down.

That night, escorted, and on the way back to our cells, Hammam starts to talk wildly. 'Help me, please… What should I do…? You can help me, I know… You see, I know the main man in the plot. Here in the palace.'

Hammam pauses. The guard is frowning at our talk. He doesn't speak a word. We walk through the chained gates into the poorly lit yard.

He gives the name. 'He knows everything. That's how they knew. That's how they know so much. How the Boss could say that he could move the President…'

Back in my cell, I straight away write down word for word what Hammam has said to me. Next morning I tell Obono and the General that it's Christmas. I know that this is what they really want. The insider's name has already come up. I hadn't known who he was, but they told me. He is someone who has lived and worked in the palace. 'So, now you owe me a pardon,' I grin. They know I mean it.

Then they start to tell me things. They are sure of US and UK involvement in the coup plot. The plot also reaches to the top of somewhat murkier international organisations.

I write a letter to the President and give it to the General, keeping it secret from Obono. I ask for a pardon, stating my case. Once out, I will work against the others on his behalf, but I have earned my pardon anyway, because I have fingered the viper in the President's bosom. I say in my letter that, as an ex-intelligence officer, I know the value of that information: it is worth a pardon anywhere. The risk of doing this is great. If Obono learns of the letter, I can be sunk.

I'm having trouble with Obono. Now it gets worse. He is told about the letter. He doesn't like my going behind his back. He becomes angry with me in an interview. He calls me a racist. In my letter to the President I imply, he claims, that Africans take bribes. Thank you, stars. I wrote the letter with the fear of such an intercept in mind.

I roll my sleeve up. The Attorney General has made me angry. I don't care any more.

'Do you see this?' I point to my arm. 'This skin is black. I was in Chikurubi for four years … and my skin is honorary black. Don't you call me a racist.'

Obono and the interpreter (not Miguel) are stunned. So am I. What had I meant, really? I wasn't sure – other than that I had meant it. I am very angry. This is dangerous. Yet being called a racist, after all this, is too much.

At my EG trial I had happily gone along with them: pleading guilty to attempted murder, terrorism and God knows what else. That was all pantomime. Everyone knew it. Even if my sentence is 35 years.

Then there is Niek du Toit.

Niek never became helpful to the EG Police, even when I showed him my notebook and statement and told him to cooperate. I told him that whatever he thought he was doing didn't matter: his unhelpfulness was damaging the chances of our other three, all held with Niek.

That wasn't fair. I wanted to get us all out of there as best I could.

Niek didn't budge, so I had to work out why. He knew that once he started to talk, then everything would come out … but so what? So what? Unless his plan had not been our plan…

Around these debriefings with Obono and the General, I have built my routine. My astronomy is a daily task, weather permitting. I watch my wall marks of the sun at 0700 move round the room. I am lucky to be able to see sky from my cell.

Sometimes I stand in awe. The fantastic heat and humidity blast away. I watch as a Cumulonimbus (Cb) forms, then grows. The instability of the air is so great that the Cb can roll up and away into a nuclear mushroom – reaching up to 40,000 feet and higher – inside an hour. Sometimes the sight takes my mind back to writing *Straw Hat*, back in Chikurubi. The Cbs of the Congo River were the dragon's breaths.

There are times that I feel so lost and alone that I fear my sadness will stop my heart from beating.

My handcuffs go. My leg-irons next. Incredible feelings. Sleeping, shitting, exercising. Everything is better. I can walk again. I start. Walking is who I am again.

The General has given me a mosquito net. I look after it like a holy object. Then I get two sets of sheets. Luxury. My body can cope with the heat better now. Because I am out of handcuffs and leg-irons, I can shower when I want, and I can wear only underpants … all day and all night.

Until they want me for more inquisition. Days. Weeks. Months.

This is true solitary confinement now. The inquisition is over, apart from rare visits, such as the British Consul, or New Scotland Yard. You may ask what they are doing there. To which the answer would be: 'Evenin' all. Just making some enquiries.' No exercise yard. No friends. Even the guards aren't allowed to talk to me. Solitary confinement is a pig. My spirit plummets. For six weeks straight, I don't leave my cell. I don't talk to another soul. I walk. I talk to myself. I imagine that my sister and my UK lawyer are in there with me. I curse them for hours.

My anger grows and grows until I again write one of the hundreds of letters that I don't ever send. That I know I won't send.

A TV crew come to interview me. It's grist to the mill. Another chance for me to show these people that I am 'all theirs'. Another chance to work towards escape.

Then a shock. Two shocks. The TV crew are working for the BBC, but the production company belongs to Jamie Oliver. Now worth £30 million, and rising. But – ha ha ha – 'Didn't Jamie used to work for you?' The crew laugh at me. They know that he did. I tell them they are right. It's true. In the old days, Amanda and I used to have lots of dinner parties. Jamie – before fame – when he was working at the River Café – used to come and moonlight for us. And, yes, we were friends with Marco Pierre White. I know that, in truth, Marco has been one of the friends who has supported Amanda and helped her. Not everyone has.

Second shock. The one leading this motley TV crew is none other than Henry Paige – the English lawyer hired by EG – except that he is now working for Jamie Oliver's production company. I never thought that I would meet Paige without a confrontation. But there isn't one. We chat.

You remember when 'Uncle' set up comms between Wilna Lubbe and me? You remember how I couldn't be disloyal? How I refused to write a letter of instruction to their lawyer?

Now Paige, with no axe to grind, answers my questions. But didn't I know, he asked, that the terms of the Charlie Wake deal had again been put on the table? When Michael Grunberg had asked? Remember how Charlie turned up at Chikurubi in 2005, with Colonel Miala, the CIO's man in charge of my case, and EG Attorney General Obono? His translator, reeking of scent? Amanda and 'London' knew nothing of it. The offer they made was straightforward. If I gave all the information that I could give – and handed over all documents – the contract between Severo Moto and me – and the bank statements – then Equatorial Guinea would make no extradition request against me. When my time is up in Zimbabwe, I will go free. May 2007.

Paige called over Obono. Did he recall when Paige had asked if those terms were still available, following Michael Grunberg's enquiry? Why, yes, of course the Attorney General remembered. He had taken the enquiry to the President himself.

Back in my cell that evening, the TV interview is nothing to me. All I can think of is what Paige and Obono had said.

There was a deal to be done then.

All there is now – for sure – is 34 long years to serve out.

My food comes from the General's hotel, *El Paraiso*. One meal once a day, plus a 1.5-litre bottle of water, bread rolls and six fruits. This food is good, but the reason for my being fed like this is not. Poison is a traditional way of dealing with problems in West Africa. There are plenty of people who want me dead and buried.

A long list: London, Madrid, Pretoria. I am a problem.

My hernia operation comes. It has only taken two years from when the doctor in Chikurubi told me that I urgently needed it. I go to the best and only private clinic in Malabo. The First Lady owns and runs the place. The President pays my bill.

We arrive at the quiet and smart clinic: me, and an escort of 20 armed troops. The General says that this is for my protection. The clinic struggles to cope with the heavily armed soldiery lying on its polished linoleum.

They give me an epidural. I thought that was for having babies. I am conscious all the way through. I can feel what is happening, but with no pain. My wrists are strapped to a cruciform. The doctor tries to tell me that this crucifixion is what they would do to anyone. Not just me.

After, the pain starts. Terrible indigestion. Guts feel ready to pop.

Twenty-four hours later I am back in my cell, alone. Thank God my cell is clean. The worst news is that the Tunisian doctors have diagnosed that I need the same operation again, this time on my right side.

Straight back from the clinic, straight back into my solitary cell, I discover that the General has given me a great gift: a plastic garden chair and a good-quality electric fan. Life will never be so uncomfy again. The blown air keeps away the mosquitoes. Combined with the fly killer that I am now able to buy, this now means that I'm winning the war. No Fly Zone.

And I am on prophylactics at last. Retrospective prophylactics – an EG first: sulfadoxine 500 mg/pyrimethamine 25 mg per tablet. Three tablets taken together, once every three months.

My pain against 'London' is terrible. I now believe that, had they listened to me, I would have been free in May '07. Instead I may die here. I write a list of my gripes against them.

Yes, I am grateful. I am grateful to anyone who has tried to help me.

Then there is Timothy Robarts, my old friend from North Foreland Court. He has never given up doing whatever he can, making a constant flood of magazines flow my way.

And yes, I can forgive. I have become Jesus in the forgiveness department. Guards. The CIO. Even the two white South Africans who not only turned state's evidence against me, all those years ago, back in Zimbabwe, but perjured themselves as well. Their lies had been deadly dangerous to me. Their lies had turned the Croc away from any thoughts of fighting our Zimbabwe case. A white witness is worth seven black – in defence or prosecution – my black Zim friends had assured me.

But I can forgive.

What gets me about 'London' is not their mistakes. Anyone can make mistakes. Me especially. What gets me is their fucking arrogance. For example: a dying man has the right to decide whether or not to allow a possibly life-saving, but very dangerous, medical procedure. Only he has that right. Others can beg and plead with him. Others can advise. Only he can decide.

But this would be news to 'London'.

I have to write again to Amanda. I don't write and say that she is 'free'. For me to say that I set her 'free' would be wrong. It tells of an ownership that neither of us ever wanted. Instead, therefore, I just say that I hope that she is having fun … getting on with her life. She will know what I mean. God it hurts, writing that.

Then there are the coup bosses. What do I really feel about them, aside from the rhetoric that I use to my captors?

Imagine a Central Asia climbing expedition, high on China's remote Kunlun Mountains, north of the Karakoram. The expedition has backers and sponsors. I am the climb leader. I find myself putting in more and more of my own money, because the chief backer isn't putting up money as promised.

I am advising the backers that the climbing season is coming to an end. The weather is bad. Heavy snow has made the climb extra dangerous. But the backers are begging us to go ahead anyway. Some of the backers are also the organisers. They hired me. Those organisers are also a part of the climb. Together we have lived and breathed the climb these past 12 months. These men have come up to base camp with us. They have posts within the climb's planning and command hierarchy.

The climb begins. Soon there is an accident. I am cut off high on the mountain. Men have been killed, others injured. Some of us are now cut off. Our route down is severed. Avalanche.

So what do they do? Fold their tents, head for London. What do they say when, halfway down the valley, they meet a rescue party coming up? They deny us. They deny their involvement. They keep going – hard – for London.

My message to them is simple: hope that I don't get off that mountain alive.

It isn't as if I expect the 'Brothers-In-Arms' to risk their lives, or their freedom, or their fortunes for us in prison. But I do expect them to do something … anything.

Throughout this time, there are the usual endless rumours and stories that, somehow or other, I will be released. Prisoner transfer, or a pardon, or whatever. But, of course, this will only come from the President. But, of course, others will need to have their wheel bearings greased as well. The legs of the goat…

I scratch my head.

I need a way of telling people in the UK one thing, when I mean the opposite. This comes about because my whole position with the EG people is that Simon Mann is 100 per cent with them. On their side.

Given that this is so, how can I refuse to pay this sum, or that sum, to this one or to that? For my song-and-dance act to work I have to be able to beg Sarah or Amanda, or my friends, to pay over money, when – at the same time – I can be confident that they will do no such thing.

Hernia two comes and goes. Throughout the op, I say out loud 'Drake's Drum'. My Tunisian doctors think it is prayer. Too much to tell them.

I had been so dreading it, but then it hurts much less. No terrible popping feeling afterwards. Carefully, I wait for the doctors' 'off games' time to run out, then – more carefully – I get my exercise routine going again.

I'm like a machine. It's me giving two fingers to everyone: home and abroad. Look! I am in this much shit, but I can still be tougher than you, and have as much fun. You see, some of the jokes that I tell myself, and some of my wit against myself, is funny. Actually.

As time goes on, I see Obono and the General decreasingly often. I become less and less hopeful that my work for EG, during the inquisition and then my trial, will pay off.

I have to face it: my 30 years might be 30, or ten, or another five. It doesn't matter much. As I tell Obono: if you don't let me out of here soon, there will be nowhere for me to go.

I will have no lover, no home.

As that route of escape closes, I think of others. In Zim, they believe that the only escape possible from a Chikurubi-style maximum security prison is by a helicopter flying over the exercise yard with a rope dangling. That was done – in the UK – at the same time as an exercise yard punch-up kicked off.

In Zim, they have a steel grid over the section, but not in EG. A helicopter could come in, to coincide with the walk from the block to my court house. The walk would be sure to happen when the British Consul visits, an event that can be found out and pinned down well in advance.

Looking out from my cell window, always quickly and carefully (my viewing public do not like me to do otherwise), I can see Cameroon, Mount Victoria, the bright-green rainforest … only 15 miles across the bright-blue sea. Amazing how beautiful nature is when denied.

My escape heli could be there – maybe on a docudrama shoot about brother-murdering chimpanzees or some such – then fly in and pluck me to safety. CS gas should take care of any guards wishing to make their weapons dirty. Low and fast should take care of any over-enthusiastic interceptors.

Once in Cameroon, we would dump the heli and jump into a King Air 200 or a Pilatus PC-12, then out. To Europe. The heli would be an old-time Jet Ranger – £200,000 at the most. The plan could work. I spend a day or two dreaming, note-taking. How? (But fear not: the notes are indecipherable to anyone but me.)

With a little bit of luck the plan could work.

Then I think about Operation Wormwood Scrubs, the Chikurubi escape plan I had made. I had been let down. Why would I be able to get backing for this heli plan when I couldn't get backing for that?

I need something cheaper.

If Uncle Bertie comes into EG as a businessman, then he could set up a microscopic business infrastructure – just enough to buy a prison officer into connivance. The officer would have to be paid to re-settle his family in Cameroon, or somewhere, but in advance. The officer would take me out of Black Beach in the boot of his car. Their security is lax. I watch.

The boot would work.

The officer would set off for Cameroon immediately in a *cocoro*, a local fishing boat.

Once out, I would set sail. I had found in my sailing mags a review of collapsible sailing dinghies. I identified the best one: the Saturn SD365. It would be easy for Uncle Bertie to smuggle one into the country. The boat was 12 feet long, but with the right kit on board I was sure I could make it to Gibraltar. From there, England would be a doddle…

A happy two days are spent in my cell plotting and planning escapes. There's nothing like working on a kit list to raise morale. Then I think again: would 'London' back even innocent little escape plans such as the one I have been dreaming up? The whole thing would cost less than £200,000. They won't go for it. They're useless. I shout at them, thinking they are in my cell, for an hour or two. Then I cry.

Next day, back in shape, I think how to do it on my own. Over the wire and into the hills. I'm an SAS jungle soldier. I can beat anyone in the jungle. And I know it. I think how to do it. The authorities don't know this but I'm hoarding the money that I am now allowed for buying toothpaste and coffee, money brought in by the Consul. I have already saved £300, with another £50 to split between the two officers for next Christmas. Tips.

I pace up and down my cell. I dream of running around in the jungle, until I can steal a fishing boat… Escape…

It won't work. Without some outside help, I will not succeed. If I try – and fail – then all my hard work making sure that the EG crowd think that I am their best friend will go up in smoke. For God's sake. I've even written a six-page security paper for them. They love it. Poacher turns gamekeeper.

I'm struggling with my exercise routine, but hanging in there. Just. Each day it's a big task to do the exercises. If I follow my weakness and don't do the exercises, I know that each day will become a bigger task.

In my daydreams about being free I think about rowing single-handed across the Atlantic. A race from the Azores to Antigua. I've read everything I can find in my mags about this race. I think of the woman who will meet me at the finish. It's always Amanda. If she'll have me…

My Concept Zero rowing machine – hanging in there by hanging off my fucking door grille – is a good way to train. Rowing training. Getting ready. But what if I'm never free? Never out of here. Ten … 20 … 30 … 34 years … my full sentence?

Suicide raises its head. Up until now, I have always believed I will escape by one means or another. But now … do I want to do 30 years, then die in here? I test myself: if they offered me a pill by which to willingly kill myself, would I take it? If the answer is YES, then I should kill myself, by whatever means I can find. It won't be hard. Not to do so would be cowardly.

I ask myself.

NO, I answer, despite the thought that YES might make things easier for Amanda and the children.

Perhaps my escape has to be virtual.

I read about the Concept 2 rowing machine – the real one – in a magazine. The British Olympic Gold Medal-holder for rowing, Sir Steve Redgrave, is advertising them. More or less £1,000, but I know they are the best. The ad has the measurements. Bingo. I measure. The thing will fit in my cell. If I can persuade them to let me have one, then persuade my family – or somebody – to buy me one, I will be all set.

What I could then do is have my own chart of the Atlantic. The Azores westward. Home! I could then row, in real time … marking out my real/virtual chart position as I go. Sleep. Eat. Row. The virtual thing is no harder than the real thing.

Piece of piss … because it's there … actually.

One of the things I miss about having my cell so clean is the gladiatorial spectator sport of Spider Wars. I used to lie on the floor and watch the spiders battle away on the ceiling and up in the corners. There is a vast number of flies. Plenty of food. I watch as different species work in different ways, forcing out others. Now that everything is clean, there are fewer. Also I am waging war on the flies with my moz net, fan, insecticide.

I, Lord of the Flies. *Mambo Makonzo Mahombe*. Species jump.

One day I am shocked to see a mess on the shower floor. I look again: many small objects … they're moving! What…?

The shower floor is covered in small spiders, shilling-size, hundreds of them. My spider-watching has been tolerant – enemies of the flies are, of course, friends of mine – but not hundreds. Not in the shower. I start stamping on them, up and down, over and over.

A green furry leg unfolds itself from the drain hole in the shower floor. Another. Two more. A Thing comes out: bright green, furry, long-legged. The size of my hand outstretched. The size of a dinner plate … and very cross. It's Mummy.

I stamp. Squelch. Yuk. I wash the floor with the hand rinse.

From that moment on, I keep something over the shower drain hole, unless I'm showering. God knows what Daddy might look like.

One night I wake up to the sound of pop-pop-pop. It cannot be small-arms fire, but that is how it sounds. I try to doze back off. It must be about 2 am. The popping grows in urgency. I take out my earplugs, worn to fend off the many ghastly night-time prison noises – coughing, idiotic screaming from malaria sufferers, praying by the godly, the crying of our very own Little Dorrit (in a nearby cell a woman is being held with her new-born baby) – and listen well.

It *is* small arms.

As a soldier, I can tell: whatever is going on is amateur stuff. The firing is the noise of undirected troops blatting off rounds more or less because they feel they ought to. I make myself lie in bed. I don't even get up for a piss.

I know they are watching me on the CCTV. I know they will be very interested to see if I am interested in what is happening. In a paranoia zoo like this, any interest by me can be easily extrapolated.

Two days later I find out: whatever it was that went on, the night of the sporadic small-arms fire, it is now being portrayed as a bungled coup attempt. Another one.

Great shortcomings and weaknesses in the security of the President's palace area, in which Black Beach prison also sits, are shown up. Then I hear: my friend General Manuel has been fired.

I sit on the floor, my head on my knees. I cry.

I tell myself that it doesn't matter, but I know it does. He is the man with whom I have my best relationship. He is the man who has come closest to making a promise that I will get my pardon. He is the man...

It is a terrible blow. My spirits dive to the bottom of the pit. I can't drag them up. For days I am listless and sad. I try to buck up. I cannot. I have to dig. Get tough with myself: I know what to do. I know my routine.

ONE – strict daily routine
TWO – physical exercise, every day
THREE – something creative, every day
FOUR – logging of the first three

All along, I've had to make myself not think of Amanda and home. It is a painful thing to do. To push away the very ones I long for. I have to do it.

I do it.

Of course, it doesn't entirely work, maybe because I don't want it to entirely work. I know that long-term prisoners often ask that their families stop all writing and visiting. It's easier not to deal with it than to have it thrust upon you. Any letter takes me a week to get over, especially Amanda's lovely notes. Letters from Sarah can wipe me out for a month. They make me so angry.

Freddy is the one who most easily gets past my defences. Although it was Peter and Jack going to war that brought home my unhappiness the most harshly. They have both done two tours by now. Peter Afghan twice. Jack Iraq, then Afghan. My life is wasted. Can't I be killed instead of one of them ... if that is how it is to be?

I have written a screenplay now. It is fiction but based on truth: *The*

Story of the Coup. The screenplay starts off where *Straw Hat* ends. Again, the officers catch me reading out loud. I have found that the dialogue only works if I have read it out loud, acted it out. The characters are wild, the accents varied and strong.

Now my low spirits need a lift. I need a creative project. Part of the Four-Legged Sanity Plan. I think of writing a fiction book for Freddy: a boy's book. Then I remember how old he is. He was seven when I left home. He's 13 now.

When I was 13 I wanted to read grown-up books: Buchan, Bond, Hornblower, Alistair MacLean, Arthur Bryant.

I'll write a book like *The Thirty-Nine Steps*. In honour of *The Thirty-Nine Steps*. It has to be different, though, so I become a girl lead, her story told in the first person, by Kass. Days pass, weeks, months. I become a dog with a bone, writing *Kass*.

Then I've written it. Finished it four times over. So I start another. Halfway through *Kass 2* – on a Saturday morning – I get taken over to my courtroom. What's up?

There are Obono and Miguel. I haven't seen them together since the trial. Not since Miguel read out my 35-year sentence. I haven't seen Obono for weeks.

I sit.

'Simon, the President is to announce the pardon of you ... and Niek ... and the other three ... the news will be out on Monday, then you will be free.'

I look at them.

This is impossible. This is what I've been waiting and praying for ... but this isn't possible. I can't speak. Obono and Miguel look shocked at my lack of reaction. I go back to my cell. I try to write *Kass*. I can't. Instead I write down how I feel. In my heart I don't believe it.

Amanda's last letter spelled it out for me: I had ruined her life.

All this time – since my arrest – I had been trying to keep thoughts of her at arm's length. All this time I had told myself how – were I ever to be free – I would be without Amanda. That was my defence. Aiming off, by getting my head around the next calamity. Hope for the best. Expect the worst.

I am about to find out. Or am I? I have heard so much rubbish. Maybe this pardon is rubbish?

I aim off again. There is no pardon.

Sunday passes, then Monday. Nothing. I was right to aim off.

There's a football match this afternoon. I can hear what's happening without climbing on my chair to watch. Even now, I have to be careful about standing on the chair. Big Brother is watching me.

These football matches are more than just football. They are an escape out of Black Beach. The teams are groups of people who get themselves together. Before the match, they line up in two rows to sing the national anthem. Referee and linesmen stand in the middle, their faces masks of officialdom.

The match starts. The sound is deafening in my cell, made worse by my being just over where the match commentator shouts away. He is pretending to be the radio reporter. He sits on the hen house to do so.

It's 4 pm on the day of my supposed pardon. Nothing like a pardon has happened. They've fucked up. The pardon is rubbish. The match is over. The crowd – all the other prisoners and the officer on duty (only ever one here, unlike Chik Max) – are dispersed. The ref must be cleaning out his whistle. The players are washing one another down at the great water tub. The chickens are back to their tireless business: pecking, babies, mating, fighting, pecking.

I stand on my chair to look out.

Two older prisoners are on their up-and-down walk, pacing the concrete that was just now the pitch. They have their transistor radios held to their ears. Long ago I gave up wanting a radio. Just as I throw out so many wants. 'I want' doesn't get.

I stretch around a little. I see Niek. Two of my others. They're sitting on one of two DIY benches placed under the old army tent, rigged for defence against the equatorial sun, whose line of passage runs over the top of us.

The two old radio listeners halt. Tense. They look at Niek, then walk over. They are grinning. They shake his hand. Everyone is grinning and shouting. Niek straight away looks up at my cell. He sees that – odds against – I am there, looking back. He gives a thumbs-up.

It's true.

We are pardoned.

I step back off my chair and sit in it, head in hands. Weeping. Tears flooding between my fingers. My whole body shaking.

I am to be free.

Tuesday.

The lieutenant and an officer bring me my suitcase at 7 am. I'm doing exercises. Still not believing. They don't believe what they see.

'Don't you know what's happening?' the lieutenant asks.

I do know. But I don't believe.

Dressed in the suit I last wore five and a half years ago, I walk out of my cell. Am I really never coming back to my cell? Do I really feel a sadness at leaving my home of 18 months?

No, I tell myself – that is nerves. Fear of the unknown future. Quite normal, I tell myself … reminding myself not to say things to me out loud any more.

I walk to my courtroom, sure that the suit fits fine. Very fine: Richard James, Savile Row, a New & Lingwood shirt, Hermes tie, the highly polished Ganes brown lace-ups, bought when I was commissioned in 1971 – all decked out in a suit several sizes too big.

The courtroom is crowded. Out of the window I see Sarah and my brother, Edward, get out of a big 4x4.

Shock.

Now I believe!

Speeches, papers, speeches, thanks. Niek du Toit refuses to thank anyone for anything. I've been told that Niek and the others will be flying out with the South African President, Jacob Zuma. I have no means of checking that.

Into the 4x4 with Sarah and Edward – and the General. We drive off.

As we go, there is a cheer from all the prisoners, the football crowd, on their pitch, the exercise yard.

I wave back, mop a tear. How many times have I watched someone else go out? It gives hope, but it unsettles.

An unreal lunch follows, and champagne, served in a private dining room in the General's hotel. I have a big tip in my pocket – my unspent escape money – that I give to the *Paraiso* staff who have fed me all this time.

Then comes the crunch: Amanda. Is she going to tell me to fuck off?

It is what I have dreaded, and at the same time tell myself: it is likely. Her last letter…

Well, I hope she doesn't. I think she might. I won't blame her if she does. I badly want to hold her to me.

'Sorry' is not a strong word.

Taking Sarah's phone, I go to my room. There's Amanda. We talk. We start to laugh. I hope, against hope. Maybe we are lovers. Laughter makes it feel as if we are at the start of a love affair. Not the end.

That night we have dinner. Obono joins us. Talk is difficult because of the language problem.

'Simon … this morning, you prisoners all agreed to never come back to Equatorial Guinea.'

'Yes, General.'

'Well … we want to tell you that this is not for you. You are welcome to come back … although we would rather you did so without your 69 men.'

Very funny.

Next morning, the Dassault 900 Falcon is straight and level in the cruise, en route from Malabo to Luton, England.

The Falcon is hired for the job. The plane is five-star, and – as I am about to find out – top-dollar. Everything feels unreal. The plane. Breakfast, elevenses, drinks, lunch. The carry-on.

Wankers' black leather biz jet executive chairs all around.

Sarah and Edward find everything as strange as I do. There is so much to say. Yet we say nothing.

I try to ask a question, about something during the five years, something that had upset me, only to see Sarah purse her lips and colour up. Behind her shoulder, dear Edward, by one sideways shake of his head, signals me: leave off.

A little later, Sarah speaks to me. 'Simon … you know – your lawyer for all these years…'

Ha ha ha (do you mean the mozzie who helped me spend £3,000,000? On legal fees? That mozzie?)

'…Well look … er … some people like him, others don't … OK?'

'And I won't?'

'Well … I just feel that maybe you and he are best not to meet. There isn't any point.'

I'm too stunned to think. Not stunned by what she has just said, but stunned by everything that is happening. Later, it strikes me how odd this business with the lawyer is. I say nothing. I'm just letting everything freewheel. I can see that they are watching me closely for symptoms of craziness, to which I have undoubtedly succumbed. I am to get used to that scrutiny.

Sitting back in my wanker's black leather biz jet chair, I close my eyes, breathe deeply and count to ten. I listen to myself about who I am, and what I have been about. The Falcon's chairs are smarter than in Pien's old Hawker.

So what the bloody hell did go wrong?

I look at the virtual instrument panel. Old, broken. But there are readings still there. The dials and lights still tell me things. Other things I have picked up. Yet other things that I have had told to me.

Hints. Lies? Who knows?

I'll never know for sure. I do know that. In this game you never know … I can be sure of that at least.

But here is how I'd bet. The Boss is well known and liked by the CIA. Having grown nervous about their own plans to put together an EG coup, the CIA have a quiet lunch with him.

They tell the Boss that President Obiang has got to go, and that Severo Moto, duly elected, would be acceptable. An operation by the Boss to that end is desirable, but wholly deniable. They will help in any way they can, so long as that deniability stays intact. 'Plausible deniability' is the slogan. There will be no CIA money. There will never be an admission.

This is a covert operation, a secret one. But more than that: this is a clandestine operation. Meaning that it is deniable. It will always be denied, no matter what.

Once Moto is in power, the Boss must keep his hands, and Moto's, off the oil concessions. Who doesn't want Obiang to crash and burn? Who doesn't want a slice of the action when he does?

So why can he not raise the cash? Today – writing this – I still don't know. With me he starts the GO STOP GO STOP. We're like an aeroplane that is both low and slow. It's a bad place to be. Plan D fucks up. The CIA take stock. They do not like what they see. Too many people know. Too many agencies are involved: South Africa is pushing to go. The UK knows but is doing nothing to stop it: tacit approval. If things go wrong, then they will go really wrong.

Then the CIA find out about the ex-USAF Boeing 727-100 that I buy in record time, very cheap, without proper export documentation. Uncle Sam's fingerprints again. Then they find out that a known CIA pilot rode shotgun on the ferry flight, making sure for me that I got my airplane on time. Uncle Sam's fingerprints are on a smoking gun.

Before the March 2004 coup attempt, all hands were versus Obiang. Many hands were helping the coup along. There was the story of the

Spanish warships. There was the US State Department report that put Obiang and Co. at the top of the tyranny class.

But, hey presto! Just months after the coup attempt, Condoleezza Rice, National Security Advisor, welcomes the great tyrant Obiang to Washington – as a friend of the American people.

Meanwhile, back at the EG ranch, Obiang is keeping his side of the bargain. Talk to anyone in EG: things there are far from perfect, but they are a thousand times better than they were in 2004. In the seven years since the coup, EG has progressed forty. Health. Education. Infrastructure. Human Rights.

Everyone that I managed to have a private conversation with in EG – about five people in eighteen months – said the same. When the 2004 coup plot failed, everything started to change. Fast.

This Falcon cockpit gives me a strange refuge. I can sit up there, on the jump seat, and talk flying to the two pilots. Later the second officer goes aft and tells Sarah (not a great flyer) that she needn't worry: I will be doing the landing, but they will keep a close eye on how I do.

For a second she loses it, then laughs.

Sitting in a real cockpit brought back many thoughts of my flying. My solitary cell. My flight simulator. We fly, chatting through the flight-deck intercom, France passing by below. Now there is a real French ATC talking to us, rather than me hamming it.

Suddenly, I hear 'London radar' – the cool voice of the very best Air Traffic Control. I swallow and brush away a tear: I've made it back to Blighty. There have been many times when I thought I never would.

It strikes me that there will be five years of new tech to catch up on. Below is the Channel, then the white cliffs. England green and little patches. How it should be.

The light is clear, the afternoon sunny. Good weather cumulus puffs. The whole place is laid out below. Welcome home. I feel there is nothing I want, everything is mine... Then I remember that Amanda may, even yet, give me my marching orders.

It dawns, my brain revving to catch up on the new hand of cards that I'm holding: life is going to hold many more problems than I'm used to. But then none will be the size of my one old big problem – getting out, getting home. Escape.

Luton is a blur. Sarah's husband, Hugh, hugs me off the plane. He has been a huge help to her, I know that. Then he sets off to fool the press. I go to the Harrods exec jet terminal (of all places), where I'm greeted by the smiles of Charlie Wake (last seen in Chikurubi, when he tried to broker the deal) and New Scotland Yard (last seen in EG, in my courtroom).

We drive up the M1 to Courteenhall in Northamptonshire, Charlie's home. Beautiful. So many funny teenage memories: so much love and laughter. There is my brother Richard, then Peter, Jack and Sophie. My head and heart spin. Then we set off to drive to the safe house. Fiona Stean's. I can only just remember who Fiona is. Amanda has set this up for us. We had agreed our plan in our phone call of the night before.

Amanda doesn't want to meet me on my turf. Or that of my family and friends. I agree.

Charlie's car draws up. As I climb out I see her. She is hiding, then peeping. Then we're holding one another for a long time. Peter and Charlie quickly take my bags in. Then they leave.

There we are. Looking at each other. Touching each other. We cry. She sizes up my suit.

'Pilot, you look like the binman... And your suitcases! They're the same ones you left with. My God – I don't believe it – you've still got your same stuff.'

I think I look good – strong and lean: Odysseus with Athene's blessings goes home to Penelope. But my Penelope looks at me, then looks away. I don't look good. I need some of Athene's magic.

I look like someone who has just escaped from somewhere awful.

She probes me for craziness, screening me before I meet our four children. She will do so for three days. She has defended them for five and a half years: they aren't now going to be messed up by me.

To say that this is an odd scenario would be an understatement. We are both aware of how odd. That night we are frightened of each other. I offer not to sleep in the same bed, but she says no, so we sleep together – but fully dressed.

I so badly want things to work between us. It also feels exciting. The start of a new love affair. Will she? Won't she? *Amor vincit omnia* – I hope – but not the way that Chaucer's Abbess thinks she means it.

When can we go home? I ask. I want to see the children. But Amanda wants to be sure that I'm safe. She can't tell me that. She hates my spindly legs. She fears that I will have lost my marbles, or become wildly intellectual ... pretty much the same thing.

She finds out that in Black Beach I used to ration myself to only two bread rolls per day. I used to write down in my book exactly what I ate. It was a part of my sanity programme. Like making sure that there was one inch of water at the bottom of that day's 1.5-litre water bottle. That was a bit crazy, but it's about the only thing.

Amanda says that there are three in our marriage now: us two and Kass. It isn't true really. Kass was everything to me in Black Beach, by the end, because she was a way for me to enjoy a proxy life. Hers.

Once I am out, then Kass quickly sinks into being something that I had created, and written, and am proud of. Nothing more. I can laugh at how shrinks would have a field day because of her – because of my writing her in the first person – but it was just a laugh.

I think my clothes are fine, but Amanda does not. She is right, so my son Peter takes us to GAP in Banbury. There is a sweater that is 20 per cent off, because of a hole in the cuff. We both like that. It makes me feel that it is an old friend. At the till, Amanda points out that the hole is big: bigger than for 20 per cent off. Maybe it's big enough for 30 per cent?

'Why? You been making it bigger?' asks the check-out girl, smiling and quick.

For me it's great to be back in England. Living with people. For so long I have lied to myself that I don't miss any of it at all.

Amanda pays with chip and PIN. I've never seen that before. Just like I'm amazed that Amanda – no techno-nerd – has mastered her iPhone. She trots off: on-line shopping on her MacBook is like rolling off a log.

I start to sob. It can happen any time. It seems to be triggered by anything. At the start it happens a couple of times a day, then less and less. It hasn't happened for a while now. It's just a huge wave of emotion that sweeps me down and around and around. Like a sea wave, I let it roll me, then I bob up. It doesn't hurt. It feels as though it cleans me.

Amanda and Peter march me to the hairdresser. It's hard to answer normal questions. What do I do? Where do I live?

I don't know. Nothing? Black Beach prison?

I have no passport, driving licence, credit card, address book, phone, laptop, money. I can't keep up when people start talking around me and making arrangements, plans for the future.

I let them finish then ask, 'So ... what are we doing?'

My brain is not used to talking to anyone but me. Multi-party conversations about time and movements are foreign. I make myself breathe well, knowing that my mind needs to get back up to speed. Everyone is keeping one eye on me. Not really believing that I can be 100 per cent OK ... but I am.

I must have passed some test because Amanda says, OK, if you're sure, we can go home, but it's full-on, the kids will be crazy – we won't be alone like we are here in Fiona's house.

I must have passed some other test as well, because – in all the many ways that lovers love – she and I are lovers again. It is wonderful. It is also scary: I'm as vulnerable as a teenager.

The Boss and Mark Thatcher send me a joint message by means of their joint lawyer. My lawyer passes it on – unadorned. They say how happy they are that I am free. They say they will welcome my putting straight the record: that they had no part in the events of 2004.

We're driving: Peter, Amanda and me. We hoot with laughter. I don't know which bit I laugh at more. Is it their cringe-making lie? Or is it their asking me to lie for them? Or is it that they have written so promptly ... now ... after their deafening and absolute silence of these past five and a half fucking years, when so often the worst of the despair has been my loneliness. Deserted in a mountainscape, into which I had set forth in the company of people I liked, loved even, but who had run away and left me.

Amanda wants to incinerate my bags and suitcase and everything in them. I can't see why, until I twig. All this stuff has been in African prisons. Malaria, TB, AIDS, filth, starvation, death... It's all contaminated. So am I. I need blood tests for everything. I know I don't really. I'm fine. But there is a sort of ceremony that has to be gone through: a protocol of detoxification. (Later I test positive for Leptospirosis, but only half positive. I don't have it. I'm clear.)

We're driving fast. South. Peter's at the wheel and I'm beside him. Amanda is in the back, iPhone embedded in her ear, or texting away. I know that however joyful this all is, everything has been thrown upside down by my having been reborn.

It is a rebirth, just as Cervantes said it was. Just how he wrote it in one of the stories within the story of *Don Quixote*. As we drive I think of all the books I've read in prison. Then I start boring Peter and Amanda with what I think is funny 'Kass' chat.

My nerves are on full alert. At home, Inchmery, a house I have dreamed of but never thought to sleep in again, wait Freddy, Lilly, Bess and Arthur – as well as Marilyn, Amanda's mother, and Mr Shamm, her … our … housekeeper. He comes from a poor farming village near Lucknow, in India. A worker of miracles, I am told.

When I left them all in the lurch, Freddy was seven, Lilly five and Bess three. Arthur was a bun only three months in the oven. Now Freddy is 13, Lilly 11, Bess nine and Arthur five. I can't think how we are all going to get along with one another. I don't know them. They don't know me.

Neither do I.

We drive into the grounds by the nanny cottage, to avoid the press at the front gate. Amanda is used to all this, and laughs at their inability to cover the ground. We drive through the garden, over the lawn, a cold grey seascape on our left. It is impossibly beautiful.

Peter starts to cry.

Then I see Freddy and we hug for a long time.

There are the girls, Lilly and Bess – Lovely and Beautiful. Then Arthur, the Viking. Marilyn. It is too much. I sit on the sofa. Not crying. I can't yet. I have missed so much that I can never get back. So much that I can never give to them.

Freddy shows me the book of photos and text that Amanda has made of his *bar mitzvah* the year before. He's proud of it. I am of him.

Arthur sits on the sofa playing with a Nintendo DS, earplugs in. He is hard at work. The Gamer. I watch, because every now and then his eyes come off the game and peek up at me. Then they dive back. I catch one peek. A tiny smile touches one side of his mouth as his eyes fall back down.

We go to bed that night and I stand out on the cold balcony. Light wind, light rain: very English Channel. The oak tree is right there. Odysseus's bower, his bed made by his hand. Penelope's trick to be sure it was him.

The beach. The sea. Tide running. Siberian geese honk, friendly. It isn't possible that I have gone from maybe a lifetime in Black Beach to maybe a lifetime of this … in less than a week.

In the morning we lie in. I forget that there is a school run (in fact being kindly taken on by Marilyn, giving us our time together). I am so in love again, but immature, excessively sensitive, jealous … aware that

Amanda has built up a life and a circle of friends in which I play no part, and of which I don't know.

Amanda? We have fallen back in love. It is very wonderful. There is anger there yet. The pain of so much time lost. But mostly we enjoy each other, each day.

We take it day by day.

POSTSCRIPT

So far as I can tell, I am physically and mentally fit … like a cartoon Napoleon fantasist, safely locked up in his loony bin. A doctor friend was kind enough to look up the medical problems that I was statistically likely to have on release: a middle-aged white man coming out of five years in tropical prisons. Messed-up kidneys was his answer. Cause: not drinking enough water, probably because the water was suspect. But my kidneys are fine. The SAS training that I remembered and carried out all the way through – always make sure your piss is clear, never yellow – was the best tip I had ever had, my friend told me.

Today, I keep my fitness training going as best I can. Now I have a bloody great stick to beat myself with. I say, 'Get going, arsehole … if you could keep training all the way through prison then you can bloody well do it now…' Looking at my charts and exercise logs gives me a strange feeling these days, but I am sure that my sanity system helped me hugely. The four legs: DAILY ROUTINE : PHYSICAL EXERCISE : CREATIVE ACTIVITY : LOGGING WHAT YOU DO.

The same doctor told me that three weeks solitary (as against my eighteen months, more or less) has been shown to be enough to wobble anyone's sanity gyros; that two months or more of solitary confinement has been shown to bring about lasting physiological damage. That's convincing. That tells me that my sanity system works.

Getting to know my children again has been interesting and fun. Easier for them than me (I hope) because children are more rubbery.

They get to the point. Almost the first thing that I had to tell them about, then show to them in full, was how I had wiped my arse, while in handcuffs and leg-irons.

Arthur (now six) wants to know about the guns. He asked me, at full volume, in a too-quiet Méribel cable car.

'Daddy, when you were in prison, what did you do with the guns?'

This was asked not for his historic interest, but because he wanted one. Others in the cable car had to work hard to hide their curiosity.

Tony Buckingham is the head of Devon Oil and Gas. He's done well! Now I know the huge lengths that he went to in order to try and help me.

Tim Spicer is the founder and head of Aegis, the most successful UK PMC of recent years. Tim hugely helped my older children while I was 'away', and helped me with the last journey from EG back to Blighty.

The death of Gerhard Merz is still hazy. What is more in focus is the lack of reaction to that death by the German government. They are not normally backward about coming forward when one of their citizens may have wrongfully died.

My old EO crowd are now all at sea, off Somalia, trying to sort out the pirates, as well as those poor people's endless tribal strife ashore. They are in big trouble with the UN. It is the old Tim Spicer story: what they are doing may be right, but it is against a UN Order. Abu Dhabi is picking up that bill. Petrodollars.

Crause Steyl has been to visit me, as charming and fun as ever.

I have some news of my old friends. I haven't been able to help anybody because Amanda and the children are my priorities one to ten.

Zeb was shot dead in a police ambush. Lucky is back in Chikurubi having been ambushed and wounded in a separate incident. Munetze and Huku have both been hanged. I dread to think what things are like in Chikurubi by now.

I have raked over some old coals. It turns out that the South African government admitted in court that their NI man in Madrid made contact with Severo Moto just as the coup was kicking off.

It seems that Niek told more than one person who was a part of the Op that the Op would never happen. He wasn't telling me that at the time. After my arrest Niek and his men up in EG stayed at liberty for 24 hours. No effort to escape. Odd, when he knew what had happened to us in Zimbabwe. When he knew what had happened to the rest down in South Africa.

Inchmery, our beautiful old home, has been sold. It was too much to keep going, and Amanda achieved an offer too good to turn down. For the move itself, Amanda and the children went away to Croatia. That meant that Amanda's mother, Marilyn (a great supporter, who had lived with and helped Amanda all the time I was away) and I, could get on with the job.

The move nearly killed me. It was a crisis of my spirit. It seemed as if I had lost Amanda and the children forever, having just found them again. Worse, in the stuff of the house was all their lives. All that I had missed.

Poor Marilyn. She couldn't work out why I kept disappearing. Over and over I found myself breaking down. Hiding from the useless movers. In fact their uselessness helped, kicking them into action a cure.

As to what went wrong with my UK legal representation, much of that is still a mystery. It'll probably stay that way. Amanda and I once spent two hours in the offices of a large City of London law firm. We had the undivided attention of four partners. Yet the charge for this extravagant show of force was zero. *Nada di nada.*

Even more amazing was that this meeting was held in order to persuade us to take my lawyer to court. The City law firm in question felt so strongly that they wanted to take on a fellow lawyer. They were sure that there was enough to go on. That my interests had not been properly taken care of.

At the end, it was our decision. Firstly, I could not bear the thought of what such a case would mean: fear and loathing. Secondly, it was clear to me what his defence would be, at every turn: I was acting on instructions...

Lastly, I have been asked by many people about technological and other changes that – following my absence – I was surprised by. Amanda – the Mercenatrix, or The Bitch of War as she now likes to call herself – had let the side down while I was away, by deserting workman's tea in favour of a huge range of what she would call lesbian tea.

More techno than that was the iPhone. Being a longtime Apple fan and a trained systems analyst, it was not surprising to find the MacBook and iPhone. The shock was to find that Amanda is now a power user of both.

Kass is alive and well, in fiction form. Maybe she will be my future voice, battling the Barrel Boyz. (And not everyone in Big Oil or the CIA or MI6 is a Barrel Boy ... but there are a few: they are the bent ones.)

The thank you that I said at the front of this book – to all who tried to help me in any way, while I was in prison – I say again: thank you.

GLOSSARY

ANC	African National Congress
APC	Armoured Personnel Carrier
ARC	Assisted Regime Change
ASL	Above Sea Level
ATC	Air Traffic Control
AU	African Union
BAOR	British Army of the Rhine
BMP	*Boyevaya Mashina Pekhoty* (Fighting Vehicle of the Infantry)
CAS	Close Air Support
Casevac	Casualty Evacuation
CCB	Civil Cooperation Bureau
CESID	Centro Superior de Informacion de la Defensa
CIO	Central Intelligence Organisation
CLSTP	Committee for the Liberation of São Tomé and Principe
COMCEN	Communications Centre
COMSEC	Communications Security
COOA	Chief Operating Officer Africa
DGSE	Direction Générale de la Sécurité Extérieure
DMW	DiamondWorks
DOG	Devon Oil and Gas
DRC	Democratic Republic of the Congo
DSL	Defence Systems Limited

DSO	Distinguished Service Order
E&E	Escape & Evasion
ECOMOG	Economic Community of West African States Monitoring Group
EG	Equatorial Guinea
ELINT	Electronic Intelligence
EO	Executive Outcomes
EOR	Earliest Date of Release
ETE	Estimated Time En Route
EUCs	End User Certificates
FAA	Forcas Armadas de Angola
FGA	Fighter Ground Attack
FLEC	Front for the Liberation of the Enclave of Cabinda
FMA	Foreign Military Assistance Act of 1998
FNLA	National Liberation Front of Angola
FUP	Forming-Up Place
GPS	Global Positioning System
INT	Intelligence
ITCZ	Inter Tropical Convergence Zone
JV	Joint Venture
KP	Key Points
KZ	Killing Zone
LAN	Local Area Network
LCT	Landing Craft Tank
LO	Liaison Officer
LURD	Liberians United for Democracy and Development
LZ	Landing Zone
MC	Military Crosses
MI	Military Intelligence
MPLA	Marxist Popular Movement for the Liberation of Angola
MTS	Military Technical Services Pty Ltd
NGS	Naval Gunfire Support
NI	National Intelligence
NM	Nautical Miles
NVGs	Night Vision Goggles
OIC	Officer in Charge
PMC	Private Military Company

PNG	Papua New Guinea
PPEG	Progressive Party of Equatorial Guinea
PW	Papa Whisky
RHIB	Rigid-Hulled Inflatable Boat
RIC	Reconnaissance Interpretation Cell
RUF	Revolutionary United Front
RV	Rendezvous
SA NI	South African National Intelligence
SADF	South African Defence Force
SAM	Surface to Air Missile
SBLO	Special Branch Liaison Officer
SBS	Special Boat Service
SEAL	Sea, Air and Land
SHs	Support Helicopters
SIGINT	Signals Intelligence
SPLA	Sudan People's Liberation Army
SPO	Senior Prison Officer
TAC HQ	Tactical Headquarters
TAS	True Airspeed
U/S	Unserviceable
UNITA	Union for the Total Independence of Angola
ZDI	Zimbabwe Defence Industries
ZPS	Zimbabwe Prison Service
ZULU	Greenwich Mean Time (military term)

APPENDIX ONE

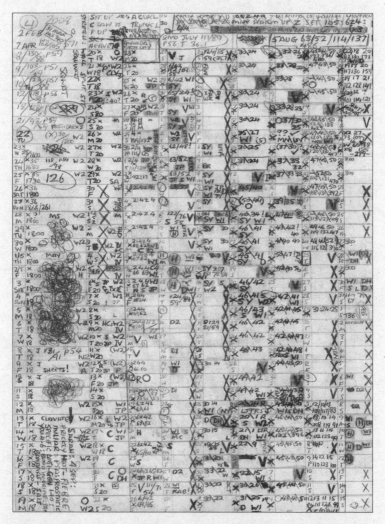

Prison Diary (see p. 309): During 2008, while in solitary confinement in Black Beach prison in EG, to maintain my sanity I obsessively kept a log to help reinforce the four legs of my daily regime. Certain symbols recur: a coronet (third column, fifth down – 27th June) refers to Amanda (Duchess) and when I spoke to her on the phone; a clock face – on that same date I also received my heart monitor to help with my exercise regime; W2 on that same date again I was interviewed not just by one interrogator but two (General Manuel and Attorney General).

343

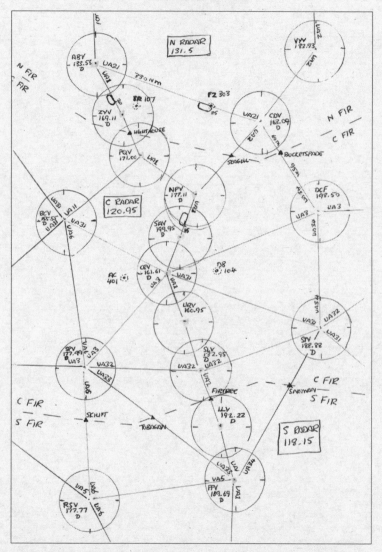

Aeronautical Instrument Flight Rules (IFR) chart (see p. 309). This chart in combination with my flight simulator (which I also drew) enabled me to fly around the world in my aircraft – N90676 – working the radio. On more than one occasion I drew a crowd of officers laughing as I mimicked the accents of the local people 'below'.

APPENDIX THREE

22 July 2003

This agreement is between Mr Severo Moto and the Provisional and subsequent Governments of Equatorial Guinea (EG) on the one hand and Captain F and his party on the other hand:

1. After a period of not greater than 60 days after their arrival in EG Captain F and the others nominated by him (up to a total of 4 to be so nominated in addition to Captain F) will each be paid US$ 1,000,000.

2. After a period of not greater than 60 days from our arrival in EG others nominated by Captain F (up to a maximum of 6) will each be paid US$ 50,000.

3. After a period of not greater than 60 days from our arrival in EG others nominated by Captain F (up to a maximum of 75) will each be paid US$ 20,000.

4. After a period of not greater than 60 days from our arrival in EG others nominated by Captain F (up to a maximum of 75) will each be paid US$ 5,000.

5. Everyone in Captain F's party and nominated by Captain F will be granted full citizenship of EG and will be issued with an EG passport to that effect within 60 days. If this is impossible for any reason then everyone will be granted multi-entry visas and work permits – as well as citizenship and passports as soon as possible.

6. Everyone in Captain F's party will each have documents (a letter and an ID card ANNEX A & B) stating that they are a member of the Armed Forces of EG. These will be issued prior to the operation taking place. The letter will give the holder immunity from prosecution by the New Government of EG for any actions taken in the course of the operation to restore the New President to power. These documents will all be duly authorised and signed by Severo Moto.

7. The letter (ANNEX A) will also guarantee that the holder is immune to any extradition proceedings whilst within the borders of EG regardless of International Laws or Agreements.

8. Captain F will hold written orders (ANNEX C) addressed to the force and to Captain F. These orders will be signed by the New President, Severo Moto, personally. They will state that Captain F and his party are contracted to act as personal protection to the New President and are to escort him home and place him in power as per his mandate of the 1995 elections.

                                              FM   S. M.

The two signed agreements dated 22 July 2003 between me and Severo Moto detailing the road map for regime change and the financial packages for me and my team.

9. Any member of the above force, as nominated by Captain F, and accepting citizenship, will be offered a place in the Armed Forces, or Security Forces, of EG, or will otherwise be allowed to work in EG in the security sector.

10. Any assets (aircraft, vessels, weapons etc) used in the operation will have their ultimate beneficial ownership transferred, in writing (ANNEX D), to the ownership of EG. This ownership will be, in writing, under the personal auspices and responsibility of the New President, Severo Moto, and will come into effect prior to the operation taking place.

11. Any handwritten alterations and additions to this agreement will be as binding as any other part of it. The number of additional pages are: ....

Signed:

For EG

Date:

For Captain F and party

Date:

Agreement Two   22 July 2003

This agreement is between Mr Severo Moto and the Provisional and subsequent
Governments of Equatorial Guinea (EG) on the one hand and Captain F and his party
on the other hand:

1. This Agreement Two is confidential between only Captain F and the new
   Government of EG and / or Provisional Government of EG.

2. After a period of not greater than 60 days from our arrival in EG Captain F
   will be paid US$ 15,000,000 (to be the US$ equivalent of UK £10,000,000 on
   the date of transfer).

3. After a period of not greater than 60 days from our arrival in EG Captain F
   will be paid back any sums of money, from his own pocket, that Captain F
   will have had at risk during the operation, or the build up to it, and PLUS the
   same amount again, in addition.

4. After a period of not greater than 60 days from our arrival in EG the
   Government of EG, or the Provisional Government, will actually buy into
   their forces any assets procured on their behalf in order to carry out the
   operation. This purchase will be at the same price as those assets were bought
   for or whatever they are worth on the open market – whichever amount is the
   greater. This clause is linked to Clause 10 in Agreement 1 but refers to the
   funds involved rather than the legal ownership.

5. All of the sums mentioned above and elsewhere in this Agreement 2, and
   those in Agreement 1, will attract interest in the event of late payment. Interest
   will compound monthly and will be calculated at LIBOR + 2%.

6. Within 60 days of arrival or as soon as possible thereafter Captain F will be
   issued with a Diplomatic Passport for EG. This Diplomatic Passport will
   properly accredit Captain F as appropriate and as Captain F requests. This
   passport will be kept valid and properly accredited for as long as Captain F so
   demands.

7. Captain F will be awarded an Honorary Rank as deemed appropriate and in
   line with the accreditation of his Diplomatic Passport.

8. ANNEX E outlines a phased programme of military procurement and build up
   that EG will undertake immediately after the New Government is in place.
   This programme will be handled by Captain F's team in all respects. Please
   note that some of these steps will have been ordered before the operation
   itself. This programme must be applied as quickly and as aggressively as
   possible. This point is specifically a part of this agreement and is not a request
   or point for later approval.

FM   *S.M*

9. Suitable documentation will be required for the above procurements (End User Certificates etc) as well as funds.

10. After the arrival in EG a new company (NEWCO) will be established. The ownership of NEWCO is still to be agreed. The ownership will be such that Captain F will keep effective control of NEWCO. Captain F will be the CEO of NEWCO and will own not less than 33% of the equity.

11. NEWCO will be warranted, contracted and paid by EG, and this contract will be granted as a renewable five year Concession (and Contract) by the Council of Ministers of the Provisional Government, and by the Council of Ministers of the subsequent elected Government, as the sole and exclusive provider of the following goods and services:

11.1 The immediate investigation and recovery of all national capital that has 'fled' the national ownership due to illegal activities of the present regime. Initially, this will be carried out 'no cure no pay'. In return EG will pay costs plus a bonus of 30% of such sums recovered. After an initial period, but not less than 60 days and not until all other financial issues mentioned in these two agreements have been paid up, this arrangement can be reviewed and changed as appropriate.

11.2 The supervision, management consultancy, procurement, outsourcing and contracting of, in UK terms, the functions of The Guard to The Head of State, JIC, SIS, MI5, SB, Armed Forces, Police, Customs & Excise, Inland Revenue and Environmental Control and Protection Agencies (including Wild Life and Parks management as well as their demarcation and patrolling and enforcement).

11.3 The Guard to The Head of State will be put in place and a contract entered into immediately after our arrival in EG. This Guard will immediately number 100 men. The contract will be calculated on the basis of US$ 6,000 per man per month plus travel and subsistence costs, equipment and services as appropriate. Payment for this Guard will always be three months in advance. Therefore a first payment of US$1.8M will be required immediately on our arrival or as soon as possible thereafter.

11.4 The actual provision of those parts, goods and services of the above functions as deemed appropriate. This will follow the modern trend of 'outsourcing'. Defence Logistics and Defence (and other) Government communications are specifically included.

12. Any handwritten alterations and additions to this agreement will be as binding as any other part of it. The number of additional pages are: ....

For EG

Date:

For Captain F and party

Date:

ANNEX E

The Armed Forces must target their build up as follows:

AIR
The Air Force must be capable of fulfilling the following tasks:

1. Defence of the two major airfields against surprise attack.
2. Close Air Support of ground troops.
3. Interdiction of enemy ground operations.
4. Detection, Interception and 'force down' throughout EG airspace.
5. Maritime surveillance and 'air to sea' attack.
6. Offering logistical support to all arms as required.
7. Ability to maintain Air Superiority within EG airspace against any likely aggressor.

SEA
The Navy must be capable of fulfilling the following tasks:

1. Defence of the two major ports against surprise attack.
2. Close Support of ground troops on coastal operation.
3. Interdiction of enemy surface and ground operations.
4. Detection, Interception and boarding throughout EG territorial water.
5. Maritime surveillance and 'sea to sea' attack.
6. Offering logistical support to all arms as required.
7. Ability to maintain Naval Superiority within EG territorial water against any likely aggressor.

LAND
1. Defence of EG, the President and Government against any surprise attack.
2. Close Support of the Civil Power whenever an Internal Security problem arises.
3. Interdiction and defeat of aggressive enemy ground operations.
4. Ground detection, interception and attack of incursive forces throughout EG territory.
5. Offering logistical support to all arms as required.
6. Ability to maintain sovereignty over EG territory against any likely aggressor.

INTELLIGENCE
As required by the above.

POLICE
As required by the local authority and by the situation within the civilian population.

BORDER CONTROL AND PARK RANGERS
As required by the border situation and by the National Parks.